JOURNAL FOR THE STUDY OF THE NEW TESTAMENT
SUPPLEMENT SERIES

255

Executive Editor
Stanley E. Porter

From Followers to Leaders

The Apostles in the Ritual of
Status Transformation in Acts 1–2

Nelson P. Estrada

T&T CLARK INTERNATIONAL
A Continuum imprint
LONDON • NEW YORK

Copyright © 2004 T&T Clark International
A Continuum imprint

Published by T&T Clark International
The Tower Building, 11 York Road, London SE1 7NX
15 East 26th Street, Suite 1703, New York, NY 10010

www.tandtclark.com

British Library Cataloguing-in-Publication Data
A catalogue record for this book is available from the British Library

Library of Congress Cataloguing-in-Publication Data
A catalogue record for this book is available from the Library of Congress

Typeset by TMW Typesetting, Sheffield
Printed on acid-free paper in Great Britain by Cromwell Press

ISBN 0-8264-6973-6

CONTENTS

Preface   ix
Acknowledgements   xi
Abbreviations   xii

Chapter 1
THE APOSTLES AND THE NEED TO CALL FOR AN ELECTION   1
    1. Methodology   8
    2. The Rituals of Status Transformation   19
    3. Summary   37
    4. Other Considerations—The Role of Commissioning
        Accounts in Luke–Acts: Contributions from
        B.J. Hubbard and T.Y. Mullins   38

Part I
SEPARATION

Chapter 2
THE APOSTLES AND THEIR LEADERSHIP ROLE   46
    1. The Ritual Elements in Acts 1.3-11   46
    2. The Initiands and their Leadership Role   52
    3. Summary   64

Chapter 3
THE APOSTLES AND THEIR SEPARATION FROM JESUS   66
    1. The Ritual Process in Acts 1.3-5   66
    2. Summary   101

Part II
TRANSITION

Chapter 4
THE UPPER ROOM: THE SETTING OF THE APOSTLES' DEFENCE   104
    1. The Ritual Elements in Acts 1.12-14   105
    2. Summary   114

Chapter 5
THE APOSTLES' MEETING WITH THE OTHER PARTIES IN
THE UPPER ROOM   115
    1. The Ritual Process in Acts 1.12-14   115
    2. The Eleven with the Women Disciples   125
    3. The Eleven with Mary and Jesus' Brothers   131
    4. Summary   149

Chapter 6
THE APOSTLES AND THEIR CASE AGAINST JUDAS   151
    1. The Ritual Elements in Acts 1.15-26   151
    2. Honour and Shame Defined   162
    3. Summary   165

Chapter 7
THE APOSTLES AND THE HORROR OF JUDAS' BETRAYAL   166
    1. The Ritual Process in Acts 1.15-26   166
    2. The Purpose of the Election Narrative from a
      Historical Method   167
    3. Twelve Apostles for Twelve Thrones?   172
    4. Is Acts 1.15-26 the Fulfilment of Luke 22.30?   176
    5. Peter's Speech: A Case of Diminished Responsibility   178
    6. The Purpose of the Criteria on the Replacement of Judas
      (Acts 1.21-22)   184
    7. The Final Choice of Judas' Replacement is Left to God   185
    8. Summary   186

Part III
AGGREGATION

Chapter 8
THE APOSTLES AS PRIMARY RECIPIENTS OF THE FATHER'S PROMISE   190
    1. The Ritual Elements in Acts 2   191
    2. Πάντες in Acts 2.1   204
    3. Summary   208

Chapter 9
THE APOSTLES TAKE ON THEIR LEADERSHIP ROLE   210
    1. The Ritual Process in Acts 2   210
    2. The Catalogue of Nations as Representative of the
        Universal Society   223
    3. The Apostles Are Formally Presented to the Society   225
    4. The Society Recognizes the Twelve   227
    5. Summary   228

Conclusion   230
Appendix: Twelve Apostles for Twelve Thrones?
    The Redaction of Matthew 19.28   238

Bibliography   249
Index of References   267
Index of Authors   278

This book is a study of Acts 1–2 using perspectives from the social sciences. The study is focused on the twelve apostles of Jesus and attempts to understand the process and purpose of their change of status from being followers to becoming the leaders of the Christian community. Specifically, this book employs the model of the Rituals of Status Transformation as its primary theoretical framework in order to clarify and define the stages and phases of the apostles' status transformation.

The primary purpose of the status transformation is to promote the leadership integrity of the apostles. This leadership integrity was put into question because Judas—a member of the Twelve—betrayed Jesus. Judas' betrayal brought social embarrassment on the apostolate and thus necessitated the author's campaign to show his readers the apostles' status transformation.

A major part of this study is the suggestion of a plausible solution to the questions surrounding the function of the pericopes of Acts 1.12-14 and 1.15-26 in relation to the Ascension and Pentecost events. Contrary to the common view that the prayer of unanimity between the Eleven apostles, the women, and Jesus' family in the upper room is simply an empty interval in preparation for the coming of the Spirit on the day of Pentecost, this study proposes that the pericope is propagandistic and intended to win support from the clienteles of the women disciples and Jesus' family. Thus, while the Rituals of Status Transformation serves as our main theoretical framework, this study uses other social-scientific models to fully explore the social conditions within the said pericopes. In the case of Acts 1.12-14, the model of patronage/brokerage together with the mechanics of social networking have been employed.

The same perspective applies to Acts 1.15-26. Again, contrary to the more popular view that the election narrative is the fulfilment of the promise of Jesus to his apostles in Lk. 22.30, I suggest that the setting is the stage of the apostles' ritual confrontation before the presence of the 120 believers. This ritual confrontation is understood within the concept of

honour and shame which works interactively with my theoretical framework. This concept is able to bring out my suggestion that Peter's speech
is an apologetic speech on behalf of the apostles—attempting to defend
their honour and leadership integrity that was marred by Judas' betrayal
of Jesus.

ACKNOWLEDGEMENTS

Thank you to Revd Dr Loveday C.A. Alexander, my thesis supervisor. Her expertise, as ever, I have relied upon, and her counsel has been invaluable.

Thank you to my examiners, Professor Philip Esler of St Andrews University and Dr Barry Matlock of Sheffield University. Their encouragement and suggestions are greatly appreciated.

Thank you for the scholarships granted by the British Overseas Research Scheme, the Langham Trust, Christ Church Fulwood, the Asian Theological Seminary, and especially the individual sponsors both from the United States of America and the United Kingdom.

Thank you to Dr Sam Tsang of the Overseas Theological Seminary. His scholarship, fellowship, and genuine friendship sustained me and my family in our most difficult times.

Thank you most of all to the three ladies in my life: my wife Mitzie, and my daughters Karen and Nikki. They, more than anyone, have had to endure the costs of my journey to a PhD degree, and they have done so without a moment's complaint. To you I dedicate this book.

ABBREVIATIONS

AB	Anchor Bible
ABD	David Noel Freedman (ed.), *The Anchor Bible Dictionary* (New York: Doubleday, 1992)
ANET	James B. Pritchard (ed.), *Ancient Near Eastern Texts Relating to the Old Testament* (Princeton: Princeton University Press, 1950)
ANRW	Hildegard Temporini and Wolfgang Haase (eds.), *Aufstieg und Niedergang der römischen Welt: Geschichte und Kultur Roms im Spiegel der neueren Forschung* (Berlin: W. de Gruyter, 1972–)
ASTI	*Annual of the Swedish Theological Institute*
ATR	*American Theological Review*
BAGD	Walter Bauer, William F. Arndt, F. William Gingrich and Frederick W. Danker, *A Greek–English Lexicon of the New Testament and Other Early Christian Literature* (Chicago: University of Chicago Press, 2nd edn, 1958)
BDB	*Brown, Driver, and Briggs*
BDF	Friedrich Blass, A. Debrunner and Robert W. Funk, *A Greek Grammar of the New Testament and Other Early Christian Literature* (Cambridge: Cambridge University Press, 1961)
BEvT	Beiträge zur evangelischen Theologie
Bib	*Biblica*
BJRL	*Bulletin of the John Rylands University Library of Manchester*
BJS	Brown Judaic Studies
BTB	*Biblical Theology Bulletin*
BZNW	Beihefte zur *ZNW*
CBQ	*Catholic Biblical Quarterly*
Ebib	Etudes bibliques
EvQ	*Evangelical Quarterly*
ExpT	*Expository Times*
HNT	Handbuch zum Neuen Testament
HTR	*Harvard Theological Review*
ICC	International Critical Commentary
IDB	George Arthur Buttrick (ed.), *The Interpreter's Dictionary of the Bible* (4 vols.; Nashville: Abingdon Press, 1962)

Int	*Interpretation*
ISBE	Geoffrey Bromiley (ed.), *The International Standard Bible Encyclopedia* (4 vols.; Grand Rapids: Eerdmans, rev. edn, 1979–88)
JAAR	*Journal of the American Academy of Religion*
JAC	*Jahrbuch für Antike und Christentum*
JBL	*Journal of Biblical Literature*
JETS	*Journal of the Evangelical Theological Society*
JHS	*Journal of Hellenic Studies*
JPTSup	*Journal of Pentecostal Theology*, Supplement Series
JQR	*Jewish Quarterly Review*
JRS	*Journal of Roman Studies*
JSNT	*Journal for the Study of the New Testament*
JSNTSup	*Journal for the Study of the New Testament*, Supplement Series
JSOT	*Journal for the Study of the Old Testament*
JSOTSup	*Journal for the Study of the Old Testament*, Supplement Series
JTS	*Journal of Theological Studies*
LCL	Loeb Classical Library
LSJ	H.G. Liddell, Robert Scott and H. Stuart Jones, *Greek–English Lexicon* (Oxford: Clarendon Press, 9th edn, 1968)
NCB	New Century Bible
NCBC	New Century Biblical Commentary
NICNT	New International Commentary on the New Testament
NICOT	New International Commentary on the Old Testament
NovT	*Novum Testamentum*
NTS	*New Testament Studies*
RSR	*Recherches de science religieuse*
SBLMS	Society of Biblical Literature Monograph Series
SBT	Studies in Biblical Theology
SE	*Studia Evangelica I, II, III* (= TU 73 [1959], 87 [1964], 88 [1964], etc.)
SJT	*Scottish Journal of Theology*
TCGNT	*Textual Commentary on the Greek New Testament*
TDNT	Gerhard Kittel and Gerhard Friedrich (eds.), *Theological Dictionary of the New Testament* (trans. Geoffrey W. Bromiley; 10 vols.; Grand Rapids: Eerdmans, 1964–)
TS	*Theological Studies*
TynBul	*Tyndale Bulletin*
VT	*Vetus Testamentum*
WBC	Word Biblical Commentary
ZAW	*Zeitschrift für die alttestamentliche Wissenschaft*
ZNW	*Zeitschrift für die neutestamentliche Wissenschaft*
ZWT	*Zeitschrift für wissenschaftliche Theologie*

Chapter 1

THE APOSTLES AND THE NEED TO CALL FOR AN ELECTION

The commission to be witnesses in Acts 1.8 together with Jesus' departure in 1.9-11 mark the beginning of the apostles' transformation from followers to leaders.[1] Their baptism and empowerment by the Spirit on the day of Pentecost in Acts 2.1-4 is seen as the completion of such a status transformation.[2] However, before the said completion, the author tells his readers of two episodes which took place in the process of the apostles' ascent to leadership. These episodes are the gathering in the upper room in 1.12-14 and the election of Matthias in 1.15-26. The question we ask is 'why'? What is the relevance of these episodes to the apostles' change of status? Why has the author chosen to tell these stories in the midst of the Ascension and Pentecost events?

The answer to these questions has solicited many opinions.[3] Most of these, however, share a common ground. For instance, with the election narrative in 1.15-26, a majority of New Testament scholars agree that the primary purpose of Matthias' election is to complete the number of the apostles to twelve. L.T. Johnson states that, '…Judas had to be replaced before Pentecost because the integrity of the apostolic circle of Twelve symbolized the restoration of God's people'.[4] J.B. Tyson feels that the

---

1. Cf. R. Stronstad, *The Charismatic Theology of St. Luke* (Peabody, MA: Hendrickson, 1984), p. 59.

2. See for example E. Schweizer, *Church Order in the New Testament* (SBT, 32; London: SCM Press, 1961), pp. 63-76; A.C. Clark, 'The Role of the Apostles', in I.H. Marshall and D. Peterson (eds.), *Witness of the Gospel: The Theology of Acts* (Grand Rapids: Eerdmans, 1998), pp. 178-80. As for the relationship of the commissioning account in Acts 1.8 and the Spirit's outpouring in Acts 2.1-4, see C.K. Barrett, *The Acts of the Apostles*, I (Edinburgh: T. & T. Clark, 1994), pp. 78-79.

3. A survey on current research concerning the purpose of the election story in Acts 1.15-26 together with bibliography is provided in my discussion of the text in Chapter 7 of this study.

4. L.T. Johnson, *The Acts of the Apostles* (Collegeville, MN: The Liturgical Press, 1992), p. 39. Further discussion and bibliography is provided later in this study.

leadership issue should be clear before the Pentecost experience takes place. He states,

> For Luke, the number of apostles must be twelve. Such is the meaning of the narrative about the selection of Matthias in Acts 1.15-26. Even before the Pentecost experience it is important that the leadership of the church be absolutely clear. In order to restore the original number of the apostles, the traitor Judas must be replaced in a ceremony intended to determine divine choice.[5]

The consensus that the purpose of the election is to bring the number of the apostles to twelve is based on the understanding that this event is the beginning of the fulfilment of Jesus' promise in Lk. 22.30. In the said passage, Jesus promises to reward his apostles for their faithfulness to serve as judges over the twelve tribes of Israel in the new kingdom. The common sense understanding is there cannot be *twelve judges* on *twelve thrones* for the *twelve tribes* of Israel when the supposed *twelve apostles* are down to eleven.[6]

What sense could we make of the election story if it is not read from the perspective we have just cited above? In other words, what if the whole election story is not primarily addressing the need to ensure that the number of the apostles should be twelve? What if we address the election of Matthias primarily as a matter of sociological concern rather than as the fulfilment of Jesus' promise in Lk. 22.30? Could it be that the enrolment of Matthias into the exclusive group of the Twelve is a response within the backdrop of a 'challenge-riposte' situation—a challenge to the honour of the apostles as a group brought about by Judas' betrayal of Jesus? And that such a betrayal has equally severe moral and social consequences for the leadership integrity of the group of apostles other than just the arrest and death of their leader Jesus?

---

5.   J.B. Tyson, 'The Emerging Church and the Problem of Authority in Acts', *Int* 42 (1988), p. 137.

6.   R. Denova, however, attempts to answer such a question. She suggests that it is the 'prophetic order of events' which forces the author to place them where they are. That the 'restoration of Jacob precedes the outpouring of the Spirit (Ezek. 39.25-29)', so should the fulfilment of Jesus' promise in Lk. 22.30 take place before the Spirit's coming in Acts 2. We will deal with Denova's view in detail later on in this study. Cf. R. Denova, *The Things Accomplished among Us: Prophetic Tradition in the Structural Pattern of Luke–Acts* (JSNTSup, 141; Sheffield: Sheffield Academic Press, 1997), p. 70. See also J. Jervell, *Luke and the People of God: A New Look at Luke-Acts* (Minneapolis, MN: Ausburg, 1972), pp. 75-112.

I raise these suggestions because of the questions which historical studies have left unanswered. For instance, historical approaches have failed to explain fully the need for Peter's elaborate speech on the death of Judas (a speech which occupies half of the whole election narrative). In other words, if the purpose of the election is for the completion of the Twelve, and that this was so in order to fulfil the promise of Jesus for the apostles to serve as judges to the twelve tribes of Israel (Lk. 22.30), then what is the need to describe Judas' death in such a grotesque manner in the first place? Could not the same goal of completing the Twelve be achieved without having to depict the betrayer's death so vividly? Furthermore, we also read later on in Acts 12.2 that James, one of the Twelve, was executed by Herod leaving another vacancy in the apostolate, yet, we do not find any call for another election.

With these issues, one begins to speculate that if the promise in Lk. 22.30 is not a factor, there must be another reason behind the urgency to conduct an election. This question is compounded by the fact that we do not recall Jesus giving any directives to the Eleven concerning the matter at all.[7] As Haenchen observes, 'It is striking that Jesus himself should not have appointed the new apostle during the forty days'.[8] So whose idea was it to replace Judas in the first place? More importantly, how is the need to replace Judas related to the whole narrative of the apostles' status transformation?

The same question applies to 1.12-14. What is the significance of this event to the apostles' transition from followers to leaders? Some have suggested that this pericope is simply an 'empty interval'.[9] Others say 'a piece of stage setting'.[10] Still others take it to be a general notion of 'preparations for Pentecost'.[11] I feel, however, that there is more to 1.12-14 than what has just been suggested. For instance, there is the issue of the presence of at least two other groups (namely, the women and Jesus'

7.   Furthermore, not even the author gives any indication in Acts that the election of Matthias is in fulfilment of the promise of Jesus in Lk. 22.30.

8.   E. Haenchen, *The Acts of the Apostles* (Oxford: Basil Blackwell, 1971), p. 164. From a tradition-historical perspective, J. Fitzmyer points to the early community as the one who is called to fill in the gap left in the Twelve by Judas' death. J. Fitzmyer, *The Acts of the Apostles: A New Translation with Introduction and Commentary* (New York: Doubleday, 1998), p. 220.

9.   J.D.G. Dunn, *The Acts of the Apostles* (Valley Forge, PA: Trinity Press, 1996), p. 15.

10.   Barrett, *Acts*, p. 61.

11.   Johnson, *Acts*, pp. 33-34.

family) in the upper room. Of all the number of people present (considering the presence of 120 brethren in the same 'upper room' [1.15]), why has the author chosen the women and Jesus' family to be those described as in unanimity with the Eleven apostles? How is this related to the general notion of 'preparations'? Some commentators suggest that the apostles, together with the women and Jesus' family, prayed in 'one accord' to prepare for the coming of the Spirit in Acts 2. Yet again, what is so special about the groups of women disciples and Jesus' family that they were honourably mentioned in favour of the other followers of Jesus? What is the author attempting to achieve by locating this occurrence in the upper room before the apostles and the whole body of 120 brethren conduct an election, and before the completed Twelve receive the Spirit's baptism?

I suggest that what is being dealt with here in 1.12-14 is the significance of the groups of women disciples and Jesus' family to the author's agenda of promoting the apostles' leadership status. On this hypothesis, Acts 1.12-14 is therefore not simply an 'empty interval', nor does it jibe with the general notion of 'preparations for Pentecost'. The women disciples and Jesus' family have a social significance in the author's campaign to promote the apostles' leadership status. We propose that Mary and Jesus' brothers represent a significant clientele in the Christian community. The same idea applies to the women disciples. While it may be true that the general status of women in ancient societies is not necessarily equal to that of men, there is enough evidence to suggest that the women disciples command an unofficial representation of the women audience in Luke–Acts or of the Christian community.[12]

Again, I submit these proposals due to the questions which the tradition-historical method have not satisfactorily answered. I believe that Acts 1–2 is not just the story of Jesus' ascension and the coming of the Spirit on the

---

12. Cf. L.C.A. Alexander, *The Preface to Luke's Gospel: Literary Convention and Social Context in Luke 1.1-4 and Acts 1.1* (Cambridge: Cambridge University Press, 1993), p. 191. Phoebe and Lydia may have had their own clientele as they too have been known to serve as Christian patrons. See also A.J. Marshall, 'Roman Women and the Provinces', *Ancient Society* 6 (1975), pp. 109-27. Quite helpful is the contribution of C.F. Whelan, 'Amica Pauli: The Role of Phoebe in the Early Church', *JSNT* 49 (1993), pp. 67-85; and B.J. Brooten, *Women Leaders in the Ancient Synagogue: Inscriptional Evidence and Background Issues* (BJS, 36; Chico, CA: Scholars Press, 1982), pp. 5-14. I will discuss more on this issue in its designated section (Chapter 5 of this study).

day of Pentecost. Rather, these chapters tell the story of the apostles' status transformation—their transformation from being the former followers of Jesus to becoming the new leaders of the Christian community. The episodes in 1.12-14 and 1.15-26 are found between the Ascension and Pentecost events because they are issues so crucial to both the author and his readers that they need to be resolved before the apostles finally receive their confirmation as leaders.

I propose, therefore, that the whole process of the apostles' status transformation is the author's means of 'legitimation'. To put it more precisely, the author of Luke–Acts needed to legitimize the apostles' change of status, from being followers of Jesus to becoming the leaders of the Christian community, not only because of the leadership vacuum created by Jesus' departure, but also because of two significant social issues: the embarrassment to the group of apostles caused by Judas' betrayal of Jesus,[13] and the significance of the apostles' relationship with other disciple groups.

I will work from the hypothesis that the replacement of Judas is primarily intended to blot out the social shame he has brought upon the apostolate. It is a hypothesis which assumes that the Lukan community of believers were gripped with the horror of the fact that Judas, a member of the Twelve, could actually have betrayed Jesus. This proposed hypothesis is not without a basis, not least in the development of tradition about Judas and his sin.[14] New Testament scholarship, for example, argues that the Judas accounts in Lk. 22.3-6 and Acts 1.16-20 are a conflation of other earlier traditions concerning who Judas is and what he stands for. The conflation is from stories and legends on how Judas has come to be known as almost synonymous with evil.[15] The evil of Judas is not only that he

---

13. E.P. Sanders, *Jesus and Judaism* (London: SCM Press, 1985), p. 100.

14. A discussion on this issue of how tradition has expanded the story on Judas' death is in Chapter 6 of this study. A detailed explanation on the conflation of traditions is provided by Kirsopp Lake in 'The Death of Judas', in F.J. Foakes Jackson and K. Lake (eds.), *The Beginnings of Christianity*. I. *The Acts of the Apostles* (London: Macmillan, 1933), pp. 22-30. See also H. Maccoby, *Judas Iscariot and the Myth of Jewish Evil* (New York: Free Press, 1991; Oxford: Maxwell-MacMillan, 1992), pp. 17, 137, 146-53; *idem*, *The Sacred Executioner* (London: Thames & Hudson, 1982), pp. 7-10; *idem*, 'Who Was Judas Iscariot?' *JQR* (1991), pp. 8-13.

15. A detailed treatment of this issue can be found in W. Klassen, *Judas: Betrayer or Friend of Jesus?* (London: SCM Press, 1996), pp. 11-27. 'To call someone Judas is the height of insult'. Fitzmyer, *The Acts of the Apostles*, p. 221.

was a follower who betrayed Jesus, but more seriously, that he was a member of the Twelve—the inner circle of Jesus' apostles.

Up until Judas' replacement by Matthias in Acts 1.15-26, Judas has not been known as a character independent from the title 'a member of the Twelve'. In other words, it is probable that his deeds and his membership in the exclusive Twelve have gravely affected the reputation of the whole group.[16]

Luke–Acts has been consistent in emphasizing that Judas was 'one of the Twelve' (Lk. 22.3, 47; Acts 1.17). Moreover, the reference to the title 'the Eleven apostles' in the early chapters of Acts immediately suggests the absence of one since they have been originally twelve. It is an absence which everyone understood to have come about, not only because of Judas' death, but also of his betrayal of Jesus. Even the reference 'he was numbered among us' (ὅτι κατηριθμημένος ἦν ἐν ἡμῖν) in Acts 1.17 emphasizes the fact that Judas was one of the twelve apostles. It is therefore most unlikely that Judas and his deeds were viewed independently from his office and membership in the Twelve. As Fitzmyer observes,

> Luke is merely echoing the horror that early Christians sensed, whenever Judas was mentioned, a horror reflected in the various qualifying phrases added to his name, as one of the Twelve 'who became a traitor' (in the list of Luke 6.16); 'Satan entered into Judas, who was called Iscariot and was numbered among the Twelve' (Luke 22.3); 'one of the Twelve, the one named Judas' (Luke 22.47); 'who betrayed him' (Mark 3.19; Matt. 10.4; cf. Mark 14.10, 43; Matt. 26.14, 25, 47; John 6.71; 12.4; 13.2; 18.2, 5). 'He had been numbered among us and was apportioned a share in this ministry of ours' (Acts 1.17). That ministry Judas chose to desert.[17]

I intend, therefore, to work from the assumption that Judas' failure could not have been viewed as his alone. The whole 'Judas tragedy' is a tragedy that has affected the status of the whole group.[18]

I will also attempt to work from the hypothesis that the author's portrayal of unanimity between the apostles and the other character-groups in the upper room (1.12-14) masks the probable differences between the apostles and the women disciples and Jesus' family. I will attempt to show why the author has specially focused on the women and Jesus' family despite the other possible groups of disciples who have followed Jesus.

16. Cf. B. Witherington III, *The Acts of the Apostles: A Socio-Rhetorical Commentary* (Grand Rapids: Eerdmans, 1998), p. 122.
17. J. Fitzmyer, *The Acts of the Apostles*, p. 220.
18. Cf. Johnson, *Acts*, p. 38.

The projection of unanimity between the apostles and the women disciples and Jesus' family is a crucial factor in uniting the Christian community of Luke–Acts to recognize the new role and status of the apostles.

The author of Luke–Acts, we believe, has succeeded in redeeming the honour and promoting the leadership integrity of the Eleven apostles. To have achieved this, the author was able to convince his readers that the Eleven apostles have gone through a serious transformation. It is a status transformation, not only of social rank, but primarily of the virtues (including 'moral') expected from leaders by (firstly) the readers of Luke–Acts, and (generally) the society (in this case, the Christian community). This required (as I have stated) a demonstration of unanimity with other known disciple groups and the excommunication of Judas from the Twelve sealed by the election of a suitable and qualified replacement—Matthias. The change of status means that the Eleven themselves are transformed from being the unreliable followers (including Peter who denied Jesus in Lk. 22.54-62)[19] to becoming the strong and reliable leaders of the Christian community.

I suggest that there is a process of transformation and that this can be understood in the events of Acts 1 and 2. Specifically, I designate Acts 1.3–2.47 as the narrative by which the author of Luke–Acts promotes the image of the Eleven apostles through such a process of status transformation. The instruction to remain in Jerusalem and wait for the promise of the father (1.3-5), Jesus' ascension (1.9-11), the enumeration of the apostles' names plus the waiting and praying in unity with the women and Jesus' family in the upper room (1.12-14), the speech of Peter on Judas' betrayal and subsequent election of Matthias (1.15-26), the outpouring of the Spirit upon the apostles (2.1-4), and the gathering of the crowd who have come from different places, together with the preaching of Peter with

---

19. I am not sure how Witherington deduced the possibility of Peter's restoration solely from 1 Cor. 15.5. While he suggests the probability of Luke being aware of the tradition in Jn 21, he has not discussed anything at all concerning the links between the two gospels. Speaking on the character of Peter in Acts 1.16, Witherington states that, 'What one notices immediately about this section is the leadership role that Peter assumes, a role that is to continue in the next few chapters in Acts. This is especially striking in view of Peter's denial of Christ, which is the last major episode prior to this in Luke–Acts in which he was a prominent figure (cf. Luke 22.54-62). This role among the disciples is presumably to be accounted for by the fact that Jesus appeared to Peter personally and restored him (1 Cor. 15.5), a tradition Luke knows *about* (cf. Luke 24.34) but either does not have sufficient data to relate or does not choose to tell the story, probably the former.' Witherington, *The Acts of the Apostles*, p. 116.

the Eleven apostles beside him (2.5-47) are all designed by the author to campaign for the apostles' leadership status.

1. *Methodology*

Issues about status transformation, the restoration of honour and integrity, and the desire to win the loyalty and support of other disciple groups are interactions between the author and his readers involving the 'inter-relations, values and symbols which characterised the early Christian communities of the NT'.[20] I propose that the episode in Acts 1.12-14 makes historical sense when read with the understanding of the social concepts of the family, kinship, and the patron-client relations in the setting of Luke–Acts. Likewise, the episode in 1.15-26 is best appreciated when read with an understanding of the social concept of honour and shame. As a whole, I suggest that Acts 1–2 is the narrative about the apostles' status trans-formation with the episodes of 1.12-14 and 1.15-26 serving as crucial social issues needing immediate attention and solution before the con-firmation of the apostles' new leadership status. The question now is how to best demonstrate this kind of reading on Acts 1–2 which primarily involves these two important tasks: (1) the author's intent to show to his readers that the apostles have gone through a serious transformation, and (2) that the episodes of 1.12-14 and 1.15-26 are necessary and crucial stages in this status transformation process?

My search for the method by which I can best demonstrate the kind of reading I have suggested leads me to the discipline of social-scientific criticism. Specifically, I intend to use models from the social-scientific approach to help show the plausibility of the proposed reading I have suggested for Acts 1.3–2.47. However, before I describe and discuss the model I have in mind, I need to briefly justify my preference to use the method of social-scientific criticism. I will do this by first defining the method. I will then discuss the current issues about the method, more specifically on what models are and how they are helpful in the inter-pretation of biblical texts.

20. P.F. Esler, *The First Christians in their Social Worlds: Social-Scientific Approaches to New Testament Interpretation* (London: Routledge, 1994), p. 2. See also D.G. Horrell (ed.), *Social-Scientific Approaches to New Testament Interpretation* (Edinburgh: T. & T. Clark, 1999), pp. 3-27.

1.1. *What is Social-Scientific Criticism?*

In my opinion, the historical method has given all it could give to make sense of the function of 1.12-14 and 1.15-26 in the narrative of Acts 1–2. Yet, despite this, the results still fall short of convincing explanations.

The development of various innovative studies in the past three decades[21] however, more particularly in the field of human sciences, has opened up new insights into biblical historical problems—problems which have been locked up through the centuries because of the wide social and cultural gap between the writers in the biblical world and the present world in which we, the modern readers, live. The questions I have raised on the narrative of Acts 1–2, especially 1.12-14 and 1.15-26, can now have plausible explanations. This method, the employment of the social sciences including sociology, anthropology, social psychology, and economics in biblical interpretation, is known as social-scientific criticism.[22]

Social-scientific criticism is defined as, '…that phase of the exegetical task which analyses the social and cultural dimensions of the text and of its environmental context through the utilization of the perspectives, theory, models, and research of the social sciences'.[23]

S.C. Barton[24] shares four important contributions of the method to biblical exegesis:

> 1. The social sciences focus attention on the 'synchronic' relations, that is on the way meaning is generated by the social actors related to one another by a complex web of culturally-determined social systems and patterns of communication.

Applied to 1.12-14, for example, I am able to ask about the significance of the meeting of the apostles with the women disciples and Jesus' family in the upper room. While the historical method focuses on the activity of the characters having unity in prayer, preparing themselves for the fulfilment of the Spirit's coming, social-scientific criticism helps readers to focus on the social relationships of the characters, relationships which

---

21. A comprehensive bibliography on social-scientific criticism and social-historical studies has been provided by J.H. Elliot in his book entitled *What is Social-Scientific Criticism?* (Minneapolis, MN: Fortress Press, 1993), pp. 138-74.

22. Esler, *The First Christians*, p. 2.

23. Elliott, *What is Social-Scientific Criticism?*, p. 7.

24. S.C. Barton, 'Historical Criticism and Social-Scientific Perspectives in the New Testament', in J.B. Green (ed.), *Hearing the New Testament: Strategies for Interpretation* (Grand Rapids: Eerdmans, 1995), pp. 69-74.

seem so important for the author and his readers that they necessitated the mention of this episode.[25]

> 2. Social-scientific analysis is useful also in helping the interpreter of the NT to fill the gaps in understanding created by the fragmentariness of the texts as sources of historical information.

One of the main 'gaps' this study will attempt to solve is the problem of who and how many were the first recipients of the Spirit's baptism in Acts 2.1-4. The sudden appearance of the 120 brethren in 1.15 can lead the modern reader to assume that this number of people are all in the same room at the same time, including the previous characters mentioned in 1.12-14 (i.e. the apostles, the women, Mary and Jesus' brothers).[26] What qualifies this as a 'gap' is the fact that only the eleven apostles have actually received instructions from Jesus to wait for the Spirit's empowerment in Jerusalem (Acts 1.4-5; 8). So, if one takes it that the Spirit has come to fill all who were in the house and that all spoke in tongues, how then do we reconcile Jesus' 'exclusive' instructions to the eleven apostles against those (the 120 brethren) who were said to be present in the same room

25. The author's representation and the readers' reading of the text involve an interaction within a given social system. In other words, the text is not independent from the social understanding which is mutually shared by the author and reader. P. van Staden strongly adheres to this view and states, '…it is immediately obvious that a text is not a sterile, clinical conveyor of meaning by means of a shared sign system. Many other equally typical human characteristics are caught up into literary text. This is recognized by literary critics, in that they study the emotional, ideological, psychological, sociological and other aspects of a text.

Now if texts do have these aspects, and we concede that they do, the next logical step is to move into the domain of the human sciences proper, and to make use of their scientific theories, methodologies and the results of their studies. In fact, this step is not only desirable, but becomes a necessity if we want to understand the text properly.' P. van Staden, 'A Sociological Reading of Luke 12: 35-48', *Neotestamentica* 22 (1988), p. 338.

26. Again, this is an issue which I will discuss later. For the reasons why some scholars view that the 120 brethren are the first recipients of the Spirit's baptism in Acts 2.1-4, see for example R. Menzies, *Empowered for Witness: The Spirit in Luke–Acts* (JPTSup, 9; Sheffield: JSOT Press, 1994), p. 176, n. 1. Menzies' reasons include, it is the most natural reading of πάντες, since the 120 are present in the preceding verses; this conclusion is supported by the repetition of ἐπὶ τὸ αὐτὸ in 1.15 and 2.1; the potentially universal character of the gift is stressed in 2.17 and 2.39, therefore it would be strange if any of the disciples present were excluded from the gift of Pentecost; more than twelve languages are recorded to have been heard, implying more than twelve were present.

when the Spirit came? The issue is compounded by the fact that Lk. 24.47-49 also portrays only the apostles to have received Jesus' instructions to go and wait in Jerusalem for the 'promise of the father'. Social-scientific criticism, specifically with the model with which I intend to read the narrative of Acts 1–2, will resolve this 'gap'. I will show that, despite the presence of the other characters in the story, the apostles serve as the main actors and become, therefore, primary recipients of the Spirit's empowerment in Acts 2.1-4.

> 3. Social-scientific criticism…offers a corrective to the strong tendency to 'theological docetism' in many circles, that is, to the assumption that what is important about the NT are its theological propositions, abstracted somehow from their literary and historical setting, and that true understanding has to do with the interpretation of the words and ideas rather than, or the neglect of, the embodiment and performance of NT faith in the lives of the people and communities from whom the text comes or for whom it was written.

As such, one of the focuses of this study is not primarily on the significance of the Ascension and Pentecost events in the narrative of Acts 1–2.[27] While these two events have inspired theological propositions (especially on Jesus and his ascension, and the Spirit on the day of Pentecost) from many modern Christian circles, my aim is to understand how the apostles (as main characters) are presented by the author in a narrative where two significant events take place. Social-scientific criticism will help me attain this objective.

> 4. Social-scientific criticism…also offers the possibility of increasing our understanding of ourselves as readers of the text… The social sciences help us to recognize that our acts of interpretation are not neutral.

The use of the conceptual model of honour and shame, for instance, will show us that it is possible to read the election narrative of 1.15-26 as a response to a challenge posed against the integrity of the apostles as leaders. The question against the apostles' integrity, as I have proposed, was brought about by Judas—a member of the Twelve. What is also helpful in this exercise is the ability to learn, not only the concept of ancient

---

27. For such focuses, see for example M. Parsons, *The Departure of Jesus in Luke–Acts: The Ascension Narratives in Context* (JSNTSup, 21; Sheffield: JSOT Press, 1987). Studies on Pentecost, on the other hand, are vast. However, for updated references, see M. Turner, *Power from on High: The Spirit in Israel's Restoration and Witness in Luke–Acts* (JPTSup, 9; Sheffield: Sheffield Academic Press, 2000).

values such as honour and shame, but to reflect, compare and contrast as well the kind of values we the modern readers have. By being able to identify and draw the line of what is ours as against what is religious tradition—a tradition conditioned by ancient values or social forces—a better and more objective understanding of the text is possible.

Scepticism about the application of social-scientific criticism to biblical texts has also been expressed. Specifically, the employment of the social sciences in New Testament exegesis has been perceived by some as completely unfruitful.[28] The objections basically fall under two categories. First are those who completely rule out the whole method simply because of its presuppositions—presuppositions which are primarily 'reductionist'[29] in nature. This means that the method reads the text from a purely scientific perspective, leaving no room for the religious factors which may have conditioned the ancient writer, the characters, the readers, and the text

28. Interestingly, the scepticism of the use of social-scientific criticism in NT exegesis has also been directed particularly against the book of Acts. Barton observes that there are three basic reasons. First, sociological or socio-scientific studies on Acts are almost non-existent. If ever there is one, they will most likely be introduced under related categories but not the specific heading of any social-scientific or sociological approach. Second is the dominance in scholarship of issues to do with the historicity of Acts. This may be attributed to: the rise of historical criticism as the recognized method of the scientific investigation of the Bible since the Reformation and Enlightenment periods; the strong ecclesiastical/doctrinal interest in the historical veracity of the apostolic witness; the particular Protestant (including Pentecostalist) interest in the testimony of Acts to the church in the apostolic times; the success and growth of archaeology as a major historical discipline able to fill out or even verify the 'historical geography' of the world and of the early church; the problem of epistemological debate. This is the question on how to respond to the issue of the supernatural in the book of Acts. It is not surprising that Acts has been approached mainly from a historical point of view. Third is the problem of how to deal with the nature of the Acts material itself. Scholars such as E.A. Judge and A. Malherbe view that 'Acts is amenable to interpretation as a source for the social history of early Christianity, but not for interpretation using the tools of the social sciences', quoted in S.C. Barton, 'Sociology and Theology', in I.H. Marshall and D. Petersen (eds.), *Witness to the Gospel: The Theology of Acts* (Grand Rapids: Eerdmans, 1998), pp. 459-72.

29. An attempt to account for a range of phenomena in terms of a single determining factor. Marxist theories, for example, have been branded as reductionist since they explain the diversity of social behaviour by reference simply to economy. 'Reductionist', in N. Abercrombie, S. Hill, and B.S. Turner (eds.), *The Penguin Dictionary of Sociology* (London: Penguin Books, 3rd edn, 1994), pp. 348-49.

itself.[30] Second is an objection to the practical functioning of the method. Here, the use of the social sciences in interpretation is deemed very limited since they are 'too dependent upon contemporary patterns to assist in understanding first century texts'. This objection finds its full expression in E.A. Judge's[31] propositions. He enumerates that,[32]

> 1. Sociological models must be historically tested or 'verified' before they can be applied. Presumably, this means that they must closely fit the historical data to which they are to be applied, otherwise they will be discarded.
>
> 2. Sociological models are 'defined' with respect to particular cultures. This hinders their being applied to first century society.
>
> 3. It is possible to carry out historical 'field work' prior to the use of models. In other words, Judge espouses an empirical hunt for 'the social facts of life characteristic' of the New Testament world, free from theoretical presupposition.

Both of these objections have aptly received rebuttals from biblical scholars who have found the method very helpful in exegesis. With regard to the first objection, sociologists begin to recognize that while the method of sociological criticism may explain a given phenomenon, such explanation is partial. Economics, political, and even religious factors may well be the other reasons behind the existence of the same phenomenon.[33] This, of course, is the same conviction I hold in my study of Acts 1.3–2.14. I do not in any way claim that the narrative of Acts 1 and 2 can only be explained from the method and models I am proposing. There are other possibilities why the narrative has been presented by the author in such a manner. Mine specifically focuses on the possible social implications behind the sequence and relationship of the events. I am convinced, however, that I find the use of models from the method of social-scientific criticism the best way to address the questions which I feel the historical method has failed to answer.

As to the second objection, social-scientific exegetes find that this is no

---

30. P.F. Esler, *Community and Gospel in Luke–Acts: The Social and Political Motivations of Lucan Theology* (Cambridge: Cambridge University Press, 1987), p. 12.

31. E.A. Judge, 'The Social Identity of the First Christians: A Question of Method in Religious History', *The Journal of Religious History* 11 (1980), pp. 201-217. Esler also identifies C.S. Rodd as an adherent of this kind of objection. Cf. C.S. Rodd, 'On Applying a Sociological Theory to Biblical Studies', *JSOT* 19 (1981), pp. 95-106.

32. Esler, *Community and Gospel*, p. 14.

33. Esler, *Community and Gospel*, p. 13.

longer the case. For instance, Esler argues that Judge's points are all inconsistent. That sociological models ought to be historically verified or validated before they are applied to the text renders them not as mental constructs or research tools but primarily akin to social laws. He strongly insists that 'as long as the comparative material has some analogy to the situation it is quite unnecessary that it correspond exactly'.[34]

Sociologists have also been aware of Judge's second observation. Those producing models and typologies have tended to strip these models of their spatial and temporal markings to increase their applicability in historical research.[35] Again, Esler adds,

> The case for using the social sciences in biblical exegesis is most thoroughly established by demonstrating not merely that this is a useful additional approach to the text, but also that the traditional historical mode of analysis is defective precisely in as much as it fails to utilise concepts and perspective from sociology and anthropology.[36]

Furthermore, to suggest the possibility of carrying out historical 'field work' prior to the use of models, Esler is precise in saying that it is quite impossible for a researcher to collect facts without subscribing to a whole range of theoretical presuppositions. In other words, there is no such thing as a purely objective approach into a specific field of inquiry. Esler believes that 'by not consciously and deliberately acknowledging and reflecting upon his or her preconceptions, the historian runs the risk of imposing modern notions of categorisation...'[37]

In reality, scholars who discourage the use of the social-scientific method in biblical studies have not been very successful. More and more exegetes are becoming aware of the significant contribution of this method in studying the biblical texts.[38] The employment of models indeed assists in 'piercing the stereotypes and conventional formulae of human action in the present, so that we can obtain a far more clear-sighted view of the past'.[39]

---

34. Esler, *Community and Gospel*, p. 14.

35. E.g. B.R. Wilson, *Magic and the Millennium: A Sociological Study of Religious Movements of Protest among Tribal and Third-World Peoples* (London: Heinemann, 1973), pp. 9-30; cited from Esler, *Community and Gospel*, p. 14.

36. Esler, *Community and Gospel*, p. 15.

37. Esler, *Community and Gospel*, p 15.

38. A point I hope this thesis will help in strengthening, especially the case against the use of the method in the book of Acts.

39. Esler, *Community and Gospel*, p. 16.

1.2. *What are Models?*

The practitioners of social-scientific criticism use models in the interpretation of biblical texts. The term 'model', according to Esler, is the general expression for the ideas and perspectives employed in exegesis, although 'typologies' and 'theories' have been used elsewhere.[40] In the end, however, the term 'model' has come to represent the 'distinctive approach integration of the social sciences and biblical interpretation characterised by a very explicit use of theory and comparative method'.[41]

Providing a simple definition of what models are has been difficult. Elliot attempts this by pulling together different definitions in order to give a dynamic description. Quoting Ian Barbour, he suggests that a model is 'a symbolic representation of selected aspects of the behaviour of a complex system for particular purposes'.[42] For Bruce Malina, on the other hand, a model ' is an abstract simplified representation of some real world object, event, or interaction constructed for the purpose of understanding, control or prediction'.[43] Thomas F. Carney suggests that,

> a model is something less than a theory and something more than an analogy… A theory is based on axiomatic laws and states general principles. It is a basic proposition through which a variety of observations or statements become explicable. A model, by way of contrast, acts as a link between theories and observations. A model will employ one or more theories to provide a simplified (or an experimental or a generalised or an explanatory) framework which can be brought to bear on some pertinent data.[44]

Models help to identify the values and perspectives of the interpreter.[45] In the investigation of the biblical text, for instance, the use of models

40. Esler, 'Review of D.G. Horrell, *The Social Ethos of the Corinthian Correspondence*', *JTS* 49 (1998), p. 254.

41. Esler, 'Review of D.G. Horrell', p. 254.

42. Cf. I. Barbour, *Myths, Models, and Paradigms: A Comparative Study in Science and Religion* (New York: Harper & Row, 1974), p. 6; quoted from Elliott, *What is Social-Scientific Criticism?*, p. 41. For further reading on this issue, see also B.J. Malina, *The New Testament World: Insights from Cultural Anthropology* (Atlanta, GA: John Knox Press, 1981); M. Black, *Models and Metaphors* (Ithaca, NY: Cornell University Press, 1962), pp. 25-47.

43. Cf. Bruce Malina, 'The Social Sciences of Biblical Interpretation', p. 231, quoted from Elliott, *What is Social-Scientific Criticism?*, p. 41.

44. Cf. T.F. Carney, *The Shape of the Past: Models and Antiquity* (Lawrence, KS: Coronado Press, 1975), p. 8; quoted from Elliott, *What is Social-Scientific Criticism?*, p. 41.

45. Esler, *The First Christians*, pp. 12-13.

brings to the surface what the properties of ancient social and cultural systems are as against what may simply be the modern reader's late-twentieth-century worldview. Because a model is consciously structured beforehand, it functions as a measuring tool, having the ability to make comparisons and thus further see what the text holds and what it does not.[46] The comparisons, however, do not function as an eliminating tool where the model is favoured and maintains its structure as it disintegrates the text. In other words, 'a model is not a set of pigeon-holes into which data is slotted... The texts must supply the answers, not the model.'[47] In reality, the model serves to expose and ask new questions. And if indeed the model is not appropriate to the text that is being investigated, the model and not the text should be adjusted, modified, replaced, or even discarded.[48]

The usefulness of models, according to Elliott, is measured by how they 'clarify and explicate the theories and assumptions of the researcher'.[49] They ought to 'reveal and explain the properties and relationships of social behaviour, social structures, and social processes'.[50] Therefore, the choice of what models to apply, Elliott adds, '...is determined by the types of social phenomena to be analysed and explained and by the theories which the researcher holds concerning the nature, interrelationships, and importance of these phenomena'.[51]

There are, however, exegetes who hold that the use of models misleads rather than helps the exegete. A common objection (a point I have just mentioned) is that models tend to impose 'alien and inappropriate frameworks on first century data'.[52] This usually happens especially when interpreters begin their investigation with a model. Such a move, according to D.G. Horrell, 'can lead the researcher to view the evidence in a particular way, or to assume that a certain pattern of conduct must be present'.[53] He emphasizes that models 'should not be a guide to research,

---

46. Esler, *The First Christians*, pp. 12-13.

47. Esler, *The First Christians*, pp. 12-13.

48. M. Finley, *Ancient History: Evidence and Models* (London: Chatto and Windus, 1985), p. 66

49. J.H. Elliott, 'Social-Scientific Criticism of the New Testament: More on Methods and Models', *Semeia* 35 (1986), p. 4.

50. Elliott, 'Social-Scientific Criticism of the New Testament', p. 4.

51. Elliott, 'Social-Scientific Criticism of the New Testament', p. 9.

52. P.F. Esler, *Modelling Early Christianity: Social-Scientific Studies of the New Testament in its Context* (London: Routledge, 1995), p. 4.

53. D.G. Horrell, 'Models and Methods in Social-Scientific Interpretation: A

but a product of it'.[54] Horrell warns that interpreters cannot avoid their own presuppositions in their choice of models and that they shape the way they see things.[55]

Model-users aptly respond back. It is argued that the issue is not whether we use models or not. In other words, any modern interpreter investigating the biblical text approaches his or her study with certain presuppositions, hence a model.[56] The question is whether the modern interpreter is conscious of the fact that he or she approaches the text with a model beforehand. As Elliott points out, 'every imagining of reconstructing of "how it was back then" necessarily involves the use of some conceptual model. "If we use them unconsciously", (quoting T.F. Carney[57]) "they control us, we do not control them".'[58] Or as Esler puts it,

> Models will have built into them certain modern assumptions and perceptions, but these are essential if we are to address cultural experience different from our own in terms we can comprehend. The debate is really about what assumptions we should adopt, not whether we model or not.[59]

The aim is whether the text will provide some answers that are historically plausible or not.[60] If it does, the goal has been achieved. If not,

Response to P.F. Esler', *JSNT* 78 (2000), pp. 83-105 (90-91).

54. Horrell, 'Models and Methods', pp. 90-91, quoting S. Barrett, *Anthropology: Student's Guide to Theory and Method* (Toronto: University of Toronto Press, 1996), p. 216. Instead, Horrell suggests the method of 'interpretivism' as a more workable social-scientific approach in biblical interpretation. Interpretivism (or interpretive criticism) involves the 'total immersion in another culture by a trained observer'. See Esler, *Modelling Early Christianity*, pp. 4-8 for the issues between model-users and interpretivists.

55. Cf. Esler, 'Review of D.G. Horrell', p. 255.

56. Horrell, however, finds the term 'model' used broadly to refer to theory or ideal-types. He believes that using this term in a very general way is highly unsatisfactory. He finds two reasons why this is so: first, the term is rendered almost entirely vacuous. For Horrell, 'if every presupposition, assumption, analogy, perspective or theory should be called a "model" then, indeed, we use models all the time, whether consciously or not, and the term becomes more little than a convenient label to describe the widely accepted truth that human perception is never purely objective or detached'. Second, the term is in danger of 'obfuscating' the significant differences between those who uses a 'model-based' approach and those who favour 'interpretative approach'. Horrell, 'Models and Methods', p. 85.

57. Cf. Carney, *The Shape of the Past*, p. 5.

58. Elliott, *What is Social-Scientific Criticism?*, pp. 44-45.

59. Esler, *Modelling Early Christianity*, p. 7.

60. Cf. Esler, 'Review of D.G. Horrell', p. 109.

the text remains intact, keeping its secrets within. The interpreter then resolves to find another model in order to make historical sense of the biblical text which has been locked up for centuries by its respective social and cultural dimensions.[61]

1.3. *Two Types of Model: The Environment and Cross-Cultural*[62]
There are at least two types of model which social-scientists use in biblical exegesis.[63] First is the model which is conceived or developed from the environment of the text.[64] In other words, these two types of model are not imported from outside the social and cultural milieu of text concerned. The first model, therefore, has been structured and defined from what is basically available or present within the biblical environment. A good example of this type has been demonstrated by W. Meeks in his book *The First Urban Christians: The Social World of the Apostle Paul*.[65] Meeks's quest to understand the formation of the *ekklesia* in the time of the apostle Paul sought to develop a model of 'group formation' solely on what is found or available in the Pauline writings and its New Testament contemporaries. His models therefore include insights from the nature and composition of the 'household', the 'voluntary associations', the 'synagogue', and the 'philosophic or rhetorical schools'.[66] In addition, Meeks also attempted to define the nature of fellowship and boundaries of Pauline Christian groups. These included the 'language of belonging', the 'lan-

61. Esler, 'Review of D.G. Horrell', pp. 109-111.
62. The need to mention this issue was brought to my attention during Dr L.C.A. Alexander's reading of her seminar paper entitled '*IPSE DIXIT: Citation of Authority in Paul and in the Jewish and Hellenistic Schools*', at the Biblical Studies Department seminar, Sheffield University, 9 October 2000. A paper originally presented by her at the proceedings of the 1997 Rolighed Conference under the seminar title *Paul beyond the Judaism-Hellenism Divide* (ed. T. Enberg-Pedersen).
63. Different from the five main types of model which T.F. Carney proposes. Mine is plainly the general type which is basically classified into two. For the discussion of Carney's five main types of model, see Carney, *The Shape of the Past*, pp. 13-34.
64. For a collection of essays on the concept, types and application of models see J. Richardson (ed.), *Models of Reality: Shaping Thought and Action* (Mount Airy, MD: Lomond Publications, 1984).
65. W. Meeks, *The First Urban Christians: The Social World of the Apostle Paul* (New Haven: Yale University Press, 1983). Also, R.S. Ascough, *What Are They Saying about the Formation of Pauline Churches?* (New York: Paulist Press, 1998); R. Wilken, 'Collegia, Philosophical Schools and Theology', in S. Benko and J.J. O'Rourke (eds.), *Early Church History* (Valley Forge, PA: Judson Press, 1971).
66. Meeks, *The First Urban Christians*, pp. 74-84.

guage of separation', 'purity and boundaries', the identity of an 'autonomous institution', and the encouragement to do mission.[67]

The second type is known as the 'cross-cultural model'.[68] Models from this type are those which are drawn from the field of the social sciences and are developed by empirical research on human behaviour.[69] The principle behind this model-type is that the investigation of the social dimensions of early Christianity can be greatly enhanced with 'the assistance of over a century of research into arguably similar areas of human behaviour conducted by anthropologists, sociologists, and social psychologists'.[70] This principle works from the assumption that certain patterns of human social activity are shared and maintained through the centuries by various societies both ancient and modern. The discipline of the social sciences has 'objectivated'[71] and formulated these patterns into theories and models by which they can be used and tested in the study of societies whether they be in the present or in the past. Social-scientific criticism is the method which enables us to 'pick and choose' among these models and theories on offer to see which are most likely to help in producing historically plausible readings of the biblical texts.[72]

In this thesis, it is the cross-cultural type of model which will serve as our theoretical framework. To explain further how this will be employed, I now move to discuss the specific model I have in mind.

2. *The Rituals of Status Transformation*

There is no doubt that one can read in Acts 1–2 the apostles' change of status from followers to leaders. As I have stated earlier, the ascension of Jesus is not only the story of his departure but also the beginning of the apostles' assumption of the leadership responsibility over the Christian community. Nor is Pentecost simply the story of the Spirit's arrival but also the event which confirms such a leadership responsibility upon the

---

67. Meeks, *The First Urban Christians*, pp. 84-107.
68. Cf. Esler, 'Review of D.G. Horrell', p. 257.
69. Esler, *The First Christians*, p. 2.
70. Esler, 'Review of D.G. Horrell', p. 253.
71. Cf. P.L. Berger and T. Luckmann, *The Social Construction of Reality: A Treatise in the Sociology of Knowledge* (Harmondsworth: Penguin Books, 1966), pp. 65-109. In particular, P. Berger is a sociologist who developed his theories from the pioneering studies of such as Max Weber (1864–1920); Emile Durkheim (1858–1917); K. Marx (1818–1883).
72. Cf. Esler, 'Review of D.G. Horrell', p. 254.

apostles. From these notions, I conclude that Acts 1–2 is a narrative telling the process of the apostles' status transformation.

One of the tasks I have aimed to do is to study this status transformation process and make historical sense of the function of the episodes of 1.12-14 and 1.15-26. I believe that we have a model from the method of social-scientific criticism which will help us achieve this aim. The model is that of a 'ritual'—the rituals of status transformation. A ritual is a means of aiding the participant in understanding the way the world is perceived by their social group and a way of participating in its patterns. It is a 'symbolic form of expression which mediates the cultural core values and attitudes that structure and sustain a society'.[73] I propose that the way the events in Acts 1–2 are sequenced and narrated yields certain social symbols, symbols which help the author convey to his readers that the apostles have been transformed from followers to leaders—their leaders. Social anthropologists have classified this process of transformation as the '*rites of passage*'.[74] It is a passage from one domain to another, from one role or status level to another higher level.

2.1. The Rites of Passage *by Arnold Van Gennep*
One of the most significant pioneers in the study of ritual behaviours in its relation to the dynamics of individual or group life is French scholar Arnold Van Gennep. His work *Les rites de passage* (originally published in 1908) has opened up new insights through the comparative analyses of social worlds.[75] His studies were moved by the desire to understand and give rational explanations on religious behaviour.[76] This meant the investigation of its 'historical origins, making comparative analyses, or presenting functional interpretations'.[77] His investigation, however, was careful not to conduct the examination of the phenomena in bits and pieces and alien from its social setting. He works from the 'tradition of positiv-

73. M. McVann, 'Rituals of Status Transformation in Luke–Acts: The Case of Jesus the Prophet', in J.H. Neyrey (ed.), *The Social World of Luke–Acts* (Peabody, MA: Hendrickson, 1991), p. 334.

74. A term first used systematically in anthropology to denote public ceremonies celebrating the transition of an individual or group to a new status, for example initiation ceremonies. Abercrombie *et al.* (eds.), *Penguin Dictionary of Sociology*, p. 360.

75. A. Van Gennep, *The Rites of Passage* (trans. M.B. Vizedom and G.L. Caffee; Chicago: University of Chicago Press, 1960).

76. Van Gennep, *The Rites of Passage*, p. vi.

77. Van Gennep, *The Rites of Passage*, p. vi.

ism—the insistence that general laws of social process should be derived from empirical research rather than from metaphysical speculation'.[78]

The major contribution of Van Gennep is his study of ceremonies which accompany an individual's 'life crises'. It is from this that he formulated his theoretical framework of *les rites de passage*.[79] In this framework, Van Gennep identifies three major phases which the individual or group goes through: separation, transition, and incorporation. These phases are based on Van Gennep's understanding of the dichotomy of things, specifically of the sacred and the profane. S.T. Kimball, writing the introduction to the English translation of Van Gennep's *The Rites of Passage*, explains:

> ...the dichotomy of the sacred and the profane...is a central concept for understanding the transitional stage in which an individual or group finds itself from time to time. The sacred is not an absolute value but one relative to the situation. The person who enters a status at variance with one previously held becomes 'sacred' to the others who remain in the profane state. It is in this new condition which calls for rites eventually incorporating the individual into the group and returning him to the customary routines of life. These changes may be dangerous, and at least, they are upsetting to the life of the group and the individual. The transitional period is met with rites of passage which cushion the disturbance.[80]

Van Gennep made it clear that his interest in not in the rite itself but in its order. He found that the order within rites was basically the same, a pattern of the rites of passage. Kimball also noticed that Van Gennep was able to show the 'existence of transitional periods which sometimes acquire a certain autonomy'.[81] Finally, Van Gennep declared that there was a connection between the actual spatial passage and the change in social position. This connection is 'expressed in such ritualization of movements from one status to another as an "opening of doors"'.[82]

The impact of Van Gennep's theoretical framework can be measured by the extent of responses to his propositions. Several have sought to use his ideas, incorporated them into the literature, attacked, defended, and expanded them.[83] Some of the more significant responses to Van Gennep

78. Van Gennep, *The Rites of Passage*, p. vii.
79. Van Gennep, *The Rites of Passage*, p. vii.
80. Van Gennep, *The Rites of Passage*, pp. viii-ix.
81. Van Gennep, *The Rites of Passage*, p. x.
82. Van Gennep, *The Rites of Passage*, p. x.
83. Earlier notable studies would include A.M. Tozzer, *Social Origins and Social Continuities* (New York: Macmillan, 1925); G. Bateson, *Naven* (Cambridge:

are those from A.R. Radcliffe Brown,[84] E.D. Chapple and C.S. Coon.[85] These scholars extended Van Gennep's identity of the 'crisis' which the group or individual experiences. According to Kimball, Chapple and Coon investigating the precise nature of the 'crisis' helps in understanding the 'disturbance' within individuals or groups.[86] Kimball states that, 'Van Gennep commented upon the disturbances which changes in status produced in the individual, and he saw rites of passage as devices which incorporated an individual into a new status in a group'.[87] Radcliffe-Brown adds to this the idea that such rites actually function as '*restorative of the moral sentiments which had been disturbed through the changes in social life of the group*'.[88]

A more popular expansion of Van Gennep's framework is that of Victor Turner. Specifically, Turner's book *The Ritual Process*[89] contributed valuable insights into Van Gennep's 'transition' phase to which Turner formulated his liminality-*communitas* stage. This stage is crucial to our study of the function and relationship of 1.12-14 and 1.15-26 within the apostles' ritual of status transformation in Acts 1–2.

2.2. The Ritual Process *by Victor Turner*

Turner is also a social anthropologist interested in the study of group life. He recognized that Van Gennep's theoretical framework indeed shows structural similarities in rites, either of status transformation, puberty, death, marriage, birth, or healing, 'to which they all operated as a way of marking life process in the experience of the people among whom he had lived and worked'.[90]

The Ritual Process is the product of Turner's study on a particular group, the Ndembu people of northwestern Zambia. This is where Turner

Cambridge University Press, 1936); C.A. DuBois, *The People of Alor* (Minneapolis, MN: University of Minnesota Press, 1944); M. Mead, *Growing Up in New Guinea* (New York: Blue Ribbon Books, 1930).

   84. Cf. A.R. Radcliffe-Brown, *The Andaman Islanders* (Cambridge: Cambridge University Press, 1922).

   85. E.D. Chapple and C.S. Coon, *Principles of Anthropology* (New York: Henry Holt & Co., 1942).

   86. Quoted in Van Gennep, *The Rites of Passage*, p. xiii.

   87. Quoted in Van Gennep, *The Rites of Passage*, p. xiii.

   88. Quoted in Van Gennep, *The Rites of Passage*, p. xiii; italics mine.

   89. V. Turner, *The Ritual Process: Structure and Anti-Structure* (New York: Aldine De Gruyter, 1995).

   90. Turner, *The Ritual Process*, p. xi.

differs from the other scholars I have cited above. 'Where Van Gennep... had sought to organize all of cultural practice superorganically, making global generalizations, Turner argued from specific field data'.[91] He applied Van Gennep's *schéma* of *les rites de passage* into a specific people-group context. Turner then was able to analyse where the tripartite processual scheme of separation, transition, and incorporation helps in the study of a particular social context. In areas where the scheme seems lacking, Turner made expansions and developed Van Gennep's framework.

One of these expansions, as I have stated earlier, is on Van Gennep's 'transition' stage. Turner introduces the term '*communitas*' into the same stage to represent the type of bonding among the initiands. This happens when the liminal subjects share comradeship with each other as class, rank, wealth, or social status is broken down even as they all submit to the ritual elders and experience the equality of sharing a common predicament.[92]

This liminality-*communitas* stage serves as an important stage in the process of the rite of passage. It is when, according to Turner, the subject experiences the 'limbo of statuslessness'.[93] The individual or group going through the process is 'betwixt and between' the status or role that has been designated.[94] This description is very helpful if we are to understand the function of the author's report about the events which happened to the apostles between the time they were commissioned by Jesus in Acts 1.8 and the confirmation of their new status by the baptism of the Spirit in 2.1-4.

But why do we find Van Gennep's theoretical framework and Turner's expansion of the same helpful in our exegesis of Acts 1–2? The answer lies in the plausibility of Mark McVann's study as he attempted to use the model on Jesus' status transformation in the gospel of Luke. McVann called his model the 'Rituals of Status Transformation' (alternatively RST).

2.3. The Rituals of Status Transformation *by Mark McVann*
Mark McVann's study is found under the category of 'social dynamics' in

---

91. R.D. Abraham's foreword in Turner, *The Ritual Process*, p. xi.
92. R.L. Cohn, 'Liminality in the Wilderness', in *The Shape of Sacred Space: Four Biblical Studies* (Missoula, MT: Scholars Press, 1981), p. 10.
93. Turner, *The Ritual Process*, p. 97.
94. Cf. Cohn, 'Liminality in the Wilderness', p. 10.

the 1991 project of the Context Group entitled *The Social World of Luke–Acts: Models for Interpretation.*[95] McVann's work, 'Rituals of Status Transformation in Luke–Acts: The Case of Jesus the Prophet' is a slightly modified version of Turner's model. What follows is a summary of McVann's propositions. From here, we will show how McVann's RST will serve as the model and theoretical framework in our investigation of the apostles' status transformation in Acts 1–2.

2.3.1. *The Elements of a Ritual.* The rite of passage involves *elements* which help effect passage to the new role and status. Ritual elements are what comprise the ritual itself. They include primarily the *initiands*; the *ritual elders*; and the *symbols* (or *sacra*):

A. The *initiands* are the people who, individually or as a group, experience the status of transformation ritual.[96] They are the ones who are ordained to take on the new roles and statuses in their society after they have gone through the ritual process.

B. The transformation from one status to another is presided over by a person or persons qualified to supervise the transition and certify its legitimacy. These persons are known as 'ritual elders'.[97] The *ritual elders* may function as models for the initiands because they are the 'professionals' who embody the core values of their society.[98] They are recognized by the society as having the authority over this field and they command respect and authority from the people within that society. These elders take the initiands into a cleansing process by which they instil new ideas and wipe out the old preconceived concepts before the new status is confirmed.[99] They need to enact these measures if the initiands are to come out of the ritual as new people and understand their new roles and statuses

95. J.H. Neyrey (ed.), *The Social World of Luke–Acts: Models for Interpretation* (Peabody, MA: Hendrickson, 1991).

96. Other terms referring to the initiand (from *initiare*—'to begin') are sometimes employed by both Van Gennep and Turner. These include, 'passengers', *novus*—'new', 'fresh', or neophyte—*neos-futon*, 'newly grown'. Cf. V. Turner, *Dramas, Fields, and Metaphors: Symbolic Action in Human Society* (Ithaca, NY: Cornell University Press, 1974), p. 232.

97. Turner, *Dramas, Fields, and Metaphors*, p. 336.

98. McVann, 'Rituals of Status Transformation', p. 337.

99. In some societies, the ritual elders may beat their initiands, withhold food or sleep, taunt or insult them, strip them of clothing, or any other measures which debases the initiands' self confidence and pride. Cf. McVann, 'Rituals of Status Transformation', p. 337.

in order to carry out their responsibilities before the people in their societies.

C. The ritual *symbols* (*sacra*) take various shapes. They are known to represent aspects of familiar things yet are combined in such a way as to make them seem bizarre. At crucial points, they are taken out and exhibited before the initiands as a part of their instruction in the basic facts of their culture.[100] They play significant roles during the ritual or at the formal induction and conclusion of the ritual. 'Ritual symbols are sacred because they are objects out of the ordinary. They provide a focus for the initiands during their liminality, and ensure that they concentrate on the values and attitudes of their society which are concentrated symbolically and highlighted in them.'[101]

2.3.2. *The Process of the Ritual.*

Regardless of the specific status transformation or the particular ritualizing society, the fundamental stages in any rite of passage remain largely the same: separation, transition, and aggregation.[102] Turner expands Van Gennep's 'transition' stage by emphasizing the liminality-*communitas* nature of such a stage. McVann's contribution is the expansion of Turner's 'liminality-*communitas*' with the addition of the phase which he calls 'ritual confrontation'. This study will adopt McVann's stage descriptions:

A. Separation. Separation is a major part of the ritual process. It 'comprises symbolic behaviour signifying the detachment of the individual or group either from an earlier fixed point in the social structure, from a set of cultural conditions (a "state") or from both'.[103] Any initiand undergoing status transformation experiences separation in three ways: separation from people, of place, and of time.

---

100. In the rituals of some cults and other religious groups, the symbols may come as skulls, masks, rings, books, or even candles. McVann, 'Rituals of Status Transformation', p. 337.

101. Turner explains further, 'These symbols, visual and auditory, operate culturally as mnemonics, or as communications engineers would no doubt have it, as "storage bins" of information, not about pragmatic techniques, but about cosmologies, values, and cultural axioms, whereby society's deep knowledge is transmitted from one generation to another'. Turner, *Dramas, Fields, and Metaphors*, p. 239.

102. Turner, *Dramas, Fields, and Metaphors*, p. 338. With primary reference to the ritual, Van Gennep uses the serial terms *separation*, *margin*, and *re-aggregation*. Likewise, with reference to the spatial transitions, he employs the terms *preliminal*, *liminal*, and *postliminal*. Cf. Turner, *The Ritual Process*, p. 166.

103. Turner, *The Ritual Process*, p. 94.

1. Separation from people takes the initiands away from the ordinary rhythm of the society. The initiands go through the ritual of separation, at times by exclusion, which is more often supervised by the ritual elders.
2. Separation of place may be the designated place of initiation. In other societies, these are places where access to it is difficult and may be deemed sacred. It can be a place known for receiving special revelations from spirits or gods; such places are ideal sites for such rituals.[104]
3. Separation of time is the moment when the initiands are thought to be removed from the normal flow of time. They are believed to leave 'secular' time and enter into a sacred 'timelessness'. It can be a time of inactivity (e.g. prayer, silence, immobility) or forced activity (singing, dancing).

B. Liminality-*Communitas*. Liminality[105] requires the initiands to abandon their previous beliefs or habits, ideas, and understandings, their personal identities and relations, with others in their society. Because they are 'lost' from the culture during the time their status is ritually recreated, any status they had is lost as well. In the liminal stage, the initiand undergoes:

> a symbolic death to his old life and is in the process of being reborn to a new one. His situation in the ritual is often likened in the lore to being in the womb or the wilderness, to invisibility, to darkness, to an eclipse of the sun or moon, to bisexuality. He is sexless or androgynous. He is out of time and space, a threshold being.[106]

The initiands (in some cultures) are perceived as dangerous or as pollution to those outside the ritual process because the initiands exist in limbo, a realm where they are always 'in between' an uncertain place.[107]

Communitas,[108] on the other hand, is the positive side of this process. Although it cannot be considered apart from liminality, *communitas* refers

---

104. McVann, 'Rituals of Status Transformation', p. 339.

105. From the Latin term *limen* meaning 'threshold'. In this case, the initiands go through the phase of liminal *personae* ('threshold people'). Cf. Turner, *The Ritual Process*, p. 95.

106. Cohn, 'Liminality in the Wilderness', p. 10.

107. McVann, 'Rituals of Status Transformation', p. 337.

108. A term in Latin preferred by Turner over 'community' to distinguish the 'modality of social relationship' from an 'area of common living'; cf. Turner, *The Ritual Process*, p. 96.

to the initiands' recognition of their fundamental bondedness or comradeship in the institution into which they are being initiated. This is the time when all inequality among the participants is broken down and is replaced by equality and unity. Liminality, therefore, suspends routine and represses status differences. *Communitas*, the focus on common humanity, can then emerge into the foreground, and an 'all for one, one for all' spirit often develops among the initiands in a rite of passage. It is the communion of equal individuals who submit together to the general authority of the ritual elders.[109]

C. Ritual Confrontation. The confrontation is usually a mock test initiated by the ritual elder or selected leaders of the community. Its purpose is to test the overall skills of the initiand before he/she is re-incorporated into the society. It appears to function as the product's 'quality test' conducted internally by people in their own camp before they are aggregated into the community which they intend to lead or serve.[110]

D. Aggregation. Aggregation (or reincorporation) happens when the ritual initiation is completed. This is the time when the initiands return to the society, taking with them their new roles and statuses, with new rights and obligations. The larger society, on the other hand, acknowledges that the initiands now have the capacities requisite for fulfilling their new roles within it. The initiands are no longer seen as threatening, dangerous, or unreliable. They can be trusted and respect can be attributed. After the ritual, the initiands become useful to the society as they take up their new responsibilities.[111]

109. Turner, *The Ritual Process*, p. 96.

110. V. Turner, *The Forest of Symbols: Aspects of the Ndembu Ritual* (Ithaca, NY: Cornell University Press, 1967), pp. 38-47; *idem, The Ritual Process*, pp. 100-102; *idem, Dramas, Fields, and Metaphors*, pp. 38-39. In certain ritual transformations, some form of ritual mock battle or hostile confrontation as a final step is seen as the initiands' achievement and public recognition of their new status. In some instances real violence occurs, while in others, there is a controlled and highly focused expression of hostility and tension such as that which occurs in a challenge-riposte situation. Cf. McVann, 'Rituals of Status Transformation', pp. 340-41.

111. McVann adds, however, that those who have been initiated into particular roles such as shamans, prophets, or priests, undergo only partial aggregation. While they provide indispensable services to the society, they remain partially on its margins since they are thought to retain access to powers and forces which make them dangerous. McVann, 'Rituals of Status Transformation', p. 341.

2.4. *The Model Applied: The Prophetic Role of Jesus in Luke 3.1–4.30*
McVann identifies Lk. 3.1–4.30 as the narrative where Jesus' ritual of
status transformation occurs. It is the narrative which shows the changing
of Jesus' role from private person to public prophet.[112]

For ritual *elements*, McVann obviously has Jesus as the initiand. The
role to which Jesus has been transformed after the ritual is that of a
prophet. John the baptizer, on the other hand, is the ritual elder. It is John
who serves, in some way, as an example of the prophet's role which Jesus
is going to be. Though Jesus is superior to John, the ritual presents John as
the one initiating Jesus into the prophet's role.[113]

Luke has consistently presented John in terms of this description. In the
infancy narratives John is already being described in the role of a prophet.
John is called a holy figure in 1.1-17; he will be separated from pollution
such as being drunk from wine in 1.15; the presence of the Spirit in him
describes him as powerful in 1.17, 41-44. John's behaviour in Lk. 3.1-20
shows that he is holy, has been set apart from society, and he acts
aggressively against sin. McVann adds,[114]

> The historical facts concerning John's actual relationship with Jesus escape
> us. But Luke's narrative presents John as Jesus' ritual elder: and exemplary
> prophet and model to be followed. Luke's story implies that Jesus, having
> studied John, learned the role into which he is initiated, as the following
> comparison suggests.[115]

112. McVann, 'Rituals of Status Transformation', p. 341.

113. McVann states, 'Luke's description of John's behaviour in 3.1-20 leaves no
doubt that John fulfils his role: (a) he remains "holy" or separate, apart from society at
the Jordan, and (b) he acts aggressively against sin'. McVann, 'Rituals of Status
Transformation', p. 343. In addition, the tradition on the miraculous conception has
been deduced from the accounts found in Lk. 1.14-17 and Mt. 1.18-20; Stephen Farris,
The Hymns of Luke's Infancy Narratives (JSNTSup, 9; Sheffield: JSOT Press, 1985),
pp. 14-98. Because of these two accounts, suggestions that Luke utilized traditional
material in forming his version is supported. Luke used this material because of two
possible reasons: first, to show the parallels between John's and Jesus' prophetic
ministries; and second, to show Jesus' superiority over John. E. Schweizer, *The Good
News according to Luke* (ed. D. Green; London: John Knox Press, 1984), p. 15; ' The
Spirit and Power: The Uniformity and Diversity of the Concept of the Holy Spirit in
the New Testament', *Int* 6 (1952), pp. 259-78 (263). For a discussion on the parallel
prophetic ministries of John and Jesus, see R.E. Brown, *The Birth of the Messiah: A
Commentary on the Infancy Narratives in Matthew and Luke* (London: Geoffrey
Chapman, 1977), p. 250.

114. McVann, 'Rituals of Status Transformation', pp. 344-45.

115. McVann argues that even in Luke 1–3, John the Baptizer is an explicit model of

	John the Baptizer	*Jesus the Prophet*
1.	holy figure (1.15-17)	Son of God (4.3, 9)
2.	conflict with sinners (3.19-20)	conflict with evil (4.3-13)
3.	discerns disguised evil (3.7-8)	discerns evil hidden in the tests (4.3-13)
4.	proclaims justice (3.10-14)	proclaims justice (4.18-19)
5.	preaches repentance (1.17; 3.3, 8)	preaches repentance (5.32; 13.3, 5)
6.	faces rejection (7.31-33)	faces rejection (4.21-30)

For ritual *symbols*, McVann first divides the narrative into three acts: Act I—John and Jesus at the Jordan (3.1-22); Act II—Jesus in the wilderness (4.1-3, with the genealogy in 3.23-38 as the narrator's lengthy aside); Act III—Jesus' re-entry into society (4.14-30).

He then identifies the symbols of the ritual in Act I (3.1-22) as the following: prophet (John the Baptizer), Jordan River,[116] Spirit (dove), and Voice from heaven.[117] McVann suggests that in the ritual context of 'baptism-investiture', this cluster of symbols informs the reader that the criteria for the transfer of prophetic power and authority from John to Jesus are firmly established within the tradition of Israel's prophets and have been divinely ordained.

In Act II (Lk. 4.1-13), another cluster of ritual elements appears. They are elements situated in the scene of a ritual combat. The elements include Jesus as the novice prophet, the devil, settings such as desert, mountain, temple, and scripture.

For ritual *process*, McVann identifies the three types of separation mentioned earlier: of people, place, and time. Jesus encounters the separation from people in three ways. First, Jesus' baptism by John signifies

---

prophet for Jesus the initiand. This is odd since Jesus as Christ is superior to John. However, in the mechanics of the ritual, Jesus is inferior to John. Jesus has not yet been transformed into the status of prophet until he undergoes the ritual of status transformation. 'Thus Luke establishes a link between Jesus and John to show that the mantle of prophecy is passed to Jesus in a valid ritual process.' McVann, 'Rituals of Status Transformation', p. 343.

116. For McVann, the Jordan river functions principally as a boundary symbol. It represents the final reach of extent of culture. As West of the Jordan is the world of humanity and culture, East is the wilderness, a place of promise and renewal, but also an unclean place of madness and starvation, tests and demons. McVann, 'Rituals of Status Transformation', p. 346.

117. Both the Spirit and Voice are ancient symbols which constitute God's intervention into human affairs. It signals that a dramatic change is about to take place. E.g. Deut. 4.33; Pss. 18.14; 68.34; Ezek. 1.24. McVann, 'Rituals of Status Transformation', p. 346.

Jesus' desire to be separated from sin.[118] Second, Jesus too had been separated from his family at Nazareth. And third, Jesus experiences separation when he abandons all human company and travels alone into the desert (Lk. 4.1).

As for separation of place, the spatial setting of Nazareth should not be disregarded. The baptism marks the point where Jesus leaves the established culture of his hometown for the wilderness of Jordan. Separation of time is found when Jesus enters the time of his testing in the desert. McVann points out that this was a place of an altered time. The narrative time is halted as the narrator narrates the encounters of Jesus with the devil. It is a time outside of the time frame of the readers.[119] At one point, Jesus sees 'all the kingdoms of the world in a moment of time' (4.5), and then Jesus is instantaneously transferred from wilderness to mountain, and then from mountain to temple.

For liminality-*communitas*, in Act I (Lk. 3.1-22), Jesus' sojourn and experience at the Jordan show how his status is unclear, that is, liminal. While it is in the role of a prophet that he undergoes the ritual, during his time of testing, his role was ambiguous. McVann proposes, however, that Jesus enjoyed *communitas* with John when he experienced his baptism, an experience he shared with others who went to John to be baptized.[120]

---

118. Again, within the ritual context of 'baptism-investiture', Jesus' baptism by John should be understood as symbolic of the transfer of 'prophetic power and authority'. Historical approaches to the same event have been a conundrum for many theologians. 'For how could Jesus have been baptized for the forgiveness of sins, when according to the Christology that developed after his death, he was divine and therefore sinless?' M. Grant, *Jesus* (London: Weidenfield & Nicolson, 1977), p. 49. Some studies see the significance of John's baptism as a ritual. However, it is not the kind of ritual we are proposing. Rather, as J. Taylor has noted, 'Often the solution is given that he [Jesus] wished to humble himself by participating with the sinful in this important ritual'. Cf. J.E. Taylor, *The Immerser: John the Baptist within Second Temple Judaism* (Grand Rapids: Eerdmans, 1997), p. 262. Thus, like A.M. Hunter who concluded that Jesus 'discerned the hand of God in John's mission, and by His acceptance of John's baptism identified Himself with the people whom He came to save'. A.M. Hunter, *The Work and Words of Jesus* (London: SCM Press, 1950), p. 36. Others have simply dismissed the historicity of the whole 'John baptizing Jesus' event. E.g. R.H. Fuller, *The Mission and Achievement of Jesus: An Examination of the Presuppositions of New Testament Theology* (London: SCM Press, 1954), p. 52. Further bibliography on this issue can be found in Taylor's *The Immerser*, p. 262, n. 4.

119. McVann, 'Rituals of Status Transformation', p. 350.

120. That Jesus shares unity with John and the others who were baptized is quite unclear from this study's perspective. I will elaborate further on this comment later on.

Furthermore, the encounter with the devil in the wilderness contains the ritual element of liminality-*communitas*. As readers see Jesus being confronted by the devil (Act II, Lk. 4.1-13), they wonder whether Jesus has really inherited the mantle of prophecy passed to him by John, and whether he is now a prophet. His status, therefore, remains unclear or liminal.

Under the ritual confrontation, Jesus' temptation by the devil is clearly the event. McVann again identifies three tests. The first is that of the devil's suggestion that Jesus should turn stones to bread (4.4). This test should be understood from the background that Jesus as initiand has just ended fasting for forty days. His abstinence from food suggests his separation from the former patterns and him undergoing the process of status transformation. The second test takes Jesus to a high place by the devil (4.5). 'This test intensifies what was implicit in the previous one: whether to be God's client and depend on God as patron exclusively for glory and authority or whether to be the devil's client and so receive these as his patronage.'[121] The third test is the setting of the temple in Jerusalem, the Holy City. McVann proposes,

> This new setting has radical implications for Jesus' identity and career. The devil suggests to Jesus that a prophet need not suffer or die, since God's messengers will protect him (4.11). But Jesus knows better. He will suffer a prophet's rejection, even death in Jerusalem, for their unyielding fidelity to God.[122]

Finally, McVann describes Jesus' aggregation. McVann finds this stage of aggregation in Lk. 4.14-15: 'And Jesus returned in the power of the Spirit into Galilee, a report concerning him went out through all the surrounding country. And he taught in their synagogues, being glorified by

---

121. McVann, 'Rituals of Status Transformation', p. 354. It is also important to note how Marshall sees the temptation event as a display of Jesus' obedience to God— obedience being one of the major features in the liminal status which the initiand experiences during the ritual of status transformation. Marshall notes that, 'The new factor in the situation is the devil, who attempts to deflect Jesus from obedience to God and hence from the fulfilment of the messianic task laid upon him by God... It has been argued that this reduces the story to the level of a rabbinic *Streitgesprach* in which Jesus overcomes the devil by a superior knowledge of Scripture..., but the point is rather that Jesus is obedient to God's will in Scripture...and not that he wins by superior dialectical skill.' I.H. Marshall, *The Gospel of Luke: A Commentary on the Greek Text* (Exeter: Paternoster Press, 1978), p. 166.

122. McVann, 'Rituals of Status Transformation', p. 354.

all.' Jesus returns from the wilderness to the society after undergoing a radical change of role and status as a result of the ritual of status transformation.[123]

2.5. *The Model Applied in Acts 1.3–2.47: An Overview*

Now that I have briefly surveyed the structure of the RST, I intend to see how this model will support the hypothesis I have proposed for the reading of Acts 1–2. In this section, I will give an overview of how this study is going to progress. This will not only show my study plan but also lay down my hypothesis in detail. Like McVann, I will first identify the ritual elements before dealing with the ritual process. I will do this in each stage of the ritual which I will designate in Acts 1.3–2.47.

My basic outline for the Ritual of Status Transformation will be the following:

First Stage—*Separation*: Acts 1.3-11.
- A. Phase One—vv. 3-5: The apostles as initiands enter into the ritual with Jesus as ritual elder.
- B. Phase Two—vv. 6-8: The ritual elder commissions the initiands.
- C. Phase Three—vv. 9-11: The initiands experience full separation as Jesus ascends to heaven.

Second Stage—*Transition*: Acts 1.12-26.
- A. Phase One—vv. 12-14: The initiands enter into the full state of liminality as they return to Jerusalem and seclude themselves into the upper room. In this phase, the Eleven apostles experience the strong camaraderie or *communitas*.
- B. Phase Two—vv. 15-26: Ritual confrontation is experienced by the initiands. The Eleven apostles defend themselves before the presence of the 120 brethren in relation to Judas and his act of betrayal.

---

123. McVann sets out the different aspects which go with Jesus' change of status and role. He cites: *from chaos to order*—contrasting the orderly world of the villages and synagogues to which Jesus returns to coming from the chaotic world of the wilderness; *from student to teacher*—that Jesus is no longer the docile child of 2.51, nor John's follower, or a novice prophet; *from follower to leader*—starting out as somewhat 'subordinate' to John but coming out of the ritual as an anointed prophet ('Rituals of Status Transformation', p. 355). It is also interesting to add that Jesus' first contact with society after the ritual is with his hometown in Galilee and home synagogue in Nazareth (Lk. 4.14, 16).

Third Stage—*Aggregation*: Acts 2.1-47.
  A. Phase One—vv. 1-4: After the transition stage, the apostles graduate from their initiation and are installed as new leaders of the community. We see the baptism and empowerment of the Spirit as a symbol of God's affirmation through the rite of installation.
  B. Phase Two—vv. 5-47: The apostles are formally presented to the crowd with the picture of Peter standing with the Eleven and delivering his speech/challenge. The acceptance of the community is reflected further until v. 47 as the apostles win their first converts.

2.5.1. *The Ritual Elements in Acts 1.3–2.47.* The apostles are the initiands. They are the ones who will undergo the ritual of status transformation. We should note that the author does not introduce any other character into the narrative until the apostles have returned to Jerusalem (1.12). The introduction of the other characters in 1.14 (the women, Mary, and Jesus' brothers) crucially happens only after the Eleven apostles have been identified individually by name (1.13). My point (as I will attempt to argue) is that Acts 1 and 2 is a story exclusively about the apostles. It is the story of their transformation. This is consistent with my hypothesis. The apostles are the only ones whose honour and leadership integrity are in question; thus, they are the ones who need justification by undergoing the transformation. This also means that when we get to the episodes where the Eleven apostles interact with other characters (such as in 1.14 and 15), the focus remains on the Eleven. The other characters play secondary or 'supporting' roles.

The ritual elder of course is Jesus. His credentials as the ritual elder are clearly emphasized even as early as in 1.3. He is the one who gives instructions to the initiands and commissions them for the mission they need to carry out.

In Acts 1.3-11, we also find the following elements: the prophet and leader (i.e. Jesus); the significance of forty days; the mention of John's baptism of Jesus and thus the baptism of the Spirit; the cloud and heaven in Jesus' ascension; and the two men in white robes.

In Acts 1.12-26, the elements include the settings in Jerusalem; the upper room; the women; Mary; Jesus' brothers; the one hundred and twenty brethren; the enumeration of the names of the apostles; the mention of the fulfilment of the scripture; Judas and the manner of his death; Peter and the meaning of him 'standing among the brethren'; the book of Psalms; and the casting of lots. There may still be other symbols I have not mentioned. I intend to discuss further all these later in their corresponding chapters of this study.

From Acts 2.1-14, we see the elements of the 'day of Pentecost'; the sound from heaven; the rushing like a mighty wind; the filling of the house; the tongues of fire; the Holy Spirit; and the utterance of other languages. We also find the symbol of Peter standing before the crowd with the Eleven as very crucial. There is also the significance of the author's particular attention to details concerning the multitude and where they have come from. The message of Peter and the miracles will likewise play a significant part as ritual elements in this act.

2.5.2. *The Ritual Process: Thesis Plan and Hypothesis.* '…we discovered that very often decisions to perform ritual were connected with crises in the social life of villages' (Turner, *The Ritual Process*, p. 10). This is exactly what we see to be the situation in Acts 1.3–2.47. For the apostles, undergoing the ritual of status transformation is the key element in addressing an impending crisis in the Christian community. It is a crisis which concerns the trust and approval of the community in the leadership of the Eleven apostles, a leadership which was seriously maligned because of the betrayal of Judas who belongs to the apostolate. What follows is the plan by which I intend to present the designated narrative of Acts 1.3–2.14 in the form and pattern of a ritual.

As reflected in my basic outline, the first stage of the ritual is *separation*. Actually, the separation of the Eleven apostles begins at the time when they enter the ritual process (1.3) and ends by the time they are aggregated into the society (2.14, 47). However, the apostles' separation is initiated and highlighted in Acts 1.3-11. In this stage there are three phases: (1) Acts 1.3-5 is the separation of the apostles as initiands from all contact with society. They are alone in the presence of Jesus—their ritual elder.

The author in this stage takes the symbols from Jesus' own ritual of status transformation in Lk. 3.1–4.30 and applies them to the apostles' situation. These symbols include the 'forty days' Jesus fasted in the wilderness as he was in confrontation with Satan (Lk. 4.2), and the reminder of the fact that John as the ritual elder baptized Jesus—the initiand (Lk. 3.15-17). I will argue that the author intends to use the same symbols in Jesus' RST in order to pattern and legitimize the apostles' status transformation; (2) the commissioning account in 1.6-8 is the second phase of the ritual separation. It is an account which presents two important issues—that the Eleven apostles were commissioned by Jesus, and that the apostles completely understood and obeyed what Jesus willed. I will argue that the absence of inside views from the apostles, despite Jesus' announcement of the *parousia* delay, is the author's method of showing the initiands' full obedience to the ritual elder's instructions; (3) the third phase is the ascension account. Jesus' ascension in 1.9-11 will be viewed primarily, not as Jesus' departure from the apostles, but as the apostles' separation from Jesus. In this phase, the apostles completely experience the utmost test of separation and segregation. I will attempt to read the drama of Jesus' ascension as the author's means of heightening the picture of separation between the apostles and Jesus their leader.

The second stage of the ritual is the *transition* and it portrays the *liminality* of the initiands. The liminal status of the Eleven apostles becomes more pronounced in 1.12-14. Liminality is emphasized when the apostles return to the city of Jerusalem, this time without their leader—Jesus. Moreover, the seclusion in the 'upper room' heightens the apostles' separation and liminal status. The apostles are at a stage where they are practically stripped of any rank or title. Their status as commissioned apostles does not come until the promise of the father is consummated in Acts 2.

It is also in this phase that the Eleven experience *communitas* and camaraderie. I suggest that the enumeration of the apostles' names in 1.13 is not merely the author's way of re-introducing who the apostles are, but rather, who they are in contrast with the other disciple groups who were with them in the upper room.

The pericope of 1.12-14 discloses quite a complex social issue. While I see this event as a time when the apostles strongly experience their *communitas*, I also find this event to be propagandic. In other words, the author (as I will attempt to argue) is subtly appealing to win more support from other groups by showing the unanimity of the apostles with the women disciples and Jesus' family. This social appeal is known otherwise as networking, a significant aspect of patronage. Under this section, I will give a brief background on the concept of patronage and discuss how networking plays a significant part in it. What we have, therefore, is the concept of patronage working interactively within the theoretical framework of RST.

More importantly, it is in this phase that the apostles as initiands

experience their ritual confrontation. Acts 1.15-26—the election narrative—depicts the apostles' defence against the incriminating evidence of
Judas' association with the Twelve. In their defence, I will point out that
Peter speaks on behalf of the apostles and not necessarily (as other
scholars claim) as a spokesman for the whole body of brethren numbering
almost 120 persons (1.15). In other words, Peter's speech on Judas' death
(1.16-20) is a speech in defence of their group—the Eleven apostles. It is a
speech declaring Judas' excommunication before the presence of the rest
of the 120 persons (a number which some suggest to be symbolically
representing the ruling body of a community).

Because I see 1.15-26 as a ritual confrontation, I will attempt to argue
that the election of Matthias can be read as primarily addressing the need
to solve the moral crisis, the crisis engulfing the honour and integrity of
the Eleven apostles. In other words, unlike most modern scholars who
place emphasis on the completion of the number of the apostles to twelve,
I will attempt to show that this is an election primarily aimed at reclaiming
the leadership credibility of the commissioned apostles. The strict criteria
which were set up in order to check the qualifications of whoever was
going to replace Judas were designed to address a 'moral' concern not just
a 'number' issue. Here too, we find the concept of honour and shame
working within the framework of RST.

Finally, the casting of lots is a method by which God got the final choice
for Judas' replacement. I will show that this is also the method which the
author uses to assure his readers that it was God himself who chose
Matthias—a divine choice which allayed the fears of a possible repeat of a
betrayal coming from the group.

After the initiands have faced and passed their ritual confrontation, they
are now prepared to be *aggregated* into society. This is the third stage of
the RST and it is also where I would want to suggest some modifications
of McVann's ritual process. As we may recall, McVann sees Jesus'
baptism by John as an event which initiates Jesus into the time of trials
and testing by the devil in the wilderness. In this study, I propose that the
apostles' baptism in the Spirit in Acts 2.1-4 may be viewed as a ritual
validation or graduation before they are incorporated into society. The
aggregation process is in two phases: (a) Acts 2.1-4 is the initiands' ritual
graduation. It is a phase where the initiands are formally recognized in
their role by the superior chancellor or ritual elder/s. This is also the rite
where the author wishes to show his readers that the apostles have
graduated complete with God's seal of approval upon them; (b) Acts 2.5-

14 is the narrative where we see the process of the initiands' aggregation. Peter and the Eleven apostles now stand before the crowd coming from different nations and begin to perform their duties as commissioned by Jesus. Finally, seeing the apostles having their first converts in 2.26-27 shows that indeed the Twelve have been redeemed in their honour and integrity as leaders of the community of believers.

3. *Summary*

I have stated that the events in Acts 1.3–2.14 show how the author of Luke–Acts promotes the leadership of the Eleven. One of the main intentions of this promotion is to blot out the effect of Judas' betrayal of Jesus. Judas' betrayal, as he was part of the Twelve, had serious social implications, especially on the honour and reputation of the apostles as a group.

I suggested that the author's campaign to promote the Eleven is best understood from a social-scientific perspective. The model by which I can study the said promotion is the ritual of status transformation. Acts 1.3–2.14, I believe, presents the transformation of the once exclusive group of Jesus' followers to be the new leaders and representatives of the people to God.

I proposed that the transformation of the apostles' status resembles the process of Jesus' status transformation in Lk. 3.1–4.30. Jesus, who was then a private person, went through a comparable status transformation, coming out of the ritual as the prophet of God.

However, I also mentioned that while the model of the Rituals of Status Transformation serves as the theoretical framework of this study, other underlying sociological issues embedded in Acts 1.3–2.14 will be studied by employing complementary interpretative models. These models primarily include the concepts of patronage, networking, and honour and shame. I will, however, define and discuss them in the narrative where they are mainly found.

Patronage, for example, will cover the issues of the apostles' role as the peoples' representative before God who is the ultimate patron. The role of representation is that of a broker. Jesus who served as the people's broker to God, now hands down this role to the Twelve. It is this role which this study wants to extend further within the theoretical framework of the RST.

One of these social issues with which patronage covers is the intent to win the approval of the patron's clientele. This objective is attainable

through what is known as the concept of networking. I suggest that the
mention of the other disciple groups in the pericope of Acts 1.12-14 is not
only to emphasize unity amongst the disciples but is this underlying intent
to win the trust of other disciple groups such as the women and those of
Jesus' family.

I would like to bring into focus the significance of the election narrative
in 1.15-26 with the help of the conceptual model of honour and shame. I
propose that the grotesque description of Judas' death, the dramatic show
of leadership on the part of Peter, more so with the strict criteria that were
set up before conducting the election, can be appreciated if one understands the concept of honour and shame in the narrative.

Finally, I will discuss the apostles' baptism in the Spirit in Acts 2.1-4
and their presentation before the crowd in 2.11, as the apostles' graduation
and aggregation. Clearly, after the apostles were baptized, the author
declares and presents the new leaders of the Christian community by
showing Peter standing with the Eleven and giving his first speech.

4. *Other Considerations—The Role of Commissioning Accounts in Luke–Acts: Contributions from B.J. Hubbard and T.Y. Mullins*

In order for this study to effectively show the benefits of the method and
models of social-scientific criticism, I find it necessary to give a brief
summary of a more common approach to the study of the same texts this
study is dealing with. This concerns the study of Acts 1 as a
commissioning account. My aim is be able to elaborate on how a tradition-
historical approach fails to provide answers to what seems to be minute
yet important issues surrounding the narrative of Acts 1–2. For this
purpose, I have particularly chosen the studies of B.J. Hubbard[124] and T.Y.
Mullins[125] on the role of commissioning accounts, in Luke–Acts.

4.1. *Commissioning Accounts: Their Form and Themes*
B.J. Hubbard[126] began his investigation with the Hebrew Bible, basing his
study on the previous works of K. Baltzer,[127] N. Habel,[128] and J.K.

---

124. B.J. Hubbard, 'The Role of Commissioning Accounts in Acts', in C.H. Talbert
(ed.), *Perspectives on Luke–Acts* (Edinburgh: T. & T. Clark, 1978), pp. 187-98.
125. T.Y. Mullins, 'New Testament Commissioning Forms, Especially in Luke–
Acts', *JBL* 95.4 (1976), pp. 603-14.
126. Hubbard, 'Commissioning Accounts', pp. 187-98.
127. K. Baltzer, 'Considerations concerning the Office and Calling of the Prophet',

Kuntz.[129] His survey claims that the commissioning accounts in the Old Testament yield a consistent structure.[130] From the OT, Hubbard attempted to analyse the non-biblical accounts and found some striking similarities. The commissioning accounts in some ancient non-biblical texts share the same structure.[131]

Hubbard's thesis is to show that, because Luke–Acts was heavily influenced by the LXX, its commissioning accounts can actually be traced from the ancient non-biblical tradition. This tradition is believed to have been passed down to Luke–Acts. Hubbard argues that the author employs such a format and becomes the vehicle of his theology.[132] The readers are familiar with such a genre and understand what literary function it serves.

Commissioning accounts in the NT were also examined by T.Y. Mullins. Mullins found thirty-seven instances:[133] six are in the gospel of Matthew;[134] two in Mark;[135] ten are in Luke;[136] one in John;[137] seventeen

---

HTR 61 (1968), pp. 567-91.

128. N. Habel, 'The Form and Significance of the Call Narratives', *ZAW* 77 (1965), pp. 297-323.

129. J.K. Kuntz, *The Self Revelation of God* (Philadelphia: Westminster Press, 1967).

130. Cf. Gen. 11.28-30; 12.1-4a; 15.1-6; 17.1-14, 15-27; 24.1-9; 26.1-6, 23-25; 28.10-22; 35.9-15; 41.37-45; 46.1-5a; Exod. 3.1–4.16 (J and E); 6.2-13; 7.1-6; Num. 22.22-35; Deut. 31.14-15, 31; Josh. 1.1-11; Judg. 4.4-10; 6.11-24; 1 Sam. 3.1–4.1a; 1 Kgs 19.1-19a; Isa. 6; 49.1-6; Jer. 1.1-10; Ezek. 1.1–3.15; 1 Chron. 22.1-16; and Ezra 1.1-5.

131. Cf. Utnapishtim's commission to build an ark: Epic of Gilgamesh, *ANET* 93; the appointment of Rekh-mi-Re as Vizier of Egypt: *ANET* 212; Thut-mose's commission by Harmarkhis to be king of Egypt: *ANET* 449; the legend of king Keret: *ANET* 143-46; the dream appearances of Isthar appointing Hattushili as priest and king: cf. A.L. Oppenheim, *The Interpretation of Dreams in the Ancient Near East* (Philadelphia: American Philosophical Society, 1956), p. 254; the dream of Djoser: Oppenheim, p. 251; the dream of the priest Ishtar: Oppenheim, p. 249; Nabonidus's commission to build the temple at Ekhulkul: Oppenheim, p. 250.

132. B.J. Hubbard, 'Commissioning Stories in Luke–Acts: A Study of their Antecedents, Form and Content', *Semeia* 8 (1977), pp. 103-26 (103).

133. For the study of the form of each NT commission account, see Mullins, 'New Testament Commissioning Forms', pp. 605-606.

134. Mt. 14.22-33; 17.1-8; 28.1-8, 9-10, 11-15, 16-20.

135. Mk 11.1-10; 16.9-20.

136. Lk. 1.5-25, 26-38; 2.8-18; 5.1-11; 7.20-28; 10.1-17; 15.11-31; 22.7-13, 14-38; 24.36-53.

137. Jn 20.19-21.

are in Acts;[138] and one in Revelation.[139] While both Hubbard and Mullins disagree on where some pericopes in the accounts belong, they nevertheless agree on the description of the elements which compose a commissioning account.[140]

1. Introduction (INT) is a brief introductory remark providing circumstantial details (time, place, overall situation of the individual to be addressed) that sets the stage of what is to follow.

2. Confrontation (CONF) is where the deity or the commissioner appears and confronts the individual to be commissioned. The person or deity giving the commission is understood as one with power and authority. The scene of commissioning normally involves the interruption of the normal activities of the person or group being commissioned. Mullins adds that after the orientation of the task the commissioned needs to undertake, there is often a radical change which the person is not prepared to undergo. The commissioned person is often in a state of bewilderment, and an air of mystery hangs over the event.[141]

3. Reaction (REAC) is where in some cases the individual reacts to the presence of the holy by way of an action expressive of fear or unworthiness. This reaction shifts the focus of the reader from the commissioner to the commissioned person. Reaction normally functions to show the unreadiness of the person being commissioned.

4. Commission (COMM) is where the individual is told to undertake a specific task which often involves assuming a new role in life (e.g. that of prophet). This element in the commissioning account signals, not only the mission which has been given, but also the official status of the commissioned as the agent duly authorized by the commissioner.

5. Protest (PROT) is where in some instances the individual responds to the commission by claiming he is unable or

---

138. Acts 1.1-12; 7.30-36; 9.1-8, 9-18; 10.1-8, 9-29, 30-33; 11.4-17; 12.6-10; 13.1-3; 16.24-34; 22.6-11, 12-16, 17-21; 23.11; 26.12-20; 27.21-26.

139. Rev. 1.10-20.

140. The following descriptions are taken from Hubbard, 'Commissioning Stories', pp. 104-105. At times, I have supplemented these descriptions with Mullin's definitions.

141. Mullins, 'New Testament Commissioning Forms', p. 607.

unworthy to carry out the commissioner's command. Or, it can also be questioning the word of the deity or commissioner. The REAC and PROT are two elements appearing with least frequency. However, Hubbard notes that, either one of the other of these elements usually is found in the commissioning account. Either way, there is the general response of the commissioned to the commissioner. For Mullins, the protest functions to measure the effect of the commission, upon the person commissioned, to indicate thus the progress of that person toward accomplishing the task, and to disclose the distance yet covered.[142] The reaction and protest serve, at times, similar functions. They also set the stage for the feature of reassurance.

6. Reassurance (REASS) is when the deity or the commissioner utters statements such as 'fear not', 'I am (will be) with you', etc. These reassuring statements are usually uttered after the COMM or PROT. Reassurances function to dispose any remaining resistance. Mullins noticed that in some cases the reassurance may be placed even before the commission is given (e.g. Lk. 5.10b; Mt. 28.10a; and Jn 20.19c, 21a). He adds that 'usually the protest will be absent where the reassurance come early; in any case, the protest has to precede the reassurance'.[143]

7. Conclusion (CONC) is the ending of the commission, usually in a less formal way. The commissioned is often seen to immediately begin to carry out the mission. At times, the conclusion functions to show the commissioned person's attitude after accepting the commission.[144]

As I have noted earlier, the largest source of commissioning stories in the NT are found in Luke–Acts (ten in Luke and seventeen in Acts). This becomes more emphasized when one understands that only eleven instances are found in Genesis and twenty-seven are in the whole of the OT.[145] In these commissioning accounts, recurring themes also defines their structure.[146]

---

142. Mullins, 'New Testament Commissioning Forms', p. 608.
143. Mullins, 'New Testament Commissioning Forms', p. 609.
144. Mullins, 'New Testament Commissioning Forms', p. 609.
145. Mullins, 'New Testament Commissioning Forms', pp. 609-10; based on B.J. Hubbard's analysis of the OT commissioning accounts in his essay *The Matthean Redaction of a Primitive Apostolic Commissioning* (Missoula, MT: Scholars Press, 1974), pp. 33-65.

1. Time and Place—it fixes the temporal or spatial relevance of the commission. Hubbard does not consider this feature as a theme: the INT does not normally indicate any temporal or spatial reference.[147]

2. Reference to a Voice or Vision—focuses on the subjective experience of the commissioned.

3. Reference to an Angel—focuses on the objective experience of the commissioned.

4. Reference to standing or a command to stand or rise—indicates that the person who stands (or is commanded to stand) is accepted as a representative of the commissioning person. Hubbard sees a similarity when the one who commissions is referred to as standing before the commissioned. The commissioner is thus pictured in an authoritative role. [148]

5. Reference to fear—which emphasizes that the commissioning person is in control of the situation.

6. Prayer—this feature is added by Hubbard as a theme to the commissioning stories. It is a final theme found in some accounts which normally places the commissioned person engaged in prayer after receiving the task from the commissioner. Hubbard indicates that this theme functions to 'indicate that the individual is in an ideal position to receive the commission from God or his messenger'.[149]

---

146. Adapted from Mullins, 'New Testament Commissioning Forms', pp. 611-12.
147. Hubbard, 'Commissioning Stories', pp. 191-92.
148. Hubbard, 'Commissioning Stories', p. 193.
149. Hubbard, 'Commissioning Stories', p. 193.

Table 1[150]

	INT	CONF	REAC	COMM	PROT	REASS	CONC
LUKE							
1.5-25	5-10	11	12	13B-17	18	13a, 19-20	21-5
1.26-38	26-27	28	29	31-33, 35	34	30, 36-37	38
2.8-20	8	9a-b, 13-14	9c	11-12	—	10	15-20
5.1-11	1-2	3	8-10a	4, 10c	5	10b	11
7.20-28	*20*	*21*	*—*	*22*	*—*	*23*	*24-28*
10.1-17	*1a*	*1b*	*—*	*2-15*	*—*	*16*	*17*
15.11-31	*11-20a*	*20b*	*21*	*22-24*	*25-30*	*31*	
22.7-13	*7*	*8*	*9*	*10-11, 12b*	*—*	*12a*	*13*
22.14-38	*14*	*35a*	*35b*	*36*	*—*	*37*	*38*
24.1-9	1-3	4	5a	6-7	—	5b	8-9
24.36-53	36a	36b	37, 41	44-48	—	49	50-53
ACTS							
1.1-14	1-2, 9	3-5, 10	6	7-8	—	11	12-14
5.17-21a	17-18	19	—	20	—	(19-20)	21a
7.30-36	*30a*	*30b, 32a*	*31, 32b*	*33-34a*	*—*	*34b*	*35-36*
8.26-30	(4-13), 27b-28	26a, 29a	—	26b, 29b	—	(39)	27a, 30
9.1-9	1-3a	3b, 4b-5	4a, 7	6a	—	6b	8-9
9.10-19	10a	10b	—	11-12	13-14	15-16	17-19
10.1-8	1-2	3	4a	5-6	—	4b	7-8
10.9-23	9-10a	10b-12	17	13, 15-16, 19-20a	14	20b	21-23
10.30-33	30a	30b	—	32	—	31	33
11.4-12	4-5a	5b-6	—	7	8	9	10-12
12.6-12	6	7a	—	7b-8	9	11	12
13.1-3	1-2	2a	—	2b	—	(2c)	3
16.8-10	8	9a	—	9b	—	(10b)	10a
18.7-11	7-8	9a	—	9b	—	10	11
22.6-11	6a	6b, 7b-9	7a	10a-b	—	(10c)	11
22.12-16	12	13	—	14-15	—	(15)	16
22.17-21	17	18a	—	18b, 21	19-20	21	—
23.11	11a	11b	—	11a	—	11c	—
26.12-20	12	13, 14b-15	14a	15-18	—	(17a)	19-20
27.21-26	21-23a	23b	—	24b	—	24a	25-26

150. Table 1 is adapted from Hubbard, 'Commissioning Accounts', p. 192. I have, however, integrated T.Y. Mullins's additional entries which are indicated in italics. Thus, in addition to the Hubbard list, Mullins considers Lk. 7.20-28; 10.1-17; 15.11-31; 22.7-13, 14-38 as commissioning accounts. Mullins does not see Lk. 24.1-9 as a commissioning account. For the book of Acts, Mullins has Acts 7.30-36 but misses 5.17-21a; 8.26-30; and 18.7-11. There are also some minor disagreements between Hubbard and Mullins on the scope of some commissioning accounts. This I have opted not to mention.

Part I

SEPARATION

Chapter 2

THE APOSTLES AND THEIR LEADERSHIP ROLE

I begin by following my suggested divisions for the narrative of Acts 1.3–2.47. Thus I have Acts 1.3-11 as the *Separation* stage; 1.12-26 as the *Transition* (Liminality-*Communitas*) stage; and Acts 2.1-47 as the *Aggregation* stage. The separation stage has three phases. Phase One—1.3-5: The apostles as initiands enter the ritual with Jesus as ritual elder. Phase Two—1.6-8: The ritual elder commissions the initiands. Phase Three—1.9-11: The initiands experience full separation as Jesus departs.

In each stage, I will first identify the ritual elements and then the ritual process. As I read the text within the framework of the Rituals of Status Transformation, I will note how the other conceptual models (patronage, networking, honour and shame) work within the narrative.

1. *The Ritual Elements in Acts 1.3-11*

1.1. *The Apostles as the Initiands*
The author does not begin his narrative with the scene where the initiands are portrayed entering into the first stage of the ritual process. Unlike in Jesus' ritual of status transformation (Lk. 3.1-2), the readers of Acts immediately find themselves right in the beginning of the ritual process itself. In Acts, the author begins with a preface including a dedication to an individual named Theophilus. While the gospel also has this dedication (Lk. 1.1-4), it is however followed by the infancy narratives of Lk. 1.5–2.52. The crucial difference between the gospel and Acts is that the apostles as initiands do not have the introductory background which Jesus has from the infancy stories in Luke. This is where McVann's information on who Jesus was before the ritual (i.e. as private person) works for him.[1] In our case, however, trying to construct who the apostles were before

---

1. McVann, 'Rituals of Status Transformation', pp. 342-43.

they became the leaders of the Christian community would have to be drawn all the way to where Luke directly points the reader in 1.1. This study, therefore, assumes the unity and continuity of the two books, an assumption I will discuss later in this study.[2]

The apostles are the initiands. And by this I mean only the Eleven apostles of Jesus. The need to establish and emphasize this point is important. The author's introduction of τοῖς ἀποστόλοις in 1.2 ought not to include any other characters in it. The fact that the number and identity of the Eleven apostles is established precisely in 1.13 establishes the scope of τοῖς ἀποστόλοις in 1.2. This would mean that the Eleven were the exclusive recipients of Jesus' commission (1.7-8); that they were the ones who primarily witnessed Jesus' ascension (1.9-11); and that the command to remain in Jerusalem and wait for the promise of the father was directed principally to them (1.3-5). Other supporting evidence for the scope of τοῖς ἀποστόλοις would include the qualifying description of the phrase οὓς ἐξελέξατο[3] ('whom he had chosen') of 1.2b, an echo of Lk. 6.13. Previous to this is the phrase διὰ πνεύματος ἁγίου ('through the Holy Spirit') which modifies οὓς ἐξελέξατο.[4] These two attributive phrases identify the initiands to be none other than the Eleven.[5]

My statements above do not in any way dispute the possibility that there were other disciples with the Eleven when they were with Jesus before his ascension. All I am simply trying to establish is the plausibility of the case that the narrative of Acts 1–2 speaks fundamentally of the Eleven apostles as the subject. And once this proposal is accepted then all other issues and characters within the narrative take a secondary place.

The need to establish the subject of the narrative is important if one has to find a working solution to what seem to be conflicting scenarios in the episodes of Acts 1–2. For instance, there is the criterion which is set up in 1.22. In this passage, the candidates for the election of Judas' replacement are required to have been with Jesus 'beginning from the baptism of John until the day he was taken up...' This means that the last two candidates, namely Joseph Barsabbas Justus and Matthias (cf. 1.23-26), would have

---

2.   A discussion relevant to this thesis is found in Chapter 3 (cf. 3.1.2.4.5).

3.   Codex D adds καὶ ἐκέλευσε κηρύσσειν τὸ εὐαγγέλιον ('and commanded them to preach the gospel'). See B. Metzger, *The Text of the New Testament: Its Transmission, Corruption, and Restoration* (New York: Oxford University Press, 1964), pp. 273-77; Barrett, *Acts of the Apostles*, pp. 67-69.

4.   Witherington, *The Acts of the Apostles*, p. 107.

5.   A related discussion on this issue is found in Chapter 8 of this study (cf. 8.2).

passed this requirement, placing them in Jesus' company until his ascension. This in effect makes it difficult to sustain the argument that the Eleven were the only ones who received Jesus' commission. As Quesnell has suggested, 'In fact, Acts 1.21 makes no sense unless Joseph Barsabbas and Matthias, as well as the larger group from among whom Luke says they were selected, have been with the Twelve constantly up to the time of Christ's ascension'.[6]

Some scholars propose solutions to break this deadlock. E. Haenchen, in brackets, adds the allusion of 'helpers' being present with the apostles in the events leading to Jesus' ascension.[7] Haenchen's proposal is open-ended and allows room to accommodate all characters that appear in the story other than the Eleven. Fitzmyer, on the other hand, simply claims 'narrative progression'. He admits that the οἷς in 1.3 indeed refers to the apostles, and that later on, the οὗτοι in 1.14 has started to include others.[8]

This is where approaching the text from a social-scientific perspective, specifically from the model of Rituals of Status Transformation is an advantage. The RST requires the interpreter to sort out early in the ritual process who the initiands are, making therefore the other characters take supporting roles. Once this is done, the initiands function consistently as the subject in the whole ritual process until the status transformation is completed.[9]

That the apostles function as the subject of the narrative is not something this study has simply concocted. Nor is it something which has been observed by the use of social-scientific approach alone. In fact, even from a literary perspective, one can detect the deliberate effort of the narrator to show that the apostles indeed take the lead role right from the very beginning of the opening scenes of Acts. For instance, the narrator places the substantive οἷς (whom) to begin the sentence of 1.3 which immediately follows what he had just stated about the apostles—that they are the 'chosen ones' of Jesus (1.2). In doing so, the narrator's emphasis falls not much on *what Jesus had done* (in contrast with Lk. 24) but *to whom Jesus did it* (his apostles). From this position, the implied reader

---

6.   Q. Quesnell, ' The Women at Luke's Supper', in R.J. Cassidy and P.J. Scharper (eds.), *Political Issues in Luke–Acts* (Maryknoll, NY: Orbis, 1983), p. 62.

7.   Witherington, *The Acts of the Apostles*, p. 139.

8.   Fitzmyer, *The Acts of the Apostles*, p. 213.

9.   I will pick up on this discussion when I reach the issue on whom really were the first recipients of the Spirit's baptism in Acts 2.1-4, a discussion I reserve for Chapter 9 of this study.

sees the apostles as lead characters in the narrative.[10] Furthermore, the narrator places the events after Jesus' resurrection within the duration of forty days. This is clearly a typological reference to the forty days Jesus was in the wilderness being tempted by the devil in preparation for his entry into his public ministry (Lk. 4.1-2). Alluding to another 'forty days' at the end of Jesus' public ministry brings a closure to the character of Jesus and paves the way for the entrance of the apostles as major characters in their own right.

As the narrator begins to focus on the apostles, a change in the mode of narration from showing to telling occurs. The change in mode is subtle. From a general description of Jesus' post-resurrection events, the narrator employs καὶ συναλιζόμενος παρήγγειλεν αὐτοῖς (and while staying with them…) to pick out what is apparently a most important episode—the charging of the apostles to remain in Jerusalem and wait for the promise of the father (1.4). The significance of this instruction is enhanced by the narrator as he emphasizes the fact that the command came from Jesus himself ('you heard from me', 1.4b). Moreover, in contrast with Lk. 24.49, the nature of the promise of the father has more details as the author associates the promise with the baptism of the Holy Spirit (1.5).

1.2. *Jesus the Ritual Elder*
The credentials of Jesus as the ritual elder are stated in 1.3-4. Jesus is said to have (1) presented himself alive after his passion by many proofs; (2) appeared to them (the Eleven apostles) during forty days; (3) spoken to the apostles about the kingdom of God; and (4) commanded the apostles to remain in Jerusalem and wait for the promise of the father.[11]

1.3. *The Symbol of 'Forty Days'*
The mention of forty days, as McVann states, 'is symbolically charged'.[12] In Lk. 4.1-2, the reference to the forty days of Jesus' testing is a time-frame ritual. In the tradition familiar to the readers, this figure resonates with the OT references to forty days or years of 'preparation, waiting, or testing'.[13] McVann suggests,

---

10. A brief description of what I mean by implied author, narrator, implied reader, and narratee is in 3.1.2.4.1, notes 43 and 49.

11. We will discuss in more detail how these credentials legitimize Jesus' role as the ritual elder in the ritual process section.

12. McVann, 'Rituals of Status Transformation', p. 350.

13. E.g. Gen. 7.4, 12, 17; Exod. 24.18; 34.38; 1 Kgs 18.8.

The single most important cluster of Old Testament references for this narrative, however, is concerned with the sojourn of Moses and Israel in the desert. Israel's forty years were a time of testing to see if it would rely exclusively on God and whether its transformation to the status of God's holy people would be effective (see Deut. 8.2, 4; 9.9, 25). Additionally, Moses spent forty days on the mountain in preparation for the climax of his prophetic career, the mediation of God's law to Israel (Exod. 34.28). So too, Jesus, who was designated 'beloved son' at the Jordan, now undergoes a forty-day period which climaxes in a ritual testing of his preparation for a public career as God's loyal prophet and holy man.[14]

But how does this mention of 'forty days' of Jesus' appearance to his apostles actually help the author's promotion of the Eleven? As we have argued earlier, the author's display of Jesus' authority is not to justify Jesus' position as the ritual elder, but to validate the apostles as the initiands (or the ones who are being commissioned). The appearance of the resurrected Jesus before the apostles for forty days, authenticated by 'many proofs' (ἐν πολλοῖς τεκμηρίοις, 1.3), not only suggests how much time they all spent together. Because the forty days is a symbol-laden ritual time, echoing how Jesus had victory over the devil, its meaning helps to validate the reasons why the apostles are designated to be Jesus' successors. In other words, just like Jesus and the other OT characters who have gone through the (forty days or years) 'tour of duty', the apostles have earned the same.

This is also why we see that M.C. Parsons's suggestion is a bit lacking. He states,

> Establishing the disciples as reliable and legitimate successors of Jesus is a major task of the opening narrative in Acts. It will be recalled that the primacy effect, that is, the effect that positioning certain material first has on the reader, is important in establishing a positive identity for the disciples in the book of Acts. The period of forty days is needed in Acts, not to allow Jesus enough time to make appearance, but to assure the reader that the disciples are 'fully instructed' (see Acts 20.20, 27, 31).[15]

The symbol of forty days indeed serves as an assurance to the readers. It is an assurance, however, not only to convey the 'full instruction' of Jesus upon the apostles. Rather, I want to add that the phrase has something of the character of validating insignia symbolically pinned upon the individual or group which functions to testify to the character's worth. In

---

14. McVann, 'Rituals of Status Transformation', p. 350.
15. Parsons, *The Departure of Jesus in Luke–Acts*, p. 195.

the context of Luke–Acts, the author deliberately takes this insignia from Jesus (and all its other representations in the OT) and places it upon the apostles as a legitimating device.

In the ritual process, as I will explain later on, the mention of forty days represents also the 'liminality' of the Israelites, the exiles, and Jesus, which is now being carried over onto the experience of the apostles in their rituals of status transformation.

1.4. *The Two Men in White Robes*

In Lk. 24.2-3, the initial signs of Jesus' resurrection indicated that the stone which covered the entrance to the tomb was found rolled away. The body which was supposed to have been laid down inside the tomb was missing (cf. Lk. 23.55b). The women who were to bring spices for the preparation of Jesus' body were said to be 'perplexed'[16] or 'uncertain' upon seeing an empty tomb. And while they were still in a state of perplexity and uncertainty, it was very fitting for the characters of 'two men in dazzling apparel' to stand beside the women and explain what had happened (Lk. 24.4). The women reacted with fear, yet with reverence ('as they were frightened and bowed their faces to the ground...' Lk. 24.5a). The reaction of reverence, coupled with the description of the attire of dazzling apparel, suggests the notion that these two men were messengers from God.

The function of the character of these two men is crucial if one is to understand the function of the other two messengers in Acts 1.10-11. The two men in Lk. 24 were there to explain to the women that Jesus has risen from the dead. The description of what they were wearing and how the women reacted when they revealed themselves convey that they were not only divine messengers, but more importantly, that the message they brought was reliable and true.

The description of the two men in Acts 1.10-11 is vital in the closing episode of Jesus' ascension in Acts. From the readers' perspective (even if one argues that the two men in Lk. 24 are not the same as the two men in Acts 1), the credibility of the two men in dazzling apparel has already been established and substantiated in Lk. 24, that is, their message about Jesus being alive is true. The effect, therefore, is that when two men in 'white robes' also appear and stand by the apostles in Acts 1.10, the validity of what they are promising the Eleven is no longer a question for

---

16. ἀπορεῖσθαι from ἀπορέω.

the readers of Acts. In our study of the apostles' RST, the assurance of Jesus' return delivered by these two divine messengers is very helpful (an issue I will further explain in the ritual process) in the time of separation of the ritual elder from the initiands.

2. *The Initiands and their Leadership Role*

The hypothesis I have laid down earlier revolves around the proposal that the author is appealing to his readers to trust and support the apostles as new leaders. The status transformation is not only because of the apostles being commissioned to be Jesus' witnesses (Acts 1.8), but also a transformation which guarantees the community that their new leaders are no longer tainted with Judas' sin, and that Matthias has made up for the absence of the twelfth apostle and the restoration of their moral integrity.[17]

I also mentioned that the author is attempting to win the trust, support, and loyalty of other disciple groups by showing the unity of the apostles with the women disciples and Jesus' family in the upper room (1.12-14). This show of unity I call networking. The language of trust, support, and loyalty; the author's programme of networking; and the replacement of the betraying apostle itself, all these have something to do with the nature of the leadership role which the apostles are expected to perform once they are installed and aggregated into the society. In other words, the role and status which the apostles will be discharging will only see its fulfilment with the full trust and support of the community to whom they will be serving. Without the community's patronage to the Twelve, the meaning and function of their roles and statuses are null and void.[18]

---

17.   The model of the rituals of status transformation has been used by social scientists in studying an individual's or group's passage from one status to another. These would include territorial passages, pregnancy and childbirth passages, birth and childhood, puberty and adulthood, betrothal and marriage, the passage from one life to another usually found in funeral rites, etc. Cf. Van Gennep, *The Rites of Passage*, p. xxiii.

18.   To define the meaning and scope of the apostles' leadership in this study is too broad and demanding. For instance, one can endlessly discuss the leadership role of the apostles as teachers. Others have focused on the apostles' role as church leaders. Yet, there are also those who have centred their studies on the apostles' performance of miracles in relation to their mission as Jesus' witnesses. My focus is on the specific nature or quality of leadership which, if absent, will render all leadership roles ineffective. This nature or quality of leadership is the knowledge and assurance that the present or incoming leaders are reliable and trustworthy. It is this quality which we

The need to convince the Christian community that the apostles are their new leaders arises, not only because of Judas' sin, but also because of the people's loss of confidence in the religious leaders in their time. The leaders who were supposed to serve as their mediator to God have made it more difficult (if not impossible) for them to access God. The apostles as new leaders will have to prove that they can better provide for the needs of their people. But with their negative track record looming over them (the case of Judas' betrayal and his membership to the Twelve) drastic measures need to be taken. This, I propose, is the essence behind the author's effort in Acts 1.3–2.47 to promote the leadership of the apostles to the Christian community.

The nature of the leadership the apostles are to assume is not heir-archical leadership but rather a leadership best explained from the perspective of the Patronage/Brokership concept. The apostles as leaders are expected to serve as brokers between God (the ultimate patron) and the people (the clients). To understand this leadership role, I opt to use the model suggested by Halvor Moxnes on the nature of Jesus' leadership, a leadership of brokerage.[19] It is a leadership role which Jesus has passed on to his apostles.

As I have stated in my Methodology section, the RST will serve as my theoretical framework for the study of the narrative of Acts 1–2. Within it are other conceptual models interactively working in this theoretical framework. The concepts of patronage, networking, honour and shame are models needed in order for us to understand the specific and individual social contexts of the episodes within Acts 1–2.

2.1. *Current Research on Patronage*
In a survey done by John H. Elliott on the status of research concerning patronage, he finds three traditional yet unrelated fields. The first were the studies of ancient historians in the context of the Roman world. The

---

believe has been shattered by Judas' betrayal of Jesus. And because Judas is one of the Twelve, the question of the leadership integrity of the Eleven persisted in the Christian community in Acts. For further discussion on the failure of the religious leaders and the effectivity of the apostles' leadership in Acts, see Clark, 'The Role of the Apostles', pp. 169-190, especially pp. 174-75. See also P. K. Nelson, *Leadership and Discipleship: A Study of Luke 22.24-30* (Atlanta, GA: Scholars Press, 1994).

19. H. Moxnes, 'Patron-Client Relations and the New Community', in J. Neyrey (ed.), *The Social World of Luke–Acts: Models for Interpretation* (Peabody, MA: Hendrickson, 1991), pp. 241-68.

second is the research by anthropologists, sociologists, and political scientists on structures and operations of social phenomena in industrial and pre-industrial societies. The third is the research by exegetes and students of the social world of early Christianity.

Ancient historians have primarily focused on the relation of earlier and later workings of patronage in the imperial period. They differ, however, on the function of the topic in the field of imperial politics. The suggestions initiated by Syme,[20] Alföldy,[21] and de Ste. Croix,[22] together with the seminal observations of Von Premerstein,[23] Badian,[24] and Gelzer,[25] have led Richard Saller[26] to understand patronage as a social institution working behind, or even inside, the language, ethics, and politics of ancient societies. Saller, like T.F. Carney,[27] was able to show how the historical and social description with attention to the perspectives and relevant research of social sciences complement each other. Elliott notes, however, that Saller's study has not considered how the Roman system of patronage functions in the broader, cross-cultural scope, or as possibly relevant for the early Christian scene.[28]

Social-scientific studies on patronage have attempted to achieve something in a field where ancient historical approaches have been very limited, and that is, the cross-cultural and political science perspectives. These perspectives include the analyses of the social characteristics of different articulations of patronage; the conditions which contributed greatly to its emergence, its development and the changes it has evolved into; its place within and the impact it has created on social systems; and

---

20.   R. Syme, *The Roman Revolution* (Oxford: Oxford University Press, 1939).

21.   G. Alföldy, *The Social History of Rome* (trans. D. Braund and F. Pollock; London: Croom Helm, 1985).

22.   G.E.M. de Ste. Croix, 'Suffragium: From Vote to Patronage', *British Journal of Sociology* 5 (1954), pp. 33-48.

23.   A. von Premerstein, *Von Werden und Wesen des augusteischen Prinzipats* (Munich: C.H. Beck'sche Verlagsbuchhandlung, 1937).

24.   E. Badian, *Foreign Clientele (264-70 B.C.)* (Oxford: Clarendon, 1958).

25.   M. Gelzer, *The Roman Nobility* (trans. R. Seager; New York: Barnes & Noble, 1969).

26.   R. Saller, *Personal Patronage under the Empire* (New York: Cambridge University Press, 1982).

27.   T.F. Carney, *The Shape of the Past: Models and Antiquity* (Lawrence, KS: Coronado Press, 1975).

28.   J.H. Elliott, 'Patronage and Clientism in Early Christian Society', *Foundations and Facets Forum* 3 (1987), pp. 39-48 (43).

also the social consequences it carries. The vast field this approach covers results therefore in an extensive amount of literature which this specific field of research has produced. Such are the essay collections of Gellner and Waterbury;[29] Boissevain and Mitchell;[30] Schmidt; Eisenstadt with Lemarchand[31] and Roniger.[32] Articles and monographs on patronage in the Mediterranean societies have been attractive to scholars who are trying to read the Mediterranean writings of the New Testament: cf. the works of Gilmore;[33] Gellner and Waterbury;[34] Boissevain;[35] and Campbell.[36]

The primary contribution of the research is its ability to develop theories, conceptual models, and methods which are instrumental in explaining the workings of the phenomenon of patronage 'as a means for structuring social relations and social exchange in accord with the structures, values, and norms of the society at large'.[37] This approach has greatly illuminated the social world of early Christianity, providing a tool both for analysis and interpretation of texts and contexts of the early Christian period.

The third field of research is that of exegesis and biblical social world analysis. Despite the extensive studies done using the social-scientific method, biblical exegetes have not paid much attention to the significance of the patronage conceptual model in biblical interpretation. Elliott observes that,

> no entries are contained in the standard reference works; few articles have patronage as their central focus; no systematic study is yet at hand. Occasional references to the institution in current studies of the early

29. E. Gellner and J. Waterbury (eds.), *Patrons and Clients in Mediterranean Societies* (London: Duckworth, 1977).

30. J. Boissevain and J.C. Mitchell (eds.), *Network Analysis: Studies in Human Interaction* (The Hague: Mouton, 1973).

31. S.N. Eisenstadt and R. Lemarchand (eds.)., *Political Clientism, Patronage and Development* (Contemporary Political Sociology, 3; Beverly Hills: Sage, 1981).

32. S.N. Eisenstadt and L. Roniger (eds.), *Patrons, Clients and Friends: Interpersonal Relations and the Structure of Trust in Society* (New York: Cambridge University Press, 1984).

33. D.D. Gilmore, 'Anthropology of the Mediterranean Area', *Annual Review of Anthropology* 11 (1982), pp. 175-205.

34. Gellner and Waterbury (eds.), *Patrons and Clients in Mediterranean Societies*.

35. J. Boissevain, *Friends of Friends: Networks, Manipulators and Coalitions* (New York: St. Martin's Press, 1974).

36. J.K. Campbell, *Honour, Family and Patronage: A Study of Institutions and Moral Values in a Greek Mountain Community* (Oxford: Clarendon Press, 1964).

37. Elliott, 'Patronage and Clientism', p. 44.

Christian social world (e.g. Meeks, 1983;[38] Stambaugh and Balch, 1986[39]) describe but fail to comprehensively explain the phenomenon.[40]

Only a handful have attempted this and they have demonstrated how the patron-client relations model can be very helpful in understanding biblical texts in their social contexts. Bruce Malina,[41] for example, was able to discuss how in the early and later church the presumed relationship of prayerful devotees to God (and later, also to the saints) replicates on the symbolic level of religious belief the social relationship of client and patron.[42] From the same series, John Pilch illustrates the nature and activity of religious prayer with reference to the gospel of Luke.[43]

One of the latest studies using the patronage model in the New Testament is that of John K. Chow. In his book *Patronage and Power: A Study of Social Networks in Corinth*, Chow attempts to investigate some of the behavioural problems in the Corinthian church by analysing the status of the patronage relationships amongst the Corinthian members. He pays closer attention to the issues of incestuous relationship, the settling of disputes before a pagan judge, the eating of food offered to idols, the baptism of the dead, and the implication of Paul's teachings in relation to the consequences brought about by the existing patronal relationships.[44]

In the study of patronage in Luke–Acts, one work stands out as it has successfully investigated the features of social conflict and economic interaction. Halvor Moxnes in *The Economy of the Kingdom*[45] and in his article 'Patron-Client Relations and the New Community' argues that Luke redefines the patron-client relations by portraying Jesus and the kingdom of God as opposing the unequal dependency relations of the patron-client system represented by the Pharisees and, in its place, shows how God is the ultimate benefactor and patron, while Jesus and the apostles are their true and reliable brokers.

---

38. Meeks, *The First Urban Christians*.

39. J.E. Stambaugh and D.L. Balch, *The New Testament in its Social Environment* (Philadelphia: Westminster Press, 1986).

40. Elliott, 'Patronage and Clientism', p. 44.

41. B.J. Malina, 'What is Prayer?' *The Bible Today* 18 (1980), pp. 214-20.

42. Elliott, 'Patronage and Clientism', p. 45.

43. J. Pilch, 'Praying with Luke', *The Bible Today* 18 (1980), pp. 221-25.

44. J.K. Chow, *Patronage and Power: A Study of Social Networks in Corinth* (JSNTSup, 75; Sheffield: JSOT Press, 1992), p. 28.

45. H. Moxnes, *The Economy of the Kingdom: Social Conflict and Economic Interaction in Luke's Gospel* (Philadelphia: Fortress, 1988); *idem*, 'Patron-Client Relations', pp. 241-68.

It is Moxnes' portrayal of the apostles as brokers which this study wishes to extend. To begin with, we need to have a general understanding of Moxnes' reading of patronage in Luke–Acts.[46]

2.2. *Halvor Moxnes' Hypothesis*
Moxnes has the following general hypotheses: First, Luke's writing of history is not in the tradition of history writing of his time. This does not primarily concern the issue of how Luke renders historical facts. Rather, the author's presentation of history (as any writer would) is with the purpose of influencing his readers.[47] His descriptions and characterizations of the actors in his two-volume work are coloured by his evaluations. The colouring serves to influence relationships between Luke and his audience.[48] The intent to influence will become very obvious and useful in our discussion of Acts 1 and 2, more particularly when we venture into the issue of how the author of Acts campaigns for the promotion of the Twelve as legitimate witnesses of Jesus.

Secondly, Moxnes discusses the significance of being able to distinguish between patronage in 'ideal' and in 'reality'. He picks up S. Silverman's advice that studies on patronage ought to first clearly 'set forth our concepts in such a way that we can investigate the interplay between values and behaviour, between belief and action'.[49] It is important to know 'how people actually behave', 'what is supposed to happen', and 'what actually happened'. In other words, the interplay between values and behaviour is crucial in the understanding of whether what is actually happening in the narrative is an application of the ideal meaning of patronage or the lack of it.

2.3. *God as Patron and Jesus as Broker*
Reading Luke–Acts from a perspective of the patron-client relations will show that God is the ultimate benefactor and patron. The author clearly

---

46. The following discussion is based mainly on Moxnes' work.
47. Cf. Marshall, *The Gospel of Luke*, p. 40.
48. F.G. Downing, 'Theophilus' First Reading of Luke–Acts', in C.M. Tuckett (ed.), *Luke's Literary Achievement: Collected Essays* (JSNTSup, 116; Sheffield: Sheffield Academic Press, 1995), p. 95.
49. Although Silverman argues that the emic/etic contrast is not the same thing as the contrast between 'real' and the 'ideal' as these terms are usually used in anthropology. Cf. S. Silverman, 'Patronage as Myth', in Gellner and Waterbury (eds.), *Patrons and Clients*, p. 10.

wants to announce this motif at the very beginning of his gospel (Lk. 1.46-55 and 1.68-79). As 'The Patron', the people look to God as their sole provider and protector. On the other hand, God demands supreme loyalty from his clients. There ought to be, as Judaism teaches, no other 'patrons' but him (cf. Lk. 16.13).

Jesus' mediation between God (the patron) and the people of Israel (the clients) presents his role as a broker. A broker is also known as a 'middleman'. He himself is a patron who has clients under him. However, he also functions as a broker when he provides access for his clients to patrons who are more powerful than he is. The broker functions as a mediator or a representative for clients of a patron who covers a large area of groups of clientele. A broker-patron may be likened to the ruler of a certain town and its population serves as the clients. To provide for major projects and needs of its constituents, funding and other resources would sometimes have to be requested from the local government to which the town or province belongs. The governor may then be viewed as the more powerful patron who heads over all the local provinces under his jurisdiction.

Relations between the broker and clients can also cover not only the economic or cultural needs of the clientele, but the religious aspects as well. Thus, there can be different brokers to the same client. This means that for every aspect of needs which a client or group of clients may require, representative brokers serve as the clients' means of access to the main source or patron. *That is why a 'holy man' can be a broker between the god and the client's spiritual relations.*[50]

The author of Luke–Acts intends to show how true brokerage ought to be. The religious leaders such as the Pharisees, priests, and scribes have not been faithful to their roles as brokers for the people to God.[51] Instead of providing access to God, these religious leaders block the peoples' need to reach for the ultimate patron. Moxnes states for example that,

> In the major part of Luke's narrative, community leaders are represented by heads of the synagogue, Pharisees and scribes. According to Luke, however, in almost every instance they do not facilitate access to God, but instead block it. This becomes the theme of several of the conflict scenes between them and Jesus. People who are in need of healing or salvation

---

50. Cf. P. Brown, 'The Rise and Function of the Holy Man in Late Antiquity', *JRS* 61 (1971), pp. 80-101.

51. For a discussion on the failure of these religious leaders as brokers for the people of God, see D. Gowler, *Host, Guest, Enemy and Friend: Portraits of the Pharisees in Luke and Acts* (New York: Peter Lang, 1991), pp. 177-319.

come to Jesus, but the community leaders try to use the Torah to stop them by means of arguments based on legality, sabbath observance etc. (5.21; 6.2, 7; 13.14). Thus, these leaders who are supposed to be 'brokers' (or 'friends') do not fulfil their function. This suggests that Jesus will fill that needed role of friend, patron, and broker.[52]

And indeed in the healing stories in the gospel, Jesus clearly functions as one who shows access to the benefactions of God.[53] Moxnes illustrates that.[54]

1. Jesus is a broker; his healings or other powerful acts are performed in the name of God or with the power of God.
2. The response of the people giving praise to God indicates that he is the ultimate source of the healing (5.25-26; 7.16; 13.13; 18.43).
3. Jesus as broker has access to that power. This poses a serious challenge to the other religious parties who claim the same access.

What we see, therefore, is a complete reversal of the concept of leadership and patronage in Luke–Acts. The representation of leadership and patronage in the narrative of Luke–Acts reveals the author's attempt to show a contrast between how patronage has wrongly functioned and how it ought to be as portrayed by Jesus. One good example is the apostles' question to Jesus of who among them was to be regarded as the 'greatest' in Lk. 22.24-27. Jesus responds by contrasting the kings who lord it over their subjects and leaders, such as himself, who actually serve. In other words, Jesus uses an established order of status and honour in his society when he says, 'Which is the greater, one who sits at table, or one who serves? Is it not the one who sits at table?' (22.27). Jesus then brings himself into his illustration by saying 'But I am among you as one who serves'.

Moxnes aptly summarizes his study on the role of Jesus as a broker by showing that the meaning of power which has always been identified with the centre, and the meaning of service, which in turn has been identified with the lowly who reside mainly in the peripheries, have both been seen as present in Jesus. In doing so, Luke discredits the temple as an institution when Jesus cleanses and strips it of its power as centre (19.45-46). The

---

52. Moxnes, 'Patron-Client Relations', p. 256.
53. Cf. Lk. 4.16-19.
54. Moxnes, 'Patron-Client Relations', p. 258.

author of Luke–Acts has always defined the true source of power as God.[55]

A new definition and form of leadership/patronage are seen in the gospel. This leadership is no longer that which oppresses and places burdens on its clients. It is not that which blocks access to God. It is a leadership which is expressed by service to its people. Thus, Moxnes adds,

> There is a strange transformation of the very concept of patronage. The institution is preserved, but the greatness traditionally associated with the role of the patron is now intimately linked with the act of serving. This transformation of roles is not only confined to Jesus; *it also becomes visible in Luke's description of the disciples of Jesus.*[56]

The transformation of roles becoming visible in Luke's description of the disciples of Jesus ushers us into one of our primary hypotheses of this thesis—the role of apostles as brokers of the people to God. It is this role that placed the responsibility of leadership upon the apostles. It is also this crucial role which was seriously marred by Judas' betrayal.

2.4. *The Apostles as Brokers*

'The Kings of the Gentiles exercise lordship over them; and those in authority over them are called benefactors. But not so with you; rather, let the greatest among you become the youngest, and the leader as one who serves' (Lk. 22.25-26).

This passage does not only speak of Jesus' teaching to his apostles about humility. Rather, the lesson is that of the complete reversal of the concept of leadership. Seizing the opportunity after his apostles are in a dispute regarding who among them is the greatest (Lk. 22.24), Jesus uses the contemporary understanding of how leaders lord over their subordinates. He corrects this wrong notion of oppressive leadership and instructs them to do the opposite—leaders live to serve and not to lord over their people.

Only after Jesus had taught his apostles what proper leadership was, did he reward them for their faithfulness and assign them a kingdom in which they would sit on thrones and judge the twelve tribes of Israel (Lk. 22.28-30). This, according to Green, is another form of reversal. He rightly observes that the transposition is only possible because of what Jesus had earlier taught his apostles (Lk. 22.24-27). He adds, '…Jesus can speak of the leadership roles of the apostles only after having transformed the

---

55. Moxnes, 'Patron-Client Relations', p. 260.
56. Moxnes, 'Patron-Client Relations', p. 260. Italics mine.

conventional relationship between the benevolent performance of leadership and the reception of elevated status. Jesus wants his disciples to lead, but in a wholly unconventional way.'[57]

Luke understands the present structures of leadership in the society but redefines it. He emphasizes the transformation of the apostles' role and their status. Greatness is defined by service. This service, however, is not reciprocated by power and honour.

This farewell scene in Lk. 22 is a clear description of the Twelve as taking on the role of brokers. Moxnes notes that even as early as Lk. 6.12-16, the apostles were called by Jesus to share in his power and authority. Their role with Jesus in preaching and healing (9.1-6), plus their call to service, places them as mediating between God and his people. Their mediation and service to people defines the role as that of a benefactor/broker.[58]

Benefactors, however, can rightly claim power and authority.[59] Benefactions by the rich elite were indeed expressed primarily by their service to the citizenry. In return, they were legitimated by the rendering of honour and status by the community. Honour and status came by placing

---

57. J. Green, *The Gospel of Luke* (Grand Rapids: Eerdmans, 1997), pp. 766-67.

58. Moxnes, 'Patron-Client Relations', p. 260.

59. Sponsorships of public events or festivals; charitable donations especially to the poor; constructions of public buildings, roads or bridges; when all these are done in the name of public service and at no expense to anyone but the patron, he is what one would call a 'benefactor-patron'. The benefactor is another form of a patron, an equivalent of the emperor on a smaller scale. As the emperor is to the empire, the benefactor is to a city or a local community. He is known to do benefactions and in return, he is honoured with recognition either through dedications by inscriptions on walls or brass plates, or the naming of bridges and roads which he financed to construct (cf. Moxnes, 'Patron-Client Relations', p. 249). The public honour, of course, becomes helpful in time of elections. The demonstration of generosity is reciprocated by the loyalty of his clients, the inhabitants of the city or the local community, especially in securing votes for a much coveted public office when the season for the local elections come.

Benefaction was also a means of maintaining social order. The maintenance of public roads also meant the assurance of an unhindered passage of supplies which the city or province regularly needs. The benefactor who is responsible for this good deed is honoured either by epigraphic inscriptions or literary declarations, the purpose of which is not only to praise the good acts of the benefactor but also to encourage other financially able people to do the same. For further discussions and examples of benefactions in the first century, see B. Winter, *Seek the Welfare of the City: Christians as Benefactors and Citizens* (Grand Rapids: Eerdmans, 1994).

them into public offices. The cycle continued only within the circle of those who had wealth. The wealthy who served received prestige. As I have stated, this prestige gets them into public positions. Public positions in government enjoyed the advancement in honour and status. Thus, the pattern of gift-giving brought with it the obligations for service and honour. Lk. 22.24-27 breaks 'with the patron-client relationship at its most crucial point: a service performed or a favour done shall *not* be transformed into status and honour'.[60]

This is not to claim that Jesus was teaching against benefactions.[61] Rather, what we can see is the emphasis on the benefactions without the reciprocity of prestige and honour. The apostles are leaders characterized primarily by service. As they are to 'sit on thrones as judges', that is, central authorities, they are at the same time to 'serve'.[62]

2.5. *An Example from the* Acts of Peter

The concept of benefactions whereby the apostles, as benefactors, do not serve in return for honour and prestige but instead give all glory to God as the ultimate patron has been evident in some traditions. One good example is found in the *Acts of Peter* (APt). In a study produced by R.F. Stoops Jr,[63] this propagandic literature written in the middle of the second century contains the earliest surviving account of the conflict between Simon Magus and the apostle Peter outside the canonical book of Acts. It promotes the apostle's victory over Simon Magus on occasions of miracle contests, showing that Peter's miracles are actually Christ's demonstrations to take care of his own.[64]

Just as Jesus has taken the opportunity to reverse the predominant understanding of benefactions in order to teach his apostles, the author of the APt has also turned around the traditional patronage concept where the Roman patron was obliged to protect and care for his client and expected

---

60. Moxnes, 'Patron-Client Relations', p. 261.

61. 'The point of Lk. 22.25 is that Christians were not to operate in an overbearing and dictatorial fashion as Gentile kings and those in authority who were commonly called "benefactors".' Winter, *Seek the Welfare of the City*, p. 40, n. 50; *contra* D.J. Lull, 'The Servant-Benefactor as a Model of Greatness (Luke 22.24-30)', *NovT* 28 (1986), pp. 289-305 (296).

62. Moxnes, 'Patron-Client Relations', p. 261.

63. R.F. Stoops, Jr, 'Patronage in the *Acts of Peter*', *Semeia* 38 (1986), pp. 91-100 (91).

64. R.F. Stoops, Jr, 'Miracle Stories and Vision Reports in the *Acts of Peter*' (Unpublished PhD dissertation; Harvard University, 1982), pp. 181-92.

to receive honour and loyalty in return. In the APt, Christ also offers protection and support in times of need. However, the author emphasizes that Christ is more than just the potential patron. As Christ rewards his loyal clients with material benefits (expressed on the level of miracle stories), he also gives knowledge, spiritual guidance, and future salvation.[65]

In the APt, the author appeals to the wealthy elite who are either already patrons or potential patrons in the Roman society. These patrons are useful, not only because the patrons' wealth usually is the means by which Jesus provides for the needs of his followers,[66] but also 'in a period of competition and expansion inasmuch as the presence of wealthy and prestigious members of society contributes to the reputation of the group as a whole... Winning a patron to the faith normally means winning the patron's clientele as well.'[67]

As the author of Luke–Acts has redefined patronage, the author of APt does the same. In the APt, there is the integration of human patrons into the community of believers in order to emphasize that Christ is the sole patron of all. The role and influence of the human patrons have been limited so as not to dilute or divert the loyalty of the clientele to Christ. Even the apostle Peter has sought to speak of his limitations and inadequacy in order to focus the reciprocation of honour to Christ. Stoops rightly suggests that,

65. Stoops, 'Miracle Stories', pp. 181-92.

66. Stoops, as an example, relates that in the story of Eubula the contest between Simon and Peter becomes a contest for both a convert and patroness (APt 17). Eubula's conversion is constructed around a vision revealing the identity of a thief (cf. Cicero, *On Divination* 1.25 and Lucian, *Alexander the False Prophet* 24). Since Simon is the thief, the story functions as part of the contest itself. It probably formed the climax of the lost part of the work set in Jerusalem. In this story Eubula must decide whether Simon or Peter is the true 'man of God'. For her it is also a question of which of the two is the appropriate channel for her benefactions (APt 17). Peter insists that Eubula must choose between Simon and the living God and that her decision must be based on deeds rather than words.

When Peter assures Eubula that her lost property will be recovered, he reminds her that the recovery of her soul is more important than the recovery of her wealth. Because Eubula is wealthy, her conversion naturally makes her a benefactress of the other believers, especially the widows, the orphans, and the poor. However, the concluding frame of Eubula's story does not treat her as a leader in the Jerusalem community. Rather, her conversion and donations are another instance of Christ's care for his own. Stoops, 'Patronage in the *Acts of Peter*', p. 94.

67. Stoops, 'Patronage in the *Acts of Peter*', p. 93.

When Peter acts a broker of the benefits that flow from Christ, he may be
worthy of honour, but he is a broker who always steps aside so that the
primary relationship between Christ and believers will be a direct one. The
apostle is allowed to function at the centre of a patronage network only for
the purpose of bringing people into the more lasting network anchored on
Christ.[68]

Stoops concludes his study by making an important observation that is
crucial to my study. He notes that despite the problems which human
patrons create in the relationship between Christ and the believers, *the
author thought the model of patronage was an appropriate vehicle for
propagation of the Christian message.*[69]

This observation is basically true in pursuing my interests in the events
of Acts 1. I believe that the values of patronage, together with the other
conceptual models (such as social networks, honour and shame) are
working interactively within this theoretical framework of RST. The
success of the author's appeal to promote the apostles as Jesus' witnesses
and leaders of the Christian community would also mean reaffirming the
reliability of the apostles' testimony which in turn is crucial to the
conversion of the people, leading to the growth and expansion of the
church.

3. *Summary*

In this chapter we have discussed two items. The first deals with the ritual
elements of the separation stage. These elements comprise the symbols of
the initial stage of the ritual process in Acts 1.3-11. They include the
apostles as the initiands; Jesus as the ritual elder; the meaning and
significance of the forty days time-span which the initiands and the ritual
elder spend together; and finally, the role and function of the two men in
white robes who played significantly in the separation between the
initiands and the ritual elder—a separation which ushered the initiands
into the complete limbo of statuslessness.

This chapter digresses slightly from the ritual discussion and is about
the leadership role which the apostles as initiands will be transformed to. I
indicated that the reason for the author's campaign for the leadership
status of the apostles is the loss of the trust and full support of the
community for the apostles. I stated that this mistrust is due to one of the

---

68.   Stoops, 'Patronage in the *Acts of Peter*', p. 95.
69.   Stoops, 'Patronage in the *Acts of Peter*', p. 99. Italics mine.

Twelve being the betrayer of Jesus. This language of trust and loyalty is a language present in patron-client relations. I suggested that if we are to properly understand the voice and tone behind the author's appeal, we can best understand this from the concept of patronage, a concept which I believe is the basis of the relationship between the apostles and the Christian community. I pursued this concept by stating that Jesus' leadership role was that of a broker, the broker who served as the middleman between God—(the ultimate patron)—and the people (the clients). This role of brokerage is now handed down to the apostles to fulfil.

The next chapter attempts to understand how all these ritual elements work within the context and the theoretical framework of the RST. The chapter is the ritual process and it primarily deals with how the apostles, as initiands, enter the stage of separation.

Chapter 3

THE APOSTLES AND THEIR SEPARATION FROM JESUS

1. *The Ritual Process in Acts 1.3-5*

I have designated Acts 1.3-11 as the *Separation* stage. I then identified its ritual elements and also defined an aspect of the leadership role to which the apostles are being initiated. In this chapter, I will now attempt to investigate the ritual process.

We find at least three phases in this stage. Phase One is 1.3-5; Phase Two is 1.6-8; and Phase Three is 1.9-11. Under each phase is a characteristic feature of a separation stage. In Phase One, we have the author legitimizing the apostles as initiands. Phase Two shows the cleansing of the initiands' preconceived ideas. Together in this phase is the initiands' absolute obedience to the teachings and instructions of the ritual elder. Phase Three portrays the initiands' experience of complete separation. Here we will find Jesus the ritual elder leaving the initiands on their own as they prepare for their ritual confrontation in Acts 1.12-26.

1.1. *Phase One—Acts 1.3-5: The Initiands are Separated from Society and Enter the Ritual Process*

1.1.1. *The Author Legitimizes the Apostles as Initiands.* Fresh in the readers' memory is the betrayal of one of Jesus' apostles (cf. Lk. 22.1-6). Thus, the first task the author needs to do is to defuse the readers' apprehensions by presenting the credentials of the Eleven apostles. The author needs to explain what qualifies the apostles as initiands and legitimate successors to the leadership.[1] This is exactly what we find in Phase One of the separation stage. The author begins his account, not with the first steps of the ritual process, but by first legitimizing the Eleven as initiands. The

---

1.   D.G. Horrell, 'Leadership Patterns and the Development of Ideology in Early Christianity', in *idem* (ed.), *Social-Scientific Approaches to New Testament Interpretation* (Edinburgh: T. & T. Clark, 1999), pp. 309-37.

author achieves this by reminding the readers of the power and majesty of Jesus (1.3a), and that this same Jesus is the one who chooses and ordains the apostles to be his successors (1.1-5).[2]

The author's legitimization of the apostles strikes an important chord in the patron-client relations. In a relationship that is primarily voluntary, clients express loyalty to the patron's representative, not only because the patron endorses the representative/broker, but also because of the representative's qualifications. This is not so in involuntary associations. In a kinship situation, a member of the family is recognized as the patron's broker or representative simply because of his blood ties with the patron. Clients are expected to honour and attribute loyalty to the patron's representative beyond his qualifications.[3] In the case of the apostles, the introduction by the author early in 1.2 with the phrase 'whom he [Jesus] had chosen' implies the legitimacy of the apostles as Jesus' representatives.[4] This phrase, coupled with the fact that the Eleven were the recipients of Jesus' instructions on 'the things concerning the reign of God' (1.3) attempts to impress on the readers that the Eleven are indeed the ones who are to follow after Jesus' leadership.[5]

1.1.2. *The Forty Days' Separation.* In Acts 1.3, we can see the start of the initiands' separation from the society. Of significance in the perspective of the RST is the meaning of the phrase 'forty days'—the time Jesus and the apostles spent together after Jesus' resurrection. For the author, it seems not enough to say that Jesus 'presented himself alive after his passion by

---

2.   For legitimization in general, see P.L. Berger, *The Sacred Canopy: Elements of a Social Theory of Religion* (New York: Anchor Books, 1990), pp. 155-71; Berger and Luckmann, *The Social Construction of Reality*, pp. 110-46.

3.   See D.A. deSilva, *The Hope of Glory: Honor Discourse and New Testament Interpretation* (Collegeville, MN: The Liturgical Press, 1999), pp. 9-11.

4.   Cf. R. Tannehill, *The Narrative Unity of Luke–Acts* (vol. 2; Philadelphia and Minneapolis: Fortress Press, 1986, 1990), p. 13.

5.   The narrative also opens with the description of the ritual elder's credentials. One of which is in 1.3 with the phrase 'presenting himself alive after his passion by many proofs'. This phrase is crucial as it emphasizes the disparity between the ritual elder and the initiands. It shows how the apostles enter the ritual with virtually having nothing to boast at all (and compounded by the fact of their humiliating association with Judas the betrayer). They, in Turner's words, '...may be disguised as monsters, wear only a strip of clothing, or even go naked, to demonstrate that as liminal beings they have no status, property, insignia, secular clothing indicating rank or role...' V. Turner, *The Ritual Process*, p. 95.

many proofs', nor that he continued to teach the apostles about the kingdom of God. The inclusion of the note of forty days in what is supposed to
be the last days together between Jesus and the apostles is very significant.[6] The author obviously uses this symbolically-laden label to parallel
the apostles' experience with Jesus' own 'forty days' wilderness experience, an experience within Jesus' own status transformation in Lk. 4.1-13.

I suggest that the author and the readers are well aware of the rich
meaning of 'forty' days (or years) which tradition has earned. Its meaning
is not just drawn from Lk. 4.2. For instance, there is the 'forty years' of
wandering in the wilderness by the Israelites (cf. Lev. 26; Deut. 28). Apart
from those things I have enumerated in the ritual elements section,[7] the
readers are reminded of the stories of the Flood which lasted for forty
days; Moses was forty days and nights in the mountain; Elijah fasted for
forty days; Ezra was not to be sought for forty days; David, Solomon,
Joash, Eli all ruled for forty years; Ezekiel lay on his side for forty days;
Goliath challenged Israel for forty days.[8]

What I seem to find particularly important about this forty-day motif, is
not only the length of the initiands' separation experience, but also their
liminality experience. This has been exceptionally vivid in the
'wilderness' stories in both the OT and NT. An example is the study by
Robert L. Cohn on wilderness motifs. He explains the unique role of the
wilderness as a narrative paradigm of a 'liminal' time and space;[9] cf. the
experience of the Israelites, who from Egypt to Canaan experienced forty

6.   Notably, there are those who simply focus on the mention of forty days in Acts
1.3 as the time separating Easter and Pentecost. It is argued, for example, that in the
days of the Valentinians, eighteen months separated the resurrection and ascension
events of Jesus; the Ophites believed that there were eleven or twelve years; Eusebius
mentions the belief that the length of Jesus' ministry after his resurrection was the
same as the length of his ministry before the Resurrection. Torrance explains, 'And so
after Easter there is something like a history of the risen Jesus who came and went
among the disciples, who spoke and ate and drank with them as he willed, in such a
way that he could be touched and seen to be no apparition, but above all it was the
personal self identification of the familiar Jesus that was the paramount factor'. T.F.
Torrance, *Space, Time and Resurrection* (Grand Rapids: Eerdmans, 1976), p. 83. These
examples are what I would raise as good examples of how historical approaches have
limited the perspective of reading the biblical text.

7.   See 2.1.3.

8.   B.K. Donne, *Christ Ascended: A Study in the Significance of the Ascension of
Jesus Christ in the New Testament* (Exeter: Paternoster Press, 1983), p. 71, n. 19.

9.   Cohn, 'Liminality in the Wilderness', pp. 7-23.

years in the wilderness. The same wilderness motif was also adopted by the exilic writers because it provided a paradigm with which to understand their own experience.[10] Cohn argues,

> Into the story of the wilderness march, the exiles projected their own fears and hopes. Like generations before them, they viewed the wilderness as a chaotic place and the march as a terrifying journey... They thus saw themselves in the 'wilderness' of exile being purged of the old and primed for the new.[11]

Likewise the Qumran community, who have isolated and regarded themselves as the true Israel, attempted to read their own situation out of the Pentateuchal story. Again Cohn adds,

> All three groups—the wilderness generation, the Babylonian exiles, the Qumranians—were or saw themselves to be societies in transition, not settled in time and space, but on the move and waiting the fulfilment of divine promises. The wilderness narrative depicts a people in transition between slavery in Egypt and freedom in Canaan. The way in which the narrative functioned paradigmatically for Israel is highlighted when its preoccupations are seen in comparative context against the background of those other transitional groups.[12]

The author of Luke–Acts understands the significance of this motif. When he has extended its application from Jesus in Lk. 4.1-13 to the apostles here in Acts 1.3-5, the purpose is not only to convey the time of instruction spent by the apostles with Jesus. I believe that the author wants to achieve two things: First, as the forty days motif carries with it the rich history depicting the trials and testing, and the training and triumph of the characters who experienced liminality in the time and space of their respective 'wildernesses', the same applies to the apostles' experience in Acts. The second, is again a function of the author's legitimizing technique. This forty days motif is for the author a paradigm or a construct. The place where Jesus was transformed from the status of private person to prophet is now adopted by the author to tell his readers of the status transformation of the apostles from followers to leaders.

---

10.   Humphreys adds, 'In the priests' narrative the chosen people are last seen as pilgrims moving through alien land toward a goal to be fulfilled in another time and place, and this is the vision, drawn from the ancient story of their past, that the priests now hold out to the scattered sons and of old Israel'. W.L. Humphreys, *Crisis and Story: Introduction to the Old Testament* (Palo Alto: Mayfield, 1979), p. 217.

11.   Cohn, 'Liminality in the Wilderness', p. 8.

12.   Cohn, 'Liminality in the Wilderness', p. 9.

1.2. Phase Two—Acts 1.6-8: Changing the Initiands' Preconceived Ideas
After justifying to the readers that the apostles were the ones chosen by
Jesus to continue his mission, and that this was done despite strong
reservations against the Eleven's moral integrity to lead the community
because of their former association with Judas, the author immediately
makes a very important move to assure his readers of the apostles' leadership worthiness. This move, in the perspective of the RST, is the changing
of the preconceived ideas of the initiands.

The changing of preconceived ideas is highly characteristic in the
separation stage. As the initiands enter into their liminal status, ritual
elders see to it that all previous 'baggages' (such as beliefs, habits, ideas,
or persuasions) must be left behind. The initiands are to be cleansed from
all factors that may hinder their full or complete transformation.[13] Turner
explicitly states that the neophyte in liminality becomes a *tabula rasa*—'a
blank slate, on which is inscribed the knowledge and wisdom of the group,
in those respects that pertain to the new status'.[14]

The author of Luke–Acts achieves this changing of preconceived ideas
in a subtle way. He particularly targets what seems to be the most hinder-
ing factor to the apostles' status transformation—their understanding of
the restoration of the kingdom to Israel. We say this because of the
following reasons:

1. The very first words which the author assigns to the apostles in
    Acts 1 pose a question about Israel's restoration (1.6). It is a
    legitimate question considering that Jesus has already been
    resurrected and is expected to lead and see the fulfilment of such
    restoration.[15]

---

13. Or as McVann puts it, 'in order to accomplish the transformation of the
initiands, the elders…see to it that the preconceived ideas about society, status, and
relationships, in short, about life itself are wiped out'. McVann, 'Rituals of Status
Transformation', p. 337.

14. Turner, *The Ritual Process*, p. 103.

15. As Fitzmyer confirms, 'Since Jesus did not wrest the governance of Judea from
the Romans during his earthly ministry, it was a natural or logical question for his
followers to put to him as the risen Lord. Cf. Lk. 24.21, where a similar remark is
made by Cleopas on the road to Emmaus. Kingship in Israel had been known in the
remote past from the time of the monarchy before the Assyrian and Babylonian
Captivities, in the more recent past in the Hasmonean priest-kings (before the Roman
occupation of Judea under Pompey in 63 B.C.), and in the case of individuals like
Herod the Great (37-4 B.C.) even in Roman times. The question formulates a hope for

2. Jesus' immediate response (Acts 1.7)—a response which is actually short of saying 'no'—not only reveals the significance and urgency of the issue but also declares that the apostles' understanding of Israel's restoration is wrong.

Jesus, the ritual elder, has to correct the apostles of this misconception. They should understand that their concept of Israel's restoration has to change if they are to be effective leaders of the community. After the initiands are corrected, Jesus gives them instructions on the next steps to take which would lead to their status transformation (1.8). This scene is consistent with Turner's observation that, '...the elders instill new ideas, assumptions, and understandings that the initiands will need to function effectively when they assume their new roles at the aggregation rite'.[16]

Did Jesus change the programme of Israel's restoration, or, did the apostles really misunderstand the concept in the first place thus necessitating correction of a preconceived idea? These questions need to be addressed in order to support my argument above. The answer to these questions dwells on Luke's eschatology, an issue which has invited varying views. A brief review of the current discussion on Lukan eschatology will be helpful. I will basically present the two popular views: Delayed and Imminent eschatology. After that, I will give my analysis and proposal.

1.2.1. *A Delayed Eschatology.* Hans Conzelmann's book *The Theology of St. Luke*[17] has become a classic in Lukan scholarship. Conzelmann proposed that Luke altered his sources to push back the original early expectation of eschatological consummation into the distant future. Luke had to undertake this alteration in response to the delay of the parousia. Conzelmann's insistence on debunking any ideas about imminent expectation in Luke–Acts deactivates the sense of urgency on the realization of Israel's restoration and the discharging of roles by its divinely appointed leaders.

Conzelmann arrived at his conclusions by weeding out the 'discrepan-

---

the restoration of an autonomous kingly rule for the Jews of Judea. Though the disciples who pose the question are Christians, they still speak as Judean Jews on behalf of "Israel". The ancient Jewish prayers, *Semoneh Esreh* 14 and *Qaddis* 2, called upon God for the restoration of the kingship to Israel and also of David's throne.' Fitzmyer, *The Acts of the Apostles*, p. 205.

16. Turner, *The Ritual Process*, p. 103.

17. H. Conzelmann, *The Theology of St. Luke* (trans. G. Buswell; New York: Harper & Row, 1961).

cies between the ideas of Luke's sources and Luke's own ideas'.[18]
Working from what should have been the intended or original meaning of
the coming of the Spirit quoted from the book of Joel in Acts 2.17
onwards, Conzelmann believes that Luke expanded the time table of the
'last days'. In other words, instead of the Spirit's arrival signalling the
eschaton, the period of the Church takes its place and the Spirit's role is to
strengthen this church in face of persecution and the fulfilment of her
missionary task.[19] The results, therefore, are transformed concepts of the
person and work of Jesus, the Spirit, and the nature of the church.[20]

Ernst Haenchen, likewise, wrote his commentary on the book of Acts
with the motif of parousia delay as his guiding rule. His statements are
more direct than Conzelmann's. He states,

---

18.   For example, he puts forward Luke's concepts of θλῖψις and μετάνοια. He
cites that as Mark uses the term θλῖψις as a definite eschatological term (e.g. 8.24),
serving as 'prelude to the cosmic dissolution', Luke totally avoids the word and
replaces it with ἀνάγκη. For Luke, according to Conzelmann, θλῖψις speaks of the
fate of believers. By changing the word to ἀνάγκη, the immediate expectation of
eschatological consummation is suppressed. With μετάνοια, Conzelmann believes that
Luke imperceptibly alters its meaning compared with how it is used in Luke's sources
(i.e. Q, Mark, special material, Acts sources). For instance, compared with Mk 1.15,
Luke omits the term, places a different message in Jesus' preaching, and is made
distinct from the repentance for which John the Baptist calls. Conzelmann, *Theology*,
p. 98.

19.   Conzelmann, *Theology*, p. 96.

20.   Of particular importance to Conzelmann is Lk. 16.16: 'The law and the
prophets were until John; since then the good news of the kingdom of God is preached,
and everyone enters it violently'. This is taken to mean that the epoch of the old order
extended to and included John the Baptist; John was a prophet in the Old Testament
mould. Then came the middle epoch—the ministry of Jesus. Finally came the epoch of
the Church when the Christian community, filled with the Holy Spirit, endeavoured to
carry on the work of its risen Lord (the story of which Luke seeks to unfold in the book
of Acts). According to Conzelmann, this third period was essential to Luke's
theological programme because some Christians were expecting the return of Jesus at
any moment, while others were becoming disillusioned that the second coming had not
already occurred. By projecting the end into the unforeseeable future, but also assuring
his readers that it would come, Luke sought to assure both parties. See also Erich
Grasser, who in 1957 argued that Jesus himself expected the parousia to be immediate;
he did not allow for a long delay, and passages which suggest otherwise actually
originated among the early Christians. *Das Problem der Parusieverzogerung in den
Synoptischen Evangelein und der Apostelgeschichte* (Berlin: Topelmann, 1957), p. 77.

This expectation of the imminent end was not fulfilled. When Luke wrote Acts, Paul had been executed and James the brother of the Lord had died a martyr; Christians had been burned as living torches in the gardens of Nero; the Holy City and its Temple lay in rubble.

Yet the world went on. By this many Christians recognized that the imminent expectation of the end was false. If, however, the end was not to come soon, when would it come?[21]

To answer the question of 'when', Haenchen presents two possibilities. Either the 'last things' are presently happening, or they are to take place in the indefinite future. Haenchen believes that the author Luke worked out his eschatology by taking 'the chronological dimension...seriously and asked himself where and how God's work of history proceeds in time'.[22]

1.2.2. *An Imminent Eschatology.* Contesting Conzelmann's theory are those who see Luke's strong call for vigilance because of an impending eschatological consummation. Both F.O. Francis[23] and A.J. Matill[24] object to the views proposed by the Conzelmann camp. Arguing for a consistent imminent expectation, Francis and Matill set out to prove that Luke was an apocalyptic activist whose only purpose in writing was to effect the imminent End.

Between the two, Matill is more enthusiastic about his findings. His study is very detailed and is determined to balance the suggestion of a parousia delay. For Matill, Luke–Acts was written also with a sense of urgency and emphasis on the imminence motif. Thus, one should expect a 'delay-imminence' picture of Lukan eschatology.

Matill outlines his study of Luke–Acts somewhat randomly. He starts off with the emphatic apocalyptic passages of Lk. 21. He builds from the discussion of the 'Apocalyptic Hope' that resounds boldly from the same chapter and then goes into smaller passages from Lk. 3.18 to Lk. 23.27-31 but which would help define Lukan Apocalypses. From the apocalyptic theme, Matill proceeds to study the 'de-apocalypticizing' found in Luke–

21. Haenchen, *The Acts of the Apostles*, p. 95.

22. Haenchen, *The Acts of the Apostles*, p. 96. Ernst Käsemann, meanwhile, drew attention to the composition of Acts and stated dryly that 'one does not write the history of the church if one daily expects the end of the world'. See W.C. Van Unnik, *Luke–Acts: A Storm-Centre in Contemporary Scholarship: Studies in Luke–Acts* (eds. L.E. Keck and J.L. Martyn; London: SPCK, 1963), p. 24.

23. F. Francis, 'Eschatology and History in Luke–Acts', *JAAR* 37 (1969), pp. 49-63.

24. A.J. Matill, *Luke and the Last Things* (Dillsboro: Western North Carolina Press, 1979), pp. 49-63.

Acts. Using Lk. 16.16 as his main text, Matill admits the neutralizing function of passages pertaining to the ministry of John the Baptist.[25]

1.2.3. *A Synthesis and Proposal.* It is possible to say that exegetes today reap the fruit of Conzelmann's hypothesis without accepting its every detail. He has certainly drawn attention to Luke's emphasis on the history of salvation, and his work on Lukan eschatology, as mentioned previously, has had a lasting influence on subsequent scholarship. It is this issue that I now want to understand.

It has been contended by Conzelmann, and by many others, that Luke's eschatology was worked out against a peculiar community situation.[26] For example, in the Thessalonian correspondence, Paul expected the Lord's return at any moment (though he was more circumspect in some of his later letters). He even had to admonish those who had given up their earthly living to await the great day (2 Thess. 3.6-13).

Mark's gospel is also thought by many to have been written at a time of high eschatological excitement.[27] But Luke, so the argument goes, was composed at a time when Christians were having to reckon with the likelihood that the end was not coming as soon as they had expected. Many people had regarded the destruction of Jerusalem and its Temple in CE 70 to be the event which would bring in the reign of Christ, but it is likely that by the time Luke was written, that event was already in the past.[28] Reactions to this delay of the parousia were two-fold. In the first place, there were those whose apocalyptic fervour led them to announce the imminent end of the world. In some cases things were getting out of hand, and some people were going so far as to identify themselves with the coming Christ. So, in his apocalypse, Luke has to warn his readers against such people (Lk. 21.8-9): 'Take heed that you are not led astray; for many will come in my name saying, "I am he!" and "The time is at hand!" Do not go after them…the end will not be at once.'[29]

On the other hand, some members were becoming disillusioned over the delay, and Luke had to assure them that the parousia would undoubtedly occur, even though its time could not be stipulated. The parable of the

---

25. Matill, *Luke and the Last Things*, pp. 182-207.

26. Conzelmann, *Theology*, pp. 131-32.

27. R. Hiers, 'The Problem of the Delay of the Parousia', *NTS* 20 (1974), pp. 145-55 (146).

28. Conzelmann, *Theology*, p. 113.

29. Cf. Conzelmann, *Theology*, p. 114, n. 3.

importunate widow (18.1-8) seems to be aimed partly at them. At one level, of course, it can be seen as teaching the value of persistent prayer, but the upshot of it is that one should not lose heart if one's prayers are not answered immediately, for God will not delay long over those who petition him earnestly. It is difficult not to see here an 'aside' for those who were becoming disheartened over the delay of the parousia.

A further pertinent feature of Luke at this point is his use of 'realized' eschatology.[30] This is the view that God's kingdom had, in a sense, already come in the person of Jesus. Of particular relevance are the following two verses: 'But if it is by the finger of God that I cast out demons, then the kingdom of God has come upon you' (11.20); 'The kingdom of God is not coming with signs to be observed; nor will they say, "Lo, here it is!" or "There!" for behold, the kingdom of God is within you' (17.20-21).

From a cursory glance, it seems likely that Luke has in mind a realized eschatology in which the end or the future is somehow able to break in upon the present. If the kingdom is to be consummated in the future, it has already been initiated in the earthly life of the believer.

Is Conzelmann's proposal valid? One of the main contentions of Conzelmann is that Luke filled the lacuna between the present and the unforeseeable future with the concept of salvation history. However, one should not overstate the case for Luke's supposed lack of interest in eschatology, for his interest in salvation was to some extent dependent on an eschatological awareness. The idea of the kingdom breaking into the present (10.9, 11; 11.20; 17.20-21) is seen as the lead to its consummation, and it is significant that the statement in 17.20-21 is followed directly by the 'Q' version of the apocalyptic discourse (17.22-37). Luke 12.35-48 is concerned with being prepared for Christ's return, and while in 12.45 the possibility of a delay has to be reckoned with, the emphasis is really on readiness for an event, the time of whose occurrence is unknown. The same message is spelled out in 21.34-36. Thus, one can say that, while Luke certainly did envisage a delay in the parousia—if only because it had already been delayed for some forty-five years by the time he was writing—he was by no means disinterested in it. Christians had to be on the alert lest they were caught out, for in Luke it is not the imminence of the end that is of importance, but rather its suddenness. John T. Carroll best explains this kind of view by stating that Luke, who was writing

---

30. A view initiated by C.H. Dodd. Refer to J. Bowman, 'Eschatology of the NT', in *IDB*, II, pp. 135-40 (140).

history, introduced the motif of delay in order to depict the present age as one of expectation. In Carroll's words,

> Luke wrote in a setting in which parousia delay and a period of worldwide mission were data of history. In such a context, in order to maintain parousia hope as a credible position, it would be necessary for him, in constructing his narrative, to show imminent expectation to have been inappropriate during the ministry of Jesus, the early years of the church's mission, and at the destruction of Jerusalem (hence the element of delay). The prominence of delay in Luke–Acts does not, therefore, rule out imminent hope in Luke's own time.[31]

Nolland confirms this. In simple terms, he adds that Luke 'continued to expect the parousia within his own generation'. Parousia delay is an indisputable fact, but parousia-delay crisis is actually hard to find.[32]

Therefore, in reference to the earlier questions I asked (that is, was there really a change of plan in the programme of Israel's restoration? Or, were the apostles wrong in their concept in the first place?), I suggest that there was really no change of plans since Jesus has already clarified this earlier, for instance in Lk. 12 especially in v. 45.[33] This means that the apostles indeed misunderstood the timing and programme of the parousia in the first place.

This fact, therefore, supports my previous suggestion. Jesus, the ritual elder, had to change the initiands' preconceived ideas about Israel's restoration. Since Luke's eschatology is already clear as early as Lk. 12, the readers are already aware of this concept. The scene in Acts 1.6-8 intends to show the readers of what and how the apostles were 'cleansed' from their preconceived ideas. In other words, Acts 1.6-8 does not primarily function to inform the readers of any changes in God's programme of restoration but to clearly show the crucial phases in the process of the apostles' status transformation.

This leads us to another important aspect in the author's quest to make his readers see and be convinced of the apostles' transformation. This has something to do with the surprisingly *non-reaction* of the Eleven to the news of the parousia delay. To be more precise, why were the apostles

---

31. John T. Carroll, *Response to the End of History: Eschatology and Situation in Luke–Acts* (Atlanta, GA: Scholars Press, 1988), p. 36.

32. J. Nolland, 'Salvation-History and Eschatology', in I.H. Marshall and D. Petersen (eds.), *Witness to the Gospel: The Theology of Acts* (Grand Rapids: Eerdmans, 1998), p. 65.

33. Nolland, 'Salvation-History and Eschatology', p. 67.

silent after learning of what was supposed to be for them a major change in the programme of God's plan for Israel? Why has there been no reference to any expression of the apostles' 'inside views' to what could be a devastating blow to a life-long expectation? In fact, this study observes that it is not simply the silence of the apostles as a group. Rather, it seems as if the apostles were deliberately muted by the author until they produced their first converts in Acts 2.46-47. This observation becomes more apparent as the author does not hold back the inside views of the other characters in the narrative. For instance, he describes the multitude with the inside views of being 'bewildered...and they were amazed and wondered' as they witnessed the alleged commotion in the house (2.6-7).

I propose that the apostles' silence is again consistent within the framework of my study—the complete obedience of the initiands who are undergoing the rituals of status transformation.

1.2.4. *The Complete Obedience of the Initiands.* Obedience through silence happens to be a key feature among the initiands undergoing the rituals of status transformation. V. Turner confirms that 'submissiveness and silence' are indeed key characteristics.[34] To demonstrate this feature of obedience through silence as being present in the narrative of Acts 1–2 we need to understand what inside views are, how they function in the narrative, and what they convey to the readers of the story.

1.2.4.1. *What are Inside Views?* 'Inside views' simply refer to the emotions and feelings of characters who are in the story. One of the main purposes of expressing inside views in a narrative is its ability to allow the reader to penetrate the mind of the character as well as to identify with that character.[35] Stanzel puts it more precisely by stating that,

> Presentation of consciousness and inside views are effective means of controlling the reader's sympathy, because they can influence the reader subliminally in favour of a character in the story. The more the reader learns about the innermost motives for the behaviour of a character, the

34. Turner, *The Ritual Process*, p. 103.
35. J. Tambling adds, '...as in ideology, the reader is placed at the centre and made to feel personally addressed. Both ideology and narrative offer individuals pleasurable images to identify with... Writers and critics encourage readers to identify with certain characters—and to demonize others—and to see fictional characters as people they might feel in "real life"'. *Narrative and Ideology* (Milton Keynes, England: Open University Press, 1991), p. 67.

more inclined he tends to feel understanding, forbearance, tolerance, and so on, in respect to the conduct of this character.[36]

Without the expression of inside views, the characters seem to be remote and distant from the reader of the narrative.[37] This may make it difficult for readers to identify with the character or occasionally may lead to the misrecognition of the character in the story.[38]

1.2.4.2. *Inside Views through Focalization.* Inside views are presented by means of focalization. Focalization happens when the subject (the point from which elements are viewed[39]) describes an object (the focalized).[40]

---

36. F.K. Stanzel, *A Theory of Narrative* (trans. C. Goedsche; Cambridge: Cambridge University Press, 1984), p. 128.

37. Because the book of Acts is a narrative it employs the services of a narrator. But what kind of narrative is Acts? Ancient Greco-Roman literature yields at least three kinds of narrative: history, biography, and novel; M.A. Powell, *What Are They Saying about Acts?* (New York: Paulist Press, 1991), p. 9. Scholars are still divided in their opinions regarding Acts' literary identity. The similarities of Luke's and Act's prefaces with other contemporary prefaces such as that of Herodutus, Polybius, Lucian and Josephus (e.g. *Jewish Wars* 1.1-2) led some scholars to conclude that Luke–Acts is an example of Hellenistic historiography (e.g. Haenchen, *The Acts of the Apostles*, pp. 136-37; D. Aune, *The New Testament in its Literary Environment* [Philadelphia: Westminster Press, 1987], pp. 78-81; C. Hemer, *The Book of Acts in the Setting of Hellenistic History* [Tübingen: J.C.B. Mohr, 1989], pp. 91-94). On the other hand, because Acts has focused on the characters of Peter, Paul, and other disciples, R. Burridge views Luke–Acts, not as a historical monograph, but primarily an ancient biography (R.A. Burridge, *What Are the Gospels?: A Comparison with Greco-Roman Biography* [Cambridge: Cambridge University Press, 1992], p. 245. Cf. C.H. Talbert, *What is a Gospel?: The Genre of Canonical Gospels* [Philadelphia: Fortress Press, 1977], pp. 133-35. Also D.L. Barr and J.L. Wentling, 'The Conventions of Classical Biography and the Genre of Luke–Acts', in C.H. Talbert [ed.], *New Perspectives from the Society of Biblical Literature* [New York: Crossroad, 1984], pp. 63-88). This is in contrast with ancient historiographies which focus more on events rather than characters. Yet, at the outset, the common consensus is that Luke–Acts is neither history, biography, or novel. The book of Acts, in particular, is believed to comprise the three kinds of genre; Powell, *What Are They Saying about Acts?*, p. 9; also M.A. Powell, *What is Narrative Criticism?* (Minneapolis: Fortress Press, 1990), pp. 8-9.

38. 'Literature can be alienating to some readers who cannot make such an identification, and it can be a source of misrecognition as we identify with people who are not us, who are themselves voices of ideological positions.' Tambling, *Narrative and Ideology*, p. 70.

39. M. Bal, *Narratology: Introduction to the Theory of Narrative* (trans. C. Von Boheemen; Toronto: University of Toronto Press, 1985), p. 118.

The subject may either be the narrator or a character in the story. The object, however, is normally another character or an event being described by the subject. For example, in Acts 1–2, the narrator is mostly the subject who focalizes on the apostles, the object. However, in 1.15-22 when Peter gives his speech about Judas, Peter becomes the subject who was describing Judas as the object.

The subject who focalizes can either take an external or internal stance relative to the story.[41] When external focalization occurs, the subject is focalizing from outside the story. In other words, the one presenting or perceiving is not internal or a character within the story. According to Rimmon-Kenan, 'external focalization is felt to be close to the narrating agent, and its vehicle is therefore called "narrator-focalizer".'[42] The narrator normally takes the external position.[43] He presents the story without him getting involved or experiencing the events themselves. His 'perception through which the story is rendered is that of the *narrating self*

40.   Bal, *Narratology*, p. 74; see also G. Genette, *Narrative Discourse Revisited* (trans. J.E. Levin; Ithaca, NY: Cornell University Press, 1988), pp. 72-78.

41.   Bal, *Narratology*, p. 74.

42.   S. Rimmon-Kenan, *Narrative Fiction: Contemporary Poetics* (London: Methuen, 1983), p. 74.

43.   A story can be an event or sequence of episodes which are connected to each other in order of happening. The author of Acts is simply an implied author as presupposed by the text itself. He or she is reconstructed by the reader from the narrative and his stance may vary from text to text; J. Knight, *Luke's Gospel* (London: Routledge, 1998), p. 29. The implied author of Acts, on the other hand, may not necessarily be the narrator of the text. Knight distinguishes the two functions better by stating that, 'Distinct from the implied author (and the characters) is the narrator. The narrator is a rhetorical agent who guides the reader through the narrative, introduces him to its world and characters and supplies the perspective from which the action can (or should) be viewed. The narrator may or may not be a character in the story (he is not in Luke). He may disagree with the implied author, in which case he is known as an "unreliable narrator"' (*Luke's Gospel*, p. 31). In other words, it is the voice of a narrator which the implied author uses in order for him to tell his story. Narrators differ in their method of narration. Some express themselves in the first person while others use the third person. For example, the narrators of the gospels speak only in the third person (with few exceptions: Lk. 1.3; Jn 1.14-16; 21.24) and are not characters in the story; Powell, *What is Narrative Criticism?*, p. 25. Also, the narrator of Acts sometimes appears to be a character in the story (e.g. the 'we' passages: 16.10-17; 20.5-15; 21.1-18; 27.1–28.16). In my case, the narrator speaks through the character of Peter as he made his appeal to the other disciples for the replacement of Judas (1.15-22).

rather than that of *experiencing self*.[44] Acts 1.12-14 is a good example of external focalization. The narrator shows his readers the upper room, the characters in it, and what takes place. The narrator is not part of the assembly, nor does he take the place of any of the characters in the said event. The narrator and his readers are just remote observers of what is taking place inside the upper room.

Internal focalization, on the other hand, takes place inside the event. This happens when the focalizer is in the story rather than outside of it. Moreover, the focalizer is no longer just a narrating self but an *experiencing self*. He is part of the event, describing another object within the story. Generally, this type takes the form of a 'character-focalizer'.[45] Again, Peter's speech on Judas is a good example (1.16-20). Not only do we see that Peter acts as the subject focalizing Judas—the object—but we also find these two apostles as characters within the event. And as the narrator perceives Judas through Peter, focalization is therefore internal.

1.2.4.3. *Focalization from Without or Within*. In focalization, Rimmon-Kenan suggests that the object can be focalized either from 'without' or 'within'.[46] Focalization from without is the subject's perception of the object with only the outward manifestations being described. A good example cited by Rimmon-Kenan is Gen. 22.3.[47]

> 'So Abraham rose early in the morning, saddled his ass, and took two of his young men with him, and his son Isaac; and he cut the wood for the burnt offering, and arose and went to the place of which God had told him'.... Abraham is about to sacrifice his son, yet only his external actions are presented, his feelings and thoughts remaining opaque.

Focalization from within is simply the opposite. The reader 'gains sure access into the story'.[48] Descriptions of feelings and emotions are present and can be carried out by either an external or internal focalizer. Both an external (narrator-focalizer) and internal focalizer (character-focalizer) can penetrate the feelings or thoughts of any given character/s in the story.[49] The difference, however, is that an internal focalizer does his focalization inside the story.[50]

---

44. Rimmon-Kenan, *Narrative Fiction*, p. 74.
45. Rimmon-Kenan, *Narrative Fiction*, p. 74.
46. Rimmon-Kenan, *Narrative Fiction*, p. 75.
47. Rimmon-Kenan, *Narrative Fiction*, p. 76.
48. Parsons, *The Departure of Jesus in Luke–Acts*, p. 179.
49. Rimmon-Kenan, *Narrative Fiction*, p. 76.
50. Parsons, *The Departure of Jesus in Luke–Acts*, p. 179.

Parsons cites the ascension of Jesus in Acts 1.9-11 as an example where internal focalization takes place. He relates that the story is told, not from the perspective of a remote narrator, but from the perspective of the disciples. The reader is, in a sense, looking over the shoulders of the disciples, hearing what they hear and seeing what they see. When Jesus ascends, he not only ascends into heaven, he is also taken from the eyes of the apostles by the cloud. When Jesus was out of sight, the reader is left standing beside the disciples, gazing heavenwards. Parsons adds that, 'The gentle rebuke of the two messengers is meant as much for the ears of the reader as for the disciples—all eyes are heaven fixed'.[51]

1.2.4.4. As the Reader Begins to Read Acts 1. Our concern in Acts 1–2 is its meaning to the actual reader's reading of the text. Again, Knight rightly explains this point by stating that,

> Just as there is a 'real reader' of a text, so there is an 'actual reader'. The actual reader is the person who reads the text, be they a Christian in the first century or a reader of Luke today. We should not restrict the term to either category, although clearly a reader today will find Luke a different text from a reader in the first century. We cannot say much about Luke's first-century readers since we do not know where the Gospel[52] was written and first read. But we can make a series of judgements about the 'implied reader' by asking how we as readers react to the signs which the author has placed in the text.[53]

When the reader reacts to the signs which the author has placed in the text, the author has succeeded in manipulating the reader. In the case of Acts 1–2, one of the ways by which the author (through the voice of the narrator) attempts to manipulate the reader is by opting not to indicate the apostles' inside views on given matters. This way, the author is able to limit the meanings created in the reading process.[54] The significance of inside views as textual markers through which the reader is able to produce meaning should not be discounted. However, when inside views are not available, the reader tends to look for other markers which will help in answering some questions resulting to some gaps in the narrative because of the author's manipulation of the text.

In order to clearly see the author's manipulation of the story, specific-

---

51. Parsons, *The Departure of Jesus in Luke–Acts*, p. 179.
52. As with the book of Acts.
53. Knight, *Luke's Gospel*, p. 36.
54. Parsons, *The Departure of Jesus in Luke–Acts*, p. 180.

ally the muting of the apostles' inside views, thus projecting their complete obedience to God's programme of Israel's restoration, I should lay down an important assumption: the unity and continuity of the gospel of Luke and the book of Acts. This is in line with how the readers of the two books would have understood the purpose of the two ascension stories from which the commission account is mainly integrated. It is also from this reading that the reader will clearly notice the absence of inside views in the commissioning account. In this section, I will attempt to demonstrate what readers encounter as they read the concluding narrative of Luke and begin to enter into the narrative events of Acts 1.

1.2.4.5. *Luke 24 and Acts 1: An Overlap of Events.* The unity and continuity of Luke–Acts is a common view.[55] While studies continue, the argument that the gospel of Luke and the book of Acts were written by a single author is unanimously accepted.[56] And whether this author wrote the two books together or with a considerable time separating them, the notion that Acts is a continuation of the gospel of Luke is widely regarded.

Like many others, I as a reader, read Acts as the continuation of the gospel of Luke. The issue of continuation is argued from different perspectives. They include:

1.   The function of the prefaces of the gospel and the book of Acts. The preface of Acts is an indication to its readers about a 'former treatise', thus, presenting the two books not as separate works but as two volumes of one continuing history.[57]

---

55.   For one of the latest compilation of papers dealing with the unity of the gospel of Luke and the book of Acts, see J. Verheyden (ed.), *The Unity of Luke–Acts* (Leuven: Leuven University Press, 1999).

56.   Arguments range from issues such as: 1. The early church tradition which is unanimous in ascribing the gospel and the book of Acts to Luke. The numerous sources include the *Anti-Marcionite Prologue*, the *Muratorian Fragment*, Iraneaus, Tertullian, and Clement of Alexandria. All these sources of evidence date from, or prior to, the third century CE. Some scholars have suggested that ascribing the gospel to Luke is little more than guesswork, but, as Leon Morris has pointed out, it is difficult to see why the church should have singled out Luke as the author when he had no apostolic pedigree and, but for his writings, played little significant part in the development of early Christianity. The only reason left is to agree that indeed Luke was the author of the two volumes ascribed to him. 2. The dedication to the same person named 'Theophilus' (Lk. 1 and Acts 1.1). 3. Similarities in composition, themes, theology; cf. Fitzmyer, *The Acts of the Apostles*, pp. 49-51.

57.   Cf. L.C.A. Alexander, 'Luke's Preface in the Context of Greek Preface-

2.   Prophecies in Lk. 24.46-49 find their fulfilment in Acts, most especially the mission of the apostles resulting to the birth and growth of the church.[58]

Nevertheless, one of its strongest evidence that shows Acts to be a continuation of the gospel is found in the ascension stories of Lk. 24 and Acts 1 (Lk. 24.1-43 // Acts 1.1-3; Lk. 24.44-49 // Acts 1.11).

The ascension story in Acts does not only begin where the ascension story in Luke ends. Both ascension narratives are complete stories in themselves.[59] Rather, what we find is an overlap[60] of accounts between the two. The overlap is done by the repetition or redundancy of scenes and phrases. For example:

1.   The apostles are to be Jesus' 'witnesses'. Lk. 24.48 // Acts 1.8b.
2.   Be witnesses beginning from Jerusalem... Lk. 24.47c // Acts 1.8b.
3.   ...(from Jerusalem) to 'all nations' // 'end of the earth'. Lk. 24.47b // Acts 1.8b.
4.   The command to stay in Jerusalem... Lk. 24.49b //Acts 1.4a.

Writing', *NovT* 28 (1986), pp. 48-74; *idem*, 'The Preface of Acts and the Historians', in B. Witherington III (ed.), *History, Literature, and Society in the Book of Acts* (Cambridge: Cambridge University Press, 1996), pp. 73-103; Witherington, *The Acts of the Apostles*, p. 9; D. Earl, 'Prologue-Form in Ancient Historiography', *ANRW* 1.2, pp. 842-56.

58.   W. Kurz, *Reading Luke–Acts: Dynamics of Biblical Narrative* (Westminster: John Knox Press, 1993), p. 21.

59.   By 'complete' I mean that both stories have a *beginning* (Jesus gathers his apostles and gives his final instructions), *middle* (Jesus ascends) and *end* (the apostles return to Jerusalem). Gerard Sorensen, commenting on the beginning of Acts and the ending of the gospel of Luke, agrees by stating that 'both the sequel and its predecessor are complete in themselves—that is...its plot is in no way dependent on its antecedent'. G.C. Sorensen, 'Beginning and Ending: The Virginians as a Sequel', *Studies in the Novel* 13 (1981), pp. 109-21 (109). Parsons adds, 'The inter-textualities ...is not to suggest that the plot of Acts is so dependent on Luke that it could not be understood by itself', *The Departure of Jesus in Luke–Acts*, p. 171.

60.   Commentators have recognized the significance of Lucian's advice to the historian which states, 'the first and second topics must not merely be neighbours but have common matter overlap'. From *How to Write History* 55, quoted from Witherington, *The Acts of the Apostles*, p. 107. Witherington seems to have neglected to give credit to L.T. Johnson as the exact paragraph appears in the latter's commentary in the book of Acts (cf. *Acts of the Apostles*, Sacra Pagina Series, 5, p. 28).

5.   ...and wait for the 'promise of the father'. Lk. 24.49a // Acts 1.4b.
6.   The apostles are to be clothed // receive 'power'. Lk. 24.49a // Acts 1.8b.
7.   Jesus ascends to heaven. Lk. 24.51 // Acts 1.9.

As the narrator of Acts repeats[61] some of the key concluding scenes of Lk. 24 in Acts 1, the reader is invited to locate similar settings in the opening scenes in Acts and pick up the story thereon.[62] What we have, on a general level, is a linkage of the gospel of Luke with the book of Acts; [63] while on a specific level, it is a movement of story plot from Lk. 24 to Acts 1. Thus, the repetitions serve as literary notches firmly bridging the two books together. It also allows a continued flow of what seems to be a single plot moving from Luke to Acts.[64]

That Acts is a continuation of Luke, as mentioned earlier, is not the problem. Commentators are quite unanimous in the view that the book of Acts is a second volume to a two-volume work.[65] Rather, the question is whether Acts 1 is a continuation of Lk. 24. To be more specific, because the ascension story of Acts 1 is in some way a 'sequel' to the ascension story of Lk. 24, the challenge for the reader is to decide where to pick up the story. Or as Parsons puts it 'one problem of any sequel is determining where to begin...'[66]

The literary critic Seymour Chatman recognizes the reader's compulsion to connect events in order for a story to make sense. He states that the reader's attitude 'depends upon the disposition of our minds, not even the fortuitous circumstances—the random juxtaposition of pages—will

61.   As R. Tannehill argues, 'The use of repetitive patterns preserves a sense of unity of purpose and action in spite of significant developments'. R. Tannehill, 'The Composition of Acts 3–5: Narrative Development and Echo Effect', *SBL Seminar Papers* (Chico: Scholars Press, 1984), pp. 239-40.

62.   M. Parsons sees this as the way by which the narrator coaxes the reader to 're-enter the story world (now Acts), with some attention paid to the exiting procedure at the end of the narrative'. *The Departure of Jesus in Luke–Acts*, p. 174.

63.   Kurz, *Reading Luke–Acts*, p. 29.

64.   Or as Uspensky states, 'when scenes are joined together the illusion of movement is produced'. B. Uspensky, *A Poetics of Composition: The Structure of the Artistic Text and Typology of a Compositional Form* (trans. V. Zavarin and S. Wittig; Berkeley and Los Angeles: University of California Press, 1973), p. 62.

65.   Alexander, 'The Preface of Acts and the Historians', p. 79.

66.   Parsons, *The Departure of Jesus in Luke–Acts*, p. 172.

deter us'.[67] While it is true that the ascension stories of Acts and Luke are complete stories in themselves, there are no indications in Acts 1 that the narrator is discouraging its readers from understanding that its ascension story is independent from Lk. 24.[68] In fact it is the opposite. The presence of repetition and redundancy between the two stories is an invitation to understand that what the reader reads is but one story and not two. When this happens, the likelihood for the reader to harmonize the two ascension accounts is high.[69]

1.2.4.6. *Jubilance or Conflict?* When the reader (consciously or unconsciously) harmonizes the ending of Luke with the beginning of the book of Acts, some problems in the narrative also appear. For example, the story of the Lukan ascension leaves us with the impression that the apostles were in a state of jubilation when they returned to Jerusalem. Lk. 24.50-53 states,

> Then he [Jesus] led them [disciples] out as far as Bethany, and lifting up his hands he blessed them. While he blessed them, he parted from them. And they returned to Jerusalem with *great joy*, and *were* continually *in the temple blessing God.*

This passage indicates that from the time Jesus had ascended until the apostles have returned to Jerusalem for the fulfilment of the father's promise, the apostles were in 'great joy' and 'continued to bless God in the temple'. The spatial settings of these events range from Bethany

---

67. Seymour Chatman goes beyond the concept of 'continuation'. He prefers to read the relationship of the two ascension stories as a 'contingency'. Proposed by Jean Pouillon, Chatman is inclined to think that the relationship of events is not a mere accident but is tied within a philosophical string. Nevertheless, whatever seems to be the relationship of events, Chatman admits that we 'should recognize our powerful tendency to connect most divergent events'. S. Chatman, *Story and Discourse: Narrative Structure in Fiction and Film* (Ithaca, NY: Cornell University Press, 1978), p. 47.

68. In fact, the first three verses summarize the story to the end of Lk. 24. The author then goes back and opens up in more detail what was happening in the final phase of that story.

69. Harmonizing the two ascension stories presents some problems. Scholars, it seems, are more settled in pointing out the parallels between the two accounts than verging into harmonization. Cf. C.H. Talbert, *Literary Patterns, Theological Themes and the Genre of Luke–Acts* (SBLMS, 20; Missoula: Scholars Press, 1974), p. 58; J.G. Davies, 'The Prefigurement of the Ascension in the Third Gospel', *JTS* 6 (1955), pp. 229-33 (30).

(where Jesus ascended) to Jerusalem (where the apostles have returned). In Acts 1, although Bethany is not mentioned, the ascension of Jesus and the apostles' return to Jerusalem are repeated (Acts 1.9-12). Because of the movement of the story from outside Jerusalem until the apostles have returned to the upper room, I (and any keen reader for this matter) have assumed the spatial settings of Lk. 24 within the same spatial and temporal settings of Acts 1.[70] In other words, from the time Jesus instructed his apostles to wait for the promise of the father until its consummation in Jerusalem (Lk. 24.44-53 // Acts 1.3–2.4), what we are reading is but one ascension story[71] with the Acts version simply being more detailed than that of the gospel.[72]

As the reader is reading one ascension story, a subtle but conflicting picture begins to arise.[73] To put it more bluntly, the apostles' attitude of jubilance as indicated in Lk. 24 does not seem to fit the context and mood of the story in Acts 1. For instance, in 1.6, the apostles come to Jesus with

70.   Uspensky adds, 'A greater reliance on temporal definition is inherent in natural language, the material from which literature is made, for the difference between language as a system and other semiotic systems is that linguistic expression, generally speaking, translates space into time... As M. Focault has noted, a verbal description of any spatial relationship (or of any reality) is necessarily translated into a temporal sequence... The specifics of the translation of space in a particular literary work are determined by the degree of concreteness of the spatial characteristics... If the work is sufficiently characterised by spatial definitions, there arises the possibility of the concrete spatial presentation of the content, and the work may be translated into such visual media as painting or drama.' Uspensky, *Poetics of Composition*, p. 78.

71.   From a tradition perspective, J. Fitzmyer sees Acts 1.3 as originally following Lk. 24.50-53. Following Benoit, he states that '...Luke came upon the precise information about the interval between the resurrection and ascension only after he had finished the Gospel, and he intended Acts 1.9-11 to be a slight correction of what he had written earlier'. Fitzmyer, *The Acts of the Apostles*, p. 192; cf. P. Benoit, 'The Ascension', in *Jesus and the Gospel*, I (New York: Herder and Herder, 1973), p. 242.

72.   And because the author does not provide any new material in the ascension narrative of Acts, and that all we get is a reworking and elaboration of the version in Lk. 24, like Johnson, any reader may be led to read Acts 1.1-11, including the gestures and words, to simply be an 'elaborate variant' of Lk. 24.36-53. Johnson, *The Acts of the Apostles*, p. 28.

73.   As B.K. Donne argues in his study of the two ascension accounts, 'Our survey of the Lukan narratives of the Ascension reveals that there are two accounts of the one event; they do not coincide in every detail because they are different in purpose...but they clearly indicate a definite and final parting which is distinct from Resurrection'. Donne, *Christ Ascended*, p. 10.

an important question. When they asked whether Jesus would now restore the kingdom to Israel, Jesus gives them an answer which is actually short of saying 'no' (1.7). The narrator does not indicate how Jesus' response might have affected the apostles who were expecting the restoration of the kingdom to Israel now that Jesus has already risen.[74] And because we as readers have assumed the settings of Lk. 24 into Acts 1, to think that the apostles were still jubilant despite the failure to meet their expectations is quite problematic.[75]

This fact is brought about by the narrator's silence on the inside views of the apostles in the ascension story of Acts. The silence of the narrator on the inside views of the apostles as a group extends until 2.46.[76] This is in relatively strong contrast with how the narrator of Lk. 24 describes the inside views of the apostles in the context of Jesus' resurrection and ascension. The narrator of the gospel makes it explicitly clear that apostles were *perplexed* (24.4), *frightened* (24.5), *looking sad* (24.17), *amazed* (24.22), *troubled* (24.38), *disbelieved for joy*, and *wondered* (24.41), and most of all, returned to Jerusalem with *great joy* (24.52).

This is also in great contrast with the characterization of the multitude

74. As Knight correctly argues, 'Part of the reader's task is to decode the signs which the author has placed in the narrative. A sign is a symbol of meaning. A collection of signs yields a pattern of thought. A text conditions its readers to react in a particular way, as for instance through the comments and presuppositions of the narrator, but the final assembly of meaning rests with the reader and not the author. This means that a reader can quite appropriately find meanings in a text which were not consciously placed there by the author—even meanings which the author might not have agreed'. Knight, *Luke's Gospel*, p. 36.

75. Citing Culpepper's observation, Parsons states, 'Variation produces movement'. The reader, according to Culpepper, 'is required to integrate the new elements into the previous patterns'. R.A. Culpepper, ' Redundancy and the Implied Reader in Matthew: A Response to Janice Capel Anderson and Fred W. Burnett' (Unpublished seminar paper read in the annual meeting of the SBL, 1983), p. 4. The movement produced in these repetitions is striking. Repetition reaffirms the link between the Gospel and Acts; variation impels the reader to leave the Gospel story and move on to the story of the church. Cf. Parsons, *The Departure of Jesus in Luke–Acts*, p. 194. See also R. Witherup, 'Cornelius Over and Over and Over Again: 'Functional Redundancy in the Acts of the Apostles', *JSNT* 49 (1993), pp. 45-66; D. Marguerat, 'Soul's Conversion (Acts 9, 22, 26) and the Multiplication of Narrative in Acts', in C. Tuckett (ed.), *Luke's Literary Achievement: Collected Essays* (JSNTSup, 116; Sheffield: JSOT Press, 1995), pp. 127-55, especially pp. 130-36.

76. Parsons, *The Departure of Jesus in Luke–Acts*, p. 174.

who have witnessed and heard of the seeming 'commotion' in the upper room. The narrator of Acts generously describes the multitude with inside views of being 'bewildered, amazed, and wondered' in 2.6-7.

1.2.4.7. No Form of Protest. In the study conducted by Hubbard and Mullins on the commissioning accounts in Luke–Acts, both have failed to address the issue which we have previously raised. Under their category of Protest,[77] they defined its function as intended 'to measure the effect upon the commissioned person'. This form is at times understood to be similar to the classification of a 'reaction'. It solicits response from the commissioned party, either by expressing unworthiness or the inability to fulfil the mission, or even in the form of a question addressed to the commissioner. Mullins understands the scene where the apostles stand to watch Jesus ascend to heaven as an expression of protest (Acts 1.10). This is a little odd since 'protest' forms in the other commissioning accounts of Luke–Acts express more clearly how the commissioned individual or party either displays an action or speaks a word of resistance before the commissioner.[78] For example: Lk. 1.18 tells about Zechariah demanding proof of the angel's message and cites a legitimate reason as to why he could not believe the authenticity of the message; Lk. 1.34 shows Mary asking the angel to explain how she could conceive when she is not married; Lk. 5.8-10a tells of Peter falling to his knees before Jesus and admitting his sinfulness; Acts 9.13-14 shows Ananias who reasons his reluctance to heal Saul's blindness because of what he had heard about Saul's activities against the 'saints in Jerusalem'; Acts 11.8 is Peter's refusal to do as he is told about the eating of unclean animals; Acts 12.9 tells about Peter's doubts of whether his vision of the angel who was about to escort him out of prison is real or not.

The absence of any form of protest from the apostles here in Acts 1–2 does not surprise Hubbard. In a survey Hubbard did on the commissioning accounts in Luke–Acts, he reckons that protests are the least common form found in the table of commissioning accounts.[79] Hubbard reflects that only thirty-two per cent of the twenty-five commission accounts he

---

77.   See 1.4 of this study.

78.   And even if it is, this adds more credence to my suggestion (a suggestion I will fully develop later on) that the author deliberately muted the apostles of their inside views in order to show to his readers the full and complete obedience of the group to the mission they were tasked to do.

79.   Hubbard, 'Commissioning Stories', p. 190.

considers in Luke–Acts register a form of protest. This even becomes less, that is, only twenty-six per cent in the whole book of Acts.[80]

However, as we have stated earlier, what Hubbard and Mullins failed to consider (probably because of the limitations set by their methodology) is the complete silence or absence of 'inside views' on the part of the group of apostles,[81] a complete silence which does not happen in any of the commissioning accounts they have enumerated. To put it more precisely, the case with the Eleven is different from the other examples of com-missioning accounts. The Eleven as a group do not get to say or express their feelings or opinions at all until they have completed the whole ritual process. The author keeps the apostles from bursting out with any emotive expressions until they see their first converts.

The absence of inside views is deliberate.[82] I argued earlier that one of the purposes of not giving the apostles the chance to react at all (beginning from the time they were daunted with the news about the delay of Israel's restoration [Acts 1.8] until the time of having their first converts [2.46]), is to project the image of complete obedience on the part of the Eleven. Again, Parsons observes,

> By being taught by the risen Lord, praying together with one accord, and performing the delicate and crucial task of selecting Judas' replacement without incident, *the disciples are presented in the opening scene as educationally, spiritually, and organisationally prepared to undertake the task of worldwide missions to which they have been assigned.*[83]

The muting of the apostles' inside views makes their role as leaders/brokers more appreciated. First, it shows that God—the ultimate patron—is the one in complete control of everything, including the plan for the restoration of Israel. Second, it paves the way to the apostles' role of

---

80. Hubbard, 'Commissioning Stories', p. 190.

81. Excluding Peter's inside views when he gave his speech on Judas' replacement (1.15-22).

82. In his study of the ascension account in Lk. 24 and Acts 1, Parsons sees a deliberate manipulation of Luke's sources to influence his audience. He states, 'At the level of the *Sitz in der Kirche*, Luke intended a veiled reference to the ascension in Luke 24.50-53 and intentionally suppressed any explicit mention of a heavenly assumption. In this way, he was able to instruct his community, who were living in the absence of Jesus, to pattern their behaviour after the disciples who were obediently, joyfully, and continually blessing God, even after the departure of Jesus.' Parsons, *The Departure of Jesus in Luke–Acts*, p. 150.

83. Parsons, *The Departure of Jesus in Luke–Acts*, p. 195; italics mine.

brokerage, that is, brokerage in the sense that while the apostles are recognized as the effective representatives between God the patron and the believers as clients their decisions and guidance depend on and represent the plan of God himself. Whatever they teach is no longer based on their preconceived ideas. Those ideas have long been corrected or changed by Jesus during their status transformation. They no longer depend on themselves but on God.[84] Now they in turn will give God's teaching which was passed on to them by Jesus.[85]

1.3. *Phase Three—Acts 1.9-11: The Initiands Experience Complete Separation*

So far, no one has attempted to view the Ascension story of Acts 1.9-11 in the way I am reading it. Most studies have focused on Jesus, the one who ascends, whereas my focus is more on the apostles, the ones who have been left behind. This focus is again consistent with another aspect in the rituals of status transformation. Initiands undergoing the ritual experience complete separation. Just as Jesus is separated from John the Baptist (the ritual elder) when he goes into the wilderness to face his ritual confrontation against the devil (Lk. 4.1-13), the apostles as well are separated from Jesus in the ascension and face their ritual confrontation in their return to Jerusalem (Acts 1.12-26).

In this section I want to focus on this concept of complete separation. I will note that the subject in the separation scene of Acts 1.9-11 is the apostles rather than Jesus (the subject in the ascension story of Lk. 24.50-53). The repetition and redundancy of scenes in the ascension story in Acts 1.9-11 attempts to highlight how the apostles have been finally left by themselves as they are separated from Jesus their leader.

I will also attempt to point out that the separation between the apostles and Jesus is a temporary one. Unlike other ascension accounts where the

---

84. In Luke's retelling of the story of Jesus and his disciples, the conflict with the religious leaders is a recurrent motif. The author's characterization of the various religious groups fall into many categories but almost consistent to that which is in opposition to what Jesus teaches. Two of the principal traits ascribed to the leaders in Luke are found in Lk. 18.9: 'they trusted in themselves and they despised others...that the latter trait is actually a manifestation of the former. Self-righteousness is the leaders' root character trait from which other characteristics are derived.' M.A. Powell, 'The Religious Leaders in Luke: A Literary-Critical Study', *JBL* 109.1 (1990), pp. 93-110 (95).

85. Cf. Clark, 'The Role of the Apostles', pp. 173-81.

ascending party leaves for good,[86] the separation of the apostles from Jesus is tentative. The apostles will stand as Jesus' representatives/brokers before God and the people of Israel until Jesus returns to complete his reign.

1.3.1. *Redundancy and Repetition in the Ascension Story of Acts 1.9-11.* We know that the ascension story in Acts 1.9-11 is a repetition of the ascension story in Lk. 24.50-53.[87] Why is this so? Suggestions vary. For instance, R. Tannehill's study of the narrative technique of redundancy in Luke–Acts mentions one of its functions as to 'combat the tendency to forget the information over a long narrative'.[88] Other scholars understand the repetitions to be an appendage (especially the version in Lk. 24.50-53) when Luke and Acts were accepted into the canon.[89] There is also the proposal that Luke was simply familiar with two distinct ascension traditions and that this has been reflected in his writings. C.F.D. Moule[90] believes that the author received new traditions after completing his gospel. These new traditions were then incorporated into Acts.[91]

J. Fitzmyer, J.G. Davies,[92] P.A. Stempvoort, S.G. Wilson,[93] and H.

---

86. E.g. the separation of Elijah from Elisha in 2 Kgs 2.

87. Cf. 3.1.2.4.5: Luke 24 and Acts 1: An Overlap of Events.

88. R. Tannehill, 'The Composition of Acts 3-5', pp. 238-40; cf. Parsons, *The Departure of Jesus in Luke–Acts*, p. 192.

89. That the ascension narrative in Lk. 24 was added after the two books were divided; cf. Jackson and Lake, *The Beginnings of Christianity*, pp. 3-4; Phillipe Menoud assumes that both ascension accounts were added when the one-volume work of Luke–Acts was divided and entered into the canon. Cf. P. Menoud, 'Remarques sur les textes de l'ascension dans Luc-Actes', in W. Eltester (ed.), *Neutestamentliche Studien für Rudolf Bultmann* (BZNW, 21; Berlin: Töpelmann, 1957), pp. 148-56; quoted from M.C. Parsons, 'The Text of Acts 1.2 Reconsidered', *CBQ* 50 (1988), pp. 58-71 (61). See also A. Wilder, 'Variant Traditions of the Resurrection in Acts', *JBL* 62 (1943), pp. 307-318 (311); Conzelmann, *Theology*, p. 94.

90. C.F.D. Moule, 'Expository Problems: The Ascension—Acts 1.9', *ExpT* 68 (1957), pp. 205-209 (207).

91. I do not fully agree with Parsons' assessment of Moule. There is no explicit suggestion from Moule that indeed the author of Luke–Acts has incorporated new traditions into Acts after the gospel has been written. Cf. Parsons, *The Departure of Jesus in Luke–Acts*, p. 190.

92. Davies, 'Prefiguration', pp. 229-33.

93. S.G. Wilson, 'The Ascension: A Critique and an Interpretation', *ZNW* 59 (1968), pp. 277-81.

Flender[94] suggest that the two ascension stories are products of the author's response to particular theological issues. Fitzmyer, for example, argues that the ascension in Luke–Acts serves as the line of distinction for the two periods of salvation history.[95] Stempvoort distinguishes the two ascension accounts by saying that,

> Here [Acts 1.9-11] it is already apparent that the second interpretation of the Ascension is totally different from the first, the doxological one. We might refer to it as the ecclesiastical and historical interpretation, with the accent on the work of the Spirit in the Church.[96]

There are also those who read the repetitions as means to emphasize a point or teaching. E. Haenchen, for instance, states that 'this technique of repetition is one to which Luke always resorts when he wants to impress something especially upon the reader'.[97] Still others find the repetition as stylistic literary variations.[98]

For the purposes of this study, I feel that the variation more than the repetition and redundancy of the ascension story in Acts 1 helps to show the motif of separation by the apostles from Jesus.

Variation 'creates uncertainty and requires the implied reader to make choices'.[99] It produces movement and also highlights the repetitions made. The more obvious variations between the two ascension accounts are:[100]

---

94.   H. Flender, 'Heil und Geschichte in der Theologie des Lukas', *BEvT* 41 (1966), pp. 16-18; quoted by Parsons, *The Departure of Jesus in Luke–Acts*, p. 191.

95.   J. Fitzmyer, 'The Ascension of Christ and Pentecost', in *To Advance the Gospel: New Testament Studies* (Grand Rapids: Eerdmans, 2nd edn, 1998), p. 420.

96.   P.A. Van Stempvoort, 'The Interpretation of the Ascension in Luke and Acts', *NTS* 8 (1958), p. 39.

97.   Haenchen, *The Acts of the Apostles*, p. 357. See also G. Schneider, *Die Apostelgeschichte* (Freiburg: Herder, 1982), p. 66; S.G. Wilson, *The Gentiles and the Gentile Mission in Luke–Acts* (Cambridge: Cambridge University Press, 1973), p. 177; and F.F. Bruce, *The Acts of the Apostles* (Grand Rapids: Eerdmans, 1990), p. 268.

98.   Talbert, *Literary Patterns*, p. 60. See also H.J. Cadbury, 'Four Features of Lucan Style', in L.E. Keck and J.L. Martyn (eds.), *Studies in Luke–Acts: Essays Presented in Honor of Paul Schubert* (Philadelphia: Abingdon Press, 1966), pp. 87-102; and G.A. Grodel, *The Acts of the Apostles* (Minneapolis, MN: Augsburg, 1986), p. 203.

99.   Parsons, following the models of repetition, variation, and context as suggested by Janice Capel Anderson, believes that repetition shows strong links between the two ascension stories and helps to move the story plot forward. Links through repetition are noticed: the characters are the same—Jesus and the apostles; in both accounts, this scene is the last appearance of Jesus to his disciples; both share Jesus' commission to

1. The chronological difference: Lk. 24 appears to show Jesus' ascension on Easter Sunday night while Acts 1 allows a 'forty day' period.

2. The site of the ascension: Lk. 24 has the place near 'Bethany' while Acts 1 has the Mount of Olives.

3. The disciples' return to Jerusalem: Lk. 24 directs the apostles to the Temple in an attitude of joy and blessing God. Acts 1 takes the apostles to the 'upper room' and engages in prayer with the other people in the room.

4. There is no dialogue account in Lk. 24 while Acts 1 is devoted to questions of the apostles and how Jesus has responded to them.

5. The 'raising of hands' and the repeated references to 'blessing' are missing in Acts.

6. Lk. 24 has the cryptic note 'he departed from them', while Acts 1 has 'he ascended into heaven'.

7. The mention of the cloud and the two messengers who assure and comfort the apostles are missing in the Lukan version.

Analysing the function of variation, repetition and redundancy in Luke–Acts, R.D. Witherup finds that one of their functions is to show the decline of one and the rise of another character within the same context as the story unfolds.[101] We find this in the ascension story of Acts 1.9-11. The variations in the ascension version in Acts focus on the character of the apostles as the subject of the story rather than on Jesus. Unlike Lk. 24, where Jesus is the hero in the ascension story, the departure story in Acts 1.9-11 centres on the apostles as the primary actors. In other words, Jesus' character declines while the apostles' character rises.

his apostles to preach to 'all nations' or ' the ends of the earth'. J.C. Anderson, 'The Implied Reader in Matthew' (Unpublished seminar paper submitted to the Literary Aspects of the Gospels and Acts, SBL Annual Meeting, 1983), p. 21; cf. Parsons, *The Departure of Jesus in Luke–Acts*, p. 192. However, I disagree with Parsons' suggestion that in both accounts the disciples seem to include a larger group than just the apostles; cf. Parsons, *The Departure of Jesus in Luke–Acts*, p. 270, n. 25. At least in the ascension account in Acts, the author clearly shows the apostles as the exclusive recipients of the commission. See my discussion on τοῖς ἀποστολοῖς of Acts 1.2 in Chapter 2 under 2.1.1.

100. Parsons, *The Departure of Jesus in Luke–Acts*, pp. 193-94.

101. Witherup, 'Cornelius', p. 54.

1.3.2. *The Separation of the Apostles from Jesus in Acts 1.9-11*. McVann listed three types of separation: separation from people, of place, and of time. In the ritual process which Jesus went through, McVann sees the way to the baptism by John as a symbol of separation. The people who were baptized separate themselves from their villages in order to go to John at the Jordan. They wanted to be baptized and therefore knew what would be required of them, and that is to seek a status transformation by being washed from their sins. Among them was Jesus of Nazareth.[102]

Jesus was not only separated from his hometown in order to be baptized but was further separated from the crowd after he was baptized by John. As the crowd return to their homes and resume their old statuses, Jesus proceeds to the wilderness for further seclusion. McVann notes that Jesus' 'baptism-theophany' (Lk. 3.22) sharply marks this second and highly dramatic separation. He adds, 'The reader thus recognizes that the descent of the Spirit and the voice of God function as the moment of the investiture when Jesus' new identity is revealed'.[103]

There is really no dispute to say that scholarship sees the ascension accounts in Lk. 24.50-53 and Acts 1.9-11 as the stories of Jesus' exaltation.[104] However, from the social-scientific perspective, Acts 1.9-11 opens a new avenue in understanding the same ascension story. In the rituals of status transformation, we suggest that as the 'baptism-theophany' marked the dramatic separation of Jesus from John, the ascension of Jesus is the 'theophany' equivalent—marking the separation of the apostles from Jesus.

This concept has three interrelated points to share:

1. In the rituals of status transformation, the apostles now enter into the state of being completely separated from any individual—a separation of the apprentice from the leader.
2. We know that the apostles' separation and not simply Jesus' ascension is equally emphasized in Acts 1.9-11. This is seen when one considers that the narrator draws attention to the sombre state of the apostles rather than to Jesus' exaltation.
3. The drawing of the reader's attention to the apostles is partly evidenced by the assurance of Jesus' return.

Let me deal with these three points in detail:

102. McVann, 'Rituals of Status Transformation', p. 348.
103. McVann, 'Rituals of Status Transformation', p. 348.
104. Cf. Parsons, *The Departure of Jesus in Luke–Acts*, pp. 29-51.

1.3.2.1. The Leader-Apprentice Type of Ascension Stories. It is particularly important to note that the ascension of Jesus is a picture of separation of the apprentices from their leader. This is the time when the apprentice breaks off from his/her dependency upon the leader and begins the process of becoming a fulfilled leader himself/herself. At this stage of the ritual process, Jesus, the ritual elder, has done all that is necessary for the initiands. They have been purged and cleansed of their habits and pre-conceived ideas in order to become the leaders which the ritual elder and the society expects them to be. All that Jesus has taught and said, 'presenting himself alive before his apostles by many proofs', 'for forty days', 'speaking to them about the kingdom of God', and 'charging them' what to do after his ascension (1.3-4), completes Jesus' responsibility as the ritual elder upon the apostles as the initiands.

Not many ascension stories have the 'leader-apprentice' relationship in their separation scenes.[105] Not even the more popular leader-apprentice relationship between Moses and Joshua has emphasis on the separation of the two. In fact, other ancient Jewish ascension stories on Moses place more emphasis on Moses's separation from his community of followers. For example, the report by Josephus in *Antiquities* IV, where more emotive description on the separation between Moses and his common followers is found rather than on the separation of Moses and Joshua:

> On his advancing thence toward the place where he was destined to disappear, they all followed him bathed in tears; thereupon Moses, by a signal of his hand, bade those in the distance to remain still, while by word of mouth he exhorted those nearer to him not to make his passing a tearful one by following him. And they, deciding to gratify him in this also, to wit, to leave him to depart according to his own desire, held back, weeping with one another... And while he bade farewell to Eleazar and Joshua and was yet communing with them, a cloud of a sudden descended upon him and he disappeared in a ravine.[106]

105. On the other hand, while indeed some ascension stories have separation as their central event, some have a totally different kind of separation in mind. Take for instance the dialogue between Hermotimus and Lycinus in Lucian. Hermotimus, lecturing Lycinus on what the conditions one finds in heaven, gives the story of Heracles's ascension as an example: 'Think of the story of Heracles when he was burned and deified on Mount Oeta: he threw off the mortal part of him that came from his mother and flew up to heaven, taking the pure and unpolluted divine part with him, the part that the fire had separated off'. Lucian, *Hermotimus* 7 (Loeb).

106. Josephus, *Antiquities* IV, 323-36 (Loeb).

However, if there is one obvious example similar to Acts 1.9-11 where the ascension account has the typical leader-apprentice type of separation, nothing can be closer than the Elijah-Elisha tandem. In 2 Kgs 2.9-14, the separation between Elijah and Elisha has similarities with the separation between Jesus and his apostles. While the manner of ascent between the two ascension stories is completely different,[107] the apprentices' reception of their leader's departure is similar in nature. To be more precise, unlike the reaction of joy by the apostles when Jesus ascended in Lk. 24.50-51, Elisha (in 2 Kgs 2.9-14) and the apostles (here in Acts 1.9-11) are not jubilant or pleased with their separation from their leaders. It is a separation which conveys the sense of loss primarily on the part of the apprentice. In Acts 1.9-11, this aspect of loss (although not explicitly stated) is the reason why there was the need to give an assurance of Jesus' return to the apostles by the 'two men in white robes'. These two men (or angelic beings) reproved the Eleven who were 'gazing into heaven' and assured them of Jesus' return (Acts 1.10-11). In the Elijah-Elisha parallel, Elisha cried out as he saw the 'chariots of Israel and its horsemen' (2 Kgs 2.12), which were probably behind Elijah's disappearance.[108]

Nevertheless, the separation in both cases is a separation where the leaders pass on their leadership role to their apprentices. It is a separation where the transformation of the apprentice to leader takes place. The transformation of Elisha is represented by the text which states that after Elijah's departure, Elisha 'took hold of his own clothes (or cloak) and rent them into two pieces' (2 Kgs 2.12a). He then 'took up the mantle of Elijah that had fallen from him...' (2 Kgs 2.13). The apostles, on the other hand, implicitly 'take on Jesus' mantle' when they are commissioned in Acts 1.7-8.

1.3.2.2. *The Focus on the Apostles.* We suggest that the ascension account in Acts does not specifically focus on the character of Jesus. Rather, we

107. A 'chariot of fire and horses of fire' plus a 'whirlwind' which takes up Elijah into heaven (2 Kgs 2.11).

108. There are two possible explanations concerning the relationship of Elijah's disappearance and the 'whirlwind' with the definite article after the chariot and horses. J. Gray, for example, suggests that since the former was a natural phenomena, the latter (chariot and horses) may also have been. He adds that the whirlwind and the sudden disappearance of Elijah may be compared with the visible progress of an accompanying dust-storm created by horses and chariots. The other explanation is the historification of a native myth or cult legend. For further discussion, see for example, J. Gray, *I and II Kings: A Commentary* (London: SCM Press, 1977), pp. 472-77.

are inclined to see that the character—the group of the apostles—considering all the circumstances which transpired, draws the full attention of the readers. These circumstances include: (1) how the apostles' expectation of Israel's restoration had just been denied in Acts 1.7; (2) the enormous responsibility of witnessing placed upon the apostles (1.8); and (3) the language of the ascension especially with the phrase ἀφ' ὑμῶν in 1.11.

With regard to the first and second points, we have already discussed at length the probable impact and effect of Jesus' negative response to the apostles' question on Israel's restoration.[109] What is peculiar in this ascension account is the use of the phrase οὗτος ὁ Ἰησοῦς ὁ ἀναλημφθεὶς ἀφ' ὑμῶν. In Parsons' comparative analysis of the vocabulary of Acts 1.9-11 with the gospels of Matthew, Mark, Luke, and John, he concludes that with the vocabulary of 1.11, there is little to be said other than the fact that the words are distinctively Lukan.[110] He argues that Luke, in his design of the ascension story of Jesus, may have been reminded of the transfiguration (Lk. 9.34) and the parousia (Lk. 21.27; cf. Dan. 7.13) and employed the elements as the 'apocalyptic stage-props' to complete the scene.[111] Other than these 'apocalyptic stage-props', Parsons' study on the vocabulary of Acts 1.11 is closed.

I contend, however, that the combination of the verb form of ἀναλαμβάνω and the prepositional phrase ἀφ' ὑμῶν is a feature worth mentioning. The way the ascension story is told by the narrator focuses on 'who is being taken away from the apostles' instead of 'who are being left behind by Jesus'.[112] The phrase οὗτος ὁ Ἰησοῦς ὁ ἀναλημφθεὶς ἀφ' ὑμῶν attests to this.[113]

Other ascension accounts use a different kind of expression. For example, the ascension passage in Mk. 16.19 reads, Ὁ μὲν οὖν κύριος Ἰησοῦς μετὰ τὸ λαλῆσαι αὐτοῖς ἀνελήμφθη εἰς τὸν οὐρανὸν καὶ ἐκάθισεν ἐκ δεξιῶν τοῦ θεοῦ (So then the Lord Jesus, after he had spoken

---

109. See my discussion 'A Delayed Eschatology' in 3.1.2.1.

110. See Table 16 of Parsons, *The Departure of Jesus in Luke–Acts*, pp. 142-43.

111. Cf. Fitzmyer, 'Ascension and Pentecost', p. 419.

112. Consider the ascension language in Lk. 24.51. Despite the phrase 'he parted from them (αὐτὸν αὐτοὺς διέστη ἀπ' αὐτῶν), the verb still modifies the character of Jesus rather than that of the apostles. In other words, the focus lies on Jesus than on the apostles. This is not the case in the ascension story of Acts 1.9-11.

113. Combined with the earlier expression in v. 9 'a cloud took him out of their sight', indeed makes the character of the apostles the focus of the narrative.

to them, was taken up into heaven and sat down at the right hand of God). What we find in this text is that in referring to the ascension, the verb ἀναλαμβάνω is not combined with the prepositional phrase ἀφ' ὑμῶν. In other words, ascension language in itself could get away with simply referring to either the ascent towards heaven or any notion of entering heaven without any reference to whom the ascending Jesus (or any character for that matter) is being taken away from.[114]

However, when emphasis is placed on the 'pains' of separation (i.e. the pain in the separation between the apprentice and the leader) the ascension language involves the prepositional phrase ἀφ' ὑμῶν. Again, referring to the example between Elijah and Elisha in 2 Kgs 2.9-14, the same expression is employed in the LXX: ἀναλαμβανόμενον ἀπὸ σοῦ.

Are the similarities between the two accounts (Acts 1.9-11 and 2 Kgs 2.9-14) coincidental? Do we have any reason to believe that the author of Luke–Acts was influenced by the Elijah-Elisha tradition? Modern scholars believe that there was indeed a degree of influence upon the author of Luke–Acts.[115] However, I would like to cite the observation that, given this striking similarity of the phrases we have just mentioned, the author of Luke–Acts may have also wanted to express and extend two lessons from the separation account between Elijah and Elisha to the separation story between Jesus and his apostles. These two lessons are the 'pains' involved in separation, and, that the focus of the separation falls on the apprentice rather than on the ascending leader.

This is also one of the main differences between the ascension stories of Lk. 24.50-53 and Acts 1.9-11. In Lk. 24, Jesus' departure did not necessitate the presence of divine messengers and the message of assurance to the apostles. In fact, the apostles are reported to have returned to Jerusalem in an attitude of 'great joy' after Jesus has ascended (Lk. 24.53). In the Acts version, however, the assurance of Jesus' return from the 'two

114. E.g. Heb. 4.14; 6.19-20; 9.24; 1 Pet. 3.22. Also the non-canonical accounts in *Acta Pilati* 16.6; *Epistula Apostolorum* 51; *Barnabas* 15.9; *The Apocryphon of James* 14-16; *The Martyrdom and Ascension of Isaiah* 11.22-33; and the ascension of Enoch in *1 Enoch* 39.1-14. In the Hellenistic literature, some examples are the ascension of Romulus into heaven in Ovid's *Metamorphoses* 14.805-851 and *Fasti* 2.481-509.

115. E.g. Johnson, *Acts of the Apostles*, pp. 30-31; Witherington, *Acts of the Apostles*, p. 112; Parsons, *The Departure of Jesus in Luke–Acts*, p. 140; T.L. Brodie, 'Greco-Roman Imitation of Texts as a Partial Guide to Luke's Use of Sources', in C.H. Talbert (ed.), *Luke–Acts: New Perspectives* (Edinburgh: T. & T. Clark, 1978), pp. 17-46; *idem*, 'Towards Unravelling the Rhetorical Imitation of Sources in Acts: 2 Kgs 5 as One Component of Acts 8, 9-40', *Bib* 67 (1986), pp. 41-67.

men in white robes' comes right after Jesus has departed and while the apostles were 'gazing at the sky' (Acts 1.10-11). There is no indication that the apostles were in a festive mood because of Jesus' exaltation.

1.3.3. *The Function of the Assurance by the Two Men in White Robes.* The pains of separation and the focus on the apprentice are supported by the need to give a soothing assurance from divine messengers. This leads us to the function of the two men in white robes in Acts 1.10-11.

T.Y. Mullins reads Acts 1.11 as a 'Reassurance', one of the major forms in commissioning accounts.[116] He sees the function of this element as,

> ...to dispose of any remaining resistance. After the reassurance, the person committed is the commissioner's agent. Since the person to be commissioned may become committed as the agent even before knowing what he is to be commissioned to do, the reassurance may be placed before the commission in some cases, as in Luke 5.10b (see also, Matt. 28.10a; and John 20.19c, 21a). Usually the protest will be absent where the reassurance comes early; in any case, the protest has to precede the reassurance.[117]

As I have argued earlier,[118] Mullins's premise in stating that 1.11 functions as a reassurance is quite unclear. He states that when the apostles stood 'gazing at the sky' in 1.9-10 it is an indication of protest or resistance. Thus, for Mullins, the reassurance from the two men in white robes functions to dispose of any remaining resistance to the commission being given to the apostles. But is the act of 'gazing at the sky' a form of protest? I do not think so. In the first place, the word ἀτενίζω simply denotes the action of looking (or to look intently, to gaze, to stare).[119] While indeed the separation between Jesus and the apostles is not one with indications of a joyful note (as in Lk. 24.52-53), there is also no clear evidence that the apostles exerted any form of protest or resistance to the commission (an issue also discussed in detail earlier). In fact, there are no emotive expressions at all on the part of the apostles. I suggest therefore that the assurance functions not to dispose of any resistance but on a different level. I propose two: the narrative and social-scientific levels.[120]

116. See Table 1, p. 43 this volume.
117. Mullins, 'New Testament Commissioning Accounts', p. 609.
118. See my discussion under 'No Form of Protest' in 3.1.2.4.7.
119. Fourteen times in the NT; two in Paul's letters; ten in Acts.
120. Scholars suggest a theological level. This is the level where the assurance functions as a prelude to the parousia of Jesus. For example, Holwerda suggests that the ascension of Acts 1 is focused on the parousia of Jesus...ascension, mission, and

1. On the narrative level, the assurance serves to heighten the intensity of separation between the apostles and Jesus. In other words, because an assurance is given, it is implied that the separation between the apostles and Jesus is tainted with an element of reluctance or uncertainty. Unlike what Mullins was suggesting, that the reassurance functions to dispose of any resistance to the commission, I say that the assurance functions to give an implication of resistance and reluctance to the fact of separation.[121]

My suggestion is further supported by the similarities of the characters who gave the assurance to the apostles of Jesus' return here in Acts 1.10-11 with the characters who also gave assurances to the women at the tomb in Lk. 24.1-11 concerning the disappearance of Jesus' body. The 'two men in white robes' of Acts 1.11 and the 'two men in dazzling apparel' of Lk. 24.4 have almost identical responsibilities—to give assurances to characters in the narrative who are in a state of perplexity or uncertainty. Lk. 24.1-9 tells us about the women who went to the tomb to prepare the body of Jesus with spices. After discovering that the body was missing, the narrator says that the women were 'perplexed' (Lk. 24.4) after which the 'two men in dazzling apparel' appeared and reminded them of Jesus' promise that he was going to be resurrected (24.7). When the author uses the same type of messengers in Acts 1.11, two intentions are possible. First it intends to tell the readers that the assurance of the messengers in Acts 1.11 is reliable. In other words, because the message of assurance by the two divine messengers in Lk. 24 was fulfilled, that is, Jesus was indeed resurrected, the assurance of the two messengers here in Acts 1.10-11 concerning Jesus' return is also going to be fulfilled. Second, I can also argue that, as there was the response of perplexity or confusion by the women in Lk. 24, the apostles might have had the same response to Jesus' departure were it not for the deliberate muting of the apostles which the author carried out until Acts 2.46.

2. From a social-scientific level, the assurance of Jesus' return does not

parousia are essentially related; 'Ascension', *ISBE*, I, p. 311. This suggestion may be acceptable that is if one looks forward to how the story is going to transpire. However, on the immediate context of Acts 1.9-11, the assurance also has an immediate function. See also Parsons, *The Departure of Jesus in Luke–Acts*, p. 144.

121. A meaning in contrast with the way the apostles left the ascension scene in jubilation as in Lk. 24.52-53. More so with the story of Romulus' ascension where the multitude rejoiced and worshipped Romulus when they learned of his ascent to heaven and his transformation from good king to a benevolent god. See Plutarch's *Romulus* 27.7-8.

completely transfer Jesus' 'mantle' to the apostles. In other words, unlike Elisha who has fully taken on the prophetic role of Elijah, the apostles' role as leaders is interim or temporary until Jesus returns and resumes his role. The assurance of Jesus' return supports my thesis that the apostles' leadership is that of a mediator-broker. They will serve as leaders, appointed and commissioned by a superior leader, who in turn will come to completely rule in the eschatological Israel.[122]

2. *Summary*

The separation aspect in the rituals of status transformation has clearly been experienced by the apostles as initiands in Acts 1.3-11. The mention of 'forty days' with Jesus tells the readers of the apostles' 'wilderness experience'. This wilderness motif represents not only the testing and trials of those who passes through it; it also, from a ritual perspective, involves the aspect of transformation—the transformation of the initiands who are leaving an old status and taking on a new one.

In this chapter, I demonstrated what happens to the initiands during their separation from society. First, the author legitimizes the Eleven as the ones chosen by Jesus. This legitimization is crucial as it, at the outset, establishes the reasons why the apostles are the rightful initiands who will go through the transformation process. Second, with regard to the moulding process, the initiands are stripped of their preconceived ideas. This is shown by Jesus' correction of the apostles' view on the restoration of the kingdom to Israel (1.6-7). Third, the aspect of obedience by the initiands to the ritual elder is displayed by the author through the apparent non-reaction of the apostles to what is supposedly a sudden change of plan concerning Israel's restoration. In fact, the author has been consistent in keeping the apostles from expressing any form of protest, either to the news of the parousia delay, or any inside views at all until they complete the ritual and are aggregated into the society (2.14, 47).

---

122. The assurance of Jesus' return gives us a fresh insight into the significance of the apostles' role as interim leaders. In other ascension stories, no assurance of the leader's return is given. That is why we find some of these characters attempt to continue their role as leaders even after their ascension or at the stage of their ascent to heaven. For example, Romulus continues to legislate even as he rises to join the gods (Ovid's *Metamorphoses* 14.805-851; cf. Ovid's *Fasti* 2.481-509). Philo's description of Moses' ascension shows how Moses continues to prophesy even as he ascends to heaven (*Life of Moses* 2.291).

Finally, in this section, we have seen the apostles' separation in the highest order. Jesus, their ritual elder, bids farewell to his apostles leaving them with such an important responsibility. Not only are the initiands changed in their preconceived ideas, but their obedience is also tested. They are compelled to return to Jerusalem and move to another stage in the process of their status transformation. Just as Jesus had travelled alone into the wilderness and faced the stage of his ritual confrontation (Lk. 4.1), the apostles travel back to Jerusalem by themselves and face their own version of ritual confrontation (Acts 1.12-26).

Part II

Transition

Chapter 4

The Upper Room: The Setting of the Apostles' Defence

Just as Jesus was separated from John the Baptist, his ritual elder (Lk. 4.1-3), the apostles experience the same with Jesus (Acts 1.9-11). However, the apostles' version of separation is not only seen in the event of Jesus' ascension but is accentuated in the scene where the Eleven have to return to Jerusalem by themselves in Acts 1.12-13, a journey usually led by Jesus when he was still with them.

As the apostles return to Jerusalem, they enter a new stage in the rituals of status transformation. This is the transition stage, a stage where the initiands experience the lowest level in their liminal status. And it is at this lowest level that the initiands experience their severe testing. This stage of testing is what I would identify as the ritual confrontation.

Despite being commissioned by Jesus in 1.7-8, the apostles have not gained any leadership status until their aggregation in 2.1-4. In between these events (i.e. the commissioning and aggregation) is the full expression of the liminality and *communitas* of the Eleven apostles.[1] This is exactly what Turner has described as the initiand's status of being in '*betwixt and between*', a status that is '*neither here nor there*'.[2] This stage of transition is found in the narrative of Acts 1.12-26.

In this transition stage, we find two phases. Phase One is 1.12-14 while Phase Two is the election narrative of 1.15-26. In Phase One, three distinctive features in the ritual process may be seen. First is the initiands' seclusion from society represented by the spatial and temporal setting of the 'upper room'. Second is the *communitas* among the initiands. This can be seen behind the purpose of enumeration of the names of the Eleven, most especially in the way the narrator subtly contrasts them with the other disciple groups in the upper room (1.13-14). Finally, there is the author's networking strategy. As I stated in the introduction of this study, I

---

1.   Cf. Chapter 5 of this study.
2.   Turner, *The Ritual Process*, p. 95; Cohn, 'Liminality in the Wilderness', p. 10.

will attempt to show that the author is indirectly appealing to the clientele of the other disciple groups in the upper room by portraying the Eleven apostles as having unanimity with them—namely the women disciples and Jesus' family (1.14).

As for the second phase—the election narrative in Acts 1.15-26—I find the whole setting as the initands' main ritual confrontation. As I have also indicated, I will attempt to argue that Peter's speech in 1.16-20 is the apostles' defence in the 'court of reputation'[3] attended by the rest of the 120 people (cf. 1.15) who serve as the jury on behalf of the community of believers. Furthermore, in this ritual confrontation, we can see the election of Matthias as a measure which the apostles have initiated in order to blot out Judas' association with them and show their innocence and sincerity as reputable and trustworthy incoming leaders of the Christian community.

I begin with the first phase—Acts 1.12-14. Again, I will first deal with the ritual elements before moving on to the ritual process.

1. *The Ritual Elements in Acts 1.12-14*

After the final separation of the initiands from their ritual elder, the initiands head for Jerusalem in obedience to Jesus' directives (Acts 1.4). The significant ritual elements in this phase are the city of Jerusalem; the upper room; the women disciples; and Mary with Jesus' brothers.

1.1. *The City of Jerusalem: The Centre of Leadership*
The return of the initiands to Jerusalem commenced from the mountain called Olivet (Acts 1.12). In Lk. 19.20, Mount Olivet is the same setting when Jesus first entered Jerusalem during his public ministry.[4] In Lk. 21.37, after teaching in the day time, Jesus went to the same Mount Olivet to lodge and to spend the night. Lk. 24.50 locates Bethany as the place of Jesus' ascension which in Lk. 19.29 is said to be near Olivet.[5] What we have, therefore, is another parallelism between the ritual elements in Jesus' RST with that of the Eleven apostles (cf. Acts 1.12-13). Jerusalem

---

3. A phrase from David deSilva's *The Hope of Glory* (p. 4), which I will expound later.

4. That is, besides the report of the infancy stories which finds the infant Jesus in Jerusalem (cf. Lk. 2.22-51).

5. However, this seems to be contrary to Josephus who locates Olivet as nowhere near Bethany; *Antiquities* 20.169. The same goes with the gospel of John in 11.18; Johnson, *The Acts of the Apostles*, p. 33.

serves as the place where both Jesus and the apostles find the fulfilment of their leadership roles.

The significance of the city of Jerusalem as a ritual element, especially in relation to the leadership role into which the initiands are being transformed, is again best explained from a social-scientific perspective. In particular, the hope that indeed the apostles have been transformed into reliable leaders of the people can be defined in part by understanding Jerusalem as the 'centre' within the 'centre-periphery' discussion. Jerusalem is the centre of power. It is the place where its leaders exercise their rule, and those in the periphery receive their directions. J.B. Chance proposes:

> Luke focused the attention of the reader on the vicinities of Jerusalem and the temple in a number of places in Luke–Acts. The birth narrative, which announces the coming of God's eschatological salvation, finds its centre at Jerusalem and the temple. Jesus' final encounter with the whole people of Israel, confronting them with the message of God's eschatological salvation happens at the temple. Near the environs of Jerusalem, Messiah Jesus is enthroned in the heavenly sphere. Finally, Luke portrays Israel as restored at Jerusalem, a community of the eschatological Spirit, ruled by the twelve apostles, those destined to rule Israel in conjunction with the reign of the Messiah.[6]

The significance of Jerusalem is crucial to the understanding of the social structures in Luke–Acts. It can be described primarily by emphasizing the social gap between centre and periphery, between the city and rural villages. These social differences affect all areas of power, namely, political, economic, and religious.[7] The centre-periphery contrast is not just a background to a religious main theme in Luke–Acts. Rather, these two themes are totally integrated in the narrative.

The centre-periphery contrast is clearly seen in the parables and narrative of Luke, especially when he describes the world of the villages (the periphery) and that of the rich elite (the centre).[8] Periphery and centre are described as culturally miles apart. For example, the rich who are dressed luxuriously lived away at Herod's court (7.25). It is when those in the

---

6.   J.B. Chance, *Jerusalem, the Temple, and the New Age in Luke–Acts* (Macon, GA: Mercer, 1988), p. 84.

7.   See also the studies of R.L. Rohrbaugh, 'The Pre-Industrial City in Luke–Acts: Urban Social Relations', pp. 125-49; and D.E. Oakman, 'The Countryside in Luke–Acts', pp. 151-79, both in Neyrey (ed.), *The Social World of Luke–Acts*.

8.   Rohrbaugh, 'The Pre-Industrial City', pp. 129-32.

centre interfere or cross paths with those in the periphery that problems arise. The problems often include the picture of oppression and the taking advantage of the marginal by the elite. Herod Antipas, for instance, interferes with Jesus who comes from the periphery. The threat to destroy Jesus is seen in the various accounts of 3.19-20; 9.7-9; 13.31-33.[9]

In reference to Moxnes' model of patron-client relations, he discusses the centre-periphery issue under three main sections. The first section deals with the topic of patrons, clients, and brokers. He argues how the concept of patronage helps one to understand the story of the centurion in Capernaum who made contact with Jesus through the 'elders of the Jews' and a group of 'friends' (7.1-10). The centurion represents the outside military and administrative power. The centurion himself is a non-Jew but apparently was able to establish himself in the role of a patron. The encounter with Jesus by the centurion was made possible by the recommendations of the town elders and friends who may have recognized the centurion's benefactions to the town. The centurion serves as patron to the remote village, he being in some way a representative of the centre to the periphery.[10]

The second section deals with a common issue in patron-client relations—the rich and the poor. For Luke, the picture of the rich is in negative terms. They are known for their luxurious clothes (Lk. 7.25;

---

9. A detailed discussion on the tensions between the city and its peripheries can be found in G. Theissen and A. Merz, *The Historical Jesus: A Comprehensive Guide* (trans. J. Bowden; London: SCM Press, 1998), pp. 162-84. In this guide, Theissen and Merz attempt to explain the various sociological issues Jesus had to contend with in the context of his environment and society. The discussions include the social and ecological tensions between the city and country (pp. 170-71); social and economic tensions between the rich and poor (pp. 171-73); social and political tensions between rulers and ruled (pp. 173-76); the religious character of Galilee (pp. 176-78); and Jerusalem as the place of the passion of Jesus (pp. 178-80).

10. The picture of military officials serving as patrons over peoples of localities under their jurisdiction is common in the Roman empire. As early as the third century BCE, evidence is found whereby Roman generals have assumed a general patronage over the conquered people. This patronage even extended and transmitted to their descendants. A. Mogmiliano recounts how C. Fabricius took the Samnites as his clients, while the Claudii Marcelli undertook to supervise after the interests of the province of Sicily, a province conquered by Claudius Marcellu in 210 BCE. In 83 BCE, the patronage of Pompey was felt all over the empire as he raised three legions of clients in Picenum, while his son Sextus gets help in Spain and Asia from the clients of his family. A. Momigliamo, 'Patronus', in the *Oxford Classical Dictionary* (Oxford: Clarendon Press, 2nd edn, 1970), p. 791.

16.19) and their sumptuous feasting and drinking (Lk. 12.19; 16.19). In Luke's time, the rich are not just an economic category but a name for members of the elite.[11]

More relevant to my study is the third section. It deals with the leaders of the people of Israel—the priests in Jerusalem who belong to the rich elite of the society. They are not only known to have access to numerous resources and wealth but they also function as brokers to the clients' access to the temple and the Torah. For example, the picture of the Pharisees as 'lovers of money' is depicted by the author in Lk. 16.14. This negative image is accentuated, according to Fowler, when read within an understanding of the image of 'limited good'.[12] Fowler argues that,

> The status-maintenance orientation in a closed system of limited good society brands such persons as thieves. Any goods that are gained in a closed system are gained at the expense of others. It is also a sign that those persons trust in their own devices and do not trust in God's care. Notice that Jesus tells the parable of the Pharisee and the Toll Collector to those 'who trusted themselves' (Lk. 18.9). Such contrasts vividly reverse the accepted categories: the Pharisees trust in themselves, but the toll collectors 'justify God' (Lk. 7.29).[13]

The expected role of religious leaders has not been met. On the contrary, the people of Israel suffer 'negative patronage'. 'Not only is there

---

11.　They are selfish and ungenerous (e.g. 'The Rich Fool', 12.16-21). Another of this kind is the parable of the rich man and Lazarus in 16.19-31. We know that the beggar Lazarus eventually was rewarded while the rich man ended in Hades. In this story, there is really no surprise at all. The readers know the rich to be evil while Lazarus is the righteous one. This is how the rich are depicted. Their disregard for the needs of the poor accentuates the inequality of the patron-client relations. The neglect of moral considerations in favour of popularity and money has been one of the downside marks of patronage in the Roman society. A patron has been known to be torn between having many poor clients—suggesting the patron's image as defender of the poor, against the few but rich clients—securing the patron's financial and social welfare. Wallace-Hadrill recalls how the play of Plautus' *Menaechmi* (571ff.), portrays Menaechmus' complaint of being trapped into the patronal system, 'What a stupid, irritating practice we have, and one the best people follow most! Everyone wants lots of clients. They don't bother to ask whether they're good men or bad; the last thing that counts is the reliability of the client, and how dependable he is. If he's poor and no rogue, he's held good for nothing; if he's a rich rogue, he's treated as a solid client'. A. Wallace-Hadrill, *Patronage in Ancient Society* (London and New York: Routledge, 1989), p. 64.

12.　Gowler, *Host, Guest, Enemy and Friend*, p. 21.

13.　Gowler, *Host, Guest, Enemy and Friend*, p. 21.

little positive contact between the elites in the urban centres and peripheries, but even their own community leaders have joined forces with the "negative patrons".'[14] This is precisely where the leadership of the apostles becomes very important. The apostles are to function as the reliable leaders of the people. And as Jerusalem is the place where leaders play their role; the apostles as new leaders are to faithfully execute their responsibilities.

1.2. *The Upper Room: The Setting of the Transition Stage*

There is a slight discrepancy between Jesus' instructions to the Eleven in Lk. 24.53 and how this is executed in Acts 1.13. Lk. 24.53 directs the apostles to return to the temple as against gathering in the ὑπερῷον[15] (upper room) which is indicated in Acts 1–2.[16] Later traditions depict this room as being in the house of Mary, the mother of John Mark (Acts 12.12). In the *Martyrdom of Polycarp*, for example, we find this type of room as being used for gatherings, for studies, and for places of prayer.[17]

Quesnell's suggestion is attractive. He states,

> Acts 1.15 takes place in a room large enough for Peter to rise in the midst of 'about 120 persons'. The place seems, by the ordinary rule of narration, to be the same place spoken of in the two preceding verses (1.13-14) as the dwelling-place for the Twelve, the women, Mary and the brothers.[18]

However, I find the symbolism of the upper room more important than its alleged physical size and structure. I suggest that the upper room provides the perfect setting and definition of the initiands' liminality-*communitas* and ritual confrontation. In other words, just as the wilderness revealed Jesus' statuslessness during his stage of transition, the confines of the upper room suitably define the 'limbo' status of the apostles. The upper room symbolically portrays the further seclusion of the initiands from the society.

Furthermore, the upper room is also the place and time of purging—the place where the initiands are to be tried for (as I have proposed) a moral accusation in line with their association with the betrayer Judas. The upper room sets the place and time where the Eleven will have to defend

---

14. Moxnes, 'Patron-Client Relations', p. 257.
15. Only occurs in Acts—1.13; 9.37, 39; 20.8.
16. Fitzmyer, *Acts*, p. 213.
17. *Martyrdom of Polycarp* 7.1.
18. Quesnell, ' The Women at Luke's Supper', p. 62.

themselves in the court of public opinion represented by somewhat like a jury of 120 brethren (Acts 1.15-26).

1.3. *The Women in the Upper Room*

There are two questions we need to answer in relation to the function of the γυναικές in 1.14. First, who exactly are the γυναικές? Second, why are the γυναικές said to be together (ὁμοθυμαδόν) with the Eleven? The first question will be addressed here in the ritual elements section while the second question will be tackled in the ritual process section.

1.3.1. Γυναικές *in Acts 1.14 as the Women Disciples.* There is still contention as to how to understand the phrase σὺν γυναιξίν in 1.14. The options are either the 'wives of the apostles' or the 'women disciples' of Jesus. The possibility that γυναικές might refer to the wives of the apostles is primarily supported by the reading in codex D which renders the whole phrase as σὺν γυναιξίν καὶ τεκνοῖς ('together with the women and children').[19] However, καὶ τεκνοῖς is regarded as an addition and is explained from three perspectives. L.T. Johnson sees it as a 'domestic touch' on the part of the editor.[20] Conzelmann simply takes it to be a failure to recognize that the list is a list of witnesses.[21] Witherington believes it to be another example of the anti-feminist reading of the Western texts similar to the tradition of Acts 17–18. He adds that the intention was to subliminate, eliminate, or change the roles women played in the early church.[22] Barrett, on the other hand, argues that the natural way to read the phrase σὺν γυναιξίν (i.e. even without the addition of καὶ τεκνοῖς) is 'with their wives'.[23] If it were σὺν γυναιξίν τισιν, then the reading will be 'with certain women'. Or, σὺν ταῖς γυναιξίν for 'with the well known women'.[24]

19. Cf. G. Lüdemann, *Early Christianity according to the Traditions in Acts: A Commentary* (London: SCM Press, 1989), p. 27.

20. Johnson, *Acts*, p. 34.

21. Quoted from Barrett, *The Acts of the Apostles*, p. 89.

22. Witherington, *The Acts of the Apostles*, p. 113, n. 39.

23. Barrett, *The Acts of the Apostles*, p. 89. Lüdemann also adds that it might have been probable to assume that the redaction of codex D was with the intention of wanting his readers to understand the phrase to mean 'the apostles' wives' since it was known that indeed the apostles had wives. Lüdemann, *Early Christianity*, p. 27.

24. For purely linguistic reasons, Gerd Lüdemann sees the absence of the Greek article before γυναιξίν as indicating a reference to the 'wives' of the disciples. This is so even without the evidence from codex D. Lüdemann believes that if the phrase

Most of the exegetes I have mentioned recognize the stronger probability that σὺν γυναιξίν refers to the 'women disciples' of Jesus. For one, up to this point in 1.14, the narrator has not mentioned any reference to the wives of the apostles. The nearest reference about women with which the readers of Acts can associate the γυναικές of 1.14 is the account of the women witnesses of Jesus' resurrection in Lk. 24. Furthermore, the fact that Mary is certainly not a wife of any of the men in the upper room supports the suggestion that the γυναικές refers to the women disciples of Jesus.[25]

1.3.2. The Identity of the Women Disciples. Despite the silence of the author there have been attempts to identify these women disciples in 1.14. Two instances in the gospel of Luke are said to fit the women's description. One is the 'women followers' of Jesus in Lk. 8.1-3, and second is the 'women at the cross' in Lk. 23.49. Lk. 8.1-3 is Lukan material since these women followers do not appear to have been derived from the same tradition as that in Mk 15.41.[26] By description, these women disciples were probably like the male followers who may have given up their home and family to follow Jesus. Mary Magdalene is one who is most likely to fit such a description.[27] Her popularity may have

meant the women disciples, then they should have been always defined more closely as they are found in Lk. 8.2-3; 10.38-42; 23.49, 55; 24.10. Furthermore, because they are no longer mentioned elsewhere in the book after 1.14, this only goes on to show that all the author wanted was to 'check off' the theme of the 'women from Galilee' for the sake of completing the scene. This also means, as Lüdemann concludes, that the author wishes to describe the composition of the people in the upper room as 'the holy family in the earliest community'. Lüdemann, *Early Christianity*, p. 27.

25. Witherington, *The Acts of the Apostles*, p. 113. Newman and Nida see some difficulty in translating the function of the conjunction καὶ in the πηρασε ὁμοθυμαδὸν τῇ προσυχῇ σὺν γυναιξὶν καὶ Μαριὰμ τῇ μητρὶ τοῦ Ἰησοῦ. They suggest that, 'It is difficult to define precisely the relationship between Mary the mother of Jesus, and the women spoken of though it is very unlikely that the women should be understood as the men involved. Perhaps Mary was included within the group of the women, but because of her unique relationship to the Lord she was given specific mention, and in any case Luke elsewhere, as in the nativity narratives, lets his high regard for Mary be known'. B. Newman and E. Nida, *A Translator's Handbook on the Acts of the Apostles* (Help for Translators, 12; London: United Bible Societies, 1972), p. 23.

26. B. Witherington III, *Women in the Ministry of Jesus: A Study of Jesus' Attitude to Women and their Roles as Reflected in his Earthly Life* (Cambridge: Cambridge University Press, 1984), pp. 116-17.

27. Witherington, *Women in the Ministry of Jesus*, p. 117.

been due to her 'bio-data' and portfolio of having been delivered by Jesus from seven demons (cf. Lk. 8.2). Also mentioned to have followed Jesus (with the exceptional description of having 'provided for them out of their means' [αἵτινες διηκόνουν αὐτοῖς ἐκ τῶν ὑπαρχόντων αὐταῖς])[28] are Joanna the wife of Chuza (who happens to be Herod's steward),[29] and Suzanna.

The women at the cross (Lk. 23.49) were probably the same who prepared Jesus for his burial (Lk. 23.55-56). Fitzmyer would include in this group the women who discovered the empty tomb (Lk. 24.2-9).[30] In contrast with Mk 15.40, Mt. 27.55, and Jn 19.25, Luke does not mention the names of the women who were present at Jesus' crucifixion. The most logical explanation is that the author invites his readers to recall the list of women mentioned in 8.1-3, 'or planned out for the reader to find out their names in Lk. 24.10'.[31]

1.4. *Mary and Jesus' Brothers*
The same questions which I have raised about the women disciples also apply to the other group mentioned as having unity with the Eleven in 1.14. Again, I will attempt to clearly define the character of Mary and Jesus' brothers here in the ritual elements section. I will discuss the function of these characters within the apostles' RST in the ritual process section.

1.5. *Mary and Jesus' Brothers as a Single Group*
The exact phrase in Acts 1.14 is σὺν γυναιξὶν καὶ Μαριὰμ τῇ μητρὶ τοῦ Ἰησοῦ καὶ τοῖς ἀδελφοῖς αὐτοῦ (together with women and Mary the mother of Jesus and his brothers). There are discussions on whether the first καὶ distinguishes Mary from the group of the γυναιξὶν and thus makes her the representative of Jesus' family.[32] If this is so, then the

---

28.   Haenchen adds that the σὺν γυναιξίν refers to 'the well-to-do followers of Jesus, some of high position'. *Acts of the Apostles*, p. 154.

29.   Lake and Jackson, *The Beginnings of Christianity*, p. 11.

30.   Fitzmyer, *The Acts of the Apostles*, p. 215.

31.   Witherington, *Women in the Ministry of Jesus*, p. 120.

32.   It is speculated that Mary, the mother of Jesus, was among the women mentioned in Lk. 23.49; 23.55, or even the 'other women' in 24.10 and the acquaintances (γνοστοι) in 23.49. Yet, Reumann is correct to say that Luke's failure to mention Mary in the said events means he finds her presence (or even that of Jesus' family) at the crucifixion insignificant. J. Reumann, *Mary in the New Testament*, p. 173, n. 393.

second καί would make Mary stand on her own since the conjunction would also distinguish her from τοῖς ἀδελφοῖς αὐτοῦ. The truth is, the two instances of καί do not divorce Mary from either the women or from Jesus' brothers. There is a certain degree of literary continuity between the group of women and the family of Jesus. While it is true that Mary is named after the women were mentioned, her association with the τοῖς ἀδελφοῖς αὐτοῦ is clearer than with the γυναικές even if she is a woman herself. In other words, Mary belongs to the party of Jesus' family rather than that of the women.

Nevertheless, the women, Mary and Jesus' brothers should be seen as distinct from the Eleven who were mentioned before them. This distinction is achieved by the function of σὺν which is placed before γυναιξὶν καὶ Μαριὰμ τῇ μητρὶ τοῦ Ἰησοῦ καὶ τοῖς ἀδελφοῖς αὐτοῦ. This argument is supported by Metzger who proposed that the second σὺν which was omitted by Codices A, D, and S and other minuscules, is a scribal addition.[33] To put it more plainly, while the women and Jesus' family were clearly not of the same group, their distinction is not from each other but against the Eleven. The fact that the women and Jesus' family are especially mentioned by the author (despite the other probable disciple groups) underlines their significant roles in the present and upcoming events.

This takes us to an important note that needs to be reiterated. While it is true that there is significance in mentioning the characters by name, and that this is Luke's first mention of Mary's name since the Infancy narratives,[34] one should be careful in assessing NT evidence concerning what is said about Mary and what is said about Jesus' brothers.[35] In other words, the naming of Mary in this specific event does not necessarily mean that she is a character on her own. Rather, as this section has consistently referred to, the phrase Μαριὰμ τῇ μητρὶ τοῦ Ἰησοῦ καὶ τοῖς ἀδελφοῖς αὐτοῦ is to be viewed as a unit or group rather than as two separate characters. 'Mary and Jesus' brothers' in this context is an alternative and synonymous with the title 'Jesus' family'.[36]

---

33. B, C3, E, Y, etc.; B. Metzger, *TCGNT*, pp. 284-85.
34. Johnson, *Acts of the Apostles*, p. 34.
35. Reumann, *Mary in the New Testament*, p. 173.
36. For further discussion on the stereotyped expression of Jesus' 'mother and brothers', see R. Bauckham, *Jude and the Relatives of Jesus* (Edinburgh: T. & T. Clark, 1990), pp. 5-19.

2. *Summary*

What I have discussed under this chapter are the significant ritual elements in the first phase of the transition stage of Acts 1.12-14. These ritual elements are the city of Jerusalem, the upper room, the women disciples, and the character of Mary and Jesus' brothers. I stated that Jerusalem symbolically stands for the centre of power where the apostles as new leaders will be executing their duties before their constituents. I proposed that the upper room serves as the spatial and temporal setting, not only for the further seclusion of the initiands from the society, but also the phase of purging of the initiands undergoing the ritual process. I added that the upper room represents the phase where the initiands experience the utter expression of the statuslessness.

In the upper room is also the time and place where the initiands continue to bond together. Their *communitas* is fully seen when contrasted with the other disciple groups who were with them. These disciple groups are the women disciples and Jesus' family.

I suggested that the women are most likely the women followers of Jesus as against the other notion that they are the wives of the apostles. I also suggested that Mary and Jesus' brothers are to be understood as a family group rather than as separate characters.

I also proposed that the presence of these two groups with the group of the Eleven apostles sets the stage for the author's networking strategy, a strategy expressed through his portrayal of exemplary unanimity between these groups in the upper room.

The apostles as initiands enter the transition stage with these ritual elements. These elements will help shape the initiands into the status they have been destined to. The next chapter in my study of the ritual process is this transition stage. We will see how these ritual elements function in the initiands' ongoing rituals of status transformation.

Chapter 5

The Apostles' Meeting with the Other Parties in the Upper Room

1. *The Ritual Process in Acts 1.12-14*

I designated Acts 1.12-26 as the stage of transition in my study of the apostles' rituals of status transformation. And just as Jesus' stage of transition is the time when he experienced his full state of liminality (Lk. 4.1-13), the apostles in the setting of the upper room, experience the same (Acts 1.12-26). This stage of transition has two phases. The first is found in 1.12-14. This phase shows how the apostles as initiands go through liminality and *communitas*. This is also the stage when the initiands prepare themselves for the ritual confrontation. This ritual confrontation is the election narrative of 1.15-26, the second phase in the transition stage. It is highlighted by the apostles' defence of their honour, the excommunication of Judas from the membership of the Twelve (1.16-20), and the election of Judas' replacement (1.21-26).

This chapter is the study of the first phase in the transition stage (1.12-14). In this phase, we will also discuss how the author succeeds in promoting the apostles' leadership status by tapping into the social network of the Christian community. We will argue that behind the author's report of unanimity between the apostles and the women disciples and Jesus' family in the upper room (1.14) is an appeal to win support from the various clienteles of these disciple groups. Finally, we will show how the unanimity between the Eleven and the women disciples and Jesus' family is crucial to what is about to take place in the upper room—the need to elect another apostle in place of Judas (1.15-26).

I began this chapter with a survey on how NT scholarship presently understands the function of 1.12-14 in the narrative of Acts 1–2. Historical methods have so far failed to submit a convincing reason as to why the author placed 1.12-14 between the Ascension and Pentecost events. I suggested that my investigation through the model of RST presents a plausible solution to this exegetical problem.

1.1. *The Function of 1.12-14: A Survey*

J. Fitzmyer sees 1.12-14 as a narrative on its own. Although he views the pericope as part of the wider story about the early Christian community (Acts 1.1-26), he argues that 1.12-14 functions 'to describe the first Christian community gathered in the city where Jesus (regarded as the founder of the movement that gave rise to its gathering) had been put to death'.[1]

For Ben Witherington,[2] 1.12-14 is also an episode on its own. However, he decides that 1.12-14 should be part of the *prologue* of the whole book since (following C.K. Barrett's observations) 'the vast majority of the material in 1.1-14 is mentioned in some form in Luke 24 or earlier…and thus it is best to see this whole section as a recapitulation, with some expansion, before breaking new ground with Peter's first speech in 1.15ff'.[3] The rest of the chapter (1.15-26) is the beginning of the whole 'rhetoric of persuasion'.

---

1.   Fitzmyer does not fully explain how the previous events (i.e. the instruction to remain in Jerusalem and wait for the promise of the father [1.3-5], Jesus' Ascension [1.6-11]) lead to the gathering of the disciple groups in 1.12-14. He also does not discuss how all these events are related with the second section—the election narrative in 1.15-26; Fitzmyer, *The Acts of the Apostles*, pp. 191-120, 212. For Fitzmyer, Acts 1 is the story of how the first Christian community began. He proposed this heading with the admission that the whole structure of Acts is indeed difficult to determine. Following the suggestion that its structure can be detected from the programmatic verse of 1.8, the layout of the whole book is based on the commission of the apostles by the risen Christ to be witnesses of his resurrection beginning in Jerusalem, in the whole of Judea and Samaria, and then to the end of the earth (p. 119). To layout the structure of Acts from this programme, however, cannot avoid the overlapping of events. This, Fitzmyer mentions, is Dupont's observation as he (Dupont) attempted to divide the account of Acts into four major sections: 2.1-8.1a; 8.1b–15.35; 15.36–19.40; 20.1–28.31 (cf. J. Dupont, 'La question du plan des Actes des Apôtres à la lumiere d'un texte de Lucien de Samosate', *NovT* 21 [1979], pp. 220-31; reprinted in *Nouvelles études*, pp. 24-36). However, Dupont's division has completely disregarded the first chapter of Acts. Fitzmyer picks this up and states that Dupont has left out 'the important matter in chapter 1'. Yet again, Fitzmyer does not explain what is this 'important matter' which characterizes the whole first chapter of Acts.

2.   Witherington, *The Acts of the Apostles*, p. 113.

3.   Witherington, *The Acts of the Apostles*, p. 105.

Again, Witherington suggests that the necessity for the author to 'persuade' his readers starts with the 'problem that needs to be solved and overcome' and that is 'the need to fill the vacancy in the Twelve'.[4] Apart from what Witherington sees as the prologue of Acts 1, the second section of the first chapter (1.15-26) is all about the election narrative and the author's literary prowess in presenting the story. With this, Witherington insists on a clear break between 1.1-14 and the election story in 1.15-26.

In contrast, L.T. Johnson sees 1.13-14 as part of the election narrative.[5] Johnson argues that Luke begins the election story of 1.15-26 with a list of the Eleven in 1.13 to highlight the failure and absence of Judas. Johnson follows this up with the view that 'the betrayal of Judas was more than simply the failure of an individual. It splintered the numerical and symbolic integrity of that group...'[6] However, Johnson arrives at this conclusion by completely taking 1.13 out from the pericope of 1.12-14. In other words, Johnson's argument would work only if 1.13 is by itself. But this is not the case. The list of names is sandwiched between the author's note that the apostles returned to Jerusalem (1.12) and the fact that they were in unanimity with the women, Mary the mother of Jesus and Jesus' brothers (1.14).

For James Dunn,[7] the only action that was taken between the Ascension and Pentecost is the replacement of Judas. 1.12-14 is an interval in the absence of the characters of Jesus and the Spirit.[8] The function of this event in the narrative is to show that the interval between the Ascension and Pentecost was a period of waiting, a 'prayerful waiting'.[9]

C.K. Barrett[10] is aware of the problem concerning how to understand the structure of Acts 1, especially the place of vv. 12-14. He believes that the issue is where the introduction of Acts ends and where the book proper actually begins. Contrary to what others claim (that the introduction ends in 1.5), Barrett agrees that a case for 1.8 can be made as the ending of the section. However, he furthers his point by saying that while the Ascension (1.9-11) may be the first independent narrative in the book, it is still a

4.   Witherington, *The Acts of the Apostles*, p. 115.
5.   Johnson, *The Acts of the Apostles*, p. v.
6.   Johnson, *The Acts of the Apostles*, p. 38.
7.   Dunn, *The Acts of the Apostles*, p. 3.
8.   Dunn, *The Acts of the Apostles*, pp. 15, 17.
9.   Dunn, *The Acts of the Apostles*, p. 17.
10.   Barrett, *The Acts of the Apostles*, pp. 59, 61.

story which finds a parallel in the gospel of Luke. The Ascension narrative therefore, ought to still be part of the introduction and recapitulation section. This also applies to 1.12-14. Barrett argues that this event functions as a 'piece of stage setting' in preparation for further action—the replacement of Judas (1.15-26). In other words, Barrett takes the whole section of 1.1-14 as the introduction and recapitulation section.[11] For Barrett, it is a 'carefully constructed piece' which achieves the following aims.[12]

> 1) It refers the reader to the following volume and indicates the continuity between the two; 2) it draws attention to the work of the Holy Spirit as an essential and characteristic feature of the new volume; 3) it underlines the function of the apostles as witnesses…; 4) it points out that the church and its witnessing activity are to extend throughout the world; 5) it emphasizes that details of the eschatological future; 6) it nevertheless lays down the eschatological framework within which the Christian story is to unfold…; 7) the church is a fellowship at whose heart are the named eleven apostles.

Barrett's argument is based on the assumption that the election narrative of 1.15-26 is totally unrelated to 1.1-14.[13] Since the election story does not find any parallel in the gospel, Barrett considers the election narrative as breaking fresh ground amongst its readers, providing new information which the readers have not read or known before.[14]

The studies of Hubbard and Mullins on the role of commissioning accounts in Luke–Acts both see the pericope as the conclusion of the commissioning story. In particular, Mullins defines the function of the conclusion as 'to show the commissioned person's approach to the task. It may show that the task was carried out or it may merely show the commissioned person's attitude after accepting the commission.'[15] Again, the studies of Hubbard and Mullins do not reflect how 1.12-14 is significant to the event that immediately follows—the election narrative in 1.15-26.

Even studies which employ narrative criticism do not seem to see a

---

11. Barrett, *The Acts of the Apostles*, p. 61.
12. Barrett, *The Acts of the Apostles*, p. 63.
13. See also F.Ó. Fearghus, *The Introduction to Luke–Acts: A Study of the Role of Lk. 1, 1-4, 44 in the Composition of Luke's Two-Volume Work* (Roma: Editrice Pontifico Istituto Biblico, 1991), pp. 71-73.
14. Barrett, *The Acts of the Apostles*, p. 61.
15. Mullins, 'New Testament Commissioning Accounts', p. 609.

strong narrative connection between 1.12-14 and 1.15-26. R. Tannehill sees the first chapter as outlining the mission of the apostles—from the time they received it from Jesus until they started executing it in Acts 2. However, Tannehill seems to downplay the function and purpose of 1.12-14 within the said 'mission' of the apostles. In fact, he completely leaves this matter out by not mentioning the episode of 1.12-14 at all.[16]

W. Kurz too finds 1.12-14 as odd in its location. He considers 1.1-11 as the introduction of Acts and separates 1.12-26 under the title 'Preparations for Pentecost'. However, he opens the discussion with the statement that 1.12-14 are simply 'transition verses' and can be treated as part either of 1.1-11 or 1.15-26.[17]

Acts 1.12-14 has also been classified as one of Luke's 'summary statements'.[18] Like the rest of the summary statements in the book of Acts,[19] 1.12-14 is seen to bear the general plan of each major division of the book.[20] This means that its descriptions are of a broader character and may suggest the chronological development of events within a certain division. A summary statement may function as a conclusion to a previous event and connects that event to the next scene. In the case of 1.12-14, the previous event is Jesus' ascension (1.10-11) while the succeeding event after the election story is Peter's speech before the gathered crowd in Jerusalem (1.15-22).

To dispute the character of 1.12-14 as a summary statement is futile. Indeed, 1.12-14 as a summary statement connects the story of Jesus' ascension with the event where Peter delivers his sermon before the crowd.[21] However, as previously argued, the flow of the narrative is still logical even if 1.12-14, or the whole upper room story (1.12-26), is not found where it is. In fact, other commentators see the upper room story as a disruption to the travel narrative of the apostles which starts from the

---

16. Cf. Tannehill, *The Narrative Unity of Luke–Acts*, vol. 2, p. 10.

17. Kurz, *Reading Luke–Acts*, p. 76.

18. Haenchen, *The Acts of the Apostles*, p. 155. See also H.J. Cadbury, 'The Summaries in Acts', in Lake and Jackson (eds.), *The Beginnings of Christianity*, pp. 392-402.

19. Acts 6.7-8; 9.32; 12.24-25; 16.5-6; 19.20-21; 28.31.

20. Cadbury, 'The Summaries in Acts', p. 392.

21. The periphrastic tense of ἦσαν καταμένοντες in v. 13 supports the idea of continuity. Barrett, *The Acts of the Apostles*, p. 87.

ascension until their return to Jerusalem.[22] In other words, after Jesus has commanded the apostles to return to Jerusalem, there is no difficulty in reading the setting of Peter's speech in 1.15-22 as immediately following 1.10-11. If this proposal is correct, then it is plausible to label 1.12-14 as a 'disruption' to the flow of the narrative.

The alleged disruption is deliberate and carries a specific purpose. But what purpose? A closer look shows that 1.12-14 does not primarily connect the Ascension story of 1.9-11 to the Pentecost event of 2.1-4. What 1.12-14 specifically does is link the ascension of Jesus with the second episode, the speech of Peter in 1.15-22. From there, it leads to the election of Matthias in 1.23-26, and then finally, with the Pentecost story.[23] Because of these closely linked sequences, I suggest that the author wants to convey more than just the notion that 1.12-14 is a summary statement.[24] As I have proposed, Acts 1.12-14 (or even the whole upper room event in 1.12-26) is a 'halting of narrative time' with the primary purpose of addressing the social issues clouding the moral and leadership integrity of the apostles. The author had to place 1.12-26 in the midst of the Ascension and Pentecost events if the readers (and the Christian community as a whole) are to be assured that all measures have been taken to prove that the apostles are the worthy successors to Jesus' leadership.

In this brief survey, we can see how other methods have attempted to explain the function of 1.12-14 in Acts 1–2. What follows is my study of 1.12-14 as the first phase in the transition stage of the apostles' rituals of status transformation. In the end, I hope to show how 1.12-14, through the model of the RST, fills the gaps which other methodologies have left unanswered. One of my main objectives is to show that 1.12-14 is a networking strategy of the author. He intends to appeal for support from the clienteles of the other disciple groups in the upper room. This support is crucial to what the apostles are about to do next, a move that is unprecedented—the search for another apostle to replace Judas (1.15-26).

---

22. E.g. Haenchen, *The Acts of the Apostles*, p. 154; Lake and Cadbury, *The Beginnings of Christianity*, IV, pp. 12-13; M. Wilcox, 'The Judas-Tradition in Acts 1.15-26', *NTS* 19 (1972–73), pp. 438-52 (439).

23. The first collective account (Acts 1.13-14) goes very uneasily at first from narrative to generalized description, but by means of the list of apostles makes best introduction to the calling of Matthias which follows... M. Dibelius, *Studies in Acts of the Apostles* (ed. H. Greeven; trans. M. Ling; London: SCM Press, 1956), p. 9.

24. Dunn prefers to read 1.12-14 as giving 'the impression of its character as an interval between the Spirit...' Dunn, *The Acts of the Apostles*, p. 15.

While all these are taking place in the upper room, I want to emphasize that the apostles as initiands are in their most vulnerable status. They are, as I have stated, statusless. Their appeal for support and their defence of their honour are apologetic and not with the command and status of a leader. At the same time, we will note that the apostles' defence as a group in turn boosts their camaraderie as initiands. It is a time when the initiands find themselves bonding as a group as they withstand the rigours of the ritual confrontation in this transition stage.

1.2. *The Initiands in Transition: Acts 1.12-14*

The instruction of Jesus is for the apostles to return to Jerusalem and wait for the promise of the Father (Acts 1.4). As I have stated, the apostles as initiands have not received their new status even if they have been commissioned by Jesus to be his witnesses (1.7-8). From the time Jesus the ritual elder is separated from the initiands (1.9-11) until the rite of installation symbolized by their baptism in the Spirit (Acts 2.1-4), the apostles are in limbo, in a state of statuslessness. At this same juncture, the initiands develop a stronger bond with each other. This bond I called *communitas*.

I shall begin with an analysis of the intent behind the list of the apostles' names in 1.13. From here, I will develop my discussion on how I see the value of *communitas* in the pericope of 1.12-14.

1.2.1. *The List of the Apostles' Names in 1.13*. After the apostles' return to Jerusalem, the narrative flow is abruptly halted by the enumeration of the names of the Eleven. The readers suddenly find themselves reading the identity of each apostle (Acts 1.13). The question, of course, is why? If one simply accepts the notion that the author wants to introduce the Eleven apostles before the narrative further develops, then why was this not done at an earlier stage? Why not in the beginning of the ritual itself, just as the author introduced Jesus in the beginning of his own ritual in Lk. 3? Moreover, why make another list here in Acts when the author has already done this earlier in the gospel (Lk. 6.12-16)?[25]

---

25.   Haenchen and Barrett attempt to resolve the re-issue of names by arguing that the list of apostles proves the separate developments of the two books of Luke. Haenchen states that if the books have appeared simultaneously, then one of the lists (either Lk. 6.14-16 or Acts 1.13) is superfluous. Haenchen, *The Acts of the Apostles*, p. 153; Barrett, *The Acts of the Apostles*, p. 87. On the other hand, Goulder claims that

It has been suggested that the list serves to show, not the identities, but the fact that there were no longer Twelve apostles—which is the very reason why the election was called for. However, this suggestion relies heavily on the historical value of the number of the apostles which is twelve.[26] Because of Judas' defection this sacred number was disrupted, and therefore they needed someone to fill the vacancy. This suggestion is quite vague. As I have raised earlier, if the whole purpose of enumerating the names of the apostles was simply to highlight that the Twelve are now down to Eleven, then why name names in the first place?[27] Moreover, why did the author neglect to come up with another replacement when the number of the apostles was again down to Eleven after James was martyred by Herod in 12.2?[28]

The enumeration of the names in 1.13 indeed shows that the author wants to identify the apostles for his readers. I propose, however, that there is more than just the intent to identify who the apostles are. I suggest that the enumeration of names primarily intends to highlight, not those *who are in the group*, but the *one who is no longer in the group*. In other words, the focus is not on the impaired number of the apostles but on the person of Judas Iscariot and the fact that he is no longer part of the apostolate. This suggestion is supported by the succeeding consequences: the elaborate speech of Peter with the grotesque description of Judas' demise (1.17-20), the criteria required to be met by the candidates for Judas' replacement (1.21-22), and the need to show that God makes the final choice of Judas' substitute (1.23-26). All of these factors focus on the character and person of Judas rather than on the fact that the number of the apostles was reduced to eleven.

Another telling piece of evidence is found in the list of the apostles' names itself (1.13). This evidence becomes more obvious when compared

---

the repetition of the names in Acts 1.13 is for emphasis; cf. M. Goulder, *Type and History in Acts* (London: SPCK, 1964), p. 20.

26.   E.g. Tyson, 'The Emerging Church', p. 137.

27.   See again our Introduction section of this study.

28.   That is why Bolt had to make an assumption that it was Jesus who ordered the replacement of Judas. Bolt argues, '…that the witnesses had to be "chosen beforehand" by Jesus (cf. 10.41) whether during his earthly ministry (as for the eleven, 1.2), or after his resurrection through the control of the lot (as for Matthias)'. B. Bolt, 'Mission and Witness', in I.H. Marshall and D. Petersen (eds.), *Witness to the Gospel: The Theology of Acts* (Grand Rapids: Eerdmans, 1998), p. 198.

and contrasted with the other lists of names in the gospel tradition. Consider the following lists.[29]

Mk 3.16-19	Mt. 10.2-4	Lk. 6.14-16	Acts 1.13b
Peter	Peter	Peter	Peter
James	Andrew	Andrew	John
John	James	James	James
Andrew	John	John	Andrew
Philip	Philip	Philip	Philip
Bartholomew	Bartholomew	Bartholomew	Thomas
Matthew	Thomas	Matthew	Bartholomew
Thomas	Matthew	Thomas	Matthew
James of Alphaeus	James of Alphaeus	James of Alphaeus	James of Alphaeus
Thaddaeus	Thaddaeus[30]	Simon the Zealot	Simon the Zealot
Simon the Cananaean	Simon the Cananaean	Judas of James	Judas of James
Judas Iscariot	Judas Iscariot	Judas Iscariot	—

The names from the lists above are unanimous in two aspects: Peter always comes first, while Judas Iscariot always comes last. The suggestion that Peter is listed first because of how he came to be recognized as the leader of the apostles can also explain why Judas has always been placed at the bottom of the list. In other words, tradition has come to know Judas, what he stands for in the Christian tradition,[31] and that is, as the one who betrayed Jesus.

The Gospel tradition carries no other description of Judas but the 'traitor'. This may have been one of the reasons why tradition has been consistent in placing him last in the list. And if the readers of Luke–Acts were aware and are able to compare the list in Acts 1.13b with the list in Lk. 6.14-16 (more so if they are aware of the tradition in the gospels of

---

29. This study will not go into the individual analysis on the authenticity and background of each name. For this purpose, see for example Fitzmyer, *The Acts of the Apostles*, pp. 213-15; Barrett, *The Acts of the Apostles*, pp. 86-88. Although there are variations they do not warrant disputing the authenticity of the tradition on apostolic names. In other words, the similarities outweigh the differences. The names in these lists are most likely authentic. (An earlier editor is said to have come up with a list based from a different tradition. The list goes as John, Matthew, Peter, Andrew, Philip, Simon, James Nathanael, Thomas, Cephas, Bartholomew, and Jude of James.) A comprehensive discussion on the possible sources and tradition of the apostolic names can be found in Lake, 'The Twelve and the Apostles', in *The Beginnings of Christianity*, V, pp. 37-59, especially pp. 42-43.

30. Other ancient texts have 'Labbaeus' or 'Labbaeus called Thaddaeus'.

31. Cf. Klassen, *Judas*, p. 34.

Mark and Matthew), then the author's deletion of Judas' name from the list in Acts 1.13b immediately reveals his intention. The author's intention, I suggest, is to make a strong statement, that is, 'the traitor is gone!' It was not just a list showing that Judas is no longer part of the Twelve. Nor is the author simply saying that the apostles were now down to Eleven. It is a list declaring that Judas Iscariot, the one who betrayed Jesus, who in turn had also tainted the honour and reputation of the apostles, has been dropped and forever banished from the exclusive list.[32]

What I have just argued above is how the list of the apostles' names in 1.13 can be viewed as suggesting that the betrayer is no longer part of the apostolate. If this argument is viable, then we can see the subtle and initial attempts of the author to clear the image of the apostles from the dishonour which Judas has brought upon them. However, I also argued earlier that the list in v. 13 does not stand on its own. The list is found within the pericope of 1.12-14. In other words, finding the list in the middle of two other verses compels any exegete to investigate how the pericope functions as a whole. This again is where I see the model of the rituals of status transformation works best. I propose that we see the concept of *communitas* among the apostles as initiands in the pericope of 1.12-14. Our clue begins from the question, why has the author enumerated the names of the apostles and then left the other characters in the upper room nameless? Why has the author taken time to individually identify the Eleven and then simply mention in passing the women and Jesus' family? Finally, and more intriguing, what is it about the women disciples and Jesus' family that captures the author's attention and wins them the right to be mentioned as having unanimity with the commissioned apostles before the election of Matthias in 1.15-26 and the outpouring of the Spirit in Acts 2.1-4?

1.2.2. *Distinction by Enumeration.* Individually naming the apostles while leaving the other disciple groups in their collective identities inevitably creates distinctions and distance between the groups mentioned in 1.13-14. The distinctions do not necessarily suggest, however, the immediate superiority of one group over the other. What seems to have been another accomplishment of the enumeration is the focus on the enumerated group. In other words, not only is the author able to tell his readers through

---

32. Detailed discussion on the role and character of Judas will be done in the section of Peter's speech, vv. 16-20.

enumeration the exclusion of Judas from the apostolate, the enumeration directs the readers to focus their attention on the Eleven apostles.

From the rituals of status transformation perspective, the focus that has been achieved through enumeration also relays the fraternal nature of the apostolate. The contrast that has been created by the author's decision to identify the apostles and leave the other disciple groups in their collective identities projects the unique status of the group of the apostles. On one hand, the contrast implies exclusivity, while on the other, it suggests the camaraderie of those who belong to the apostolate. This, I suggest, is a subtle expression of *communitas* among the initiands.

While indeed the enumeration of the names of the apostles suggests the unique status of the Eleven over the other disciple groups in the upper room, the author's option to leave the other groups individually unnamed does not render their characters insignificant. In fact, I find the presence of the other disciple groups mentioned in 1.12-14 more intriguing. As I have asked earlier, 'what is it about these groups that they deserve the honour of being mentioned at precisely this point?'

My suggestion is simple. I propose that the author is attempting to win the support of the clienteles of these other disciple groups for the apostles' leadership status. More specifically, I find that this networking strategy in 1.12-14 is crucial to what the apostles as initiands are about to face, that is, the event which is about to take place in the upper room—the initiands' ritual confrontation. To explicate this proposal, I need to get an idea of the relationship between the Eleven and the other disciple groups mentioned in 1.12-14. The next section deals with this issue.

2. *The Eleven with the Women Disciples*

At first I thought it possible to make the case that the author of Luke–Acts made special mention of the γυναῖκές in Acts 1.14 to show the reconciliation of the Eleven with the women disciples. This thought is based on two interrelated points of reference: the Eleven's recent rejection of the women's testimony about Jesus' resurrection (Lk. 24.10-11), and more significantly, my general assumptions that Luke–Acts advocated raising the status of women. Unfortunately, these assumptions crumbled.[33]

---

33. Borrowing from S. Davies' expression in 'Women in the Third Gospel and the New Testament Apocrypha', in A. Levin (ed.), *'Women Like This': New Perspectives on Jewish Women in the Greco-Roman World* (Atlanta, GA: Scholars Press, 1991), p. 188.

There is really no reconciliation needed with the women disciples by the Eleven since, in the first place, there was no particular problem with them being women witnesses.[34] The rejection of the women's testimony about Jesus' resurrection is not because they were women, but because the event itself was too incredible to believe.[35] Such an outlook also applies to many of the Lukan scenes where the encounters of Jesus with women are sometimes misconstrued as emphasizing Jesus' exceptional concern. For instance, Luke's story of a handicapped and possessed woman in Lk. 13.10-17 should be seen as stressing the healing of the woman on the Sabbath and not the fact that Jesus healed a woman.[36] Likewise, the story of the sinful woman in Lk. 7.36-50 which brought strong criticism against Jesus by his host, a Pharisee, emphasizes not that Jesus was anointed at his feet by a woman, but primarily because she was a sinner.[37]

That the author was campaigning to elevate the lowly status of women is only one of the standard views of Luke–Acts.[38] There were also those

34. Ben Witherington III discusses the conditions and weight of a woman's witness in both the legal and social contexts. *Women in the Ministry of Jesus*, pp. 9-10. For further discussion on this issue, see also T. Ilan, *Jewish Women in Greco-Roman Palestine* (Tübingen: J.C.B. Mohr, 1995), pp. 163-66.

35. I.R. Reimer, *Women in the Acts of the Apostles: A Feminist Liberation Perspective* (trans. L.M. Maloney; Minneapolis: Fortress Press, 1995), p. 233. Luise Schottroff explains further that 'the disciples cannot believe any longer that Jesus still is the liberator of Israel since he had died after all (see Luke 24.20-21)'. Their disbelief continued despite witnessing an empty tomb (Lk. 24.24) and hearing the testimony of two of their male colleagues (24.13-35). It was only after Jesus showed himself personally that the apostles believed (24.36-43), *Let the Oppressed Go Free: Feminist Perspectives on the New Testament* (trans. A.S. Kidder; Westminster: John Knox Press, 1991), p. 103.

36. Davies, 'Women in the Third Gospel', p. 188.

37. Davies, 'Women in the Third Gospel', p. 118; cf. 5.17-26.

38. See, for example, A. Plummer who suggested that 'the Third Gospel is in an especial sense the Gospel for women', *A Critical and Exegetical Commentary on the Gospel according to St. Luke* (eds. C.A. Briggs, S.R. Driver and A. Plummer; ICC Series; New York: Charles Scribner's Sons, 1906), p. 528; F.W. Ferrar, *The Gospel according to Luke*, Cambridge Greek Testament for Schools and Colleges (ed. A. Carr; Cambridge: Cambridge University Press, 1912), p. xxxv; H. J. Cadbury, *The Making of Luke–Acts* (London: SPCK, 1958), pp. 263-64; V. Taylor, *Behind the Third Gospel: A Study of the Proto-Luke Hypothesis* (Oxford: Clarendon Press, 1926), p. 214; also R. Bultmann who finds Luke as having a 'sentimental feature' for women, *The History of Synoptic Tradition* (rev. edn; New York: Harper & Row, 1968), p. 367; R.J. Karris

who promoted the view that the author was primarily egalitarian.[39] Up until today, there are some modern scholars who pursue the idea that the third evangelist showed special favour upon women.[40] For example, Dennis M. Sweetland, in an article entitled 'Luke the Christian' believes that the author is 'more progressive than his Jewish or Greco-Roman contemporaries' for suggesting that there is equality between men and women.[41] Constance F. Parvey reads the stories of women in Luke–Acts as offering to instruct the women believers in the early church in the radical revision of the roles of women.[42]

The multiplication of stories about women, especially that of the author's tendency to pair stories about women with stories about men, is one of the reasons why others see Luke as having special concern towards women.[43] These parallel pairs of stories of men and women showing

provides a further list of those who hold this view in 'Women and Discipleship in Luke', *CBQ* 56 (1994), pp. 1-20 (2, n. 4).

39.   That the author believed that, 'man and woman stand together and side by side before God. They are equal in honour and grace, they are endowed with the same gifts and have the same responsibilities (cf. Gal. 3.28)'. H. Flender, *St. Luke Theologian of Redemptive History* (trans. R.H. Fuller and I. Fuller; London: SPCK, 1967), p. 10.

40.   E.g. C.F. Parvey states that both Luke and Acts 'have been compiled in a Hellenistic setting and may well reflect the more emancipated attitudes toward women in that setting', in 'The Theology and Leadership of Women in the New Testament', in R.R. Ruether (ed.), *Religion and Sexism* (New York: Simon & Schuster, 1974), pp. 139-46 (138); E.J. Via, 'Women, the Discipleship of Service and the Early Christian Ritual Meal in the Gospel of Luke', *St. Luke's Journal of Theology* 29 (1985), pp. 37-60; Quesnell, 'The Women at Luke's Supper', pp. 59-79.

41.   D. M. Sweetland, 'Luke the Christian', in E. Richard (ed.), *New Views on Luke and Acts* (Collegeville, MN: Liturgical Press, 1990), p. 60. Likewise, R.J. Cassidy believes that Luke gives an outlook on women which is 'extremely progressive'. R.J. Cassidy, *Jesus, Politics, and Society: A Study of Luke's Gospel* (Maryknoll, NY: Orbis, 1978), pp. 23-24.

42.   Parvey, 'Theology and Leadership', p. 138.

43.   For example, the story of the centurion's servant who was rescued from death in Lk. 7.1-10 (cf. Mt. 8.5-13) is seen as a pair to the healing of the widow's son in 7.11-17; cf. E.J. Via, 'Women in the Gospel of Luke', in U. King (ed.), *Women in the World's Religions: Past and Present* (New York: Paragon House, 1987), pp. 38-55. Mary Rose D'Angelo gives a complete list of the 'pairings' in Luke–Acts which includes: two first miracles: for possessed man and Peter's mother-in-law (Lk. 4.31-39 // Mk 1.21-31); two lists of named disciples: men apostles (Lk. 6.12-19 // Mk 3.12-19) and two women ministers (Lk. 8.1-3); two penitents: the paralytic (Lk. 5.19-26 // Mk 2.1-12) and the penitent woman (Lk. 7.35-50 // Mk 14.1-11?); two 'releases': the bent-

Luke's regard for women as being equal with men have met strong objections from more recent exegetes. Stevan Davies, in his work 'Women in the Third Gospel and the New Testament Apocrypha', explains that the more 'obvious motives should take precedence'.[44] For example, with the centurion's servant and the widow's son who were both rescued from death (Lk. 7.1-17), Davies argues that,

> ...one of Luke's christological perspectives is that Jesus is a prophet in the manner of Elijah or Elisha. Jesus' introductory sermon in Nazareth is evidence for this claim, and from that sermon one might expect Jesus to raise the son of a widow as did Elijah and to heal a leper as did Elisha. Luke does add to Mark a story of raising of a widow's son (7.11-17) similar to 1 Kings 17.17-24, and the story of Jesus' healing of ten men with leprosy (17.12-19). Thus the pericope depicting the widow of Nain cannot to be adduced as evidence of the evangelist's concern for women in general or widows in particular; it is primarily an attestation of Jesus' likeness to Elijah.[45]

over woman (Lk. 13.10-17) and the dropsical man (Lk. 14.1-6 // Mk 3.1-6?); 2 taken: men (?) sleeping, women grinding (Lk. 17.32-35 // Mt. 24.40-41); two examples of prayer: widow, Pharisee and publican (Lk. 8.9-17); two attitudes to worship: scribes and widow (Lk. 20.45-21.4 // Mk 12.37-44); two sets of followers: Simon and women (Lk. 23.26-32 // Mk 15.21); two groups of watchers: women and all his acquaintances (Lk. 23.49 // Mk 15.40-41); two groups of resurrection witnesses (Lk. 24//Mk 16.1-8); M.R. D'Angelo, 'Women in Luke–Acts: A Redactional View', *JBL* 109.3 (1990), pp. 441-61. D'Angelo also suggests that there are two kinds of pairing methods. First is a unit of two brief stories with 'an identical point or similar function, one about a male and one about a female'. These techniques may have had some influence from Q, while others are probably from Mark. Basically, D'Angelo explains, this kind of pairing shows the story about the man to be traditional, while that of the woman is special to Luke. For example, the man who had a hundred sheep (Lk. 15.1-7 // Mt. 18.10-14) and the woman who had ten coins (Lk. 14.8-10). The second kind is labelled as 'architectural' pairs. These, as D'Angelo claims, as 'similar stories told in different contexts to bind the narrative together and to manifest the coherence of "God's plan of work" (cf. Acts 5.38-39 with 2.23; 13.36; 20.27)'. While pairings also exist in Acts, their occurrences are fewer and of a different nature. The signature 'both men and women' or even the names of couples are used instead of paired stories (p. 445). On the other hand, O'Toole reads these pairings as suggesting that 'Men and women receive the same salvific benefits. God, Christ, and the disciples act in their lives in similar fashion. Women and men experience and fulfil similar functions. They believe and proclaim the gospel message.' Cf. R. O'Toole, *The Unity of Luke's Theology: An Analysis of Luke–Acts* (Good News Studies, 9; Wilmington: Glazier, 1984), p. 120.

44.   Davies, 'Women in the Third Gospel', pp. 185-97.

45.   Davies, 'Women in the Third Gospel', pp. 188-89. It is also worth noting that the pairing technique is not original to Luke. The evidence shows that Luke follows

For Davies, the alleged exaltation on the status of women in Luke–Acts is primarily a methodological concern. He believes that to effect the liberation of an apparent marginalized group there ought to be the literary evidence of both the subjugation and liberation.[46] If the case is so obvious that evidence for subjugation is unnecessary, Davies argues that there should be evidence 'in contemporary texts or from common human experience'.[47] Luke's concern for the poor needed no explicit demonstration on their status in society. What we clearly see is the author's portrayal of Jesus' sympathy towards them. No such subjugation is shown or implied with the women. Davies adds that,

> Luke depicts women, without needing Jesus' intervention, as self-reliant. The widow who demands justice from the unjust judge eventually achieves her goal (18.1-8); Anna, Elizabeth, and Mary the mother of Jesus act independently and with self confidence; and so forth… I see no elevation of women's status in Luke. Unless one presumes the society of the time to be pathological to the extent that women were regarded as despised, disreputable, beyond the pale of respectable society, and so forth (as some scholars do although Luke, Mark, Matthew, Paul, John, Josephus, etc., do not), then Jesus' actions in regard to women are nothing unusual.[48]

Further objections have been raised by recent feminist scholars. Elisabeth Schüssler Fiorenza observes that the multiplication of stories about women, plus the pairing technique, makes the author of Luke–Acts more transparent about his attitude towards women. Fiorenza argues that while the author was well aware of the ministries in which the women of Luke–Acts were involved (such as prophets, missionaries, deacons), he did not attempt to reflect these in his narratives.[49] Likewise, Barbara E. Reid warns that,

> Although it is indisputable that there were women disciples in Luke and Acts, a closer study reveals that they do not participate in the mission of

---

Mark in the stories of the healings of both a man and a woman in Lk. 4.33-39//Mk 1.23-31. The parable of the shepherd in Lk. 15.1-7 is paired with the parable of the woman who lost ten coins in Lk. 15.8-10 which may have been original to Q. In short, Luke is not doing anything new. The pairing technique may have been from his sources which do not necessarily advocate the exaltation of women.

46.   Davies, 'Women in the Third Gospel', p. 185.
47.   Davies, 'Women in the Third Gospel', p. 185.
48.   Davies, 'Women in the Third Gospel', pp. 186-87.
49.   E. Schüssler Fiorenza, *In Memory of Her: A Feminist Theological Reconstruction of Christian Origins* (New York: Crossroad, 1983), p. 50.

Jesus in the same way that the men disciples do. If we are looking to Luke's narrative to show that women and men shared equally in Jesus' mission in the first century, we will be disappointed.[50]

Davies rightly concludes that the whole issue on the multiplication of stories on women, plus the pairing of women stories with stories about men, simply reflects *the author's attempt to engage the attention of his female audience.*[51] We can further assume that the need for the multiplication of stories about women arises because of the possibility that a greater proportion of Luke's audience were women,[52] and that, in some way or the other, these women played significant roles in the community, which the author of Luke–Acts (and also the male readers) fully recognizes.[53] If this assumption is correct, I now have a good background from which I can base my hypothesis as to why the women disciples are figured to be one of the groups which the author wanted to project as having unanimity with the Eleven.

Evidence that certain women played significant and influential roles in the society, and that some of these women were instrumental to Christian leaders who were carrying out their Christian mission, is supported by the example we find in Rom. 16.1-4. These passages serve as a window in understanding why Paul may have wanted to tap the services of Phoebe— a woman of high social status in the Roman community. For instance, Robert Jewett argues that Phoebe, a deaconess of the church in Cenchreae and a patron to Paul and his churches, was the answer to the problems the apostle was facing in his quest for a Spanish mission.[54] Because there was no apparent Jewish population in Spain on which Paul could establish

---

50.   B.E. Reid, *Choosing the Better Part: Women in the Gospel of Luke* (Collegeville, MN: The Liturgical Press, 1996), pp. 3-4.

51.   See also Parvey, 'Theology and Leadership', pp. 140-42; Davies, 'Women in the Third Gospel', p. 190.

52.   And probably even children as 'households' had been baptized together which meant the presence of children.

53.   The assumption that women were definitely part of Luke's audience is made by Downing. In his work 'Theophilus' First Reading of Luke–Acts', Downing suggests that the wider audience of Luke were men and women who met together to listen to the reading of either Paul's letters or that of Luke. However, while the assembly was composed of both women and men, the status remained of unequal terms (pp. 92-93).

54.   R. Jewett, 'Paul, Phoebe, and the Spanish Mission', in J. Neusner *et al.* (eds.), *The Social World of Formative Christianity and Judaism: Essays in Tribute to Howard Clark Kee* (Philadelphia: Fortress Press, 1988), p. 151.

his mission base, and because of Paul's inability to speak Latin—the predominant language (apart from the variety of languages spoken in Spain during the first century) used at that time—Phoebe and her vast network of contacts or clientele together with her presupposed wealth and social prominence justifies Paul's endorsement and 'recommends' (συνίστημι) this woman patron to his churches (Rom. 16.1).[55]

Arguing that Paul's letter to the Romans was actually intended for Ephesus and not Rome, C.F. Whelan nevertheless agrees with Jewett on the significance of Phoebe and her social influence on Paul's missions strategy. Whelan states that,

> Whether Paul expected her support and patronage for a proposed Spanish mission as Jewett proposes, or whether, as I have argued, her destination is Ephesus, it is reasonable to assume that he expected her to play some role in support of his efforts, and hence was an integral part of his proselytizing activity.[56]

That women like Phoebe greatly helped in drawing support and influence from either the political, missions, and other propagantic purposes of the apostles is not at all surprising. Women in the Roman society had enjoyed many privileges and freedom which placed them in a position to acquire wealth and freely dispose of it.[57] This wealth and social influence has made it more probable that women like Phoebe gained positions of leadership. This same position is what became to be very attractive amongst those who wanted to seek support and backing for their own agenda.[58]

3. *The Eleven with Mary and Jesus' Brothers*

Surprisingly, the family of Jesus also gets to be mentioned here in Acts 1.14.[59] Although they are absent from the majority of significant events in Jesus' life and ministry, Luke finds it important to name Mary and Jesus' brothers as the other group present in the upper room. Acts 1.14 is the second and last instance where Jesus' family is noticed.[60] And in this last

---

55. Jewett, 'Paul, Phoebe, and the Spanish Mission', p. 151.
56. Whelan, 'Amica Pauli', p. 73.
57. Whelan, 'Amica Pauli', p. 75.
58. For further examples of these women patrons, see again Whelan, 'Amica Pauli', pp. 71-85.
59. J. Dunn concurs. Cf. *The Acts of the Apostles*, p. 16.
60. The first being Lk. 8.19-21.

instance, the author tells his readers that Jesus' family were in unanimity with the Eleven in the upper room before they faced the group of 120 brethren (Acts 1.15-16).

So why did the author choose to tell his readers that the Eleven were in unanimity with Jesus' family before the election of Matthias takes place? In the rituals of status transformation perspective, we may ask, 'As a ritual element, what is the role of Jesus' family in the transition stage of the initiands?' To answer this question, we need to know what the author of Luke–Acts has so far informed his readers about Jesus' family.

3.1. *Jesus' Family in Luke–Acts*

The study of Jesus' family in Luke–Acts can come from two sources. First is an extensive set of references on Mary (Jesus' mother) in the infancy narratives of Lk. 1–2;[61] and second, there are merely two references to Mary and Jesus' brothers in the rest of the gospel and the book of Acts.[62] While indeed the infancy narratives present vast information about the mother of Jesus, they cannot however serve as an objective source for my study on Jesus' family. One of my main reasons is that Mary is presented as a character in her own right in the infancy stories. In other words, Mary is not presented with Jesus' brothers as a family unit. This has been so, not only because of the uniqueness of Mary's character, but primarily because of the uniqueness of the whole infancy narratives of Lk. 1–2. The arguments for the uniqueness of the infancy stories include: (1) that the gospel of Luke originally begins in ch. 3;[63] and (2) the genre of the infancy

---

61.   Reumann, *Mary in the New Testament*, p. 105.

62.   I disagree with Reumann as he sees Lk. 11.27-28 as another passage which speaks of Jesus' mother. The text does not show any evidence which directly refers to the character of Mary. Cf. Reumann, *Mary in the New Testament*, p. 171.

63.   In line with this, for example, R. Brown argues, 'The solemn beginning of John's ministry in Lk. 3.1-2 could well have been served as the original opening of the gospel; Both the gospels of Mark and John open the gospel story with the events surrounding the baptism of Jesus; The reference to Jesus' baptism by John the Baptist as the beginning in Acts 1.22; The placing of the genealogy in the third chapter of Luke makes more sense if that had been before and the infancy narrative had been prefixed; As was true also with Matthew's gospel, none of the Lukan infancy narratives have had a major influence on the body of the gospel, so that if the first two chapters had been lost, no one could have ever suspected of their existence.' For an exhaustive discussion on the nature of Luke's infancy narratives, especially on issues of composition history and its incorporation into the gospel, see Brown, *The Birth of the Messiah*, pp. 25-38; 239-55.

narratives is different from the rest of Luke–Acts.[64] Because of our agenda, therefore, there are only two accounts in Luke–Acts which tell about Jesus' family. These are Lk. 8.19-21 and Acts 1.14. I will present my discussion of Acts 1.14 in the ritual process section.

Lk. 8.19-21 is a parallel to Mk 3.31-35.[65] According to J. Reumann, Luke has significantly altered his sources in order to project a positive image of Mary and Jesus' brothers in contrast with the family's negative image in Mk 3.31-35. In Reumann's words,

> Luke removes any element of hostility from the fact that the mother and brothers are outside: 'They were not able to reach him on account of the crowd'. In Mark/Matthew when the news is given to Jesus about the presence of his mother and brothers outside, he replies with a question which challenges their status as his true family: 'Who are my mother and my brothers?' No such question is asked in Luke.[66]

Green's analysis is more subtle. For Green, Luke uses Jesus' family as a unit or party in contrast to another party, the disciples. He does not praise or reject his physical family. Rather, he uses them as a 'catalyst'[67] to drive home to his hearers (the disciples and the crowds) the true meaning of kinship. 'Kinship in the people of God is no longer grounded in physical descent, he contends, but is based on hearing and doing the word of God'.[68] When pitted against Mk 3.30-35, the redaction in Luke's version indeed makes a statement. Although the lesson may fall on the true meaning of kinship, Luke teaches this lesson by a make-over of the negative image of Jesus' family in Mark into a positive one in his gospel. Reumann is correct to observe the Lukan redaction as an attempt to influence a change in the perception of Jesus' family by his readers.[69] While, for some, the changes may not necessarily be projecting a positive

---

64. So Barrett, *The Acts of the Apostles*, p. 89.
65. A study on the redaction of the Markan parallel by Luke on this specific passage may be found from my ThM thesis 'A Redaction-Critical Study on the Relationship of the Spirit, Proclamation and Miracle-Working Power in Luke–Acts' (Asia Graduate School of Theology, Philippines, 1994). The same thesis has been modified as an article and published in *Phronesis*, 'The Spirit, Prophecy, and Miracle-Working Power', Asian Theological Seminary (vol. 2; 1996), pp. 1-53.
66. Reumann, *Mary in the New Testament*, p. 168.
67. Green, *The Gospel of Luke*, p. 330.
68. Green, *The Gospel of Luke*, p. 330.
69. See also Johnson, *The Acts of the Apostles*, p. 34.

image of the family,[70] they are enough to redeem them from a negative image pictured in Mark's and Matthew's versions. Other than Lk. 8.19-21 and Acts 1.14, the author does not tell much about Mary and the brothers of Jesus.[71] Either the evangelist does not have any other information, or he opts not to say anything more.[72]

This attitude is relatively the opposite when it comes to the other women in Jesus' ministry. Similar to Mark and Matthew, Luke mentions the presence of the women disciples of Jesus during his crucifixion, the burial, and the finding of the empty tomb. Luke even takes it a step further by naming some of the women who were involved. In contrast, Luke does not mention the presence of Mary, Jesus' mother, or even some of the brothers, in the same significant events.[73]

If one is to speculate on the tradition concerning Jesus' family based on the only available information (i.e. Lk. 8.19-21 and its corresponding parallels in Mark and Matthew, plus the single passage in Acts 1.14) certain factors stand out. First, tradition indeed speaks of a family of Jesus. This family is always billed as the 'mother' and the 'brothers' of Jesus.

Second, it is a tradition which rarely speaks of Mary as an individual, and likewise, does not present Jesus' brothers separate from the character of Mary their mother. In other words, the characters 'mother and brothers' have not been primarily introduced as independent from each other. This

---

70.　Johnson, *The Acts of the Apostles*, p. 34.

71.　The brothers of Jesus are named James, Joses, Simon and Judas in Mk 6.3 (par. Mt. 13.55). These brothers were not known to be Jesus' disciples (cf. Jn 7.5) until the resurrection where Jesus is said to have appeared before James (1 Cor. 15.7). Other sources (e.g. Ephipanus in *Panarion* 78) say that Joseph had a former wife with whom he had sons making these therefore Jesus' half brothers. On the other hand, Tertullian (*Against Marcion* 4.19) insists on the view that Jesus really had full brothers. This view was later on strongly promoted by the Roman Christian, Helvidius, who was known to be against the teaching of the Virgin birth. In reply, Jerome (*Adv. Helvidium de perpetua virginatate b. Mariae*) suggested that the brothers were actually Jesus' cousins, sons of Alphaeus by 'Mary of Clopas' whom he inferred from Jn 19.25 to be the Virgin's sister. Bruce, *The Acts of the Apostles*, p. 107; for a detailed discussion on the various views on Jesus' brothers, see R. Brown, K. P. Donfried, J. A. Fitzmyer, and J. Reumann (eds.), *Mary in the New Testament*, pp. 289-92; also J. McHugh, *The Mother of Jesus in the New Testament* (London: Darton, Longman & Todd, 1975), pp. 200-54.

72.　Not even James is presented as Jesus' brother (12.17; 15.13; 21.28).

73.　Reumann, *Mary in the New Testament*, p. 173.

is why B. Malina's and J.H. Neyrey's suggestion is helpful. They claim that because Mary was a widow, she now probably lives on her own and, therefore, lacks the protection of a male, either husband or son. She becomes vulnerable but Luke changed that. Luke, according to Malina and Neyrey, 'defends the honour of Jesus by guarding the shame of Mary and by locating her in a new family, an honourable household, the Church'.[74] If Malina's and Neyrey's social reading of Mary's status is correct, then it supports my understanding that the gospel tradition, when presenting the said characters (or at least the evidence in the synoptic gospels minus the infancy stories), has rarely separated Mary from the brothers of Jesus. This also supports the probability that Mary, while being a widow, has been understood by tradition as maintaining a stable status because of Jesus' brothers. From this idea (an idea I have already reiterated earlier in the ritual elements section), I submit that the phrase 'Mary and Jesus' brothers' (especially in 1.14) can be understood as referring to a group—a 'family group'—rather than emphasizing the separate identities of Mary as Jesus' mother, and the brothers of Jesus as Jesus' brothers.

Third, if Reumann is correct in saying that the reason for the Lukan redaction of Mark's and Matthew's version of Jesus' family is to project a more positive image, then tradition could have originally known the family with a passive or negative image—an image probably understood in terms of the family's reservations against Jesus and his ministry (cf. Mk 3.31-35). This idea of a negative image has been supported by Bauckham's study of Jesus' relatives. He states, 'During his ministry Jesus' relationship with his family was not entirely smooth (Mark 3.19b-21; 6.4; John 7.5)'.[75]

Luke's attempt to mellow down the negative image of Jesus' family may be related to the way the book of Acts has shown that at least one of Jesus' brothers ended up as a great church leader.[76] Gospel tradition in general confirms this. Again Bauckham argues that, '...the references to and naming of relatives of Jesus in the Gospel traditions indicates that they were well-known figures in the early church',[77] and that the popu-

---

74. B. Malina and J.H. Neyrey, 'Honor and Shame in Luke–Acts: Pivotal Values of the Mediterranean World', in Neyrey (ed.), *The Social World of Luke–Acts*, p. 64.

75. R. Bauckham, *Jude and the Relatives of Jesus* (Edinburgh: T. & T. Clark, 1990), p. 56.

76. E.g. The role of James in the Jerusalem council in Acts 15.

77. Bauckham, *Jude and the Relatives of Jesus*, p. 56.

larity of Jesus' relatives may have had real influence in the period of the development of Gospel tradition.[78]

From the ideas I have just presented, we can now draw some probable reasons as to why the Eleven apostles are projected to have unanimity with the women disciples and Jesus' family in the upper room. The author picks the right place to relay such an encouraging scene. The author understands that the picture of unanimity between the Eleven and the two influential disciple groups would be very helpful for the apostles who are about to have an audience with the 120 brethren (and the wider Christian community) in the upper room (Acts 1.15-26). In the RST context, these two disciple groups serve as ritual elements which the initiands take with them as they are about to go through what is apparently a difficult ritual confrontation.

My argument is not hollow. I find concrete evidence in the way the author emphasizes this scene of unanimity between the Eleven and the two disciple groups in Acts 1.14. The author uses the unusual word ὁμοθυμαδόν ('with one accord' or 'with one mind') in order to convey the idea that the apostles have the backing of these two influential groups as the Eleven propose to take the unprecedented step of choosing another apostle to replace Judas. The next section investigates and explains this evidence.

3.2. ῾Ομοθυμαδόν *in Luke–Acts*

Commentators agree that while the word ὁμοθυμαδόν may have originally meant 'with one accord' or 'with one mind', its present usage in the NT is none other than the simple 'together'. To them, the meaning of ὁμοθυμαδόν has lost its original force and has become greatly weakened in the NT. In other words, the notion of unanimity among those who are gathering together is obsolete. This view was originally proposed by Edwin Hatch and has become quite influential in Lukan studies.[79] In his book *Essays in Biblical Greek* which investigates the value and use of the Septuagint for understanding the meaning of words and psychological terms in Biblical Greek,[80] Hatch argues that ὁμοθυμαδόν started to lose its primary notion of 'with one accord' in the LXX.[81] He cites three obser-

---

78. Bauckham, *Jude and the Relatives of Jesus*, p. 57.

79. E.g. Barrett, *The Acts of the Apostles*, I, p. 89; Newman and Nida, *A Translator's Handbook*, p. 23.

80. Originally published in 1889, E. Hatch, *Essays in Biblical Greek* (Amsterdam: Philo Press, 1970), p. 63.

81. Including the non-canonical writings, there are thirty-six occasions: Exod. 19.8;

vations: (1) It is used to translate Hebrew words which means simply 'together';[82] (2) It is interchanged with other Greek words or phrases which mean simply 'together';[83] (3) It occurs in contexts in which the strict etymological meaning is impossible.[84] Together with the word's occurrences in the NT, Hatch concludes that ὁμοθυμαδόν can mean nothing else but the simple 'together'.[85]

Hatch's conclusion has some merit. The employment of ὁμοθυμαδόν in the LXX is varied and inconsistent. Indeed, in some cases, translating the word with its etymological meaning of 'with one accord' is clearly inappropriate for the contexts concerned.[86] However, extending this observation into the NT raises some significant questions. For one, apart from Rom. 15.6, all of the occurrences of ὁμοθυμαδόν are in the book of Acts. And it is the evidence in Acts that invites some doubts to Hatch's observations.[87]

The gospel of Luke has at least twelve occasions[88] on which the words

---

Num. 24.24; 27.21; 1 Esd. 5.46, 56; 9.38; Job 2.11; 3.18; 6.2; 9.32; 16.10; 17.16; 19.12; 21.26; 24.4, 17; 31.38; 34.15; 38.33; 40.13; Jer. 5.5; 26.21; Lam. 2.8; Jud. 4.12; 7.29; 13.17; 15.2, 5, 9; 3 Macc. 4.4, 6; 5.50; 6.39; Wis. 18.5, and 12.

82.   Replaces either יחד, e.g. Job 3.18 ('There the prisoners are at ease together, they hear not the voice of their taskmaster'); or יחדו, e.g. Job 2.11 ('They made an appointment together to come to condole him and comfort him').

83.   Such as ἅμα in Gen. 13.6, 22.6; ἐπὶ τὸ αὐτό in Deut. 22.10, Jos. 9.2; κατὰ τὸ αὐτό in Exod. 26.24, 1 Sam. 30.24.

84.   As in Num. 24.24 where reading ὁμοθυμαδόν as 'with one accord' would not fit the context ('And one shall come forth from the hands of the Citians, and shall afflict Assur, and shall afflict the Hebrews, and they shall perish together', αὐτοὶ ὁμοθυμαδόν ἀπολοῦνται); 1 Chron. 10.6 'So Saul died, and his three sons on that day, and all his family died at the same time' (ὅλος ὁ οἶκος αὐτοῦ ὁμοθυμαδόν ἀπέθανε); Job 38.33 'And you know the changes in heaven, or the events which take place together under heaven?' (ἐπίστασαι δὲ τροπὰς οὐρανοῦ ἢ τὰ ὑπ' οὐρανοῦ ὁμοθυμαδόν γινόμενα). English translations from Sir Lancelot C.L. Brenton, *The Septuagint with Apocrypha: Greek and English* (Grand Rapids: Zondervan, 1851).

85.   Hatch, *Essays in Biblical Greek*, p. 64.

86.   For example, Num. 24.24; Job 6.2; 17.16; 24.17; 34.15; 38.33; etc.

87.   Dunn believes that ὁμοθυμαδόν is typical of Luke but fails to explain why the word was not used in the gospel, Dunn, *The Acts of the Apostles*, p. 16. One possibility is that the author did not want to completely alter his sources since he was simply replicating scenes or events from Gospel traditions. For this discussion, see A.J.P. Kenny, *A Stylometric Study of the New Testament* (Oxford: Clarendon Press, 1986), p. 72.

88.   The RSV's translation submits fifteen. However, both Lk. 6.38 and Lk. 23.18

'together' or 'gathered together' rightly translates its corresponding Greek term. With the exception of Lk. 24.33 where ἠθροισμένους from ἀθροίζω emphasizes the 'collective' gathering of the Eleven apostles (thus the number ἕνδεκα immediately follows),[89] most of these terms are from words with συν-prefixes.[90] Συν-prefix words are compound verbs which basically carry the intention of the preposition συν, 'together with' or 'including'.[91] When these are prefixed before a verb, most of the time, the meaning of the root verb is retained and the action is executed co-operatively, not by an individual, but by groups to which the prefix συν applies.

In the book of Acts, there are thirty-two occasions in which the author wants to convey the meaning of characters being or gathering 'together'. Out of these thirty-two, ten instances are occupied by the adverb ὁμοθυμαδόν while the rest are again of the συν-prefix verbs.[92] With this proportion (including that of the gospel), we can assume that the author was fairly used to employing the συν-prefix words in contexts involving the assembling together of characters in a given situation. It is also this assumption that leads us to believe that the author would not have employed the word ὁμοθυμαδόν simply for the convenience of having alternative expressions to convey the meaning 'together'. It is possible, therefore, to say that the author understands and applies the word's etymo-

can be read without the word 'together'. In Lk. 23.18, the use of the phrase Ἀνέκραγον δὲ παμπληθεὶ λέγοντες instead of a sun-prefix verb places emphasis on the act of 'crying out' by the multitude rather than on their presence as a group gathered together in a context where they demanded for the release of Barabbas over Jesus.

89.	BAGD, 'ἀθροίζω', p. 21.

90.	Lk. 8.4 συνιόντος; 9.1 συγκαλεσάμενος; 12.1 ἐπισυναχθεισῶν; 13.34 ἐπισυνάξαι; 15.6 συγκαλεῖ; 15.9 συγκαλεῖ; 17.37 ἐπισυναχθήσονται; 22.55 συγκαθισάντων; 22.66 συνήχθη; 23.13 συγκαλεσάμενος; 24.15 συζητεῖν; 24.33 ἠθροισμένους.

91.	Cf. 'Συν' in *BDF*, p. 119.

92.	Acts 1.6 συνελθόντες; 1.14 ὁμοθυμαδὸν; 2.6 συνῆλθεν; 2.44 ἦσαν ἐπὶ τὸ αὐτὸ; 2.46 ὁμοθυμαδὸν; 3.11 συνέδραμεν; 4.5 συναχθῆναι; 4.24 ὁμοθυμαδὸν; 4.26 συνήχθησαν; 4.27 συνήθησαν; 4.31 συνηγμένοι; 5.9 συνηφωνήθη; 5.12 ὁμοθυμαδὸν; 5.21 συνεκάλησαν; 7.57 ὁμοθυμαδὸν; 8.6 ὁμοθυμαδὸν; 10.24 συγκαλεσάμενος; 12.12 συνηθροισμένοι; 12.20 ὁμοθυμαδὸν; 13.44 συνήχθη; 15.6 συνηχθῆσαν; 15.25 ὁμοθυμαδὸν; 15.30 συναγαγόντες; 16.13 συνελθούσαις; 18.12 ὁμοθυμαδὸν; 19.25 συναθροίσας; 19.29 ὁμοθυμαδὸν; 19.32 συνελελύθεισαν; 20.7 συνηγμένων; 21.30 συνδρομη\; 25.17 συνελθόντον; 28.17 συγκαλέσασθαι.

logical meaning, and that is, to convey the 'inner unanimity' between the groups who were gathered together.[93] In other words, when the author prefers the adverb ὁμοθυμαδόν to the more common συν-prefix verbs, special attention is given to the bonding or unity of the group/s involved. For instance:

1. Chapter 2 of Acts has a series of 'coming together' scenes. In 2.1, the narrator tells that 'when the day of Pentecost had come, they were all in one place (ἦσαν πάντες ὁμοῦ ἐπὶ τὸ αὐτό)'.[94] In 2.6, the narrator speaks of the multitude who 'came together' (συνῆλθεν) into Jerusalem to celebrate Pentecost. After Peter gives his Pentecost speech, the narrator describes the same multitude who believe and are converted with the phrase ἦσαν ἐπὶ τὸ αὐτὸ καί in 2.44, commonly translated as 'together'. Suddenly, the author switches to ὁμοθυμαδόν in referring to how the same crowd who got converted attended the temple 'day by day' and 'breaking bread in their homes, they partook of food with glad and generous hearts'.

What we have here, therefore, are distinctions in the nature of the gathering. In 2.1, the emphasis falls on the fact that the people were in 'one' place as the Spirit came to fill the 'house' where they were (2.2b). This explains why the author uses ὁμοῦ (occurs only once) instead of ὁμοθυμαδόν in 1.14.[95] In 2.6, the author uses the typical συν-prefix word συνῆλθεν simply to indicate that the multitude are assembling together to observe the phenomenon which was taking place (i.e. the 'noise' they were hearing).

From the same multitude came 3,000 who repented and were baptized (2.41). These new believers 'devoted themselves to the apostles' teaching and fellowship'. In 2.44, the author uses the phrase ἦσαν ἐπὶ τὸ αὐτὸ καὶ similar to v. 1 except for πάντες ὁμοῦ. Again, while the phrase may be translated as meaning 'together', it literally suggests that the new believers were staying with each other or have 'continued' to be in the company of

---

93. It signifies the group's 'exemplary unity' (Fitzmyer, *The Acts of the Apostles*, pp. 213, 215); or 'spiritual unity' of the believers says (Johnson, *The Acts of the Apostles*, p. 34).

94. There is a considerable discussion on whether the reference to the 'place' means the same 'upper room' (ὑπερῷον) in 1.14, or a 'house' (οἶκος) as stated in v. 2. From a discourse level, I think the matter is irrelevant. The author simply intends to say that the people were at the same place together, not even as a group or a community, but emphasizes the 'locality' (hence the use of ὁμοῦ ἐπὶ τὸ αὐτό). Cf. Barrett, *The Acts of the Apostles*, p. 112.

95. This is also probably why the scribes of C3, E, Y, and M have maintained ὁμοθυμαδόν so as to be consistent with 1.14.

each other.[96] This explains the corresponding descriptions that 'they all held things in common' (2.44b) and 'they sold their possessions and distributed to the poor' (2.45).

When the author switches to ὁμοθυμαδόν in 2.46, he is not simply creating variety with terms. Rather, he completes the whole picture of the conversion of the people who were once scattered and have come from different places (2.7-11) but now become a united community of believers. Their unanimity is climaxed by the descriptions of attending the temple 'day by day' and with the corresponding communal activities such as 'breaking bread in their homes, partaking of food with glad and generous hearts, praising God and having favour with all the people' (2.47).

2. Chapter 4 gives a clearer picture of how the author again suddenly switches to the adverb ὁμοθυμαδόν from a series of συν-prefix verbs. In v. 5, we have the typical 'gathering together' (συναχθῆναι) description which places attention on the act of being assembled in a certain locality. It describes the gathering of the rulers, elders and scribes in Jerusalem with Annas the high priest, Caiaphas, John and Alexander, together with the high-priestly family. The agenda is to interrogate Peter and John about their illegal preaching activities (4.5-32).

Unable to find any concrete offence, plus the fear of going against the people who found favour for the apostles after having witnessed the healing of a forty-year-old man, they released Peter and John with a stern caution. The two apostles returned to their friends and reported what they had just gone through in the hands of the top religious leaders (4.23). After hearing their testimony, the narrator describes the friends' response with the phrase 'they lifted their voices together' (ὁμοθυμαδόν ἦραν φωνὴν) to God (4.24). The response includes a quotation from Ps. 2.1-2 where a typological connection is made between the rulers during king David's time who were 'gathered together (συνήχθησαν) against the Lord', and with the leaders Herod and Pontius Pilate, who, like the rulers, were 'gathered together' (συνήχθησαν) in the city of Jerusalem against Jesus (4.25-27).

It makes sense to understand the etymological meaning of ὁμοθυμαδόν

---

96.   The construct ἐπὶ τὸ αὐτο (which appears here and in 1.15; 2.1; 2.47 and 4.26) is debated concerning its precise translation. Either 'in assembly', or 'in the community'. However, its Hebrew equivalent יחד is something more technical referring to the community at Qumran (cf. 1QS 1.1; 3.7). Witherington, *The Acts of the Apostles*, p. 162; Fitzmyer, *Acts*, p. 271.

in 4.24. The expression of praise conveys not only that it was done by a group, but adds substance to the meaning of unanimity in response to the deliverance of Peter and John from the religious leaders. On the other hand, when describing the simple assembly, either in a place or because of an event, the author uses the συν-prefix words readily. Such is in 4.31, where the narrator emphasizes the 'place' of gathering (συνηγμένοι) as being shaken after the people who were gathered had prayed.

In 3.11, the people who witnessed the healing of the lame man by Peter and John are described as having 'run together' (συνήρδραμεν) to the apostles into a place called 'Solomon's portico'. The same description and place is depicted in 5.12. The people who had just witnessed the signs and wonders of the apostles are said to have gathered together in 'Solomon's portico'. This time, however, the author employs ὁμοθυμαδόν instead of the συν-prefix word he used in 3.11 despite having mentioned the same location, Solomon's portico. Nevertheless, the reason for the distinction is clear. In 5.12, the author places emphasis on the unanimity of the apostles who were gathered in Solomon's portico. The context speaks of the probable fear of the people to approach the apostles after having heard of the death of Ananias and Sapphira in 5.1-11. The function of ὁμοθυμαδόν also distinguishes the apostles as a unified group in contrast with 'the rest' (τῶν λοιπῶν) 'who dared not to join them'. Their unanimity is further enhanced when the narrator describes how the people held the apostles in 'high honour' (5.13).

Finally, not even the occasion when groups are said to have gathered to pray is described by the author with ὁμοθυμαδόν. One may think that this is the perfect occasion by which the author might have wanted to emphasize the group's unanimity.[97] Unfortunately, this is not always the case. Take for example 12.12 where Peter walked away from prison by the help of the Lord's angel (12.6-11). After realizing that he had escaped, the narrator tells his readers that Peter went straight to the house of Mary, the mother of John. This house was the place where many were 'gathered together' and were praying. The author employs συνηθροισμένοι καὶ προσευχόμενοι instead of ὁμοθυμαδόν in describing the group and their activity. The focus falls on the place where Peter had gone to, a place where the apostle found his support-group praying for him. It also sets up the story for the appearance and surprise of Rhoda, a member of the group.

97. Compare 1.14.

When she answered the door and saw Peter already standing before her, the group was still engaged in prayer (12.13-17).

While there is no clear pattern by which we can predict when and at what context will the author of Luke–Acts prefer ὁμοθυμαδόν over the συν-prefix words or any other construct, we can, however, see common narrative features where ὁμοθυμαδόν has been employed:

1. In contexts where people respond to the preaching of the word, signs and wonders.

After the multitude who were gathered together listened to Peter's speech (Acts 2.14-40), there were those (numbering about 3,000 [2.41b]) who received the apostle's message and were converted and baptized that day. The same language 'and they devoted themselves to...prayer' in 2.42 is used by the narrator as in 1.14. Come 2.43, the narrator gives the impression to his readers that fear (φόβος) or awe came upon the people as he immediately reports the many wonders and signs (πολλά τε τέρατα καὶ σημεῖα) which were performed by the apostles.[98]

The narrator uses two ways to describe the gathering of those who believed. In 2.44, he states that 'all who believed were together' (πάντες δὲ οἱ πιστεύοντες ἦσαν ἐπὶ το αὐτό), while in v. 46 he uses ὁμοθυμαδόν to mean the gathering with feasting, rejoicing,[99] generosity amongst them, and the praising of God.

In Acts 5.12, the death of Ananias and Sapphira had caused great fear (φόβος μέγας) upon the whole church. Keeping to themselves some of the proceeds of the land which they had sold, Peter sees this as lying against the Holy Spirit and against God himself. It is the awe of God and his righteousness that has overcome those who have heard of such an incident.

The incident is immediately followed up by the author with a summary statement (5.12-16). The narrator begins by reporting the 'many signs and wonders' (σημεῖα καὶ τέρατα πολλά) that were done by the apostles among the people. He adds that these people were all together (ὁμοθυμαδὸν) with the apostles in Solomon's portico.[100]

---

98.   The force of the imperfect tense ἐγίνετο is such as to indicate that the apostles were continuously causing miracles and wonders and that the people were constantly filled with awe. Newman and Nida, *A Translator's Handbook*, p. 64.

99.   Or 'gladness' from the word ἀγαλλιάσις which suggests eschatological joy in the presence of the Lord. Johnson, *Acts*, p. 59. Cf. Lk. 1.14, 44, 47; 10.21. Compare LXX Pss. 9.2; 12.5; 19.5; 20.1; 30.7; 39.16, etc.

100.   Witherington views that 'the signs and wonders are not done within the

In Acts 8.6, the multitudes of Samaria found themselves being 'with one accord' (ὁμοθυμαδόν) in response to Philip's preaching of the word and the signs he performed. This event is presented by the narrator as having taken place after the scattering of those who were on the run from Saul's persecution of the church (8.1-3).[101]

2. In contexts of praise.

Acts 4.24 is in some ways similar to the first three passages. The narrative talks of Peter and John who were boldly preaching about Jesus. They also performed signs by healing a crippled man (4.5-11). This activity caught the attention of the priest, the captain of the temple, and the Sadducees (cf. 4.1). The bid to stop the two apostles from their activity was unsuccessful. The popularity of the two amongst the people who witnessed the healing of the crippled man prevented the protagonists from holding Peter and John much longer. They were eventually released and the two headed back to their friends, testifying to what had just happened (4.13-25). The narrator describes the friends' response as a 'united (ὁμοθυμαδόν) lifting of voices' in praise to God (v. 24). Just like 2.46, 5.25 and 8.6, 4.24 is a 'unanimity in response' to something; in this case, a response to the testimony of Peter and John.

The rendering of ὁμοθυμαδόν as a 'united voice' here in 4.24 finds an almost similar expression in Rom. 15.6. While the contexts are different, and while the combination ὁμοθυμαδόν ἦραν φωνὴν in 4.24 is rendered with the more literal ὁμοθυμαδόν ἐν ἑνὶ στόματι δοξάζητε (that together you may with one voice glorify), the intention of inviting a *united declaration of praise to God* is identical.

A good example outside the NT is in the *Letter of Aristeas*.[102] The word ὁμοθυμαδόν in this epistle is found in line 178. We pick up the story from line 172 where the narrator, speaking in the first person, is with his companion Andreas, together with some envoys and heavy security. They

confines of the house church but among the "people" (λαὸς), which here must surely mean the Jewish people who are not yet converts'. Witherington, *The Acts of the Apostles*, p. 224.

101. Heidland describes the substance of ὁμοθυμαδόν in these three examples as 'stressing the inner unanimity in response to' the teaching, preaching, accompanied by signs and wonders. H.W. Heidland, 'ὁμοθυμαδόν', *TDNT*, V, pp. 185-86.

102. H. Meecham, *The Letter of Aristeas: A Linguistic Study with Special Reference to the Greek Bible* (Manchester: Manchester University Press, 1935), p. 25. See also, 'The Letter of Aristeas', in R.H. Charles, *The Apocrypha and Pseudepigrapha of the Old Testament in English*, II (Oxford: Clarendon Press, 1913), pp. 110-11.

are dispatched by Eleazar to meet with the King of Alexandria and personally hand over gifts of parchments. These valuable parchments contain the Law, written in Jewish characters and inscribed in gold. When the king finally sees this gift from Eleazar, he is very pleased with it, extending his gratitude even to them, the couriers of the parchments. Seven times, the king bows down before the couriers to express his joy and gratitude. Seeing this, the envoys and all who are present before the king shouted out 'at one time with one voice (ὁμοθυμαδόν): God save the King!' These exaltations and praises from everyone made the king burst into tears of joy. From thereon, the king has decreed to make that day a great day in their history. The couriers are treated with high respect and receive special treatment during the course of their stay.

3. In contexts of anger and rage.

The next set of ὁμοθυμαδόν passages comes from a context opposite to the previous two classifications we have just mentioned. This time, the unity of the people is instigated, not by signs and wonders or praise, but by anger and rage. In 7.57, 18.12 and 19.29, crowds of people were enraged by the preaching of Stephen and Paul. Chapter 7 verse 57 speaks of the martyrdom of Stephen by the united effort of the people in stoning the disciple to death. Likewise, 18.12 and 19.29 relate the two instances where the audience of Paul's teaching were offended, and thus, united themselves to mount an attack against the apostle. The only difference between these two accounts is that in the latter Paul was able to avoid harm due to the wise counsel of the other disciples who were with him.

The use of ὁμοθυμαδόν in contexts of groups united by rage against their opponents is also evident outside the NT. Striking similarities are found between the martyrdom of Stephen and that of Polycarp. The narrative goes on to say that in the presence of the Pro-Consul, Polycarp is being asked to renounce his faith while the crowd who is eager to hear his defence awaits outside the court. The Pro-Consul has threatened Polycarp with death by wild beasts. And if Polycarp defeats the beasts, he will then have to be consumed by fire. Finally, the Pro-Consul has given up on Polycarp as he was challenged to make good his threats.

Sending the Pro-Consul's herald to the waiting crowd, the herald breaks the news that Polycarp has strongly confessed to being a Christian. The narrator states that when this news has been heard from the herald, 'all the multitude of heathen and Jews living in Smyrna cried out with uncontrollable wrath and a loud shout: "This is the teacher of Asia, the father of the Christians, the destroyer of our Gods, who teaches many neither to offer sacrifice nor to worship" '. This multitude then asked Philip the Asiarch to let loose the wild beasts to devour Polycarp. However, because the hunting time is closed, such an act would be illegal. The multitude then 'found it good to cry out with one mind (ὁμοθυμαδόν)' that Polycarp should be burnt alive, a manner of execution which Polycarp himself has seen through a vision.[103]

4. In contexts of petitions and appeasement.

The narrative in Acts 15 tells of the coming together of a group who needed to appease an offended party. Chapter 15, verses 22-29 speak of the letter from the council of apostles and elders to the gentile believers concerning the choosing of Silas and Judas (also called Barsabbas). These two are described to be chosen 'from among their own men' (ἐκλεξαμένους ἄνδρας ἐξ αὐτῶν) and are to accompany Paul and Barnabas to Antioch. The mission of the four was to serve as witnesses that indeed the letter of instructions pertaining to the believers' dilemma genuinely came from the council. Apparently, there were some teachers, not sanctioned by the council, who arrived and taught them disturbing instructions about the partaking of food sacrificed to idols, the eating of blood from strangled animals, and sexual immorality.

The context speaks strongly of the need for the apostles and elders to

---

103. Other classic examples include Josephus' *Antiquities* 15.277. The author explains that on every fifth year, Herod held athletic competitions in honour of Caesar. He built a theatre in Jerusalem and a large amphitheatre in the plain. They were reckoned to be great and lavish occasions and structures. All around the theatre were trophies of the nations which Herod defeated in war. These trophies were made of pure gold and silver, displayed for people to see, including other precious stones and garments. Other highlights included the combat of condemned men to fight each other and men against wild beasts. All these spectacle were found to be very entertaining to the foreigners but very offensive to the natives of Jerusalem, the Jews. For the Jews, the sight of throwing men to be devoured by wild beasts for the pleasure of spectators is a challenge to their custom. However, what was most objectionable was the display of trophies in the belief that they were images surrounded by weapons. Herod noticed the Jews' anxiety and displeasure against him and his trophies. However, he thought it best not to force the trophies on them and therefore made reassurances to the Jewish leaders in the hope of winning back their confidence. Herod did not succeed in his attempt to pacify the people. The Jews 'cried out with one voice (ὁμοθυμαδόν)' that although everything else might be tolerated, the sight of images of men being brought into the city was a blatant attack against their custom. Herod finally summoned the leaders of the Jews into the theatre and ordered that the trophies be stripped of the lavish garments and weapons which adorned them.

assemble and make a decision in order to appease the gentile believers. The council states, 'it seemed good to us, having come to one accord (ὁμοθυμαδόν) to choose men and send them to you...' In other words, the apostles and elders had to come together for a consensus in order to solve the present problem with the gentile Christians.

From my study of the use of ὁμοθυμαδόν in Acts and in some classical examples, I note the following observations. First, the word is exclusive in showing the unanimity of people in groups. Ὁμοθυμαδόν has not been applied to individuals assembling or meeting together. Second, it is not used for inanimate characters, presumably because they do not emote feelings and inner views in order to express unanimity. Third, the word has been used to describe the unanimity not only with believers but also with their opponents.[104] Fourth, the call or reason for unanimity is often compelling and urgent. Finally, it is also used to show the unanimity of opposing or socially distinct groups.[105] With these observations, I am confident that Hatch's conclusion about ὁμοθυμαδόν in the NT, which bears the simple idea of being together, is weak.

3.3. Ὁμοθυμαδόν *in Acts 1.14*

This leads us to see how ὁμοθυμαδόν functions in 1.14. While it is the first instance in Acts where the word is used, it appears to be quite distinct from the others. Its distinction lies in the specific reason why the narrator calls for the unanimity of the characters in the upper room. In other words, as we have described the various instances where the author employed ὁμοθυμαδόν, the agenda in Acts 1.14 is not as clear as the others. The following are possible scenarios:

First, the call for unanimity in the upper room is in response to the need to elect Judas' replacement. This scenario is indeed very attractive. For one, its context exhibits striking similarities with the narrative of ch. 15. For example, just as the replacement of Judas was chosen among the rest of the disciples in the upper room (a company of 120 [1.15]), Judas called Barsabbas and Silas who were chosen 'from among their own men'

104. For the believers—Acts 1.14; 2.46; 4.24; 5.12; 8.6; 15.25; for their opponents—Acts 7.57; 12.20; 18.12; 19.29. Witherington, *The Acts of the Apostles*, p. 113; Johnson, *Acts*, p. 34.

105. E.g. on the concept (although in a negative way) 'men and women should not at all follow the same pursuits "with one accord" (ὁμοθυμαδόν) with all their might'. *Plato on Laws, Book VII* (Loeb); also, the unanimity of the heathen and the Jews in their bid for Polycarp to be immediately executed, *The Matryrdom of Polycarp* (Loeb).

(ἐκλεξαμένους ἄνδρας ἐξ αὐτῶν) and are to accompany Paul and Barnabas to Antioch (15.22b). Both contexts speak of Jerusalem as the place of gathering (1.12//15.2b). Both mention the presence of groups or parties (1.13-14//15.5-6). There is the 'gathering together' to consider a matter (1.14//15.6). After the gathering, Peter stands among the brethren (1.15//15.7). Peter gives a speech (1.16-22//15.7b-11). A quotation from Scripture is given (1.20//15.16-18). Both assemblies participate in the choosing of at least two men from amongst them (1.23//15.22).

While the two stories indeed exhibit some parallels, their differences are also clear in such a way that the reason for the use of ὁμοθυμαδόν in 1.14 may not necessarily be the same as that of Acts 15. In other words, as ὁμοθυμαδόν expresses the unanimity of the apostles, elders, and the whole church in Acts 15 in response to the need of choosing and sending two disciples to tackle the problem with the gentile Christians in Antioch, the unanimity in the upper room happens even before the problem about Judas' replacement was expressed. To put it more precisely, most of our ὁμοθυμαδόν examples state their reasons beforehand which then is followed by the need to demand unanimity amongst the participants. Because we do not find this in 1.14 (that is, the problem concerning the need to replace Judas which we expect to occur before the occurrence of ὁμοθυμαδόν, then, there must be other compelling reasons why the author has opted to use the word.

The other option is to understand the commission by Jesus of his apostles in Acts 1.8 as the reason for the need to have unanimity amongst the characters in the upper room. If this assumption is correct, then we have ὁμοθυμαδόν in its proper place, namely, after the reason which eventually calls for the unanimity of the participants. Yet again, this scenario also presents some legitimate questions, one of which is the fact that the apostles were the only direct recipients of Jesus' commission in 1.8. The women, Mary the mother of Jesus, and Jesus' brothers only enter the scene after Jesus had ascended, and before the apostles even have returned into Jerusalem. In other words, why would the narrator include the other group characters to be in unanimity with the apostles if they were not recipients of the commission? While it is true that the reader eventually understands the inclusion of other characters as recipients of Jesus' divine instructions,[106] it still does not comply with the common narrative

---

106. As Fitzmyer argues, 'It must now spread abroad (the news of Jesus' resurrection) through such testimony borne by Jesus' followers, first of all by apostles, but then by others; they are all to become ministers of the Word...' Fitzmyer, *Acts*, p. 206.

features mentioned earlier on the characteristic use of ὁμοθυμαδόν in Acts.

The last plausible option is to understand that the reason for the use of ὁμοθυμαδόν lies within the confines of Acts 1.12-14 itself. What I mean is that, both the narrator and the reader understand that the call for unanimity applies, not only in response to Jesus' commission in 1.8 or in solving the problem about Judas in 1.15-26, but also for the mending of social differences which had long been understood about the groups represented in the upper room. In other words, the author attempts to show that the preparation events in Acts 1 include both the replacement of Judas and the election of Matthias stories (1.15-26), and crucially, the breaking down of social barriers between the known groups of Jesus' followers.

The author of Luke–Acts achieves two significant goals in mentioning the unanimity of the parties in the upper room. First, he is able to show that the Eleven apostles enter the 'court of reputation' (Acts 1.15-26) with the backing of two important disciple groups. This in turn suggests to the audience that whatever is about to take place in the upper room, the two disciple groups already find favour for the Eleven apostles. Second, the author also finds the influential standing of the women disciples and Jesus' family within the Christian community as key to the community's acceptance and approval of the apostles' succession to Jesus' leadership. As we have mentioned before, this is typical of ὁμοθυμαδόν contexts, that is, the call for unanimity even between different parties. This assumption, therefore, can explain the sudden mention of the groups of women disciples and Jesus' family as those present in the upper room before the election of Matthias in Acts 1.15-26 and the outpouring of the Spirit in ch. 2.

From the perspective of the RST, the apostles as initiands now have on their side crucial ritual elements as they prepare to enter into the phase of ritual confrontation. Where Jesus' ritual confrontation was with his encounter with the devil in Lk. 4.1-13, Jesus was equipped with the fullness of the Spirit (Lk. 4.1). The apostles, likewise, enter their stage of ritual confrontation equipped with the approval and recognition of what could be two of the most significant disciple groups (apart from the apostles) in the Christian community.

4. *Summary*

Acts 1.12-14 is the first phase of the apostles' stage of transition in the rituals of status transformation. In this phase, the initiands' status is unclear and undefined. Despite being commissioned by Jesus to be his witnesses in Acts 1.7-8, the fullness of their status does not come until they complete the ritual of status transformation. The road to completion involves experiencing that state of liminality and *communitas*.

The concept of the initiands' *communitas* may be read behind the enumeration of the names of the Eleven apostles (v. 13). This concept of *communitas* becomes more prominent when contrasted with how the author has opted to simply mention the other characters in v. 14 collectively rather than by their names. With the women disciples, for example, we know that the author could name names if he wanted to do so just as he does with the women disciples of Jesus in Lk. 24. But here in 1.14, the reference to the women did not go further other than by stating their presence in the upper room as a group. The same goes with Jesus' family. Although Mary is mentioned by name, she is mentioned not as an individual but in the company of Jesus' brothers.

We also suggested that this first phase of the transition stage provides the scene of the initiands' preparation for the ritual confrontation. The preparation is seen in the way the apostles are portrayed as having unanimity with the two disciple groups, namely the women and Jesus' family. The author employs the unusual word ὁμοθυμαδὸν which translates as 'with one accord'. This word is apparently used mostly in Acts and only with occasions involving urgency or groups with distinct social differences. I proposed that the author wants to convey the unanimity of the Eleven apostles with other disciple groups who may have had strong reservations against the group to which the traitor Judas belonged. Yet when the apostles had these two groups behind them, the probability of the Christian community accepting their leadership status is no longer remote.

This picture of unanimity is instrumental on the part of the author in pursuing his campaign to promote the leadership image of the apostles. Within the terms of patron-client relations, the apostles as brokers ought to win the support of other disciple groups. This the author has achieved by tapping the web of social networks through which the women disciples and Jesus' family may have played influential roles. The sight of these two disciple groups having unanimity with the Eleven apostles conveys approval and social acceptance. The author hopes that this will pave the way for other patrons/brokers and their vast network[107] of clientele to recognize the leadership of the Eleven apostles.

107. A network is a 'web of relationships between any combination of friends, clients, brokers and patrons that acts overtime with numerous exchanges of gifts, favours, and commitments. Networks may vary in size, mutuality and duration', K.C. Hanson and D.E. Oakman, *Palestine in the Time of Jesus: Social Structures and Social Conflicts* (Minneapolis: Fortress Press, 1998), p. 200. Modern social anthropologists have classified the characteristics of social networks (characteristics which will be helpful in my analysis of the narrative of Acts 1) under two criteria: morphological and interactional. The following discussions were summarized from J.C. Mitchell, 'The Concept and Use of Social Networks', in J.C. Mitchell (ed.), *Social Networks in Urban Situations: Analyses of Personal Relationships in Central African Towns* (Manchester: University of Manchester Press, 1969), pp. 12-36.

Chapter 6

The Apostles and their Case against Judas

1. *The Ritual Elements in Acts 1.15-26*

After the Eleven have secured the support of the two disciple groups (the women disciples and Jesus' family) they now enter the second phase in the transition stage. This phase is the ritual confrontation. Recalling McVann's description, he states,

> Certain status transformation rituals require some form of mock battle or hostile confrontation as a final step in the initiand's achievement and public recognition of the new status. In some instances there is real violence, in others, only playful and harmless insults. In others, however, there is controlled and highly focused expression of hostility and tension such as occurs in a challenge-riposte situation.[1]

Contrary to the common notion that Acts 1.15-26 is about the reconstitution of the Twelve, I see a more consistent flow of the narrative when the same text is viewed as the apostles' defence in a 'challenge-riposte' situation. I say this because of the following features in Acts 1.15-26:

First, I read Peter's speech not as a speech *per se* but as an apologetic speech. I will attempt to show that Peter acts as the apostles' spokesman and delivers their defence (or riposte) concerning the apostles' relationship with the 'traitor' Judas. This relationship, as I have proposed, is the basis for the challenge against the apostles' honour and leadership integrity.

Second, there is the presence of the rest of the 120 brethren. We read this group as the representative of the Christian community in general who were in the same room prepared to hear the defence of the apostles.

The third factor is the apostles' concession to resolve the situation. This involves two important steps: the immediate excommunication of Judas from the apostolate; and the setting up of the strict criteria for choosing

---

1. McVann, 'Rituals of Status Transformation', p. 340.

Judas' replacement. I suggest that the criteria do not only serve as guidelines in choosing the new apostle but as a crucial move on the part of the Eleven to assure the community that the traumatic experience created by Judas will not happen again. The concession on the part of the Eleven is even sustained by the fact that they do not choose the twelfth apostle themselves but by simply putting forward the final two candidates.

Fourthly, there is the apostles' move to place the responsibility upon God to make the final choice from the two candidates for Judas' replacement. This move not only exonerates the Eleven from their shameful association with Judas but also gives the community the assurance that, because the new apostle was divinely chosen by God, their fear of another 'Judas' within the apostolate is remote.

The next section discusses the ritual elements in Acts 1.15-26. These include the characters of Peter, Judas, and the manner by which the replacement for Judas was conducted—the casting of lots. The characters of Joseph Barsabbas, Matthias, God, and the 120 people are secondary and thus their descriptions will be incorporated into the ritual process section.

In order to fully grasp the atmosphere of a confrontation in a challenge-riposte situation, I will present a brief discussion on the concept of honour and shame. As stated, I intend to use this conceptual model as a backdrop in bringing out the social issues embedded in the narrative of Acts 1.15-26.

1.1. *Peter as Spokesman*

When Peter stood up 'among the brethren' (1.15) and gave his first speech, commentators conclude that Peter acts as a leader[2] of the 120 people who were in the upper room. Such a conclusion does not seem to fit the scenario we see in the text. From the very time the apostles were introduced by the author in Acts 1.3, until they are aggregated and formally stand in the presence of the multitude in 2.14, the apostles are the focus of the narrative. It is therefore more plausible to suggest that all the author speaks of in Acts 1–2 centres on the Eleven apostles of Jesus.

The election narrative of 1.15-26 is not an exception. The subject of the narrative is not any other group of people but the apostles. The other characters involved (such as the women, Jesus' family, the 120 persons,[3]

---

2.   E.g. Dunn, *The Acts of the Apostles*, p. 18. See also K.P. Donfried, 'Peter', *ABD*, V, p. 253.

3.   Which would probably include the women and Jesus' family in the count.

Joseph Barsabbas, and Matthias) are, thus, all but secondary characters or they play supporting roles. Peter, therefore, speaks for and on behalf of the subject of the narrative—the apostles.

When viewed from this perspective, we can see how the plot which I have suggested earlier works well. We find Peter portraying the role of a spokesman for their group.[4] As I proposed, the 120 people serve as the body representing the Christian community who are to hear the case of the apostles concerning their defence on the challenge against their honour and leadership integrity brought about by their association with the betrayer Judas. The women disciples and Jesus' family serve as witnesses and support group for the defendants. The presence of these two disciple groups in the 'court of reputation' helps to strengthen the credibility of the Eleven apostles as the ordained group to lead the Christian community in the temporary absence of Jesus.

1.2. *Election by the Casting of Lots*

Another significant ritual element in this phase of ritual confrontation is the use of the lot in choosing the apostle to replace Judas. As I initially proposed, the decision to cast lots to determine God's choice in place of Judas has two underlying intentions: (1) to allay the fears of a 'Judas' comeback; and (2) to repair the damage Judas had done to the reputation of the apostolate by electing a righteous and trustworthy replacement.[5] The following section looks into the background of the casting of lots.

The use of lots in judicial decisions within the OT is found in the story of Achan (Josh. 7.10-21); the choosing between David and Jonathan (1 Sam. 14.40-42); the decision between the two goats on the Day of Atonement, and also the distribution of priestly tasks in the temple.[6] The casting of lots in Hebrew and Jewish religious life has also been used within the context of confrontation with Yahweh or with legal decisions. At times, the practice was for playful purposes.[7]

What is quite important in the Hebrew-Jewish tradition in the use of lots

---

4. Cf. Fitzmyer, *Acts*, p. 222.
5. Cf. Introduction section at 1.2.5.2.
6. E.g. Lev. 16.8; 1 Chron. 25.8; 26.13; Josephus, *Antiquities* 7.7.366-67.
7. 'Heads I win, tails you lose' story of the *Midrash Rabbah*, Lam. 1.1, 6. For the lot in legal decisions, see b. *Baba Bathra* 106b (division of land among the heirs), where the technical legal questions lead to the idea of the division of Canaan by lot, but the awareness of divine presence in the lot is entirely confined to the remembered ancient instance.

is its theological significance. The need for a supernatural intervention on crucial decisions, ruling out any human influence on the outcome, made the casting of lots the most welcome way. For example, there is the division of the land among the tribes by lot.[8] This suggests that the land was God's gift and not achieved by the recipient.[9] There may have been a relation, therefore, with the metaphor of 'inheritance' to which in Greek they are linguistically related. Thus, the statement in Ps. 16.5 'The Lord is my chosen portion and my cup, thou holdest my lot…' is significant. Used also in great decisions or actions of God, the text in Isa. 34.17 is important. 'He has cast the lot for them, his hand has portioned it out to them with the line; they shall possess it forever'.

In the Greco-Roman world, the casting of lots was strongly associated with the fatalistic apprehension of the divine. The choice of responsible officials attributed by Aristotle to Solon is a good illustration.[10] Also in situations of conflict, the ambition to seize power, and the desire to evade responsibility can be found in Homer's writings.[11]

The use of lots in relation to the divine eschatological decision of God is particularly common in the Qumran writings. The dualistic concept in Qumran bears the language of 'two lots'. Thus, one finds the phrase 'the lot of the sons of light' in contrast to the 'lot of the sons of darkness'.[12] It must be stressed, however, that the lots are God's decisions and they do not necessarily represent a strong dualism. In other words, God's lot will decide the person's destiny, either that of God's side or not (1QS 4.25-26). The term 'lot' has come to mean 'the station assigned by God within the community'. Thus, 'No one shall either fall from his station, or rise from the place of his lot' (1QS 2.23; cf. 1QSa 1.9, 16). This idea of the lot

---

8. Num. 26.55-56; Josh. 18.6. Also, the procedure associated with the transfer of tribal land rights; cf. Josh. 18.6 and 18.9-10. A.M. Kitz, 'Undivided Inheritance and Lot Casting in the Book of Joshua', *JBL* 119.4 (2000), pp. 601-18 (602).

9. 'Yahweh's right to bestow the land as a gift', W. Rast, 'Joshua', in *Harper's Bibile Commentary* (New York: Harper & Row, 1988), p. 241.

10. Aristotle, *Ath. Resp.* 8; see also 'Roman Egypt' by Frank F. Abbott and Alan Johnson, in *Municipal Administration in the Roman Empire* (Princeton: Princeton University Press, 1926), pp. 78, 520-21.

11. Homer II.VII.170-79; see also the references in Plutarch cf. *Timoleon* 31.3-4.251. On Philo's awareness of the uncertainty of the lot, see *The Decalogue* 4.I.151.

12. 1QS I.9-11; 1QM II; 13.5, 9; cf. 1QH 3.22-23; 4.13. Cf. related phrases in 1QS 2.17; 4.24; CD 13.12); the 'men of God's lot and the men of Belial's lot' (1QS 2.2, 4; Wernberg-Moller's translation), cf. 3.24; 1QM 13.12, 18.1.

associated with God's decision may explain why such a concept is infrequent in the Manual of Discipline where decisions are made by the community. Scholars therefore suggest that the phrase 'the lot comes forth' in texts such as 1QS 5.3 and 9.7 is metaphorical and not literal.[13] It was the community who stated 'the fixed measure of the lot shall go forth with regard to every matter'. The word 'decision' is literally rendered 'lot' and is spoken in connection with admission of members in the community.[14] In the Damascus Document (13.3-4) the term 'lot' is used to mean decision and not the literal casting of lots.[15] Again Beardslee states, 'Whether the decision in question was reached by a majority vote is another matter. Such a conclusion should be viewed with some reserve, as the actual procedure may have been closer to what would today be called oligarchical rather than democratic.'[16] For example, the relation of the decisions of the priest and that of the community is not clear.[17]

The suggestion that the casting of lots, especially in the Qumran community, as primarily figurative or metaphorical was recently challenged by P.S. Alexander and G. Vermes. In their study of some of the scrolls found in Qumran Cave 4, these scholars claim that actual lots have been identified with Qumran, and thus, 'the possibility cannot be ruled out that divination by the (literal)[18] casting of lots was used for some purposes within the Community'.[19] From this idea,[20] Alexander and Vermes suggest that the casting of lots in the appointment of Matthias in Acts 1.23-26 may have involved actual lots. However, be it as it may, the result of the

---

13. Cf. P. Wernberg-Moller, *The Manual of Discipline* (Leiden: E.J. Brill, 1957), p. 92, n.15.

14. 1QS 4.18-19 (Wernberg-Moller's translation); cf. 6.16, 21-22.

15. Suggested long ago by Solomon Schechter, *Documents of Jewish Sectaries*, I (Cambridge: Cambridge University Press, 1910), p. 52, n. 18.

16. W. Beardslee, 'The Casting of Lots at Qumran and in the Book of Acts', *NovT* 4 (1960), p. 248.

17. Compare 1QS 9.7 with column 5, and cf. Wernberg-Moller, *The Manual of Discipline*, p. 134, n. 16.

18. My addition.

19. P.S. Alexander and G. Vermes, 'Qumran Cave 4, XIX: Serekh Ha-Yahad and Two Related Texts', *Discoveries in the Judaean Desert*, XXVI (Oxford: Clarendon Press, 1998), p. 222.

20. Although the theological meaning of the choice of Matthias is similar to that of the lot-metaphor at Qumran and in general Jewish apocalyptic examples, drawing relations between Luke and Qumran is not strongly recommended since the understanding of the divine purpose through the lot was widespread tradition, *BDB*, p. 174.

casting of lots is always understood as God's predestined choice of the successor to Judas and not simply how the lots fell.[21]

1.3. *Judas*

The question of how the reputation of Judas has affected the honour and leadership integrity of the Eleven will be dealt with in the ritual process section. However, before I can show that indeed such a reputation has disgraced the apostles, we need to know who Judas is by briefly looking into how tradition has portrayed him. In this section, three identifying aspects about Judas will be discussed: (1) the meaning of the suffix 'Iscariot', (2) the meaning of being 'one of the Twelve', and (3) the meaning of being a 'traitor'.

1.3.1. *The Suffix 'Iscariot'*. The suffix 'Iscariot' is believed to be not originally attached to the name Judas. C.C. Torrey in 1943 from Yale University first proposed that the appellation of the surname is related to the deed of Judas. Torrey believes that because there was no evidence at all that Judas was ever called with the surname Iscariot during his lifetime, the surname may have been a reproach or (in Torrey's exact words) 'an opprobrious appellation given the man because of his deed'.[22]

This proposal from Torrey was later disputed by A. Erhman who argued that, while it is true the suffix Iscariot may have been derived from the Jewish Aramaic *sharai, sheqarya*, and with the addition of the *alef, ishqarya* meaning 'false one, liar, hypocrite', Torrey has failed to consider the fact that all changes of name or the addition of nicknames in the NT are always explicitly noted.[23] Ehrman cites the examples of James and John—Boanerges (Mk 3.17); Simon—the Zealot (Lk. 6.15); Simon—Peter (Jn 1.42); Joseph—Barnabas (instituted by the apostles in Acts

---

21. Alexander and Vermes, 'Qumran Cave 4, XIX', p. 222. The Qumran example provides evidence for the practice of lots, and that especially in an eschatological setting, the term lot means 'a decision reached by the community' which mirrors the decision of God himself. As Beardslee states, 'Luke's source told of the decision of the community, using the metaphorical language which is evidenced from Qumran. Luke understood its theological meaning, that this was God's choice, not man's; and in shaping his story he objectified the mechanism of the divine choice in a literal casting of responsible officials, in the tradition of the Gentile world.' Beardslee, 'The Casting of Lots', p. 251.

22. C.C. Torrey, 'The Name "Iscariot" ', *HTR* 36 (1943), pp. 51-62 (58).

23. A. Ehrman, 'Judas Iscariot and Abba Saqqara', *JBL* 97.4 (1978), pp. 572-73 (572).

4.36); and Judas—Barsabbas (Acts 15.22).[24] In other words, the absence of the explicit reason as to why Iscariot was suffixed to Judas' name does not warrant the conclusion that Iscariot is related to Judas' deeds.

Other suggestions to the meaning of the surname include: (1) that Judas may have belonged to the group of the 'Sicarii' which were known to be 'dagger-wielding assassins' probably related to the Zealots;[25] (2) some believe that it indicates the person's hometown.[26]

While this issue focuses on why Iscariot is attached to the name Judas, and what this surname really means, there is one simple suggestion that helps the reader of the narrative; the surname Iscariot distinguishes the apostle from the other characters who bear the same name.[27]

1.3.2. *One of the Twelve.* The term 'the Twelve' occurs once in Paul,[28] nine times in Mark,[29] seven in Matthew,[30] eight times in Luke–Acts,[31] and four in John.[32] It is a term which does not simply indicate how many apostles Jesus has. Rather, this term is used to refer to the inner circle of Jesus' disciples.[33] It designates the special and exclusive group of twelve individuals whom Jesus himself has hand-picked, trained, travelled and lived with throughout the course of his public ministry.[34]

Studies on the meaning and function of the title 'the Twelve' in the NT have particularly been interested in knowing whether it was coined by the early church or whether it goes back to Jesus himself.[35] Those favouring the early church as the original source of the title are more inclined to believe that there was actually no exclusive twelve followers of Jesus. To them, the concept of the Twelve was a development of tradition probably in keeping with the OT tradition of having twelve tribes for the nation of

24. Ehrman, 'Judas Iscariot', p. 572. See also the review of A. Ehrman's study by Y. Arbeitman, 'The Suffix Iscariot', *JBL* 99.1 (1980), pp. 122-24.
25. Cf. O. Cullmann, *The State in the NT* (New York: Scribner, 1956), p. 15.
26. E.g. H.J. Klauck, *Judas—Ein Junger des Herrn* (Freiburg, 1987); quoted from W. Klassen, 'Judas Iscariot', *ABD*, III, pp. 1091-96 (1091-92).
27. Cf. Lk. 6.16; Acts 1.13; Jn 14.22. Klassen, 'Judas Iscariot', p. 1091.
28. 1 Cor. 15.5.
29. Mk 4.10; 6.7; 9.35; 10.32; 11.11; 14.10, 17, 20, and 43.
30. Mt. 10.2, 5; 19.28; 20.17; 26.14, 20, and 47.
31. Lk. 6.13; 8.1; 9.1, 12; 18.31; 22.3, 47 and Acts 6.2.
32. Jn 6.67, 70, 71; and 20.24.
33. Klassen, *Judas*, p. 34.
34. Jervell, *Luke and the People of God*, pp. 75-79.
35. Maccoby, *Judas Iscariot*, pp. 22-33; 34-49; 75-79.

Israel.[36] On the other hand, there are those who firmly believe that the Twelve did really exist, and that it was Jesus who formed this group to serve as his trainees and main protégés.[37]

Despite the debate on the origin of the title and concept of 'the Twelve', scholars agree that the term primarily carries with it the distinctive character and elite nature of the group which served as Jesus' main followers.[38] It is a group which is a class on its own, not to be mistaken with the other disciples or followers of Jesus. The fact that an apostle is named as a member of the Twelve, therefore, means that he is identified not only with an ordinary group but with an exclusive and elite group which commands honour and authority,[39] most especially after Jesus has departed and has left all leadership responsibility to this group.[40]

It is in line with this concept of membership in the Twelve that Judas' character should strongly be associated. In other words, any study on the identity, character, and apostleship of Judas conducted separately from the meaning and function of 'the Twelve' is not a good study at all. Judas is not Judas in the first place without the accompanying description of being 'one of the Twelve'. Judas would not have been the popular 'betrayer' if he was not a member of the Twelve.

The gospels have almost always introduced Judas Iscariot with two accompanying descriptions: the first is that he is one of the Twelve, and the second is his act of betrayal.[41] These descriptions seem to have been exclusive to Judas. His betrayal is not independent from his title 'one of the Twelve'. Other apostles who are also introduced individually in the gospels need not be described as being 'one of the Twelve'.[42] I propose,

---

36. See for example W. Horbury, 'The Twelve and the Phylarchs', *NTS* 32 (1986), pp. 503-27 (503-505); R. Schnackenburg, 'Apostles before and during Paul's Time', in W.W. Gasque and R.P. Martin (eds.), *Apostolic History and the Gospel: Biblical and Historical Essays Presented to F.F. Bruce on his 60th Birthday* (Exeter: Paternoster: 1970), p. 282.

37. For instance, R. Meye, *Jesus and the Twelve* (Grand Rapids: Eerdmans, 1968).

38. Cf. J.A. Kirk, 'Apostleship since Rengstorf: Towards a Synthesis', *NTS* 21 (1975), pp. 249-64 (253).

39. Gottfried Schille (as Klassen quotes) has suggested that, to be addressed with the description 'one of the Twelve' is a 'current designation of honour' for individuals; the predicate had its origin 'not fixed in a circle of people but from the church's recognition of the earliest followers of Jesus'. Cf. Klassen, *Judas*, p. 34.

40. Kirk, 'Apostleship', p. 253.

41. Mt. 26.14, 27; Mk 4.10; 14.10, 20, 43; Lk. 22.47; Jn 6.70-71.

42. For example, the apostle James who is introduced as a 'servant of God' yet

therefore, that the title 'one of the Twelve' is not used simply to distinguish Judas from the other Judases who are in the apostolate or are identified to belong to the other group of followers of Jesus;[43] the surname Iscariot is used to serve this purpose. Rather, I suggest that introducing Judas with the title 'one of the Twelve' combined with his act of betrayal ought to be understood with an element of sarcasm suggesting the horror of how an apostle who belonged to the inner circle of disciples could have betrayed Jesus.

This suggestion is supported by the two other occurrences in the NT whereby an apostle is introduced with the title 'one of the Twelve' (or a member of the Twelve) coupled with his identifying 'sin' against Jesus. For instance, Peter's denial of Jesus in the passion narrative can best be appreciated when reminded of the scene where the apostle was recognized as being a Jesus follower.[44] Furthermore, a most important example is the first and only instance where the apostle Thomas is introduced as a character in the NT. In Jn 20.24, Thomas like Judas bears the title 'one of the Twelve'. After such an introduction, the succeeding story presents how this apostle seriously doubted Jesus' resurrection from the dead (20.25). Thomas was later confronted and disabused of his doubts by Jesus' personal appearance complete with full evidence of the 'print of the nails' and 'mark on the side' on Jesus' body (Jn 20.26-31).

1.3.3. *The Traitor.* There are four references in Luke–Acts which deal with Judas in relation to his betrayal of Jesus: Lk. 22.1-6, 21-23, 47-53, and Acts 1.16-20. Lk. 22.1-6 opens the narrative by immediately introducing the brains behind the plot to kill Jesus—the chief priests and the scribes. These groups are portrayed as having resolved to destroy Jesus. But the question of how to carry out this plan without getting retaliations from the people is another matter.[45] By stating this devious plan up front and to execute such a plot without the crowd knowing it, the author portrays the religious leaders as the ones who are primarily responsible for Jesus' death.

While the primary responsibility of Jesus' death may rest upon the

without the title 'one of the Twelve' (Jas 1.1).
43. Cf. Judas son of James in Lk. 6.13-16.
44. Lk. 22.54-62.
45. The retaliation as implied by the phrase 'for they feared the people' in Lk. 22.2b.

religious leaders, Judas' role as betrayer is equally emphasized.[46] For example, in 22.3, the betrayer is presented in such a way that he is not to be mistaken with any other character in the scene as he is strongly and specifically described as, 'the one no other but Iscariot, that who is a member of the Twelve'.[47] This description is followed up with the phrase 'he went away and conferred with the chief priests and officers how they might betray him to them' (22.4).[48] The story goes on to show that the religious leaders were glad of Judas' plan of betrayal, and have agreed to reciprocate him with money (22.5). The plot to kill Jesus has been finalized and summarized by the author in 22.6. All the elements, therefore, of what is supposed to be a 'verbal contract' in order to destroy Jesus are laid out.[49] (1) Judas—the inside man, agrees; (2) Judas finds the perfect opportunity to betray Jesus; (3) Judas is to do this without the knowledge of the crowd. All these elements indeed lead any reader to agree that there is no better description to depict Judas other than the 'traitor'.

There is, however, one important aspect in the story which mitigates the role of Judas as traitor. The author, while indeed portraying Judas as the betrayer, adds the fact that 'Satan entered into Judas' (Lk. 22.3a) before the deal with the religious leaders was contracted. Klassen rightly observes that 'only in Luke does Satan enter Judas'.[50] Although Klassen's comment that 'Luke, furthermore, sets Judas on equal footing with the chief priests and officers of the Temple because he goes to negotiate with them',[51] I believe that it is more precise to say that Judas' meeting with the religious leaders aims to show the reversal of allegiance (i.e. from Jesus' camp to the enemies' camp) by one of the Twelve.[52]

---

46. K. Hein, 'Judas Iscariot: Key to the Last-Supper Narratives?', *NTS* 17 (1970–71), pp. 227-32 (228).

47. My paraphrase.

48. In contrast with Mk 14.10 and Mt. 26.14, Luke has the phrase καὶ στρατηγοῖς (officers) suggesting that temple authorities were involved in the plot to destroy Jesus (cf. 22.52). Cf. Marshall, *The Gospel of Luke*, p. 788.

49. Or, as Green terms it, 'human stratagems', *The Gospel of Luke*, p. 752.

50. Klassen, 'Judas Iscariot', p. 1093.

51. Klassen, 'Judas Iscariot', p. 1093.

52. Unlike in Lk. 22.3-6 where Judas is named as the betrayer of Jesus, Lk. 22.21-23 mentions the presence of a traitor but does not identify Judas to be that person at all. Cf. Maccoby, *Judas Iscariot*, pp. 52-53. I am not suggesting that Judas is not the betrayer. However, Green's observation on this passage is significant. He suggests that,

Finally, Lk. 22.47-53 speaks of the drama of Jesus' arrest. The cutting off of the ear and the manner by which Judas was supposed to betray Jesus, all make the scene of betrayal quite dramatic and intense. Here, the author identifies the traitor, not by his surname Iscariot (as he did in 22.3), but by his title of being 'one of the Twelve' (22.47b). Moreover, the addition of the descriptive phrase 'the man called Judas' makes no mistake as to who the author wants to identify as betrayer. Lastly, the attempt to betray Jesus with a 'kiss' does not heighten the relationship between the 'apostle and his leader' but primarily, the extreme treachery of the apostle's betrayal.[53]

From the descriptions by the author of Judas and his betrayal in Lk. 22, we find the following features: first is the consistent use of the term 'betray'; second is that the act of betrayal points to no other than Judas; and third is that Judas is referred to as 'one of the Twelve'. The next issue I want to resolve now is how these Judas features have affected the Christian community and the readers of the narrative. Recalling what G. Schille has suggested about the prestige and honour of being counted as a member of the Twelve,[54] I want to know what status the Twelve now have in relation to the fact that Judas, 'one of the Twelve', led Jesus to his capture, and eventually, to his death. I suggest that, as much as the number of the apostles was reduced to eleven because of Judas' betrayal and demise, what greatly affected the apostolate was their reputation, their honour, and leadership integrity before the Christian community. Judas and his apparent membership of the apostolate poses a serious challenge to the Eleven's honour and leadership integrity. Therefore, in order to fully understand how the apostles strongly defended themselves against the way Judas had tainted their reputation, we need to orient ourselves briefly with the concept of honour and shame in the NT period.

'the author shows no interest in naming the betrayer, and his identity is unknown to those at the table. Luke leaves the apostles to discuss among themselves who it might be; this is troubling, since it suggests that any one of them is capable of breaking faith with Jesus.' Green, *The Gospel of Luke*, p. 764. In other words, the role of betrayal is open to anyone from the Twelve. And rightly so for in the same chapter another 'betrayer' comes into the picture. Peter denies Jesus three times before Jesus' interrogation by the religious leaders in 22.54-62.

53. Green, *The Gospel of Luke*, p. 782.

54. See my discussion in 6.1.3.2.

2. *Honour and Shame Defined*

Honour (τιμή[55]) is the sense of value or self-worth understood by the person or group towards him/herself or themselves. This understanding of self-worth depends (especially in ancient societies) on the value perceived or acknowledged by the society towards that individual or group.[56] This perception, however, also depends on how the individual projects him or herself to the society according to the set of values which is understood by the same society. In Neyrey's words, 'honour basically has to do with evaluation and social perception: What do people think of this person? How is he evaluated, positively or negatively?'[57] Honour, therefore, is one of the primary bases in measuring the person's or the group's social standing within the society.[58] Social anthropologists of the classical world look at the concept of honour in the Mediterranean world as a 'pivotal value'.[59] It is no surprise to see that honour is associated with the qualities of power and wealth, the same qualities patrons are supposed to have, and which their clients count on.[60]

Shame, on the other hand, may be defined from two perspectives. First, it can be seen as a positive quality. It is the quality of 'sensitivity' to the opinions of the society. The sense of being concerned with anything that will ruin the reputation of the individual, group, or family is viewed as a good quality. Second, shame can also be understood as the negative correlate of honour: 'That is, to lose honour, be humiliated, be ashamed, act shamefully, be disgraced, be ridiculed'.[61]

55. The Greek word meaning 'the price and value of something', BAGD, p. 817.

56. DeSilva, *The Hope of Glory*, p. 2.

57. J.H. Neyrey, *Honour and Shame in the Gospel of Matthew* (Westminster: John Knox Press, 1998), p. 5.

58. J.H. Hellerman, 'Challenging the Authority of Jesus: Mark 11.27-33 and Mediterranean Notions of Honor and Shame', *JETS* 43 (2000), pp. 213-18 (217).

59. For an understanding of the label 'Medtiterranean', see Malina and Neyrey, 'Honour and Shame in Luke–Acts', p. 41. Also Neyrey, *Honour and Shame in the Gospel of Matthew*, pp. 8-9.

60. Moxnes, *The Economy of the Kingdom*, pp. 36-38.

61. Hanson and Oakman, *Palestine in the Time of Jesus*, p. 203. It is interesting to note that honour and shame also have a male and female component. It has two aspects, the sexual and moral divisions of labour (Malina and Neyrey describe this component under the title 'Gender-Based Honour', Malina and Neyrey, 'Honour and Shame in Luke–Acts', pp. 25-65, especially p. 41. Also Malina, *The New Testament World*). Although studies in the concept of honour and shame have largely been

2.1. *How Honour is Gained*

Honour is either ascribed or achieved. Ascribed honour takes place through birth, family connections, or the endowment of someone who is superior in status and power. The honour which the individual or group receives, therefore, is something that is not laboured or worked for. It is received primarily from being born into it, that is from family or kinship, or bestowed by a person of power (such as a king or governor upon loyal friends).[62]

Achieved or acquired honour is something received or earned by the individual or group through merits. This is normally attained by doing benefactions, military duties, athletic excellence and other services to superior people, the community, or even to the whole nation or kingdom. Patrons or groups, especially those who have political ambitions, engage in a highly competitive market to acquire honour and be recognized. This method serves a very useful purpose particularly when local elections come.[63]

The sense of competition for honour is heightened because of constant challenges to the honour of a person or a group. In fact, 'any social interaction that takes place outside one's family or one's circle of friends is a challenge to honour, a mutual attempt to acquire honour from one's

influenced by social anthropologists such as Campbell, *Honour, Family and Patronage*; see also J.G. Peristiany (ed.), *Honour and Shame: The Values of Mediterranean Society* (London: Weidenfeld & Nicholson, 1965).

The sexual division understands honour primarily as a male aspect. This means that the concept of shame for males is the loss of honour. See D.D. Gilmore, 'Honor and Shame and the Unity of the Mediterranean', in *idem* (ed.), *American Anthropological Association Special Publication* 22 (Washington, DC: American Anthropological Association, 1987), pp. 4, 8-17. The female aspect views shame as the sensitivity to preserve honour. Thus, while the issue of shame has a negative connotation for males, it has a positive value for females.

The moral division of labour, on the other hand, is that which defines honour and shame from the moral values viewpoint of the society. Thus, female honour covers issues such as the 'female sexual exclusiveness, discretion, shyness, restraint, and timidity'. It concerns primarily with the preservation of the female sense of sexual 'purity'. Males concern themselves with their duty to protect their wives', sisters' and daughters' purity. The shame of any these females means the dishonour of the male who is the leader of the household (Malina and Neyrey, 'Honour and Shame in Luke–Acts', p. 42).

62. Hellerman, 'Challenging the Authority of Jesus', p. 218.

63. Hanson and Douglas, *Palestine in the Time of Jesus*, pp. 70-73.

social equal'.[64] This social interaction is known as 'challenge-riposte', a constant social tug of war, a game of social push and shove.

2.2. *Group Honour*

An important element in the concept of honour and shame which is very relevant to this study is that of collective or group honour. These social groups have two dimensions: natural or voluntary. Natural groups refer to families, villages, or regions which possess honour collectively and all members participate in their preservation or protection.[65] Voluntary groups are groups in which memberships are not based on kinship derivations. Parties such as the Pharisees, Sadducees, Essenes, and Zealots are examples of these voluntary groups. As such, the group of apostles especially that of the Twelve, may be viewed as belonging to this classification.[66] A significant observation by Malina and Neyrey should be emphasized at this point. They argue that,

> In voluntary groupings, the members have no sacred qualities as persons because of who they are in relationship to others (kinship). Rather the posts, offices or functions in these groupings bear the qualities otherwise embodied by persons in natural groups. Now it is these posts, offices, and functions which are considered sacred and pure, although many different people can hold them. As for the group in general, the heads of both natural and voluntary groupings set the tone and embody the honour rating of the group, so to speak. While the internal opinion as well as public opinion are at work in natural groupings, *in voluntary groupings public opinion is sovereign.*[67]

Thus, for example, the honour rating of the Twelve apostles was set by Jesus himself. The honour which the group acquired was at a standard Jesus had received, and the loss of this honour, either from one or any of the Twelve, is a loss of honour for the whole group. The loss of the group's leader is also the loss of the group's identity. Much worse, the loss

---

64. Malina and Neyrey, 'Honour and Shame in Luke–Acts', p. 29.

65. Malina and Neyrey, 'Honour and Shame in Luke–Acts', p. 38.

66. Cf. Neyrey, *Honor and Shame in the Gospel of Matthew*, pp. 27-29; B.J. Malina, 'Early Christian Groups: Using Small Group Formation Theory to Explain Christian Organizations', in P.F. Esler (ed.), *Social Scientific Studies of the New Testament in its Context* (London: Routledge, 1995), pp. 106-108, also *idem*, 'Patron and Client: The Analogy behind Synoptic Theology', *Foundations and Facets Forum* 4 (1988), pp. 3-33 (20-27). See also Meeks, *The First Urban Christians*, pp. 75-81.

67. Malina and Neyrey, 'Honour and Shame in Luke–Acts', p. 28. Italics mine.

of the group's leader due to the betrayal by one of its followers is the loss of the group's honour in its full extent.[68]

3. *Summary*

In this section, I identified the ritual elements in the ritual confrontation of Acts 1.15-26. These include the characters of Peter, Judas, and the method of the casting of lots. I also briefly discussed the concept of honour and shame. This concept serves as the background to what I have proposed as the challenge-riposte situation between the Eleven apostles and the 120 brethren in the upper room. I suggested that the challenge was to the leadership credibility of the apostles as this is related to the issue of Judas the 'traitor' being a member of the Twelve.

68. I will expand on this aspect when I get to analyse the text in Acts 1. Cf. Chapter 7.

Chapter 7

THE APOSTLES AND THE HORROR OF JUDAS' BETRAYAL

1. *The Ritual Process in Acts 1.15-26*

As I have proposed, I am reading the election narrative of Acts 1.15-26 as the event where the apostles face their ritual confrontation. This ritual confrontation is the final phase in the transition stage. It is the phase where the initiands are tested and tried as to whether they will be able to measure up to the status to which they are being ordained. In the case of the apostles, Acts 1.15-26 is the stage where the Eleven respond to the challenge which questions their honour and leadership integrity.

In order to have a better understanding of how the election narrative works best from the perspective of a ritual confrontation, significant historical issues need first to be addressed. This chapter, therefore, is divided into two major sections. In the first section, I will review and respond to the issues concerning the purpose of the election narrative from the perspective of the historical method. This review will pay particular attention to two prominent views: (1) that the election was to complete the number of the apostles to twelve; (2) that the election is the beginning of the fulfilment of Jesus' promise to his disciples in Lk. 22.30.

The second section is my study of the election narrative as a ritual confrontation. This primarily entails the study of Peter's speech about Judas and how the former leads the whole assembly in the upper room to the election of Judas' replacement. I intend to show that the speech is a defence speech and the election process is structured to resolve the damaging effect of Judas' association with the apostolate. As a whole, I will argue that the election narrative has the features of a ritual confrontation according to the perspective of the rituals of status transformation.

2. The Purpose of the Election Narrative from a Historical Method

The many titles which have been ascribed to Acts 1.15-26 testify to the contrasting emphases defined by various readers of the text. Many scholars see the presence of two independent traditions moulded together to form the present narrative.[1] As a result, one may favour the title 'election of Matthias'[2] over the 'Defection of Judas'.[3] Others see it as the 'Death of Judas'[4] as against the 'Choice' or even the 'Enrolment of Matthias'.[5] And there are also those who see Peter addressing his 'First Speech'[6] as the heart of the narrative.[7]

The different titles which have been ascribed to the narrative of Acts 1.15-26 reveal the difficulty in finding the focus of the whole election story. In other words, the ability to answer the question 'why the elections?' is the key to understanding the many related issues embedded within the entire election account. Below is a survey of the two major arguments concerning the intention and purpose of the election narrative.

2.1. The Twelve as a Distinct Entity
The first argument is a view which places its emphasis on the Twelve as distinct from all the 'apostles'. Karl Heinrich Rengstorf popularized this

---

1.   Of Judas, 1.17-19, while of Matthias, 1.21-26. The NT preserves two accounts of Judas' fate. The other one is in Mt. 27.3-10. This fact serves as evidence that the Judas tradition in Acts may have been traditionally separate before the composition or its inclusion within the election narrative by the author. Cf. Barrett, *The Acts of the Apostles*, p. 92; also Wilcox, 'The Judas-Tradition', p. 445.

2.   E.g. K.H. Rengstorf, 'The Election of Matthias in Acts 1.15ff.', in William Klassen and Graydon F. Snyder (eds.), *Current Issues in New Testament Interpretation: Essays in Honor of Otto Piper* (London: SCM Press, 1962), pp. 178-92.

3.   E.g. J. Dupont, 'La destinee de Judas prophetisee par David (Act 1, 16-20)', *CBQ* 23 (1961), pp. 41-51 (41).

4.   A.D. Knox, 'The Death of Judas (Acts 1.18)', *JTS* 25 (1923–24), pp. 289-95 (289).

5.   L.S. Thornton, 'The Choice of Matthias', *JTS* 46 (1945), pp. 51-59. M.L. Soards, *The Speeches in Acts: Their Content, Context, and Concerns* (Louisville, KY: John Knox Press, 1994), p. 26.

6.   Cf. G.J. Steyn, *Septuagint Quotations in the Context of the Petrine and Pauline Speeches of the Acta Apostolorum* (Netherlands: Pharos, 1995), p. 40.

7.   See J. Crehan, 'Peter according to the D Texts of Acts', *TS* 18 (1957), pp. 596-603.

idea in his 1962 article 'The Election of Matthias in Acts 1.15 ff'.[8] Rengs-torf attempts to answer the question 'What was Luke's aim in reporting nothing but this one event, the election of Matthias, between Jesus' ascension and the outpouring of the Holy Spirit?' Although he admits that there is merit in speculating that the original intention of the narrative 'between the Ascension and Pentecost, the group of the Twelve, having been made incomplete by the betrayal and the death of Judas, was made complete again through the by-election of Matthias',[9] Rengstorf was quick to see that this assumption is insufficient. Initially, he relies on E. Haenchen's[10] method of looking into the significance of the Matthias narrative within its function in the book of Acts, and furthermore, with the theology of the author of Acts himself. However, he found that Haenchen eventually failed to answer his own questions. Rengstorf argues that the 'Matthias Narrative deals with a single event which seems to have no further importance for the continuity of events as Luke deliberately relates them in Acts'.[11]

Rengstorf, therefore, advances his own presuppositions concerning the intention of the narrative.[12] For Rengstorf, it appears that 'the apostolate of the Twelve in its existence and function appears to be independent of the will of those who became members of the group'. Also, the decision to come up with apostles was entirely up to Jesus. This means that as Jesus had originally appointed apostles before, the choice of the twelfth is still his. And third, the completion of the Twelve did not point to any function of the apostles as hierarchical leaders of churches. Rather, what is indicative is that after the completion, the new set of apostles was prepared for a leadership of service.[13]

From these presuppositions, Rengstorf concludes that the election narrative, by the completion of the Twelve, shows the 'continuing un-broken claim of Jesus on Israel as his people'. After Pentecost, Luke lets

8. Rengstorf, 'The Election of Matthias', pp. 178-92.

9. Rengstorf, 'The Election of Matthias', p. 182.

10. Cf. E. Haenchen, *Die Apostelgeschichte* (Meyer, *Kritisch-exegetischer Kommentar* [Göttingen, 12th edn, 1959]), III, p. 123.

11. Rengstorf, 'The Election of Matthias', p. 180.

12. Haenchen, *The Acts of the Apostles*, p. 184.

13. Lk. 22.26; cf. K. Giles, 'Is Luke an Exponent of "Early Protestantism?" Church Order in the Lukan Writings (Part 1)', *EvQ* 54 (1982), pp. 193-205; (Part 2), *EvQ* 55 (1983), pp. 3-20.

the Twelve disappear so as to place emphasis on the work and guidance of the Spirit, placing secondary importance on church organizations.[14]

Max Wilcox furthers the idea of the completion of the Twelve. While his arguments come from several points, his main contention revolves around the phrase ὅτι κατηριθμημένος (lit. *numbered*) ἦν ἐν ἡμῖν. He recognizes that while Judas occupied a special role, it was his failure to perform this role which necessitated his replacement.[15] Wilcox's lead came from his parallel study of the Palestinian Targumim to Gen. 44.18, a narrative that is absent in the MT, the LXX, and even in the major Targums such as Targum Onkelos. The Targum to Gen. 44.18 narrates an extended story of the Haggadah which deals with the story of Benjamin being caught with Joseph's silver cup in his sack. In this commentary, Judah states how,

> ...Simeon and Levi had avenged the humiliation of their sister Dinah 'who was not numbered with us' among (lit. *from*) the tribes and will not receive a portion and share with us in the division of the land... How much more, he argues, will his sword not return to its sheath until it has slain the whole population of Egypt for the sake of Benjamin who—unlike Dinah—was 'numbered' with us among the tribes and will receive a portion and share with us in the division of the land.[16]

For Wilcox, there is a formula present in these parallel texts. The mention of the phrase 'for he was numbered among us' (first in the negative sense with Dinah, and then positively with Benjamin) shows how the concept of being 'numbered' has been developed and used. This same phrase is strikingly similar with how Judas was referred to in Acts 1.17. Wilcox concludes that the similarity of the phrase in Acts 1.17 with that of both the Dinah and Benjamin accounts in the Palestinian Targum of Gen. 44.18 highlights Judas' central significance in the Twelve, and thus, the urgency to replace him because of his failure to carry out his office.[17]

2.2. *The Election Narrative as the Fulfilment of Jesus' Promise in Luke 22.30*

The second argument comes from a slightly different premise. According to Jacob Jervell, Luke's concept of Israel's return to sovereignty is comprised of significant events leading to the establishment of the eschatological

---

14. Rengstorf, 'The Election of Matthias', pp. 191-92.
15. Wilcox, 'The Judas Tradition', p. 448.
16. Wilcox, 'The Judas Tradition', p. 447.
17. Wilcox, 'The Judas Tradition', p. 448.

kingdom. The significant events include the restoration of the Temple, the return of the remnant and the gathering of the twelve tribes, the inclusion of the Samaritans and Gentiles into the fold, the rule of the new Davidic king, and the role of the apostles as 'Judges' of the twelve tribes of Israel.[18]

Of these events, the role of the apostles as judges is my interest. There are those who say that the role of the Twelve in the book of Acts is the fulfilment of the promise of Jesus in Lk. 22.28-30. The text states, 'You are those who have continued with me in my trials; and I assign to you, as my father assigned to me, a kingdom, that you may eat and drink at my table in my kingdom, and sit on thrones judging the twelve tribes of Israel'.

Opinions slightly differ on whether the fulfilment of the promise in Acts is partial or purely eschatological. The 'partial fulfilment' view believes that the apostles have started exhibiting their roles as rulers in Acts. For instance, in Acts 5.1-11, Peter displays his role as a judge deciding the fate of Ananias and Sapphira. Thus, R. Denova argues that,

> Acts 1.15-26, the replacement of Judas, is a story which both reaffirms the authority granted to the apostles in Lk. 22 and demonstrates that the restoration of the twelve has to happen before the outpouring of the Spirit in Acts 2, 'upon the house of Israel'. Subsequently, we find Peter literally serving in his capacity of judge over Ananias and Sapphira (Acts 5.1-11), thus, confirming Lk. 22.30.[19]

Likewise, the teachings (2.43), miracles (2.44), and most especially, the community's laying of possessions at the apostles' feet (4.32-37) show the submission of the people to the new leaders of Israel. An example of this view is J.B. Chance who states that, 'The opening chapters of Acts present, therefore, the fulfilment, or at least a proleptic fulfilment, of the promise of Lk. 22.28-30. The twelve apostles in conjunction with the messianic king, rule the twelve tribes of eschatological Israel'.[20]

On the other hand, the 'eschatological fulfilment' view contends that since the twelve tribes have not been restored and Jewish resistance in Acts prevents the apostles from functioning as governors of the whole

---

18. Cf. Jervell, *Luke and the People of God*, pp. 75-77.

19. Denova, *The Things Accomplished*, p. 70.

20. Chance, *Jerusalem, the Temple*, p. 81. Also L.T. Johnson, *The Literary Function of Possessions in Luke–Acts* (Montana: Scholars Press, 1977), pp. 166-67; E. Franklin, *Christ the Lord: A Study in the Purpose and Theology of Luke–Acts* (London: SPCK, 1975), pp. 97-99.

Jewish people, the apostles will exercise their rulership only in the eschatological Israel.[21]

While both the 'partial' and the 'complete fulfilment' views contest the realization of Jesus' promise to the apostles, few scholars dispute that Acts 1.15-26 is the scene which effects the promise of Jesus in Lk. 22.28-30. Acts 1.15-26 speaks of the replacement of Judas by the election of Matthias as the twelfth apostle, thereby completing the number of the twelve apostles for the twelve tribes of Israel. Right after the completion of the twelve, the outpouring of the Spirit takes place (Acts 2.1-4). According to prophetic traditions the Spirit's outpouring signals the start of Israel's restoration (e.g. Ezek. 39.25-29). Thus, some scholars see this as the reason why Luke placed the election narrative before the Spirit's arrival. Again Denova argues, 'Hence, a prophetic order of events forces the replacement of Judas, as well as other elements of the story, to be put precisely where they are located; it would make little sense to place them anywhere else'.[22]

The completion of the number of the twelve apostles paves the way for the fulfilment of the prophecy on the restoration of the twelve tribes. Acts 1.15-26 is, therefore, the induction of the twelve apostles into their rulership of the restored Israel. Apart from Denova and Chance, Jervell and Nelson share the same reasoning. Jervell mentions that the need to have a complete number of twelve apostles was only for a certain duration. In his book *Luke and the People of God*, he states that,

> In the unique farewell discourse in Luke 22.24-30 the Twelve are given an eschatological role as the future regents over Israel. The text signals Luke's conception of the apostolate. In the question from the Twelve (Acts 1.6) the resurrection and the outpouring of the Spirit are interpreted as heralding the restoration of Israel. [23]

Jervell's study picks up the idea that the election of Matthias was a direct result of Jesus' promise to his disciples in Lk. 22.30.[24] Likewise, Peter K. Nelson in his *Leadership and Discipleship: A Study of Luke 22.24-30*, discusses in detail the relationship of Lk. 22.30 with the purpose of the election in Acts. Nelson ends up by saying that, 'The need to

---

21. R.C. Tannehill, *Luke* (Nashville, TN: Abingdon Press, 1996), p. 319.
22. Denova, *The Things Accomplished*, p. 70.
23. Jervell, *Luke and the People of God*, p. 76.
24. J. Jervell, *New Testament Theology: The Theology of the Acts of the Apostles* (Cambridge: Cambridge University Press, 1996), p. 75.

describe at length the replacing of Judas (Acts 1.15-26) reveals Luke's concern to show the reconstituted circle of twelve apostles as corresponding to the twelve tribes of Israel'.[25]

The two views surveyed agree on the purpose of the election story as the completion of the Twelve apostles. They, however, slightly differ from the premise of the purpose itself. The first view places emphasis on the completion of the number of the Twelve. This is in keeping with the identity of the Twelve as being established by Jesus himself and also being distinct from the other apostles. The second view strongly brings in the function of Lk. 22.30 and uses the concept of the 'Promise-Fulfilment' method in understanding the purpose of the election story. This view argues that the purpose of the election was to complete the Twelve in order to see the fulfilment of Jesus' promise to his apostles of being judges to the twelve tribes of the new Israel. Judas' betrayal had caused a vacancy and therefore had to be filled in by a new apostle.

3. *Twelve Apostles for Twelve Thrones?*

As indicated by our survey above, many scholars argue that the need to complete the Twelve is to fulfil Jesus' promise to the apostles in Lk. 22.30. Apparently, there are supposed to be twelve apostles to serve as judges to the twelve tribes of the new Israel. To put it in other words, Acts 1.15-26 is seen as the start of the fulfilment of Jesus' promise in Lk. 22.30, in that Peter has to call an election to fill in the post of the twelfth apostle to replace Judas. Judas' betrayal of Jesus cost him his privileged seat on the supposed 'twelve thrones' made available for the 'twelve apostles' who were to serve as judges over the 'twelve tribes' of the new Israel.[26]

The election in Acts as the beginning of the fulfilment of the promise in Lk. 22.30 would have been a perfect scenario if not for one disturbing problem. The phrase δώδεκα θρόνοι (twelve thrones) in Lk. 22.30 does not exist. Strictly speaking, Jesus did not promise twelve thrones to his twelve apostles in the context of Lk. 22.30. Instead, what we have is simply the word 'thrones' (θρόνων);[27] and the suggestion that each

---

25. Nelson, *Leadership and Discipleship*, p. 222.

26. See Denova, *The Things Accomplished*, p. 70; Chance, *Jerusalem, the Temple*, p. 81. Also Johnson, *Literary Function of Possessions*, pp. 166-67; Franklin, *Christ the Lord*, pp. 97-99; Tannehill, *Luke*, p. 319; Jervell, *Luke and the People of God*, p. 82.

27. See line 2 of the parallel passage I have provided on the next page.

apostle will get to sit on a throne and rule one of the twelve tribes of Israel is an idea obviously imported from its only extant parallel—Mt. 19.28.[28]

	Mt. 19.28	Lk. 22.30
1	καὶ ὑμεῖς ἐπι	καὶ καθήσεσθε ἐπι
2	δώδεκα θρόνους	_____ θρόνων
3	κρίνοντες	κρίνοντες
4	τὰς δώδεκα φυλὰς	τὰς δώδεκα φυλὰς
5	τοῦ Ἰσραήλ	τοῦ Ἰσραήλ[29]

Transferring the idea of 'twelve' thrones from Mt. 19.28 to Lk. 22.30 raises some important concerns. For example, the context from which the 'reward' saying appears in Matthew is radically different from its Lukan counterpart. Closely similar to the Markan material, Matthew has the saying in a context beginning with the 'household' instructions (Mt. 19.1-15 // Mk 10.1-16), the Rich Young Ruler (Mt. 19.16-22 // Mk 10.17-22), and entering God's kingdom (Mt. 19.23-30 // Mk 10.23-31). Luke, on the other hand, places his version of the saying at the beginning of the so-called 'Passion Narrative', specifically right after Jesus' and the disciples' celebration of the Passover feast (Lk. 22.1-38). The Lukan parallel to Matthew's and Mark's contexts is found in Lk. 18.15-30. In these stories, both Matthew and Luke follow Mark up until the question of Peter in Mk 10.29 (// Mt. 19.27 and Lk. 18.28). The response of Jesus to Peter's question becomes longer in Matthew as the reward-saying appears at this point.

The majority of modern scholars read Lk. 22.30 with the Matthean parallel in mind. For many of these scholars, the absence of δώδεκα in Lk. 22.30 is not a problem. The reasons why Luke may have dropped δώδεκα before θρόνων are all circumstantial and therefore do not warrant vetoing the reading of the quantitative word 'twelve' before thrones in Lk. 22.30 from Mt. 19.28.[30] These reasons include: (1) Luke had difficulty assigning

---

28. The concept that each apostle will rule one of the twelve tribes of Israel is also an inferral from the text. Neither Matthew nor Luke directly suggests the reason for the individual rulership of each tribe. Jacob Jervell understood it otherwise as he rationalizes that James was not replaced by the apostles when martyred by Herod in Acts 12.2. This is to avoid having thirteen regents for only twelve tribes available to rule. See Jervell, *Luke and the People of God*, p. 82.

29. This phrase comes right after κρίνοντες in Luke's version.

30. Hence, 'It may be presumed, however, that Luke's text still implies twelve thrones to match the "twelve tribes of Israel". So the necessity to replace Judas (Acts

a throne to Judas. Fitzmyer and others[31] believe that the author of the third gospel had a problem of designating a throne for Judas whose plan of betrayal had just been revealed by Jesus. Luke, therefore, altered Q[32] by deleting δώδεκα and thus eliminated Judas from the list of Jesus' beneficiaries; (2) Luke wanted to widen the application of the promise.[33] Peter Nelson objects to this suggestion since the idea of judging or ruling 'becomes distorted when access to thrones is significantly limited';[34] (3) Luke, for purely stylistic reasons, often replaces a repeated noun with a pronoun, sometimes apparently just to avoid repeating the same noun;[35] and (4) Luke and Matthew simply had two different sources other than Q.[36]

The weakness of the reasons I have just listed lies in the great degree of assumption that Luke was the one who has altered his sources. It seems that, for some, the Lukan redaction of Lk. 22.30 has become a fact rather than a theory, making the possibility of a Matthean insertion of δώδεκα strongly remote. One must constantly be reminded that Q is no more than a working hypothesis to explain the agreement between Matthew and Luke on a large body of Jesus' sayings, and, barring the unlikely event of such a document being discovered, always will be. Moreover, it may also have been possible that (as I.H. Marshall concurs) the two evangelists could have been dependent on two different sources, 'or more probably, on two different recessions of Q'.[37]

But, for argument's sake, there are also viable reasons to believe that Matthew was the one who has altered his version of the saying. One example is C.K. Barrett who has raised an interesting scenario. He

1.12-26)'. Nelson, *Leadership and Discipleship*, p. 212, also n. 179.

31. E.g. J. Fitzmyer, *Luke* X-XXIV, p. 1419; Nelson, *Leadership and Discipleship*, p. 216.

32. Very helpful in this area of discussion is J.S. Kloppenborg, *The Formation of Q: Trajectories in Ancient Wisdom Collections* (Philadelphia: Fortress Press, 1973), pp. 1-102.

33. E.E. Ellis, *The Gospel of Luke* (Grand Rapids: Eerdmans, 2nd edn, 1981), p. 256; cf. Marshall, *The Gospel of Luke*, p. 814.

34. Nelson, *Leadership and Discipleship*, p. 216.

35. H.J. Cadbury, *The Style and Literary Method of Luke* (Cambridge, MA: Harvard University Press, 1920), p. 83 onwards.

36. Hunter, *The Work and Words of Jesus*, p. 160, 186; B.F. Streeter, *The Four Gospels* (London: Macmillan, 1924), p. 288.

37. Marshall, *The Gospel of Luke*, p. 815.

suggests that Matthew[38] (1) affixed the phrase 'in the new world (παλιγγενεσία)'; (2) dropped the phrase 'I appoint you...' since the clause is assumed by the free variant in Rev. 3.21; (3) added 'Whenever the Son of Man sits on the throne of his glory' and then further added the word 'twelve' before 'thrones' in order to enhance the parallelism between Jesus and his apostles. The idea of parallelism is also welcomed by Gundry as he sees the new context in Matthew mentions no betrayer.[39] Jacobson strongly supports this view. He adds,

> Matthew, but not Luke, specifies 'twelve thrones'. This is important because 'twelve thrones' may imply the notion of the 'Twelve' (disciples or apostles). But Luke's version, 'on thrones judging...' does not specify how many thrones there are, and thus need not entail the idea of the 'Twelve'. Here Matthew is probably secondary. It is possible that Luke eliminated the first 'twelve' because it will have implied the inclusion of Judas, who figures prominently in this context. But this seems unlikely, because Luke knew that Judas's place among the twelve was unalterable; he tells us about Judas's replacement (Acts 1.15-26). It is more likely that Matthew added 'twelve' (he refers to the disciples in his context) than that Luke omitted it.[40]

Yet beyond the redactional[41] issues involved between the reward-sayings of Lk. 22.28-30 and Mt. 28.30, the question of whether the election of Matthias is the fulfilment of Jesus' promise in Lk. 22.30 can best be answered only by Acts 1.15-26. In other words, does the author of

38. Barrett, *The Acts of the Apostles*, p. 55. See also J. Baumgarten, 'The Duodecimal Courts of Qumran, Revelation, and the Sanhedrin', *JBL* 95 (1976), pp. 59-78.

39. R.H. Gundry, *Matthew*, p. 394.

40. A.D. Jacobson, *The First Gospel: An Introduction to Q* (Sonoma, CA: Polebridge, 1992), p. 247. Fledderman raises three reasons why Matthew could have added δώδεκα: Matthew uses numbers quite freely. Although he occasionally omits numbers from his sources, he more frequently adds them; he repeats numbers he finds on his sources (e.g. 'forty days' from Mk 1.3); he identifies the disciples and the twelve. He refers three times to the twelve disciples (Mt. 10.1; 11.1; 20.17) and once to the 'twelve apostles' (Mt. 10.2); cf. H.T. Fledderman, 'The End of Q', *SBL Seminar Papers* 29 (1990), pp. 1-10 (6-7). See also S.C. Barton, *Discipleship and Family Ties in Mark and Matthew* (Cambridge: Cambridge University Press, 1994), pp. 207-208; R.E. Menninger, *Israel and the Church in the Gospel of Matthew* (New York: Peter Lang, 1994), p. 156; J.S. Kloppenberg, 'The Sayings Gospel Q and the Quest of the Historical Jesus', *HTR* 89 (1996), pp. 307-44 (327).

41. A redaction-critical study of the saying in Mt. 28.30 and Lk. 22.30 is in the Appendix of this study.

Luke–Acts indeed direct the reader to understand that Acts 1.15-26 is the fulfilment of Lk. 22.30? My investigation has led me to believe otherwise.

4. *Is Acts 1.15-26 the Fulfilment of Luke 22.30?*

If Acts 1.15-26 is the story by which the author wants to tell his audience that Jesus' promise in Lk. 22.30 can now be fulfilled, then this is probably one of the most indirect or vague ways the author has conveyed such a message. For instance, the only parallel between Acts 1.15-26 and Lk. 22.30 is the number of the inner circle of Jesus' apostles which is twelve. Apart from this, the author leaves no clue or evidence at all whatsoever for the reader to understand that the reading of the election narrative should be taken as the fulfilment of Lk. 22.30.

Scholars point to the phrase which Peter uttered in his speech which states 'for he [Judas] was *numbered* among us and was allotted his share in this ministry' in Acts 1.17 as the all important evidence to understand Acts 1.15-26 as the fulfilment of Jesus' promise in Lk. 22.30. If this is so, why has the author opted to say it this way? Why is it so indirect? Why has the author not clearly identified the election of Judas' replacement as the fulfilment of Jesus' promise in Lk. 22.30? While Peter was clear in stating that Judas' fate was the fulfilment of what was prophesied in the book of Psalms (1.20), he gives no statement that the election is in any way also a fulfilment of what Jesus had earlier promised them during their last supper with him.

Does Acts 1.17 necessarily imply an invitation for the readers to recall the promise of Jesus in Lk. 22.30? Commentators are divided on this issue. While there are some who see that indeed the promise in Lk. 22.30 is echoed here in Acts 1.17,[42] others simply refer to the earlier use of the term in Lk. 22.3 where Satan is said to have entered Judas who was from the 'number (ἀριθμοῦ) of the twelve'.[43] What is widely agreed among exegetes is the reference to the casting of 'lots' in 1.26 with the phrase 'allotted his share in the ministry' here in 1.17.[44] Biblical tradition knows of the distribution or sharing of lands among the tribes 'by lot' from God (see Num. 16.14; 26.55; 33.53). As also the Levites (Num. 18.21-26) have been known to have received their share of ministry of service by 'lot'

---

42. E.g. Fitzmyer, *Acts*, p. 223.

43. E.g. Johnson, *Acts*, p. 35.

44. See my discussion on the 'Casting of Lots' in 6.3; cf. Johnson, *Acts*, p. 35; see also Dunn, *The Acts of the Apostles*, p. 18.

(since Levites do not receive properties of lands like the other tribes), the same language is understood in Peter's description of Judas' share in the ministry.

With 1.17, therefore, I am suggesting that it is possible to see the author's emphasis on the concept of Judas as being 'identified with the group' rather than 'being numbered in the group'. In other words, Judas completes the essence of the group as the inner circle of Jesus' apostles rather than simply a character who completes the number of the apostles which is twelve. This is why, as I have argued, the need to replace Judas does not necessarily fall on simply completing the number of the apostles but rather because of how the Twelve as a group has been seriously affected by the betrayal from one of them.

Another significant point against the argument that Acts 1.15-26 is the fulfilment of Lk. 22.30 is the apparent silence of Jesus about the whole 'replacement of Judas' issue. While Jesus was very clear to the Eleven on his instructions for them to remain in Jerusalem and wait for the promise of the Father (Acts 1.4), there is no instruction at all to make sure that Judas is replaced or that their number should be twelve. For sure, the narrative assures the readers that Jesus was aware of Judas' absence (not to mention the fact that it was Judas who betrayed him), especially during the forty-day period he was with the Eleven before his ascension (cf. 1.3), yet Jesus did not question nor make any implications to such an issue. Of course, this is also the case against the author. In other words, why has the author kept the character of Jesus silent on this matter?

Then there is the issue on the criteria that were set to choose the candidates for Judas' replacement (Acts 1.21-22). The author gives us the impression that the criteria were strict for the one who is going to fill in Judas' place. Yet again, there is no implication at all that these strict criteria are the standard demanded for those who are to serve as future judges to the twelve tribes of the new Israel.

Finally, when Matthias was elected, and thus, had completed the Twelve, no reference is given for the reader to understand that the promise in Lk. 22.30 is now back on its right track. The narrative of Acts 1 simply flows smoothly into Acts 2, leaving no room at all for the readers to be inspired by the reality that the promise in Lk. 22.30 is now on its next phase of its fulfilment.

It is from these observations that I am actually challenging the notion that the narrative of Acts 1.15-26 is the beginning of the fulfilment of Lk. 22.30. In other words, what I am suggesting is that the election narrative of Acts 1.15-26 has a more demanding reason other than the need to complete the number of the apostles to twelve. I contend that the whole election narrative is best understood from a social-scientific perspective. And as I have been impressing since the beginning of this study, the election is the measure which the apostles had to take in response to the social shame which Judas' scandalous act of betrayal has created upon the apostles' reliability to be leaders of the Christian community. If this suggestion is correct, then the beginning of the fulfilment of Jesus' promise in Lk. 22.30 is pushed further beyond Acts 1.15-26.[45]

5. *Peter's Speech: A Case of Diminished Responsibility*

In the perspective of the rituals of status transformation, in particular the ritual confrontation, Peter's speech is a defence speech. He delivers this on behalf of the Eleven apostles. The title of this section immediately suggests that whatever has happened to Judas, especially his evil deeds, should not in any way implicate the rest of the members of the apostolate. The following important aspects in Peter's speech support my suggestion. First, that the evil deeds of Judas were the fulfilment of scripture ('Brethren, the scripture has to be fulfilled...' 1.16a). Second, the grotesque description of Judas' death depicts the evil nature of Judas (1.18-19), and this implies the extirpation and excommunication of Judas from the membership of the apostles.

Before I proceed to discuss the two aspects in Peter's speech, and in order for me to put the speech in the perspective of a ritual confrontation, let us again be reminded of the suggested scenario I painted earlier:

1. The election of Matthias is the step which the apostles are taking in order to show the people (those in the upper room and the readers of the text) that Judas is gone and is going to be replaced by someone capable and reliable. In the broader context, Acts 1.15-26 is part of the author's promotion that indeed the apostles have been transformed; that Judas the 'traitor' is no longer part of the group, and that Matthias is ordained by God himself to fill in the place of Judas.[46]

---

45. For an excellent discussion on the issue of when the apostles fully realized the fulfilment of Jesus' promise in Lk. 22.30, see Nelson, *Leadership and Discipleship*, pp. 224-32, esp. n. 211, pp. 224-25.

46. Klassen's observations fit well in the sociological scenario which I have just suggested for Acts 1.15-26. In fact, Klassen has stated that 'It is possible that the main point of these stories for the writers of Matthew and Luke was the indication that Judas

2.   Peter's role in Acts 1.15-26 is that of a spokesman.[47] He speaks, not on behalf of the 120 people but (a member of) the Eleven apostles. That Peter speaks on behalf only of the apostles is supported by the consistent focus of the narrative on the Eleven apostles. In fact, from the very time the apostles were introduced by the author in Acts 1.3, until they are integrated and formally stand in the presence of the people in Acts 2.14, the apostles are the focus of the narrative. It is therefore not a forced assumption that all the author speaks of in Acts 1–2 centres on the Twelve apostles of Jesus.

3.   Peter's speech as a defence speech on behalf of their group is designed to argue that the responsibility for the arrest and death of Jesus falls on Judas alone and that the Eleven should not be held accountable for what Judas had done. Furthermore, Peter not only defends the honour and integrity of the group of apostles but also encourages the company of people to agree with the action they are about to take (the election of Judas' replacement) in order to assure the community that such a traumatic experience from Judas will and should never happen again.

4.   The author's placement of the events (i.e. Acts 1.12-14 and 15-26) suggests that the assembly of the people happened in the same setting.[48] If this is a correct understanding of the sequence of events in the upper room, then it is plausible to assume that the picture of unity between the Eleven and the other disciple groups in 1.14 has some bearing on what is about to take place in 1.15-26. What I am, therefore, suggesting is the attempt of the author to show that the Eleven have first secured the support of the other known disciple groups (such as the women disciples and Jesus' family) before they embarked on their defence in the presence of the larger group of believers numbering about 120 persons (1.15).

5.   The 120 persons in the upper room represent the body of the Christian community to whom the apostles will serve as leaders. Some commentators suggest that the inclusion of the statement 'the company of persons[49] was in all about 120' (1.15b) is simply a parenthetical clause. In

---

no longer was a member of the Jesus community'. Klassen, *Judas*, p. 171.

47.   As we have also stated, Peter is the author's mouthpiece in telling his readers of the transformation of the apostles.

48.   The temporal reference 'in those days' (ἐν ταῖς ἡμέραις ταύταις) connects this event to the previous events. Cf. Johnson, *Acts*, p. 34.

49.   The only time the author of Luke–Acts uses the term ὄνομα to mean 'person'. For discussions on the author's employment of the term, see Barrett, *The Acts of the Apostles*, p. 96.

other words, it is an unexpected statement; it does not originally belong in the pericope. Or as Fitzmyer bluntly puts it, 'strange!'[50] It is so strange that Barrett had to conclude that the statement may have been 'an unfortunate lapse which Luke omitted to remove from his work'.[51] From the sociological context I am suggesting, the delivery of Peter's defence speech to a larger group of believers seems to fit the scenario well. How is this so?

There is the remotest possibility that the author wanted to make a parallel picture with the current decision-making or approving body known as the Sanhedrin. Even while this assumption of a parallel is seen by some as near absurdity, some commentators still consider the possibility of equating the number of '120 people' with what is found in *M. San.*[52] 1.6. Lake and Cadbury believe that, 'It can scarcely be an accident that this number is that of the Twelve multiplied by 10. It is remarkable that *Sanhedr.* 1.6 enacts that the name of officers in a community shall be a tenth of the whole, and that 120 is the smallest number which can hold a "small Sanhedrin".'[53]

Although Lake and Cadbury's conclusion has long been challenged, no satisfactory answer has been given to explain the mention of the '120 persons' before Peter's speech. All that has been consistently posited concerning this issue is the inappropriateness and sudden inclusion of the phrase in the text.

If, however, Lake and Cadbury's suggestion is correct, then what we see is the author's attempt to show his readers that the apostles were tried by 120 persons representing the Christian community. Moreover, what is about to take place (i.e. the election of Judas' replacement) is not only decided by the Eleven or a smaller band of disciples, but rather by the representative council of 120 people.[54] Such an idea is the essence of how B. Blue sees the purpose of this Lukan interjection, 'The primary purpose of the specific mention of the 120 people assembled together (Acts 1) might well be an articulation of a new, autonomous, self-governing

---

50. Fitzmyer, *Acts*, p. 222.

51. Barrett, *The Acts of the Apostles*, p. 96.

52. I.e. *Mishnah Sanhedrin*.

53. Lake and Cadbury, *The Beginnings of Christianity*, Part 1, vol. IV, p. 12.

54. A further explanation of the possible parallels of the number can be found in Barrett, *The Acts of the Apostles*, p. 96. This includes parallels from Qumran such as 1QS 6.3-4 and 1QSa 222 where the 120 may be understood as 10 multiplied by 12, or one leader for each of ten members.

community (cf. *M. San.* 1.6) in which women were included in the count'.[55] Bearing in mind this scenario, I now come to discuss the two aspects in Peter's speech.

5.1. *The Deeds and Death of Judas as the Fulfilment of Scripture*
'Brethren, the scripture had to be fulfilled...' 1.16a. This statement from Peter comes before the whole speech in Acts 1.16-17. Because it does so, whatever follows after it is governed by this guideline. In other words, the death of Judas, a death associated with his betrayal of Jesus ('concerning Judas who was guide to those who arrested Jesus', 1.16b), was planned by God.[56]

Such a statement also conveys the dissociation of anybody else from acting as accessory to Judas' betrayal of Jesus, and consequently, Judas' death. If this is correct, when viewed from the perspective we are suggesting, Peter is dissociating the Eleven from any responsibility relating to the arrest and death of Jesus.

Klassen has made an important observation that supports my proposal. This has something to do with the redaction of Luke concerning Judas and his deeds. He says, 'Missing is any reference to Satan; instead, Peter through Luke's redaction, speaks of the way in which scripture was fulfilled through the deeds of Judas'.[57] In other words, while Lk. 22.3 mitigates Judas' evil act by associating it with the character of Satan, Judas alone is portrayed to take all responsibility for Jesus' arrest and the betrayer's death here in Acts 1.16.[58]

---

55. B. Blue, 'The Influence of Jewish Worship on Luke's Presentation of the Early Church', in I.H. Marshall and D. Peterson (eds.), *Witness to the Gospel: The Theology of Acts* (Grand Rapids: Eerdmans, 1998), p. 480.

56. Soards, in his analysis of Peter's speech, claims that Peter associates to scripture, not only Judas' death, but also his betrayal of Jesus. All that had happened was of 'divine necessity', *Speeches in Acts*, pp. 27-28.

57. Klassen, *Judas*, pp. 168-69.

58. Klassen, in his study of the Judas death accounts, compared and contrasted Acts 1.16-20 with the account in Mt. 27.3-10; Klassen, *Judas*, pp. 169-70. He came up with the following observations: For similarities: 1. They draw on popular traditions; 2. Both agree that Judas died an unusual death; 3. Both are fond of bringing out the application of Old Testament quotations; 4. Both say that land was purchased with the money Judas received; 5. They are linked to concrete details of the topography of Jerusalem; 6. The name of the land purchased is virtually identical in both accounts. Their differences are: 1. The manner of death is different. In Matthew he hangs himself; in Luke he falls to his death; 2. The time of death is different. Matthew places

5.2. *The Purpose of the Grotesque Description of Judas' Death*

'The way that Judas died is not important', Fitzmyer makes this conclusion regarding the author's description of how the betrayer's life ended. For Fitzmyer, the recounting of Judas' demise falls under the 'stereotypical literary form' of folkloric elaborations utilized for notorious characters who were known to have been enemies of the church.[59] Judas, therefore, belongs to the group of people who in some way or the other have caused serious offences either against Jesus, his apostles, or any of the heroes of faith. This exclusive group would include people such as Herod the Great, Antiochus IV Epiphanes, Herod Agrippa I.[60]

Folkloric elaboration, in this case, is the addition of gruesome details about the death of a person. This tradition is mostly associated with the

the death before Jesus himself dies; in Luke there is no indication of time; 3. The purchase of the field is brought about by different circumstances and by different people; 4. The location of the field is well known as being near Jerusalem, according to Luke, while in Matthew no such indication is offered; 5. Matthew records remorse on the part of Judas, but Luke mentions nothing about it.

59. Fitzmyer, *Acts*, p. 220.

60. Klassen asks what could have been the reason why the early church had to record the death of Judas when there are no other death accounts for any of the other apostles of Jesus. He later concludes that such a phenomenon is attributed to the practice of the later church who follows in the genre of death stories of other evil men and how they died. He cites the examples from Papias who tells the story of Antiochus Ephipanes (2 Macc. 9.7-12); Josephus' story of Herod the Great (*Ant.* 17.6, 5, para. 169); and Luke himself of Herod Agrippa (Act 12.23). Klassen further remarks that both Luke and Matthew (see n. 89 under section 7.5.1) may have probably been handed down with the tradition belonging to the category of 'aetiological legends' that seek to explain causes. In the case of Judas' death, one is to seek for its deeper intention. Thus, Klassen argues that 'the intention is to assert the link between the "field of blood" which everyone knows and the tragic end of Judas' (p. 171). For further discussions and examples of Death of Tyrant Type Scenes, see O.W. Allen Jr, *The Death of Herod: The Narrative and Theological Function of Retribution in Luke–Acts* (Atlanta, GA: Scholars Press, 1997).

Klassen's observations are helpful to the extent of understanding how tradition was passed down to the authors of both accounts. However, the same observations, most especially those concerning the version in Acts, are also significant to our study, particularly in the study of the social implications involved in Judas' death. These factors (we will attempt to argue) support the view that Peter's speech on Judas' death is apologetic on behalf of the Eleven apostles (including himself) as a group to which Judas formerly belonged (B. Witherington III, quoting G. Kennedy, reads this first speech of Peter as 'a brief example of deliberative rhetoric—an act of persuasion meant to produce a certain course of action...' *The Acts of the Apostles*, p. 115).

concept of divine retribution against known tyrants or persecutors of the church. It is folkloric in the sense that the stories developed as they passed through from one tradition to another, having conflated several individual tales into a unified and larger tradition.

The Judas tradition may be a piece of folklore. The details of his death in 1.18-19 may also be a conflation of smaller traditions. However, would the conflation or even the development of a folkloric tradition about the death of Judas say something about the purpose and substance of the speech itself? I believe it does. Even if tradition has always associated 'evil men' with gruesome deaths, the reason for the association is significant. In our case, 'association' is in effect 'dissociation'. In other words, as Peter describes the gruesome death of Judas, he is in fact formally declaring Judas' extirpation and excommunication from the Twelve.

Extirpation and excommunication of serious offenders find parallels, both in the Second Temple Judaism and the Qumran community. In particular, excommunication from a group is found in Qumran examples.[61] The extirpation and excommunication is normally expressed by the description of how the offender met his demise. Three elements comprise the description: a ban, a curse, and a divinely inflicted death.[62] The description of Judas' death seems to fall into this category. Klassen supports this theory,

> It is possible that the main point of these stories for the writers of Matthew and Luke was the indication that Judas no longer was a member of the Jesus community. He removed himself from them. There could possibly be a link, then, between the way the Second Temple Judaism dealt with the defector, the way Qumran in particular extirpated or excommunicated someone, and the way the early church told stories about Judas' death. Judas could not live on among the disciples, for his role in the death of Jesus was too complicated. Thus, for some sectors of the Second Temple Judaism, the acts of banning, expulsion, and premature death were connected. Being 'cut off' from the people could take the form of excommunication or premature death.[63]

In our study, however, the picture of Peter 'removing' Judas rather than Judas 'removing himself' from the Twelve is more appropriate. The 'cut-

---

61. Cf. W. Horbury, 'Extirpation and Excommunication', *VT* 25.1 (1985), pp. 13-38.

62. Horbury, 'Extirpation and Excommunication', pp. 13-38.

63. Klassen, *Judas*, pp. 171-72.

ting off' of Judas from the Twelve is a significant step in rebuilding the confidence of the brethren in the leadership of the apostles.

The rebuilding of confidence is even more strengthened when the apostles, through Peter's representation, appeal for the replacement of Judas by an election. After Peter's speech on Judas' death practically 'cuts off' the latter from the 'Twelve', the apostles make another important step in reclaiming their honour and integrity—the appeal for Judas' replacement. We are now, therefore, in a position to fully understand that such an appeal is not simply for the completion of their number into twelve. The criteria in Acts 1.21-22 were not primarily designed to make sure that the replacing apostle lives up to being a twelfth member. Rather, the criteria are to assure and satisfy the community that whoever replaces Judas is credible, in keeping with the honour and integrity of being a member of the Twelve.

In some way, the criteria appear to be an appeal for approval from the audience. Within the context of the election narrative, it is an approval which the apostles seek from the 120 persons in the upper room. In the context between the author and his readers, it is an approval which the author seeks from the Christian community on his campaign on behalf of the Twelve. The next section further explains this point.

6. *The Purpose of the Criteria on the Replacement of Judas (Acts 1.21-22)*

My interest lies not on the criteria themselves but on why they were set up in the first place. To begin with, one may notice that it is still Peter who speaks in the forum. He alone is portrayed by the author as responsible for setting up the criteria in choosing the candidates for Judas' replacement.[64] However, because Peter speaks on behalf of the Eleven, the criteria may be understood as a proposal coming from the group of apostles with Peter serving as their spokesperson.

The proposed criteria (Acts 1.21-22) come crucially after the apostles have publicly submitted and declared Judas' excommunication (1.18-19). This may be viewed as suggesting the apostles' sincerity to resolve the

---

64. Johnson adds, 'A small but fascinating variant in Codex D makes "presented" singular, which would make Peter the nominator rather than the community. This would clash with the procedure suggested by Acts 6.5-6, but would delight later ecclesiastics eager to find Petrine primacy in the NT texts'. Johnson, *Acts*, p. 37.

social harm of Judas' betrayal, not only to the group of apostles, but also to the whole Christian community.

The show of sincerity does not stop at the announcement and the act of excommunication and extirpation of Judas. The suggestion to replace Judas is a further step to the reconciliation between the group of apostles and the brethren (whom we have suggested earlier as representing a wider group or body of believers). One may ask, of course, why the need to replace Judas? Why not settle with Eleven apostles, the original apostles who were commissioned by Jesus in Acts 1.7-8? Again, contrary to the suggested reason, namely, the urgent need to complete the number of the eleven apostles to twelve, I believe that the election primarily addresses a moral and social problem. The election is a proposal submitted by the apostles to the brethren in order to mitigate and appease the problem Judas had caused. Thus, when Matthias is eventually enrolled into the Twelve, the apostles as a group have finally redeemed themselves.

This is also why I believe that the issue of James' martyrdom in Acts 12.2 is no longer seen as creating a vacancy among the Twelve. There was no need to redeem the honour and integrity of the apostles as a group after Acts 1.26. This is also why the group of the Twelve have slowly faded out from the narrative after Acts 2.46. Their leadership, honour, and integrity have been reclaimed after the enrolment of Matthias, and substantiated by God after Pentecost. Their honour as apostles was recognized even as they have individually carried on in their ministries and mission. Moreover, this is also why the issue of Paul's apostleship is not discussed by the author of Acts within the concept of the Twelve. The discussions all along about the Twelve in Acts 1–2 are about the sociological implications of Judas' betrayal and not the completion of their number. That is why the author of Acts has not in any way made any implications about Paul being part of the Twelve. Paul's honour is not at all affected by Judas' betrayal.

7. The Final Choice of Judas' Replacement is Left to God

Another measure which the apostles take in assuring the brethren that the stigma of the Judas problem is struck out from the reputation of the Twelve is the decision to leave the final choice of Judas' replacement to God. This is the crucial feature which is missing in the council at Jerusalem meeting in Acts 15. The choice of Judas and Silas (who also have passed strict criteria themselves—'men who have risked their lives for the sake of our Lord Jesus Christ' [15.26]) was conducted completely by the apostles and the elders themselves. The assembly in Acts 15 does not make any reference at all to having prayed over or consulted God before making their choice.[65] While it is true that the Holy Spirit is mentioned in Acts 15.28, its direct involvement in the choice of Judas and Silas is not stated.

The casting of lots, as I have discussed in the ritual elements section, is practically an exercise which declares God's choice over the nominees. Again, there is no reference of this sort in the Acts 15 meeting.

8. *Summary*

In this chapter, I was able to demonstrate the plausibility of reading the election narrative of Acts 1.15-26 as a story in which the apostles defend themselves from a moral and social dilemma. This dilemma is the question on the honour of the apostles as successors to Jesus' leadership. The question has been brought about by Judas' membership of the apostolate and his betrayal of Jesus.

I have attempted to show that the apostles' defence of their honour and leadership integrity represents the ritual confrontation in their rituals of status transformation. This ritual confrontation is the final phase of the apostles' stage of transition. From here, the apostles as initiands enter the last stage of the RST—the stage of aggregation.

My description of this phase has necessitated the discussion of some vital historical issues. These issues need to be established in order to help us understand the place of the election narrative of Acts 1.15-26 in the perspective of a ritual confrontation. Thus, I divided the presentation of this chapter into two major sections. The first section dealt with the current research on the purpose of the election narrative. Under this, I find two prominent views: that the election was conducted to complete the number of the apostles to twelve, and that the election is the fulfilment of the promise of Jesus to his apostles in Lk. 22.30.

I found out that the idea concerning the election of a new apostle as a

---

65. In the Acts 15 meeting, the apostles are not the only ones described as a group who are actively participating. The elders are with them in an agenda almost similar to Acts 1—the choosing of persons to address a pending problem. Moreover, Peter is not the only one described as one directing the meeting. James, another leading figure in the leadership of the Christian community, is also pictured presenting his views (15.13-14). Both meetings (Acts 1 and 15) address a gathering of people referred to as the 'brethren'.

response to the need to complete the number of the Eleven apostles to Twelve is not necessarily the primary concern of Acts 1.15-26. I made this conclusion because of the absence of concrete evidence in the text itself. My further investigation shows that the concept of the urgency to have twelve apostles before the Pentecost event in Acts 2 was popularly drawn by some scholars from the promise which Jesus made to his apostles in Lk. 22.30. In this passage, Jesus promises his apostles that in the new Israel they will sit on thrones and serve as judges over the twelve tribes. I stated that the absence of the word 'twelve' before the word 'thrones' shows the general scope of the promise in Lk. 22.30. Furthermore, I argued that the idea that there should be twelve apostles for the twelve thrones was imported from the parallel saying in Mt. 19.28. I stated that it was more likely that Matthew was the one who inserted the word 'twelve' before the word 'thrones' because of the context where the saying appears. I concluded that the version of the reward-promise in Lk. 22.30 is closer to the original saying.

I pursued my argument about how the election narrative in Acts 1.15-26 does not primarily concern itself with the completion of the Eleven apostles to twelve, and that its primary agenda is to replace Judas in order to finally blot out the social and moral embarrassment he has caused the apostolate by analysing the extent of the relationship between Lk. 22.30 and its alleged fulfilment in Acts 1.15-26. I found out that one of the major points as to why I should doubt the suggestion about the promise-fulfilment relationship between Lk. 22.30 and Acts 1.15-26 is the absence of any direct or indirect claim either by the author or the characters in the narrative that the election of Matthias is indeed the fulfilment of Jesus' reward in Lk. 22.30.

After having dealt with the important historical issues surrounding Acts 1.15-26, I proceeded to show how the narrative can be viewed as the defence of the apostles against the Judas problem. I started by proving how the author portrays Peter as speaking on behalf of the Eleven apostles and not the 120 brethren as some would claim. Instead, I showed the plausibility of the scenario that Peter acts as the defence spokesperson for the group of the apostles while the rest of the 120 brethren act as the jury or representatives of the Christian community.

I then enumerated the evidence in Peter's speech (and in the rest of the narrative) which shows how the apostles distanced themselves from their association and the guilt of Judas. The reasons include: (1) that the betrayal and death of Judas was the fulfilment of scripture. That because it is the fulfilment of scripture, there was no way that anyone could have prevented it nor do the apostles have any responsibility towards it; (2) that the grotesque description of Judas' death shows the evil nature of Judas and that his actions were his and his alone; (3) that the apostles through Peter publicly declared Judas' extirpation and excommunication for the apostolate, cutting off any ties with the group of apostles; and (4) to finally heal the damage which Judas has caused to the reputation and honour of the apostles, the Eleven proposed the election of a trustworthy and reliable replacement. The proposal comes with the strict criteria which all the candidates should meet in order to qualify for the vacant post; (5) the choice between the candidates was left to God through the casting of lots. This expresses the apostles' sincerity and assurance that whoever is going to be Judas' replacement is God-ordained and the fear of the repeat of Judas' betrayal is no longer possible.

Just as Jesus' ritual confrontation with the devil in Lk. 4.1-12 ends up with victory over his adversary, the apostles complete their version of the ritual confrontation with a solution to the Judas problem—the election of Matthias. All the concerns which were left hanging from the time Jesus was arrested until the time he departed were answered during this assembly in the upper room. The matters about Judas' death, and more importantly, the degree of the Eleven's participation and accountability in Judas' betrayal of Jesus, were all cleared up in the apostles' defence before the 120 brethren in the upper room.

The apostles as initiands now complete their stage of transition. Whether they have been vindicated or denied their appeal to regain their honour and leadership integrity remains to be seen in the events that are to follow.

Part III

AGGREGATION

Chapter 8

THE APOSTLES AS PRIMARY RECIPIENTS OF THE FATHER'S PROMISE

The excommunication of Judas from the exclusive group, plus the election of Matthias as his credible replacement, finally solves the one problem which has constantly shamed the reputation of the apostles—that the 'traitor' was a member of the Twelve. By electing Matthias, Judas is officially struck off from the exclusive list and his seat is filled in. Matthias, therefore, is a 'solution' to a moral problem more than just a statistical settlement to complete the number of the apostles to twelve.

Facing and solving the Judas problem is the last phase in the apostles' stage of *transition*. The training of the initiands is over and the next stage is the confirmation and installation of their new status and role as leaders of the Christian community. This stage is *aggregation*, the time when the initiands have come out from their liminal status and are incorporated into society with defined rights and obligations. The apostles 'become useful again to society as they take up the roles for which the ritual has prepared them'.[1]

As I have previously done, I will first identify the ritual elements before I move to the ritual process. What follows are the ritual elements in Acts 2. One particular element that defines the setting of the whole of Acts 2 is the Feast of Pentecost. To be precise, the author's intention to locate the Spirit's outpouring on the Day of Pentecost is vital to the understanding of the apostles' aggregation into society. I will begin with a brief background study of Pentecost.

1.   McVann, 'Rituals of Status Transformation', p. 341; Turner, *The Forest of Symbols*, pp. 251-60.

1. *The Ritual Elements in Acts 2*

1.1. *The Feast of Pentecost*

There are three great feasts observed annually in ancient Israel. They are the pilgrimage feasts (חג) of the Passover[2] which was eventually combined with the feast of the Unleavened Bread (מצות),[3] of Weeks (שבעות), and of Tabernacles (סכת).[4] Of these three, the Passover and the feast of Weeks came to be recognized by the Christian tradition. The feast of Tabernacles, although mentioned in Jn 7.2 and Mt. 9.5 (and parallels) has not really found its way into being one of the celebrated Christian festivals.

Next to the Passover,[5] the feast of Weeks is the second most celebrated in the NT times. Known also as the feast of Harvest (or wheat harvest; Exod. 23.16),[6] the 'feast of Weeks' (חג שבעות)—its name and how it is dated—is found in Deut. 16.9-10,

> You shall count seven weeks; begin to count the seven weeks from the time you first put the sickle to the standing grain. Then you shall keep the feast of weeks to the Lord your God with the tribute of a freewill offering from your hand, which you shall give as the Lord your God blesses you...

In Lev. 23.15-21[7] (cf. Num. 28.26-31) we find more details of how the ritual is conducted. The date of the feast is determined by counting fifty

---

2.　From the Hebrew word פסח (e.g. 2 Sam. 4.4; 1 Kgs 18.21; with the meaning 'to jump over', or 'left out', Exod. 12.13, 23, 27).

3.　R. de Vaux, *Ancient Israel: Its Life and Institutions* (trans. J. McHugh; London: Darton, Longman & Todd, 1961), pp. 484-93.

4.　The name סכת may be found for example in Deut. 16.13, 16; Lev. 23.34. The term 'tabernacles' is from the Latin *tabernacula*. The term 'tents', on the other hand, may be misleading since the feast did not in any way involve the erection of tents. סכת literally means 'huts' and may be related to what Exod. 23.16 and 34.22 refer to as the 'feast of Ingathering'. Cf. Vaux, *Ancient Israel*, p. 495.

5.　The Passover became the principal feast in Second Temple Judaism. It was primarily observed in the second month of the year according to the religious calendars most especially in Exod. 12. Cf. Exod. 23.15; 34.18, 25; Deut. 16.1-8; Lev. 23.5-8; especially the rituals in Num. 28.16-25 and Ezra 45.21-24; and the story in 9.1-14.

6.　It was one of the main periods in the agricultural calendar of Palestine (Gen. 30.14; Judg. 15.1; 1 Sam. 6.13; 12.17), and in the calendar of Gezer. Vaux, *Ancient Israel*, p. 493.

7.　'And you shall count from the morrow after the sabbath, from the day that you brought the sheaf of the wave offering; seven full weeks shall they be, counting fifty days to the morrow after the seventh sabbath'.

days (i.e. seven weeks plus a day) from the day when the first fruits of the harvest was offered to the priest.[8] The 'fifty days' count explains why the Greek-speaking Jews understood and translated the feast with the term Πεντηκοστή.[9] Later on, a fixed date was understood for Pentecost after the Priestly tradition related it to the joint feasts of the Passover and Unleavened bread.[10] The feast later on came to be celebrated in the third month of the year.[11]

Again, my aim is to understand how the events of the Spirit's outpouring in Acts 2 relates to the aggregation of the Twelve into society. We know that the coming of the Spirit is an event very much anticipated by the apostles as Jesus himself instructed them to remain in Jerusalem and wait for its fulfilment (Acts 1.8a). Acts 2.1-27 narrates such a fulfilment. Yet, how is it that such an awaited event happens to coincide with a great Jewish festival—the day of Pentecost? Why, of all the many days in the Jewish calendar, does the outpouring of the Spirit occur on the day when a significant pilgrimage feast is being celebrated in Jerusalem? To rephrase my initial question above: 'How is the Spirit's baptism of the apostles which happens on the day when the great pilgrimage feast of Pentecost is being celebrated relate to the aggregation of the Twelve into the society?'

1.2. *Pentecost as a Covenant Renewal?*

I indicated earlier that the feast of Pentecost was eventually fixed on the third month of the year as the time for commemoration. Scanning through other evidence, certain sectarian celebrations are held on the same date which is designated for Pentecost. For example, in 2 Chron. 15.10-12[12] the 'gathering in Jerusalem on the *third month* in the fifteenth year of Asa's reign' (15.10) and the 'offering of the first fruits' (15.11) highly characterizes the feast of Pentecost. But what is interesting in this gathering is

---

8.   Cf. I.H. Marshall, 'The Significance of Pentecost', *SJT* 30 (1977), pp. 347-69 (347-48).

9.   The 'fiftieth' day is first mentioned in Tob. 2.1 and 2 Macc. 12.31-32 along with the name 'feast of Weeks'.

10.   Cf. Fitzmyer, 'The Ascension of Christ and Pentecost', p. 281.

11.   For an idea on the disagreement between the Pharisees and Sadducees on the exact date of Pentecost, see Fitzmyer, 'The Ascension of Christ and Pentecost', p. 281.

12.   2 Chron. 15.10-12: 'They were gathered at Jerusalem in the third month of the fifteenth year of the reign of Asa. They sacrificed to the Lord on that day, from the spoil which they had brought, seven hundred oxen and seven thousand sheep. And they entered into a covenant to seek the Lord, the God of their fathers, with all their heart and with all their soul;...'

the aspect of the renewal of the covenant with God, a covenant which 'their fathers had made'. This renewal of the covenant is an allusion to either the Noahic or the Sinai covenant (15.12). In other words, what transpired on the third month of Asa's reign was a pilgrimage in Jerusalem characterized by the offering of the first fruits of harvest and the peoples' renewal of the covenant with God. The Sinai event, in particular, is dated by Exod. 19.1 on 'third month of the new moon' after their departure from Egypt. What we have, therefore, is the feast of Weeks (Pentecost) and the renewal of the Sinai covenant being commemorated on the same date. Could Pentecost then have evolved from just being the feast of harvest to a celebration of the giving of the Torah at Mount Sinai?[13] Some scholars think so.[14] The most suggested pieces of evidence are discussed below.

1.2.1. The Book of Jubilees. Evidence alluding to the feast of Pentecost as being characterized by a renewal of covenant is found in the book of Jubilees[15] ch. 6.[16] Verses 15-18a speak of God's promise to Noah concerning not to destroy the earth by flood:

> He gave Noah and his children a sign that there would not again be a flood on the earth. He placed a rainbow in the clouds as a sign of the eternal covenant that flood waters would not again be on the earth to destroy it as long as the earth remains. For this reason, it has been ordained and written on the heavenly tablets that they should celebrate the festival of weeks during this month—one time each year—to renew the covenant annually. This entire festival was celebrated in heaven from the time of creation until Noah's day—for twenty-six jubilee-periods and five weeks of years (1309 years).[17]

13. Cf. Marshall, 'The Significance of Pentecost', p. 348.

14. E.g. J. Dunn, 'Pentecost', in *Christ and the Spirit: Pneumatology*, II (Grand Rapids: Eerdmans, 1998), p. 211; see also the bibliography of A.J.M. Wedderburn, 'Traditions and Redactions in Acts 2.1-13', *JSNT* 55 (1994), pp. 27-54.

15. Written approximately between 150–140 BCE, the book of Jubilees is said to be the account of the revelation which Moses received from God in Mt Sinai. Its primary theological teaching focuses on the author's eschatological teaching in the context of the Law and Israel's future. J.C. Vanderkam, 'The Book of Jubilees', in *ABD*, pp. 1030-32.

16. It is also in this text that we find the connection between the Noahic and the Sinai covenants.

17. M. de Jonge, 'The Book of Jubilees', in *idem* (ed.), *Outside the Old Testament World* (trans. J.C. Vanderkam; Cambridge: Cambridge University Press, 1985), pp. 122-23.

Noah's descendants are instructed to observe the covenant annually. His children kept but later on corrupted it until God had to renew it with Moses at the 'mountain' (6.18b-19):

> Noah and his children kept it for seven jubilee-periods and one week of years (350 years) until Noah's death. His children corrupted it until Abraham's time and would not eat blood. Abraham alone kept it; then his sons Isaac and Jacob kept it until your [Moses'] time. In your day the Israelites had forgotten it until I renewed it for them as this mountain.[18]

We know that the mountain being referred to is Sinai as this is clearly described in 1.1-2:

> In the first year of the Israelites' exodus from Egypt, the third month, the sixteenth of that month, the Lord said to Moses: 'Come up to me on the mountain, and I will give you two stone tablets of the Law and the commandment which I have written so that you may teach them'. [So] Moses went up onto the mountain of the Lord. Then the Lord's glory settled on Mt. Sinai, and a cloud overshadowed it for six days.[19]

1.2.2. The Essene Sect in Qumran. The Qumran community is another of the sectarian groups which may have observed Pentecost as a covenant renewal feast. 1QS 1.8–2.16[20] instructs the community to conduct the covenant renewal on an annual basis.[21] Although the feast of Pentecost is not specifically mentioned in this text, yet because the Qumran sect is

---

18. De Jonge, 'The Book of Jubilees', pp. 122-23.

19. De Jonge, 'The Book of Jubilees', pp. 122-23. Marshall adds that for the author of Jubilees, the Law-giving is associated with the feast of Weeks. This issue appears to have been discussed early in the second century CE by R. Akiba. See Marshall, 'The Significance of Pentecost', p. 349, n. 2; cf. B. Noack, 'The Day of Pentecost in Jubilees, Qumran and Acts', *ASTI* 1 (1962), pp. 73-95 (81).

20. Especially 1QS 1.13b-20, 'They shall not stray from one of all God's orders concerning their appointed times; they shall not advance their appointed times nor shall they retard any one of their feasts. They shall not veer from his reliable precepts in order to carry out all that he commands and in order not to stray from following him for any fear, dread, grief or agony (that might occur) during the dominion of Belial. When they enter the covenant, the priests and the levites shall bless the God of salvation and all the works of his faithfulness and all those who enter the covenant shall repeat after them: Amen, Amen.' Text and English translation from F.G. Martinez, *The Dead Sea Scrolls Translated: The Qumran Texts in English* (trans. W.G.E. Watson; Grand Rapids: Eerdmans, 2nd edn, 1996), p. 3.

21. 1QS 1.19, 'They shall act in this way year after year…'

known to have followed the Jubilees calendar,[22] the likelihood of this observance being done on the third month of the year[23]—the same date for the feast of Pentecost—is not remote.[24] Turner adds that the recently published 4Q266 confirms this as lines 17-18. They show the requirement of the 'formal coming together in the third month to curse those who depart from the Torah'.[25]

1.2.3. *Some Rabbinic Writings.* Evidence from R. Jose ben Halafta (c. 150 CE) which states, 'The Israelites immolated the Passover lamb in Egypt on the fourteenth of Nisan and it was a Thursday... The third month, the sixth day of the month, the Ten Commandments were given to them, and it was a sabbath day';[26] for which Exod. 19 was the appointed lesson to be read on the feast day.[27] Compare the statement from R. Eleazar (c. 270 AD), 'It [the feast of Weeks] is the day on which the Torah was given'.[28]

22. Fitzmyer, 'The Ascension of Christ and Pentecost', p. 282. Also S. Talmon, 'The Calendar Reckoning of the Sect from the Judaean Desert', in *Scripta Hierosolymitana. IV. Aspects in the Dead Sea Scrolls* (Jerusalem: Magnes Press, Hebrew University, 1967), pp. 177-79.

23. Fitzmyer discusses the celebration by the Qumran sect of three Pentecostal feasts which makes a complete cycle. Evidence from the Temple scroll in Qumran Cave 11, most specifically 11QTemple 18.10-13—the Feast of Weeks or Feast of First Fruits, third month, fifteenth day; 11QTemple 19.11-14—the Feast of New Wine, fifth month, third day; and 11QTemple 21.12-16—the Feast of New Oil, sixth month, twenty-second day. Cf. Fitzmyer, 'The Ascension of Christ and Pentecost', pp. 283-84. See also Y. Yadin, *The Temple Scroll: The Hidden Law of the Dead Sea Sect* (London: Weidenfeld & Nicholson, 1985), pp. 91-96.

24. R. Le Deaut, 'Pentecost and Jewish Tradition', *Doctrine and Life* 20 (1970), pp. 254-56; Marshall, 'The Significance of Pentecost', p. 349; Fitzmyer, 'The Ascension of Christ and Pentecost', p. 282; J.T. Milik, *Ten Years of Discovery in the Wilderness of Judaea* (Naperville, IL: Allenson, 1959), pp. 103, 116-18; G. Vermes, *The Dead Sea Scrolls: Qumran in Perspective* (Cleveland: Collins & World, 1978), pp. 177-79.

25. Turner, *Power from on High*, p. 281. R. Le Deaut also finds evidence from the *Damascus Document* suggesting that the feast of Weeks was celebrated as a feast of covenant. Cf. Le Deaut, 'Pentecost and Jewish Tradition', pp. 254-56.

26. *Seder 'Olam Rabba* 5, English translation from Le Deaut, 'Pentecost and Jewish Tradition', pp. 256-57. Text from H.L. Strack und P. Billerbeck, *Kommentar zum Neuen Testament aus Talmud und Midrasch*, II (Munich, 1956), p. 601.

27. Marshall, 'The Significance of Pentecost', p. 349. This is set by the Targums in Exod. 19.1 as fifty days after the Passover, and the meal in Exod. 24.11 is described, according to Turner, 'in the language of the harvest covenant meal of Deut. 16.11. Cf. Turner, *Power from on High*, p. 282, n. 42.

28. *B. Pesahim* 68b. English translation from Menzies, *Empowered for Witness*,

Based on what I have just cited, the renewal of the Noahic covenant and the giving of the Torah to Moses at Mt Sinai happen to coincide with the feast of Weeks which takes place on the third month of every year. There are grounds, therefore, to assume that the feast of Weeks was no longer just a feast of harvest but also the commemoration of covenant renewals.

1.3. *That Luke was Influenced by the Moses/Sinai Traditions*
Others argue that the author of Luke–Acts himself was influenced by the Moses/Sinai traditions when he composed the Pentecost story. Thus, when the readers read of the outpouring of the Spirit in Acts 2, those who are familiar with the Jewish Sinai traditions are reminded of the story when Moses received the Torah from God at Sinai.[29] This suggestion is based, not only on the evidence I have cited above, but also on the various literary, language, and imagery parallels between other traditions and the Acts 2 account.[30] The following are some of the more prominent parallel examples.

1.3.1. *Exodus 19 and 20.*
One of the reasons why some scholars consider the possibility that the author of Luke–Acts may have written his Pentecost story within the tradition of Moses and his Sinai experience is the striking verbal parallelism between Acts 2 and Exod. 19 and 20.[31] For instance, (1) the adverb ὁμοῦ and its variant ὁμοθυμαδόν[32] is parallel with Exod. 19.8 referring to how 'all (ὁμοθυμαδόν) the people gathered

---

p. 190, n. 5; see also J. Neusner, *The Talmud: A Close Encounter* (Minneapolis: Fortress Press, 1991).

29. Turner, *Power from on High*, p. 280.

30. What we find are allusions and not strictly the literary dependence of Luke on the said traditions. Nevertheless, Turner suggests that, '…Luke's account was selected and shaped in a milieu which had contacts with such tradition, and in which the Pentecost account (in the form we have it) would have been especially striking'. Turner, *Power from on High*, p. 280; see also R. Maddox, *The Purpose of Luke–Acts* (Edinburgh: T. & T. Clark, 1982), p. 138; Lüdemann, *Early Christianity*, pp. 41-42; L. O' Reilly, *Word and Sign in the Acts of the Apostles* (Rome: Pontifical Biblical Institute, 1987), pp. 21-29.

31. J. Dupont argued for these verbal allusions in his work 'The First Christian Pentecost', in *idem, The Salvation of the Gentiles* (Ramsey, NJ: Paulist Press, 1979), pp. 35-59. My summary above is based mainly from Fitzmyer, 'The Ascension of Christ and Pentecost', p. 283.

32. A variant employed in C3, E, M, Y. See my discussion on ὁμοθυμαδόν in section 5.1.3.

together'; (2) the sound which came from heaven as stated in Acts 2.2 is ἦχος and φωνή in 2.6. Exod. 19.16 reads ἐγίνοντο φωναὶ which may be read as 'there were sounds' (or as Fitzmyer suggests 'thunders'), also φωνὴ τῆς σάλπιγγος ἤχει μέγα ('a sound of the trumpet blasted loudly'); (3) Acts 2.2 also indicates that the sound came from heaven (ἐκ τοῦ οὐρανοῦ), the same source in Exod. 20.22—'I have spoken to you from heaven' (ἐκ τοῦ οὐρανοῦ λελάληκα πρὸς ὑμᾶς);[33] Fitzmyer also adds that 'Yahweh's descent to Mt. Sinai in fire (Exod. 19.18) provides an Old Testament background for "the tongues of fire" in Acts 2.3'.[34]

1.3.2. *Examples from Philo*

1.3.2.1. *De Decalogo*. Philo's *Decalogue* is a treatise which basically deals with two issues. First are issues concerning the giving of the Torah at Sinai. The second pertains to issues on adultery. Our interest lies on the first part. Consider both the verbal and imagery parallels with the Pentecost story in Acts 2. I have italicized and underlined the words and phrases to show the apparent parallels:

The Decalogue[35]	*Acts 2*
(v. 33) I should suppose that God wrought on this occasion a *miracle*[36] of a truly holy kind by bidding an *invisible sound to be created in the air more marvellous than all instruments* and fitted with perfect harmonies, not soulless, nor yet composed of body and soul like a living creature, but a rational soul full of clearness and distinctness, which giving shape and tension to the *air* and changing it to *flaming fire, sounded* forth like the *breath* through a trumpet an *articulate*	(v. 1) When the day of Pentecost had come, *they were all together in one place* (v. 2). And *suddenly a sound came from heaven like the rush of a mighty wind,* and it filled all the *house where they were sitting* (v. 3). And there appeared to them *tongues as of fire,* distributed and resting on each one of them (v. 4). And they were all filled with the Holy Spirit and began to speak in other tongues, as the Spirit gave them utterance (v. 5). *Now there were dwelling in*

---

33. The verbal and imagery parallels may also be found in Deut. 4.11-12: 'And you came near and stood at the foot of the mountain while the mountain burned with fire to the heart of heaven, wrapped in darkness, cloud, and gloom. Then the Lord spoke to you out of the midst of the fire; you heard the sound of words (φωνὴν ῥημάτων ὑμεῖς ἠκούσατε), but saw no form; there was only voice (φωνήν).'

34. Fitzmyer, 'The Ascension of Christ and Pentecost', p. 283.

35. Text and English translation from Philo, *The Decalogue* 32-36, 44-46 (Loeb).

36. Compare θαυματουργῆσαι with ἐθαύμαζον of Acts 2.7. Cf. Turner, *Power from on High*, p. 283.

voice so loud that it appeared to be equally audible to the farthest as well as the nearest (v. 35). But the new miraculous voice was set in action and kept in flame by the power of God which breathed upon it and spread it abroad on every side and made it more illuminating in its ending than in its beginning by creating in the souls of each and all another kind of hearing far superior to the hearing of ears. For that is but a sluggish sense, inactive until *aroused by the impact of the air*, but *the hearing of the mind possessed by God* makes the first advance and goes out to meet the spoken words with the keenest rapidity (v. 36). So much for the divine voice. But we may properly ask why, when *all these many thousands were collected in one spot, He thought good in proclaiming His ten oracles to address each not as to several persons but as to one*, Thou shalt not commit adultery, Thou shalt not kill, Thou shalt not steal, and so too with the rest. (v. 44b)…*the rush of the heaven-sent fire…* (v. 46). Then from the *midst of the fire that streamed from heaven there sounded forth to their utter amazement a voice, for the flame became articulate speech in language familiar to the audience, and so clearly and distinctly were the words formed by it that they seemed to see rather than hear them*.

Jerusalem Jews, devout men from every nation under heaven (v. 6). *And at this sound the multitude came together,* and they were bewildered, because *each one heard them speaking in his own language* (v. 7). And they were *amazed and wondered,* saying, 'Are not all these who are speaking Galileans? (v. 8). *And how is it that we hear, each of us in his own native language?* (v. 9). Par'thians and Medes and E'lamites and residents of Mesopotamia, Judea and Cappadocia, Pontus and Asia (v. 10), Phrygia and Pamphylia, Egypt and the parts of Libya belonging to Cyrene, and visitors from Rome, both Jews and proselytes (v. 11), Cretans and Arabians, *we hear them telling in our own tongues the mighty works of God*' (v. 12). And all were amazed and perplexed, saying to one another, 'What does this mean?' (v. 13). But others mocking said, 'They are filled with new wine'.

Despite the fact that Philo is describing a totally different event, not to mention the disparity of time, date, and place of writing, one cannot help but notice that Luke's Pentecost account shares striking similarities with the vocabulary of Philo. This strengthens the possibility that Luke and other earlier and contemporary writers wrote their accounts in a milieu of OT tradition.

1.3.2.2. *De Specialibus Legibus*. Philo's *Special Laws* extend the theophanic descriptions of the 'sound' which comes from heaven and the mighty signs which come with it. In II.189, the celebration of the 'Trumpet feast' is being described. The text goes,

> For then the sound of the trumpet pealed from heaven and reached, we may suppose, the ends of the universe so that the event might strike terror even into those who were far from the spot and dwelling well nigh at the extremities of the earth, who would come to the natural conclusion that such mighty signs portended mighty consequences.[37]

The phrase 'those dwelling in extremities of the earth' (ἐν ἐσχάταις κατοικοῦντας) reflects what Acts 1.8 has—('Ιερουσαλὴμ καί ἐν πάση τῇ 'Ιουδαια καὶ Σαμαρεια καὶ ἕως ἐσχάτου τῆς γῆς ('Jerusalem and in all Judea and Samaria and to the ends of the earth').[38] Likewise the phrase τά οὕτως μεγάλα μεγάλων ἀποστελεσμάτων ἐστὶ σημεῖα is reminiscent of Acts 2.11—τά μεγαλεῖα τοῦ θεοῦ.[39]

1.3.3. *The Babylonian Talmud Shabbath 88b*. An important parallel to the account in Acts 2.5-13 where the multitude which came together heard their own language being spoken is reflected in the later era of the traditions in the Babylonian Talmud (*b. Šab.* 88b).[40] For example, Rabbi Jochanan (c. CE 279) had referred to the divine word at Sinai as saying 'Every single word that went forth from the Omnipotent was split up into seventy languages'. Likewise, from the school of Rabbi Ishmael came the tradition which claims that 'Just as a hammer is divided into many sparks, so every single word that went forth from the Holy One, blessed be He, split up into seventy languages'.

---

37. Philo, *Special Laws*, II.189.
38. Turner, *Power from on High*, p. 284.
39. Cf. Acts 2.19, 22. The Targums of *Pseudo Jonathan* on Exod. 20.2 and *Neofiti* on Exod. 19.16ff. show expansions of the Sinai episode sharing familiar imagery of the Pentecost account in Acts 2. In *Pseudo Jonathan* it states, 'The first word, as it came forth from the mouth of the Holy One, may his Name be blessed, was like storms and lightning, and flames of fire, with a burning light on His right hand and on His left. It winged its way through the air of the heavens, and was made manifest unto the camp of Israel, and returned, and was engraven on the tables of the covenant that were given by the hand of Mosheh...' English translation from J.W. Etheridge, *The Targums of Onkelos and Jonathan Ben Uzziel on the Pentateuch* (New York: Ktav, 1968), p. 551.
40. H. Freedman, 'Shabbath', II (1938) in I. Epstein (ed.), *The Babylonian Talmud* (London: Soncino, 1935–52), p. 420.

The literary, language, and imagery parallels I have just described have encouraged a majority of NT scholars to view that the author of Luke–Acts may have been using the Sinai episode as a platform for the event of the outpouring of the Spirit. Jacques Dupont's analysis of these allusions expresses this view well.[41]

1.　By the time Luke penned Acts, Pentecost was regarded as a feast commemorating the giving of the law on Sinai;

2.　The Pentecost account contains numerous literary allusions to Sinai traditions and therefore was shaped with this event in mind;

3.　Acts 2.33 is based on Ps. 67.19 with reference to Moses, who at Sinai, ascended into heaven to receive the Torah in order that he might give it to humanity. In Acts 2.33 the psalm is applied to Jesus who ascended to the right hand of God, received the Spirit, and poured it out on the disciples. Thus the gift of the Spirit is viewed as the essence of the new covenant and the new law—an interior law, written on the heart (Jer. 31.33; cf. Ezek. 36.26).

Fitzmyer, on the other hand, admits that none of the alleged allusions is unambiguous. He, however, recognizes that if ever there is any validity to them is that 'they may supply an OT and Palestinian Jewish background for the first Christian Pentecost when the newly reconstituted Twelve, filled with and emboldened by the Spirit, (Acts 15.7) on the Feast of its Assembly for the renewal of the Sinai Covenant'.[42]

1.4. *Against Pentecost as a New Sinai*

There are, however, strong objections raised against viewing the Pentecost story in Acts 2 as a 'new Sinai'. R. de Vaux, for example, doubts the relationship of the Christian feast of Pentecost with the Sinai event. For him, Acts 2 which was marked by the gift of the Spirit and by the calling of all nations into the new Church, does not coincide with the feast of Weeks in the manner the Qumran community celebrated the event. 'The story in Acts contains no allusion to the Sinaitic Covenant nor to the New Covenant of which Christ is the mediator'.[43]

A much stronger objection comes from Robert Menzies. In his mono-

---

41.　Cf. J. Dupont, 'La nouvelle Pentecôte (Act 2, 1-11)', in *Nouvelles études sur les Actes des Apôtres* (Paris: Cerf, 1984), p. 193; English translation from Menzies, *Empowered for Witness*, pp. 189-90.

42.　Fitzmyer, 'The Ascension of Christ and Pentecost', p. 283.

43.　De Vaux, *Ancient Israel*, p. 495.

graph *Empowered for Witness: The Spirit in Luke–Acts*,[44] Menzies responds to the evidence above as lacking and inadequate to substantiate the 'new Sinai' argument.[45] For instance,

1. With the implications from some rabbinic writings such as R. Jose ben Halafta (c. 150 CE) and that of R. Eleazar (c. 270 CE), both of which place the giving of the law on the day of Pentecost, Menzies argues that these evidence are 'late and of little value for reconstructing Jewish attitudes toward the feast before the destruction of the temple'. He adds, 'The transformation of the feast from a harvest festival to a festival commemorating the law was undoubtedly given impetus through the destruction of the temple. Without the temple the rituals of sacrifice so central to the harvest feast could no longer be performed.'[46]

2. Suggestions that Jub. 1.1 and 6.19 speak of the Sinai covenant are primarily based on the perception that the giving of the Torah is related to the renewal of the covenant with Noah. In other words, while the feast of Weeks may be linked with the covenants made with Noah (6.1-20) and Abraham (15.1-24), Menzies does not find any strong evidence to connect the feast with the Sinai covenant.

3. The evidence from 1QS 1.8–2.18 showing that the Qumran community observed the renewal of the covenant annually may be true. What Menzies doubts is how this annual observation relates to the feast of Pentecost. The suggestion that because the community adopted the Jubilees calendar, Qumran's view of Pentecost as a covenant renewal festival should be doubted since none of the scrolls explicitly supports it.

4. The similarities between Luke's Pentecost account and the Sinai traditions of Philo are dismissed by Menzies as simply the common acquaintance with the language of Jewish theophany.

5. As to the traditions found in the Babylonian Talmud, the parallel of communicating the divine word in different languages is explained as simply the 'writers' (of both the Sinai and Lukan traditions) interest in the universal significance of the events which they describe'. Thus, according to Menzies, 'it is not surprising that a parallel of this nature is found in these accounts'. He further adds that,

---

44. Menzies, *Empowered for Witness*, was a slightly revised thesis version originally published in 1991 by the same publisher with the title *The Development of Early Christian Pneumatology with Special Reference to Luke–Acts*.

45. Menzies, *Empowered for Witness*, pp. 190-97.

46. Menzies, *Empowered for Witness*, p. 191.

the theory that Luke was influenced by these rabbinic legends can also be questioned on the grounds that it anachronistically reads Acts 2 in light of rabbinic texts from a later era. Although it is possible that these texts reflect traditions which stem from the first century, support from such an assumption is lacking.[47]

Summing up his investigation of the alleged evidence in arguing for Pentecost as a new Sinai, Menzies offers the following points: First, there is no sufficient support to view that Pentecost was celebrated as a festival which commemorates the giving of the law at Sinai in the time of Luke's writing; second, the examples from some first-century sectarian circles which celebrate Pentecost as a covenant renewal do not necessarily lead to the conclusion that Judaism in general has viewed the same feast as in like manner; and third, that the mere mention of τὴν ἡμέραν τῆς πεντη-κοστῆς in Acts 2.1 is not enough to suggest that the images of Moses, Sinai, or covenant renewal ceremony were evoked into the minds of the readers of Luke–Acts. Menzies caps his findings by stating that,

> The evidence suggests that Luke neither shaped the Pentecost account with Sinai traditions in mind nor unconsciously used material significantly influenced by them. The Pentecost account indicates that Luke did not view the gift of the Spirit as the power of the new law of Christ. According to Luke, the Spirit of Pentecost is the source of prophetic inspiration and, as such, the Spirit of mission.[48]

Does Menzies have a point? Unfortunately, I am inclined to dismiss Menzies's proposal. I say this because most of Menzies's arguments rely on the perils of parallelism. Heeding primarily to S. Sandmel's warning of 'parallelomania',[49] Menzies finds most of the evidence simply as sharing a broad milieu rather than direct dependence. Menzies cites at least four examples which also share the same language and imagery but have nothing to do with the giving of the law at Sinai: 4 Ezra 13.1-10; 1 En. 14;

---

47. Menzies, *Empowered for Witness*, p. 197.
48. Menzies, *Empowered for Witness*, p. 201.
49. Cf. S. Sandmel, 'Parallelomania', *JBL* 81 (1962), pp. 1-13. Menzies notes Sandmel's cautions as: 'That the similarities may reflect a shared milieu rather than direct literary dependence. For this reason it is imperative not only to isolate the parallels between Acts 2.1-13 and various Sinai traditions, but also to determine the parameters of the milieu in which these parallels are found... That distinctions are often more important than similarities... Warns of the anachronistical reading of late rabbinic citations as "persuasive parallels" for the New Testament documents.' Cf. Menzies, *Empowered for Witness*, pp. 193-94.

2 Sam. 22.8-15; Isa. 66.15-16.[50] For Menzies, dissimilarities ought to say more than similarities.

This issue has been taken up by Max Turner, a response which I find more credible. Turner agrees that indeed there is no direct literary dependence by Luke on the said traditions. However, he rightly points out that,

> Luke, by contrast, is not attempting to 'describe' Sinai, but another event, so we should anticipate great differences in detail... The real question then is, would the Pentecost account strike a Jewish reader as sounding 'like' Sinai, despite the differences? Are there sufficient 'structural', linguistic and conceptual points of contact to be liable to evoke a comparison?[51]

With the similar features I have cited between Acts 2 and the Sinai traditions, including the striking parallels between the examples from Philo, we can assume that indeed the Pentecost story ought to evoke from its readers some comparisons with the Sinai event. This assumption (which I will expand later) is important in understanding why the aggregation of the apostles happened in the time of the Pentecost celebration.

Having said that Pentecost is not just a feast of Harvest but also a celebration of the renewal of the covenant and the giving of the Torah at Sinai; and having said that the outpouring of the Spirit as narrated by the author of Luke–Acts evokes the Sinai tradition upon its readers, I can now attempt to study the significance of the whole Pentecost narrative in Acts 2 in relation to the aggregation of the apostles into society. However, there is still another significant ritual element which needs to be consistently emphasized. This element is the character of the apostles as the subject/focus of the whole ritual process. In other words, because I am reading this study from the perspective of the Ritual of Status Transformation, my methodology assumes the apostles to be the subject in the narrative. I have initially discussed this issue in Chapter 2 (i.e. 2.1.1). However, my discussion was focused only on the introduction of the apostles by the author into the narrative in Acts 1.3-4. The issue that the apostles are the primary focus of the narrative (it seems) becomes more difficult in Acts 2.

The difficulty comes from a single and ambiguous word—the πάντες in Acts 2.1. On this word, the recipients of the Spirit's baptism, the question of who spoke in tongues and testified to the crowd in Jerusalem, and eventually, the subject of the whole narrative of Acts 2, are completely dependent. The popular view is that πάντες refers to the 120

---

50. Menzies, *Empowered for Witness*, pp. 195-96.
51. Turner, *Power from on High*, p. 283.

people mentioned in 1.15 and not just to the Twelve apostles. If this is so, then our suggestion that Acts 2 as the ritual stage which presents the Twelve initiands being incorporated into society is weakened. The next section deals with this issue.

2. Πάντες *in Acts 2.1*

There are at least four reasons why πάντες is commonly understood as not only referring to the Twelve apostles.[52] First is that it happens to be the natural reading of the term since the 120 persons are introduced in the preceding verses. Second is the repetition of the phrase ἐπὶ τὸ αὐτό in 1.15 and 2.1. Third is the 'potentially universal character of the gift of the Spirit'.[53] Arguing that the apostles were the only ones who received this gift would be uncharacteristic of Luke. Finally, because the crowd of more than twelve who had gathered in Jerusalem claimed that they heard their own languages being spoken, it is therefore implied that there were more than twelve recipients of the Spirit's gift who blurted out in tongues.

2.1. *The Natural Reading of* Πάντες *in 2.1*
That the natural reading of πάντες should be the 120 persons referred to in 1.15 may have a point. However, 'natural' readings can only work under two conditions. First, if there is indeed ambiguity in the word or phrase which is being questioned. Second, if there are clearly no other possible alternative reasons which may explain the ambiguity of the said word or phrase other than the 'natural' reading.

As to the first condition, the employment of the word πάντες is indeed ambiguous.[54] This is how many of the English versions have chosen to translate the word. The problem, of course, is that the translation 'all' is

---

52. Cf. Menzies, *Empowered for Witness*, p. 176, n. 1.

53. Cf. Menzies, *Empowered to Witness*, p. 176.

54. Cf. J.R. Royce, 'Scribal Tendencies in the Transmission of the Text of the New Testament', in B.D. Ehrman and M.W. Holmes (eds.), *The Text of the New Testament in Contemporary Research: Essays on the Status Quaestionis* (Grand Rapids: Eerdmans, 1995), p. 242. The addition of the phrase οἱ ἀποστόλοι by some manuscripts may have been an intention to explain the ambiguity of πάντες. However, since the addition is found only in secondary manuscripts, some scholars were quick to read them against the major codices of A, B, C* which bear only the word πάντες. The addition, then, has been understood as an intention to mislead rather than to explain.

not necessarily an 'absolute all'.[55] Witherington has opted to understand the term 'all' as rhetorical since 'it is unlikely that Luke is thinking of a Christian house holding 120 people'.[56]

It is, however, the second condition which makes us find the so-called natural reading doubtful. The subject of the whole promise-fulfilment context of Acts 1–2 are the apostles. The recipients of Jesus' instructions to return to Jerusalem and wait for the 'promise of the father' are clearly the apostles (1.4). The commissioning to become witnesses for Jesus is again only for the apostles (1.7-8). The subject of the whole election narrative (1.15-26) again points only to the apostles. It is, therefore, more logical and consistent to assume that, while indeed other characters play alongside the apostles in Acts 1–2, the apostles fit more into the description of πάντες. Bolt correctly observes that,

> Despite others being in the background (1.14-15), Acts 1 focuses upon and ends with the twelve (1.26), who are the most likely subject in 2.1. This is confirmed by the flow of the chapter. Whoever is the subject of 2.1 receives the Spirit (2-4) and a crowd comes together (5-13). This sets up two groups: those receiving the Spirit—who are all Galileans (2.7; cf., 1.11)—and the crowd. The identity of the first group is revealed when Peter stands up with the eleven (2.14; cf., 2.37) to address the crowd. Promising an explanation of what has gone on for 'these men' (15-16), his address provides further confirmation. When he eventually gets to this explanation, these men have become 'witnesses' (32-33), a group which has already been limited to twelve.[57]

2.2. *The Repetition of* Ἐπὶ Τὸ Αὐτό

The repetition of ἐπὶ τὸ αὐτό in 1.15 and 2.1 is understood by some as indicative of the presence of the gathering of people (specifically the 120) in the house apart from the Twelve apostles. I suggest, however, that ἐπὶ τὸ αὐτό, in this context, can also mean the emphasis on the 'place' of the gathering rather than on the 'people' who had gathered.[58] If the author

---

55. Cf. Newman and Nida, *A Translator's Handbook*, p. 33.

56. Witherington, *The Acts of the Apostles*, p. 131, n. 8; Green, avoiding the issue of the number of people, opted to identify πάντες as merely referring to those 'persevering in prayer together' (1.14; cf. 1.24), those 'with one mind'. That is, the eleven apostles, the women disciples, and Mary with Jesus' brothers. *Witness to the Gospel*, p. 91.

57. Bolt, 'Mission and Witness', p. 199.

58. Fitzmyer concurs, 'Luke uses the phrase *epi to auto*, "together", which may say

intended to emphasize the gathering of the people, just as he did in 1.15, then why has he employed the word ὁμοῦ (a word which basically means 'together') in 2.1? Why has he not simply used the same phrase ἐπὶ τὸ αὐτό? My suggestion is that ἐπὶ τὸ αὐτό, in this context, emphasizes the gathering in the 'single' and the 'same' place in order to pave the way for what is about to be emphasized in v. 2b—the temporal and spatial setting—'and it filled all the house where they were sitting'.[59]

2.3. *The Universal Character of the Gift of the Spirit*

Barrett has suggested that the gift of the Spirit was not narrowly confined to the Twelve.[60] Menzies, likewise, has argued that 'the potentially universal character of the gift of the Spirit is stressed in 2.17 and 2.39; therefore it would be strange if any of the disciples present was excluded from the gift at Pentecost'.[61] The issue in Acts 2, however, is not on whether the gift of the Spirit is available to all or not. There is no doubt that 2.17 and 2.39 state that the Spirit's gift is for all. I believe that the question one ought to ask is whether the initial outpouring of the Spirit was indeed received by the alleged 120 disciples being referred to by the πάντες in 2.1 or was it first confined to the Twelve. From my perspective, especially as I have argued that the Twelve have consistently been the subject of the narrative beginning from Acts 1 until the last episode of ch.

no more than the preceding adv. *homou*, but it can be used in the sense of "at the same place", which suites the context'. Fitzmyer, *Acts*, p. 238.

59.   Our earlier suggestion that πάντες refers to the Twelve also solves the problem of how the 120 can fit into the οἶκος. Zahn was one (if not the earliest) to suggest that Luke actually referred to the Temple as the place of gathering. This suggestion was intended to explain the accommodation of the 120 people in what was understood to be a common small size NT house. However, as most commentators have observed, apart from Acts 7.47 (a context which makes it clear why οἶκος is meant 'Temple'), the author of Luke–Acts has consistently used the term τὸ ἱερόν for 'temple'. Cf. T. Zahn, *Die Apostelgeschichte des Lucas* (2 vols.; Leipzig/Erlangen: Deichert, 1927), p. 77; reference taken from Fitzmyer, *Acts*, p. 238. Some patristic and medieval writers have resolved to understand the οἶκος as the Cenacle, the same place where the Last Supper was held; Fitzmyer, *Acts*, p. 238; C. Kopp, *The Holy Places of the Gospels* (New York: Herder and Herder, 1963), pp. 330-34. See also J. Murphy-O'Connor, 'The Cenacle and Community: The Background of Acts 2.44-45', in M.D. Coogan *et al.* (eds.), *Scripture and Other Artifacts: Essays on the Bible and Archaeology in Honor of Philip J. King* (Louisville, KY: Westminster, 1994), pp. 296-310.

60.   Barrett, *The Acts of the Apostles*, p. 112.

61.   Menzies, *Empowered for Witness*, p. 176.

2,[62] it is exegetically possible to assume that the Twelve were the initial recipients of the Spirit's gift. For while there is no concrete evidence to disprove the presence of the 120 disciples in the same house when the Spirit arrived, there is also no concrete evidence to support it.[63] Πάντες, as I have stated, is ambiguous. And from what the rest of Acts 2 indirectly says of the identity of those who were 'filled by the Spirit' in the οἶκος (see vv. 14, 37, 42, and 43), it is plausible to argue that πάντες refers to the Twelve.

2.4. *The Number of Languages Spoken*

Because there were more than twelve different nationalities (who at that time were on a pilgrimage in Jerusalem to celebrate Pentecost) claiming that they have heard their own languages being spoken (Acts 2.11), it has been deduced that more than twelve persons were simultaneously yet individually speaking a different language. This means, therefore, that there were not only twelve persons (or Twelve apostles) who received the baptism of the Spirit and spoke in foreign tongues.[64]

This argument can be challenged. First, the text does not specifically say that the crowd of more than twelve nationalities heard their language being spoken all at the same time.[65] This allows for the possibility that each or any of the Twelve apostles has spoken a different language one after the other.[66] Second, when Peter stood up to explain to the crowd what was

---

62. Only the apostles were commissioned to be witnesses and were instructed to remain in Jerusalem (Acts 1.7-8); only the apostles returned to Jerusalem, they were introduced individually; they waited and prayed in the upper room (1.12-14); the apostles elected Judas' replacement (1.15-26); the apostles were baptized by the Spirit (2.1-4); and finally, the apostles performed their task of being witnesses and had their first converts (2.14-47).

63. This is why I think that Witherington's comment is less convincing. He stated that 'there is no indication that this phenomenon (speaking about the Spirit's outpouring) was only experienced by the Twelve, as some sort of empowerment for leadership'. Cf. Witherington, *The Acts of the Apostles*, p. 132. I have consistently shown, that from a status transformation perspective, the narrative of Acts 1–2 which focuses on the Twelve apostles as the subject, can be read as a narrative which promotes the leadership of the Twelve apostles.

64. Menzies, *Empowered for Witness*, p. 176, n. 1.

65. It was originally A. Harnack who suggested that the original text of the list of nations in the pericope of vv. 5-11 is only twelve. Cf. Lake and Cadbury, *The Beginnings of Christianity*, V, p. 112.

66. Some commentators see the gift as *glossolalia* meaning 'ecstatic utterance' (e.g. Johnson, *Acts*, p. 42), while others prefer to understand it as *xenologia*, that is,

going on—an explanation to suffice the crowd's bewilderment (2.6), perplexity, and amazement on hearing about God's mighty works being spoken in their own language, and also to those who had mistaken them for being drunk (Acts 1.11b-13)—the text says he stood with the Eleven and not with the alleged 120 (2.14-15). For if Peter's speech was necessitated by the event (most especially to explain to those who had accused them of being drunk, cf. 2.15a), why is Peter standing only with the Eleven and not with the 120 disciples?[67] Furthermore, after Peter had finished explaining to the crowd what had just happened, the crowd is said to have been 'cut to the heart' and directed their response *specifically* to 'Peter and the rest of the apostles' (2.37) and not *generally* to any of the other 120 disciples.[68]

What I have just argued above is the possibility of reading πάντες in Acts 2.1 as primarily referring to the Twelve apostles. I find this reading more consistent with how the character of the apostles has been projected as the main subject in Acts 1–2. The subject, viewed from the rituals of status transformation framework, are the initiands and are now (here in Acts 2) in the process of being aggregated into the society.

3. *Summary*

In this chapter, I have discussed the ritual elements in the aggregation stage of the apostles. I stated earlier that I would attempt to argue for the outpouring of the Spirit upon the apostles as the symbol of God's formal endorsement of the Twelve to be leaders of the Christian community. Because of this, I find Pentecost to be one of the most significant ritual elements in this stage. Thus, I asked the question, 'What is the intention behind the outpouring of the Spirit upon the apostles in Acts 2 happening on the same day as the pilgrimage festival of Pentecost is being celebrated?'

'speaking in a foreign language' (e.g. Barrett, *The Acts of the Apostles*, p. 109). The author of Luke–Acts seems to have indicated this to be a miraculous gift since it was understood by foreigners only here in Acts 2. When the same phenomenon is used in Acts 10.45-46://. 19.6, the adjective ἑτέραις is no longer used. Fitzmyer, *Acts*, p. 239. Moreover, if Luke regards this event as a miracle, it is a miracle of hearing. Thus, the number of speakers is irrelevant.

67.   Thus, Lake and Cadbury comment, 'Peter stands up with the other apostles as though it were on them that the Spirit had descended'. *The Beginnings of Christianity*, IV, p. 17.

68.   Again, further emphasis on the Twelve and not on the 120 disciples is seen in vv. 42-43.

I tried to trace the history of Pentecost (or feast of Weeks), hoping to find some clues leading to the said intention from the evidence that it was being celebrated on the third month of the year, to suggestions that it came to be a commemoration of Israel's covenant renewal, and until the feast evolved to be the day to remember God's giving of the Torah to Moses in Mt Sinai. Some exegetes, therefore, have concluded that the feast of Pentecost is being related and used by the author as a backdrop to the giving of the Spirit in Acts 2.

I also weighed the evidence of the camp of scholars who disagree in understanding Pentecost as a parallel to the Spirit's outpouring in Acts 2. And after much consideration, I found the suggestion that, while indeed the author may not have intentionally related the two events together, the characteristics found from the event of giving of the Spirit in Acts 2 would have surely evoked upon the readers to relate it with the giving of the Torah to Moses.

This study, however, finds a relevant connection as to why the aggregation of the apostles has to happen during Pentecost. I will show that from the perspective of the rituals of status transformation the gathering of the crowd from different nations to celebrate the annual feast is not only circumstantial. I will argue in the ritual process section that the enumeration of the names of the many nations that have gathered for the Pentecost pilgrimage is actually the author's attempt to show the universal nature or scope and acceptance of the apostles as the new leaders of the Christian community.

In this same chapter, I have also finally resolved the issue of the narrative's focus. Because I encountered again another hurdle in proving my theory that Acts 1–2 speaks primarily of the apostles, I showed that the πάντες in 2.1 can be understood as simply pertaining to the Twelve apostles and not necessarily the 120 in the upper room (cf. Acts 1.15).

The next chapter attempts to put these ritual elements in their proper place in the ritual process of the initiands' stage of aggregation.

Chapter 9

THE APOSTLES TAKE ON THEIR LEADERSHIP ROLE

1. *The Ritual Process in Acts 2*

Whether Pentecost in Acts 2 was eventually the commemoration of the giving of the Torah at Sinai, or whether it has remained simply as a harvest feast, the discussions continue. What is a fact, however, is that scholars from both camps agree that the Pentecost narrative reflects significant OT traditions. And it is this fact that is particularly important in my study of the apostles' installation of their new status and aggregation into the community.

The heritage of OT language and imagery in the Pentecost story are recognizable. The mention of fire and wind in Acts 2.1-4, for instance, reminds us of the Exodus narrative where God's pillar of fire served as guide during the night for the Israelites (Exod. 13.21) and the wind as protection against the charging Egyptian armies (Exod. 14.21).[1] 'The wind and fire on the day of Pentecost do not, however, attest to a new exodus. Rather, in concrete terms familiar to all, they demonstrate that God was present and active.'[2]

But what happens to be a particularly striking heritage of OT tradition in Acts 2 is that of the Mosaic tradition in Num. 11. The story of Moses and the distribution of the Spirit (רוח) upon the seventy elders share some similarities (although not exact parallels) with the apostles' Pentecost experience. These would include: a *leadership crisis* which needed the appointment of the seventy elders; the *status transformation* of the elders to meet the leadership needs of the people; the *endowment* of the Spirit

---

1.   In Sinai imagery (Exod. 19.18), fire is a common element. It has also been often associated with the meaning of cleansing and purification. However, Marshall is right to observe that here in Acts 2.4, its appearance is most likely associated with power. Cf. Marshall, 'The Significance of Pentecost', p. 354.

2.   Stronstad, *Charismatic Theology*, p. 58.

upon the elders during the process of their installation as leaders; and finally, the elders prophesying after the Spirit has *rested* upon them.

What follows is a comparison and contrast of the Moses tradition in Num. 11.10-30 with the apostles' Pentecost experience in Acts 2. Again, it is never my intention to see Num. 11 as a parallel with the Acts 2 event. What I want to show is that the author of Luke–Acts shares similar theophanic expressions (or even traditions) with the OT, especially with stories about Moses. If this assumption is correct, then I am hopeful that the milieu which the author of Luke–Acts shares with the tradition of Num. 11 may lead us to better understand the apostles' experience of aggregation in Acts 2.[3]

1.1. *A Leadership Crisis: Reflections from Numbers 11*

My concern with Num. 11 begins in v. 4. The narrative gives the account of the children of Israel complaining to Moses about their discontent with food. It seems that the Israelites are tired of eating manna (11.6b) and are craving to eat meat (11.4b).[4] They have expressed their demand to Moses by 'weeping again', an expression analogous to their experience when Yahweh responded by providing manna on which they were to live from then on.[5] This time, however, the Israelites' dissatisfaction has reached a level where it is no longer simply the desire to eat meat but at a level where even Moses' leadership is questioned (11.10-13).[6]

The effect of the people's complaint upon Moses is seen in 11.11-15. Moses himself begins to doubt his own ability to lead the people. As 11.14-15 indicates, Moses reacts, not against the people's complaints and their rejection of God's provision, but against the fact that his job as a leader has become more difficult. He then questions Yahweh for giving him this leadership task.[7] Moses' burden and disappointment is reflected

---

3. A helpful discussion on this issue may be read from B. Capper, 'Reciprocity and the Ethic of Acts', in Marshall and Peterson (eds.), *Witness to the Gospel*, pp. 510-11.

4. It is argued that the discontent among the people originated not with the Israelites but with the 'rabble that was among them' (11.4a). Some scholars suggest that the 'rabble among them' refers to the people of various nationalities 'who had accompanied the Israelites during the exodus'. E.W. Davies, *Numbers* (NCBC; Grand Rapids: Eerdmans, 1995), p. 105.

5. M. Noth, *Numbers: A Commentary* (London: SCM Press, 1968), p. 85.

6. We also see this discontent with Moses' leadership by Miriam and Aaron in ch. 12.

7. T.R. Ashley, *The Book of Numbers* (NICOT; Grand Rapids: Eerdmans, 1993), pp. 209-10.

by his statement that 'he would rather be killed by Yahweh' in view of the present difficult situation. For this reason, God instructs Moses to appoint seventy elders who were known to be leaders of the people.[8]

The crisis necessitated the appointment of seventy elders. It was not just a crisis concerning the discontentment of the people about their diet. It had actually led to a crisis of leadership—the ability of Moses to lead the people. My point is to emphasize that this leadership crisis results in a status transformation of the elders for the people of Israel.

In Acts, the apostles' status transformation is also in response to a crisis which the community is facing. And as with Num. 11, the crisis in Acts 1–2 is a leadership crisis. I suggested that the leadership crisis in Acts is not only because Jesus has departed, nor is it only because the supposedly Twelve apostles who were to serve as judges (cf. Lk. 22.30) are missing one due to Judas' death. Rather, I pointed out that the episodes in Acts 1, especially the events leading to the election of Matthias as a replacement to Judas (Acts 1.12-26), present primarily a moral crisis. Judas' betrayal of Jesus has caused serious moral problems to the integrity of the apostles as leaders—the very apostles whom Jesus has appointed to be his witnesses.

1.2. *A Status Transformation*

The designation שֹׁטֵר[9] (cf. v. 16) may be misleading. Indeed, the term suggests that the seventy elders were already leaders about the people. Thus, what had just transpired may be misconstrued as simply the confirmation of an added, or probably, more specific responsibility other than their general responsibilities as leaders. If this is true, then there was really no significant status transformation at all.

However, choosing seventy elders from among the 'elders of Israel' does not necessarily mean that we are talking about designated leaders of Israel. For one, it is possible to view the phrase 'from the elders of Israel' as an expression which means the choice from the very numerous 'heads of the families'. Noth confirms this idea. He suggests that the title was originally understood as 'officials' within the tribal organization set up. That the 'relative clause in 11.16a, which is surely to be regarded as a

---

8. See also 1 Sam. 4.3; 8.4; Ezek. 10.14.
9. Can mean the leaders appointed over the people by the Egyptians (Exod. 5.6, 10, 14-15, 19); or those who organize the people for marching (Jos. 1.10; 3.2). May also convey the role of 'judges' (cf. the term שֹׁפְטִים). Cf. Ashley, *Book of Numbers*, p. 210.

secondary aside, inserted particularly unskilfully,[10] while it designates the chosen men specifically as "officers"—literally "writers"—gives expression to this 'official' character of the elders…'[11]

What we have, therefore, is a definite status transformation—a transformation needed to meet the present crisis which is plaguing the leadership of the people of Israel. It is a change of status from the ordinary 'heads of families' to being 'heads of the whole people'. This status transformation is the agenda behind the meeting in the tent and Yahweh's endowment of the Spirit upon the chosen seventy elders.

The selection of Judas' replacement also involved certain criteria. Just as the seventy elders were chosen among the present leaders of Israel, the candidates for the twelfth apostle also had to be chosen among those who had only been with Jesus, 'beginning from the baptism of John until the day when he was taken up…' (1.22). As it was made clear to Moses by Yahweh that he was to choose seventy men whom Moses know 'to be the elders of the people and officers over them…' (Num. 11.16), Peter also made clear to those present in the election the qualifications which the candidates needed to have in order to vie for Judas' seat.

1.3. *The Endowment of the Spirit in an Installation Rite*

There are other leadership themes in the Moses tradition comparable with Num. 11. For instance, in Exod. 18, we find the story of Jethro, Moses' father-in-law, giving counsel to Moses concerning the choosing of able men (or leaders) who would help him in the rulership of the Children of Israel (Exod. 18.13-26). Following Jethro's advice, Moses chose for himself leaders who served as judges, leaving only the difficult yet fewer cases to himself (18.24-26).

Numbers 11.10-35 show Moses choosing seventy elders who would assist him in attending to the crisis that befell him and the people of Israel. The major difference from the Exodus account, however, is Yahweh's endowment and distribution of the Spirit among those who were chosen to assist Moses in leadership.

The endowment of the Spirit by God to the seventy elders shows that

---

10.   For the discussion on the issues of the P and J traditions being placed together, especially on this specific context, see De Vaux, *Ancient Israel*, pp. 138, 152-53; Davies, *Numbers*, pp. 107-108; J. Van Seters, *The Life of Moses: The Yahwist as Historian in Exodus and Numbers* (Westminster: John Knox Press, 1994), pp. 220-44.

11.   Noth, *Numbers*, p. 87.

this story is not simply a doublet of Exod. 18.[12] This also cannot be fully compared with the 'Elijah-Elisha leader-apprentice' relationship even if we find similarities like the sharing of the Spirit (2 Kgs 2.15) between two parties. For one, the case is that of leadership succession and the transfer of Spirit from a single individual to another individual and not to a group. The only comparable scenario with Num. 11 happens to be in Acts 2 (cf. v. 33).

Despite the objections expressed by some NT scholars against the use of Mosaic traditions in the study of the Pentecost event in Acts 2, it is really difficult not to be reminded of the experience of Moses and the seventy elders in Num. 11 when one reads of the apostles' Pentecost experience. Just as with the elders appointed by Moses, the apostles in Acts 2.1-4 also go through the rite of installation as they finally complete their status transformation.

Installation rites for a group of initiands normally take place in one specific setting. This is in contrast with initiands who are being installed individually and into different statuses or ranks. With a group, however, confinement in a specific temporal and spatial setting is important. Being gathered together in one place is significant especially as the symbolic union of the initiands has to be emphasized.

The symbolic union can be expressed in various ways: either through a communal meal; the exchange or sharing of gifts or tokens; the performance of blood compacts; or the sharing of precious possessions. All these are done to emphasize and establish the binding/union of the ones being installed. When this happens, the group's identity as peers and as a single unit is affirmed.[13]

Against this backdrop, we suggest that the opening verses of Acts 2 bear the traits of an installation rite. First, the author informs the readers that the apostles were 'all together in one place' (v. 1). This note may be deemed unnecessary considering that the previous episodes (1.12-26) already make clear that the apostles had been together as a group since Jesus' ascension and had been assembled in one place because of Jesus' instruction to wait in Jerusalem for the promise of the father (1.4).[14]

---

12. Ashley, *Book of Numbers*, p. 211.

13. Van Gennep, *Rites of Passage*, p. 29.

14. Understandably, a tradition-historical approach sees the significance of this note in relation to Acts 2.2b. For it would really not make sense to portray the coming of the Spirit as being preceded by 'an engulfing sound of a mighty wind which fills the whole house' if the apostles were all widely scattered all over Jerusalem. In other

However, from the perspective of a ritual, the initiands being together is needed if they are to establish their strong identity and union as a group. This, similarly, is what we witnessed with the seventy elders in Num. 11. After Moses received the instruction to choose seventy elders who would assist him in the leadership role, God instructs Moses to take them into the tent of meeting.[15] The elders suddenly found themselves identifying with each other in contrast to their individual statuses before they were selected by Moses.

Second, is the aspect of equality. In the symbolic union of the initiands, there is no superior or inferior among them. As with the Twelve apostles, this aspect may be represented by the equal distribution of the 'tongues of fire which rested on each one of them' (2.3). What we have is not just a single tongue of fire resting on an individual or leader of a group. Rather, there are individual tongues shared to each apostle. No apostle within the group is presented to be dominant or greater than the others.[16]

There is, however, a slight difference between the scenarios in Acts 2.1-4 and Num. 11. In Num. 11, when the choice of the seventy elders was finally made they all gathered in the tent standing beside Moses (11.16). Included in God's instructions was that the Spirit which he would give to

words, the presence of the Spirit in the whole house is related with the understanding that the apostles are gathered together inside it.

However, if the main purpose of the Spirit's coming is primarily to empower the apostles (a purpose stated in 1.8), what is the need of this happening only when they are gathered together? Would this not be accomplished if the Twelve are found in different places yet within the vicinity of Jerusalem? Indeed, this set of questions are purely hypothetical, or probably even irrational to some. But it is exactly this scenario that leads to my suggestion that Acts 2.1-4 can be viewed as having the elements of an installation ritual. To be precise, the symbolic union of the initiands cannot be ritually conducted if the initiands are not assembled together in one place.

15.   Yahweh directed Moses to take the seventy elders to the tent in order to give his further instructions (to be more precise, the place where God distributed his Spirit among the elders, v. 16a). What used to be God's place of revelation, the mountain, is changed to the tent of gathering. It is quite odd that Yahweh had to do this since even when Moses and the elders have gathered, Yahweh still intended to speak only to Moses and not with the elders (cf. Ashley, *Book of Numbers*, p. 210). The echo I am intending to show is obvious. The mountain where Jesus had ascended (Mt Olivet in 1.12) is not necessarily the place where God will pour out his Spirit. Rather, the apostles had to travel to Jerusalem to wait for the Spirit's outpouring (1.4).

16.   This becomes more obvious when one considers the fact that before and after Acts 2.1-4 are episodes which portray Peter as leader or spokesman of the whole group (cf. 1.15-22 and 2.14-42).

the elders would partly be taken from Moses himself (11.17a).[17] This rendering significantly implies that Moses' status was not equal to that of the seventy elders.[18] This is true since we know that Moses stood as the superior leader over all the other leaders of the people of Israel.

Nevertheless, what is interesting to point out is that the seventy elders had equal standing with each other. We are told that when the Spirit was taken from Moses, it was placed upon all of the seventy elders. Other than Moses, no elder stood prominent within the chosen group.[19]

1.4. *Prophecy—When the Spirit Rested upon Them*

In Num. 11, the direct result of the Spirit being placed[20] upon the elders was prophecy (11.25). How and what the elders had prophesied is contested. It seems that the Hithpael verb ויתנבאו is denominative (i.e. it serves as a verb where its root is actually a noun) from נבא which can basically suggest two meanings. The first is prophesying with ecstatic behaviour. The NEB translates 'fell into prophetic ecstasy'. The elders then, after receiving the Spirit, 'were flung into a state of divine frenzy'.[21] Some scholars relate the elders' experience to 1 Sam. 10.6; 19.24; and even to Jer. 29.26 'where the one who prophesies (in this case, Jeremiah) is virtually equated with a madman'.[22]

The second view understands the verb to mean 'proclaiming Yahweh's

---

17.   Does this mean that the source of the Spirit is Moses and not God? The phrase 'I will set apart some of the spirit that is upon you, and I will place it upon them…' (ואצלתי מ⁻הרוח אשר עלי ושמתי עליה) may suggest that the Spirit is already *upon* Moses. It could be understood, therefore, that the source of the Spirit originally placed upon (על) Moses is God. Ashley rightly adds, 'This case is only partially parallel to 2 Kgs 2.15, which deals with the succession of Elijah by Elisha. Compare the phrasing of Num. 11.17 with 2 Kgs 2.15 *(rûaḥ 'elîyahû 'al-' lîšä')*. The spirit here is not simply *rûaḥ mošeh* but *rûaḥ 'ašer 'al mošeh*, i.e., the Spirit is not only *upon* the elders, but also *upon* Moses (i.e. it is not his).' Ashley, *Book of Numbers*, p. 211.

18.   Davies, *Numbers*, p. 109.

19.   While it is true that Eldad and Meldad are said to have received the Spirit, their case is different from the seventy elders. First, they were not part of the seventy; and second, they remained in the camp and not in the tent. This special situation is why they are mentioned in the first place. (Cf. Num. 26-30.)

20.   A different verb is used here in 11.25 to convey the 'placing' of the Spirit upon the elders. In contrast with 11.17 where שם is used, the verb נתן which literally means 'to give' may suggest that the Spirit was a 'gift' from God. Cf. *BDB*, pp. 680-81.

21.   *BDB*, pp. 680-81.

22.   Ashley, *Book of Numbers*, p. 214, n. 46.

word' without the ecstatic behaviour. However, since the text does not give any indication that the elders were proclaiming any message from Yahweh, the former suggestion (i.e. ecstatic behaviour) is favoured.

In Acts 2 there is a similar experience. Although symbolized by the tongues of fire, the Spirit in Acts 2.1-4 also rested on each of the apostles.[23] Moreover, the direct result of the apostles being filled by the Holy Spirit was prophecy. What we can see in both cases (i.e. Num. 11 and Acts 2) is that the transfer[24] of Spirit results in an outburst of prophecy.[25]

The clear difference in the Num. 11 account, however, is that the apostles in Acts 2 prophesied by uttering a clear message coming from God. First, the reaction of the crowd who heard the 'sound' which was supposed to be coming from the οἶκος was that of amazement (2.12). They were amazed that they heard the mighty works of God being proclaimed by the apostles in their own language (2.11). Second, Peter's subsequent speech (2.17-36) after he and the Eleven had prophesied spoke about the fulfilment of the prophecies of Joel (cf. Joel 2.28-32). Joel's prophecy was a message from God.

1.5. *The Significance of the Endowment of Spirit upon the Seventy Elders*
We now come to what is probably the main crux of the Moses tradition in Num. 11, 'the significance of the endowment of Spirit upon the seventy elders'. As I stated earlier, there are other leadership-appointment themes in the Moses tradition but it is only in this episode that we find the character of the Spirit being involved. Martin Noth (like other scholars) asks why? He states, 'This is very strange in the present context. Moses is supposed to be "relieved of his burden" (vv. 14-17). How this goal is achieved by putting the seventy elders into a state of ecstasy is difficult to imagine; moreover, nothing is said on this subject.'[26]

Noth arrives at the conclusion that the purpose of the endowment of Spirit upon the elders is to show the 'derivation of ecstatic "prophecy" from the "spirit" of Moses'.[27] He adds, 'It is true that it is not said that from then on this phenomenon existed in Israel; but it emerges here as a

---

23. Fitzmyer, *Acts*, p. 238.
24. The transfer of Spirit from Moses to the seventy elders is a type of the transfer of Spirit from Jesus to the Twelve apostles.
25. Stronstad, *Charismatic Theology*, p. 59.
26. Noth, *Numbers*, p. 89.
27. Cf. 1 Sam. 10.10-12; 19.23-24.

prototype for the first time in the history of Israel in direct connection with the figure, envisaged as unique, of Moses'.[28]

Yet again, Noth's suggestion does not really answer the question of how the elders prophesying helped in the crisis which both they and Moses faced. Moreover, if the purpose of the whole event is to show that 'ecstatic prophecy' can be traced back to this specific event, then why did it cease immediately after it happened (Num. 11.25b 'but they did so no more')?[29] The only plausible explanation is to understand the elders' 'prophesying' feat as directly linked to their newly appointed office. In other words, the reason why the seventy elders prophesied when the Spirit had rested upon them is primarily to legitimize the new status they all had been transformed to. Davies puts it more precisely by stating that,

> It seems preferable, therefore to view the 'prophesying' of the elders in this instance as merely a visible sign of their authorisation to a position of leadership in the community…it serves, in effect, as a mark of their instal- lation to a particular 'office'…it appears that the narrative was intended to distinguish a particular group of elders as having specific administrative functions in Israel, and their ecstatic behaviour was a token of their divine election to fulfil this role. Viewed in this way, the bestowal of the spirit upon the elders was an entirely appropriate response to Moses' request for help to bear the burden of caring for the people (vv. 11f., 14f.).[30]

The apostles' baptism in the Spirit in Acts 2.4 has primarily been understood as the empowering for witness, and for some, miracle-working power. After what has been discussed above, we want to know if it is also possible to understand the event as more than just the empowering of the apostles. Is it possible that, just as in Num. 11 where the Spirit legitimizes the seventy elders into their leadership role, the Spirit in Acts 2.4 (from the perspective that the Twelve apostles are going through a status transforma- tion) also legitimizes the apostles into their new role as witnesses and reliable leaders of the Christian community?[31] We submit that it is, beyond the overwhelming view that the role of the Spirit in Luke–Acts, especially in 2.4, is to endow the recipients with prophetic power, producing special

---

28.   Noth, *Numbers*, p. 89.
29.   Cf. Davies, *Numbers*, p. 104.
30.   Davies, *Numbers*, pp. 104-105.
31.   Again, we are not suggesting the legitimization of the Twelve into the office of an apostle. Rather, it is the legitimization of their leadership credibility.

insight and inspired speech, primarily for the purpose of effective witness and with miracle-working power.[32]

The idea that the Spirit's baptism of the apostles in Acts 2.4 affirms them in their role as representatives or brokers between God and the Christian community has not been fully explored. I think that there are two reasons why this is so. First is the persistent reluctance of exegetes to accept the possibility that the subject, and therefore focus, of the whole outpouring of the Spirit in Acts 2.4 is primarily the Twelve apostles. Second (and it is strongly related to the first reason) is the perspective from which we are approaching the narrative of Acts 1–2—the status transformation of the apostles (i.e. from followers to leaders). From this outlook, I suggest that it is indeed possible to understand the event in Acts 2.4 as, not only the endowment of power for witness and/or the ability to perform miracles, but also as a means for the author to show his readers that the apostles had been transformed and legitimized by God himself as his appointed overseers over his people.

The concept of the Spirit as having an active role in affirming or legitimizing statuses can be seen in other Lukan examples:

---

32.   There are at least two prominent views concerning the Lukan concept of the Spirit's relationship with proclamation and miracle-working power. First is the view that the Spirit was the one who empowered Jesus and the disciples to preach and perform miracles. This empowerment is said to have been accomplished during Jesus' baptism (Lk. 3.21-22), as well as during the disciples' reception of the Spirit on the day of Pentecost (Acts 2.4). Some of the most significant works in this area are that of Max Turner (*Power from on High*) and James Shelton (*Mighty in Word and Deed: The Role of the Holy Spirit in Luke–Acts* [Peabody, MA: Hendrickson, 1991]). Both Turner and Shelton support the view that the Spirit's empowerment upon Jesus and his disciples is both to 'heal and reveal'. This view goes against Eduard Schweizer's suggestion that no text indirectly associates the Spirit with the miracles of Jesus and the disciples in Luke–Acts (cf. 'Pneuma', in G. Kittel [ed.], *TDNT*, VI [Grand Rapids: Eerdmans, 1968]). Furthermore, parallel passages in the gospels of Matthew and Mark involving the Spirit with miracle-working activity are altered, or sometimes omitted, in the gospel of Luke. Schweizer's suggestion has been supported and argued further by Robert Menzies in his book *Empowered for Witness*. Picking up from where Schweizer left off, Menzies believes that the Intertestamental period's concept of the Spirit strongly influenced Luke to distance the Spirit from miracles. During this period, the Spirit is said to be a Spirit of prophecy and not primarily a Spirit of miracles. Thus, Luke is cautious in the way he relates the Spirit to miracles and chooses to associate the Spirit directly only with inspired speech.

1. The Spirit legitimizes John's prophetic ministry. This is seen in Lk. 1.15b and 1.17. In 1.15b, the prophecy about John's greatness is coupled with the fact that he will be filled with the Holy Spirit. In 1.17, John's role as a prophet is described as 'in the spirit and power of Elijah'. 'John's unique reception of the Spirit while still in the womb points to John's special status and role...'[33]

2. In 1.39-56, especially vv. 41-45, the Spirit legitimizes the status and role of Mary through the prophetic outburst of Elizabeth. After Elizabeth received Mary's greeting (Lk. 1.41a), the text states the baby in her womb 'leaped'. Elizabeth then was 'filled[34]

---

33. Menzies, *Empowered for Witness*, p. 108. Both 1.15 and 1.17 bear the strongest possibility that these verses were originally Lukan ideas which were incorporated into an existing story (cf. J. Fitzmyer, *The Gospel according to Luke I-IX* [AB, 28; New York: Doubleday, 1981], p. 319). For example, R. Menzies states that 'the use of πίμπλημι (filled) with the anarthous usage of πνεῦμα ἀγίον (Holy Spirit) in v. 15 and the collation of πνεύματι (spirit) and δυναμίς (power) in v. 17 indicate that these are Lukan' (cf. *Empowered for Witness*, p. 108). On the basis of this evidence we see here the author's desire for his readers to know that John's prophetic ministry is one which is sanctioned by the Spirit.

34. Luke's description of John, specifically with the use of the word πίπλημι, is viewed by many scholars as exclusively Lukan (Cf. Marshall, *The Gospel of Luke*, p. 58). Πίπλημι is often used by Luke in reference to the Holy Spirit (Cf. 1.41, 67; Acts 2.4; 4.8, 31; 9.17; 13.9). Although πίπλημι is exclusive to Luke, some exegetes have concluded that the usage of the word does not necessarily suggest uniqueness in meaning or concept on the part of the author. Therefore, Luke does not emphasize any new or unique point concerning the Spirit, nor should we see any relation with John's prophetic calling (Estrada, 'A Redaction-Critical Study', pp. 32-33).

This view is, however, inadequate. Though all of the Lukan πίπλημι references may be considered a common word to the author, and that it is attributed to his literary style of describing the infilling of the Spirit, it does not necessarily follow that in all of the πίπλημι references in the gospel of Luke the word bears the same meaning. More often, the intention of the author within the specific context serves as the key in understanding the meaning of the word. For example, in 1.15, John is said to 'filled with the Spirit' ἐκ κοιλίας μητρὸς αὐτοῦ ('in his mother's womb'). The same Greek phrase is repeated in 1.41-44. However, the focus of the latter falls on the 'praises of Elizabeth' upon Mary. The difference between the two πίπλημι passages is clear. With 1.15, the association of the 'infilling' of the Spirit is with and upon the person of John, the one who is to come as prophet like Elijah. The focus of πίπλημι in 1.41-44, on the other hand, is to highlight the message of Elizabeth. It tells the immediate 'filling' of Elizabeth who in turn uttered pneumatic praises (cf. J. Shelton, ' "Filled With the Holy Spirit" and "Full of the Holy Spirit": Lukan Redactional Phrases', in

with the Holy Spirit' and gave affirmation of Mary's role as the 'mother of the Lord'. After hearing this, Mary herself uttered praises about the role she had been blessed to carry out (Lk. 1.46-56).

3.   Zechariah's prophetic outburst after being filled by the Spirit, likewise, affirms John's role as a prophet. Specifically, 1.76 indicates the role or relation of John to Jesus. John will act as a prophet, preparing the way for Jesus.[35] Again, this affirmation of John's status comes only after Zechariah was filled by the Spirit.

4.   The Spirit affirmed Jesus' role as a prophet after Jesus went through his own ritual of status transformation. Coming out from the wilderness (Lk. 4.1-13), Jesus is said to have returned in the power of the Spirit into Galilee (v. 14). However, it is not until 4.18-19 that we see the full picture of how the Spirit is understood by the author of Luke–Acts in relation to Jesus' role and status.

The Nazareth pericope in 4.16-30 is viewed to be one of the most crucial sections in the study of Jesus and his role in the gospel of Luke. NT scholars agree that this pericope, especially vv. 18-19, is programmatic. It serves as the framework for Jesus' public ministry, and for the programme of Luke's theology.[36] What is important, however, is to note that the attempt to describe Jesus' role as a prophet like Elijah and Elisha comes with the affirming description of being 'Spirit-anointed'. Lk. 4.18-19 not only describes what Jesus would literally do, but also what Jesus stands for—the long-awaited Messiah and Prophet of God.

Lk. 4.18-19 refers to two Isaiah passages, 61.1-2 and 58.6. The author's quotations of these passages reveal his own

---

P. Elbert (ed.), *Faces of Renewal: Studies in Honour of Stanley M. Horton* (Peabody, MA: Hendrickson, 1998), pp. 80-100.

35.   Marshall, *The Gospel of Luke*, p. 93.

36.   Brawley claims that placing the Nazareth event instead of Capernaum which is in Mark and Matthew shows that Luke wanted the event to be programmatic. Cf. R. Brawley, *Luke–Acts and the Jews: Conflict, Apology, and Conciliation* (Atlanta, GA: Scholars Press, 1987), p. 8. See also C. Evans, ' Luke's Use of the Elijah/Elisha Narratives and the Ethic of Election', *JBL* 106.1 (1987), pp. 75-83 (79). Johnson relates the programmatic layout of vv. 18-19 with Jesus' role by stating that the placing of the pericope in the initial chapters of the gospel meant to show that every act that Jesus did in his ministry was an act by the Spirit-anointed Messiah. Cf. Johnson, *Literary Function*, p. 93.

interests. For instance, Seccombe observes that Luke showed eagerness in the fulfilment of scripture. He states that Luke's usage of the Isaiah passage shows the author's appreciation for Isaianic themes.[37] One such theme is the anointing of the Messiah. 'Anoint' in Isaiah is often used in the metaphorical sense. In fact, as J. Skinner recalls, only in 1 Kgs 19.16 can one find an actual anointing with the accompaniment of oil. Brawley adds that the appropriation of the anointing of the Spirit of the Lord over Jesus is an appropriation done for the prophet. The anointing power and role of the Spirit over Jesus affirms his status as prophet.

5.   In Acts 6, one of the major qualifications for the role of deacons is being 'full of the Spirit'. Read the other way around, being full of the Spirit affirms the status of being qualified as a deacon (cf. 6.2-3). This qualification leads to the choice of Stephen in 6.5-6. Acts 6.5, specifically, describes Stephen as a man 'full of faith and of the Holy Spirit'. This description serves as a colourful backdrop for the story of Stephen's martyrdom (cf. 6.10 and 7.55).

6.   The prophetic role and the impact of Agabus' message to the church in Antioch is authenticated and affirmed by the description that the Spirit had foretold about the famine that is about to come to the world. In other words, the association of the Spirit with the prophetic message and the prophet who utters it gives credence or affirmation to both the message and messenger (Acts 11.27-30).

The Holy Spirit is also associated with (or even responsible for) the setting apart of Barnabas and Saul as missionaries in Acts 13. Verse 2, in particular, states that it is the Holy Spirit himself who has declared Barnabas and Saul to be sent for the missionary task. In the succeeding events, it is interesting to note how the author makes a contrast between Bar-Jesus, a Jewish false prophet and magician, and Paul. Being summoned by the proconsul (who by the way was described as being intelligent, v. 7b) to hear the word of God, the magician attempted to turn away the proconsul from the faith (v. 8). The narrator comes into the scene with the strong descriptions about Paul being 'full of

37.   D. Seccombe, 'Luke and Isaiah', *NTS* 27 (1981), pp. 252-59 (253).

the Holy Spirit' before Paul rebuked the magician (v. 9). While the proconsul is described as being intelligent, Paul is described as being full of the Holy Spirit. In other words, what we see here are three titles being affirmed or legitimized by their attributes: the magician as being a 'false prophet'; the proconsul as being 'intelligent'; and Paul the missionary as being 'filled with the Holy Spirit'.

7.   In Acts 19, Paul meets the twelve disciples in Ephesus. Paul's immediate question was whether these disciples had been baptized by the Holy Spirit. The context suggests that discipleship is affirmed by the Spirit's baptism. As Paul laid his hands upon them, these twelve disciples spoke in tongues and prophesied.

8.   Acts 20.17-35, especially v. 28, shows how the Spirit has affirmed and enabled the elders in the church in Ephesus to serve as 'overseers' in the community.

From these examples alone, we can see how the Spirit is understood to have an active role in legitimizing the statuses of characters in their respective narratives. And just as we have seen the seventy elders in Num. 11, and the seven deacons in Acts 6, the presence of the Spirit with the twelve apostles in Acts 2 is strongly related to the affirmation of their new status and role which they all have been appointed to fulfil. These role and status, as I have suggested, are not only being witnesses for Jesus but primarily being credible and reliable representatives between God and the community.[38]

What I have just demonstrated above is the possibility of how to understand Acts 2.1-4 as the rite of installation for the Twelve apostles. What follows next is how the apostles are finally accepted and recognized by the society in which they have been appointed to serve.

2. The Catalogue of Nations as Representative of the Universal Society

One of the most intriguing issues in the study of Acts 2 is the function of the catalogue of nations in 2.5-13. First, the narrator seems to interrupt the flow of his narration by taking time to enumerate the names of countries and people which are represented.[39] Second, the order of the nations, why

---

38.   Cf. Stronstad, *Charismatic Theology*, pp. 60-61.
39.   After the apostles have been installed, and a ritual conducted within the walls

they are named and not others, and whether they are composed at random or have been acquired from an existing list, are topics for heated debate among NT scholars.[40] As usual, my aim is not to find out the function of the list of nations from the historical perspective. I would not really want to add more confusion to the theories that have been posited concerning this issue. What I want to know, however, is how this enumeration of the nations and people in 2.5-13 relates to the aggregation of the twelve apostles as the latter successfully complete their ritual of status transformation?[41]

My suggestion is quite simple. It has been posited that the enumeration of the nations and people in 2.5-13 in effect represents the universality of the Spirit's gift and the message of the gospel to 'every nation under heaven'. From the perspective of the apostles' ritual aggregation, the catalogue of nations also appropriately symbolizes the universal scope of the apostles' status and role as witnesses and leaders.[42]

---

of the οἶκος (2.1-4), the aggregation process of the Twelve takes its first step. This step is represented by the change of scene 'from inside to the outside of the house' (Haenchen, *The Acts of the Apostles*, p. 168). The ritual of status transformation, a process which started when Jesus commissioned his apostles in Acts 1.3, was primarily an internal affair. But when the Twelve have finally been filled with the Spirit (an event which I interpreted as the legitimization of their status and role as witnesses and brokers) their aggregation has begun. The Jews (who have come to Jerusalem for the pilgrimage of the feast of Pentecost—2.5-13) reacting to what they have just heard and witnessed, signal the change of scene from an internal to an external affair. (A transition from a 'private to a public event'. Barrett, *The Acts of the Apostles*, p. 117; reacting to H. Conzelmann's observation on the same passage. Cf. H. Conzelmann, *Die Apostelgeschichte* [HNT, 7; Tübingen: J.C.B. Mohr, 1963], p. 25).

40. Cf. Fitzmyer, *Acts*, p. 240.

41. S. Weinstock was the first to suggest that the list of nations in Acts 2.9-11 has striking similarities with the astrological catalogue by Paulus Alexandrinus (4 BCE). S. Weinstock, 'The Geographical Catalogue in Acts 2.9-11', *JRS* 38 (1948), pp. 43-46. See also B.M. Metzger, 'Ancient Astrological Geography and Acts 2.9-11', in W.W. Gasque and R.P. Martin (eds.), *Apostolic History and the Gospel* (Exeter: Paternoster Press, 1970), pp. 123-33.

42. Cf. Capper, 'Reciprocity and the Ethic of Acts', pp. 510-11. Cf. Lüdemann, *Early Christianity*, pp. 39-41. Of course, it is only correct to assume that Peter's speech is mainly directed to the Jews (the ἄνδρες Ἰουδαῖοι) of the world (both local and foreign) and not to the whole world. On this issue, see Witherington, *The Acts of the Apostles*, p. 141. While it is true that representatives of the Jewish Diaspora were actually the ones who came to celebrate Pentecost, it is nevertheless plausible to understand the enumeration of the countries as primarily intending to suggest the universality of the occasion.

3. *The Apostles are Formally Presented to the Society*

Earlier, I attempted to use Num. 11 as a backdrop for the study of the apostles' installation rite in Acts 2. Specifically, I mentioned the example from Moses, and especially, the seventy elders whose ritual installation of their new status as leaders (cf. Num. 11.4-25) strikingly resembles the apostles' experience in Acts 2.1-4.

There is another frame in the Num. 11 story which I feel worth noting in order to illustrate my point in this section. What I am particularly interested in is the way Yahweh instructed Moses to stand with the seventy elders in the tent of meeting as they were to be formally installed as leaders.

There is really nothing particularly special about the employment of the word 'stand' (וְהִתְיַצְּבוּ from יצב is rendered תַנְסֹהָתֶם from ἵστημι by the LXX) in this context. But what seems to be interesting is that Moses had to stand *with* the elders instead of *before* them. In other words, Moses, who had always been God's representative and spokesman before the people, became the representative of the elders before God. This observation is supported by the fact that (as I have argued earlier) God spoke only to Moses (11.17a) but his message and instructions were for Moses and the elders. Furthermore, the seventy elders were not to take all the leadership responsibility from Moses, but rather, to share with Moses.

Again, from a ritual standpoint, Peter is said to be 'standing'[43] with the Eleven (Acts 2.14) after the crowd have heard them speak God's message in their own languages. Just as Moses was the representative of the elders, Peter's role as the representative of the Twelve is emphasized.[44] I say this against what I have observed to be a commonly sidelined note in the many studies on Peter's speech at Pentecost. For instance, Soards observes that,

> Prior to Peter's opening address one reads that he 'stood' (σταθείς) and 'lifted up his voice' (ἐπῆρεν τὴν φωνὴν αὐτοῦ). The stance is that of a Greek orator, and speakers assume such a position in 2.14; 5.20; 11.13;

43. Σταθείς from ἵστημι, a term common with characters about to make a speech similar to Greek orators; cf. 'ἵστημι', in BAGD, pp. 381-82.

44. This is also consistent with my argument earlier that the apostles are the primary subject of the narrative of Acts 1–2. Peter does not serve as representative of the whole 120 disciples as other exegetes have claimed. If he was, would it not make more sense for the author of Luke–Acts to have simply portrayed Peter as standing, either by himself or with the 120 disciples, explaining to the crowd what had just happened?

17.22; 25.18; 27.21. Indeed, σταθείς ('standing') occurs in 17.22 and 27.21.[45]

Soards failed to observe that this speech was given by Peter on behalf of the Twelve apostles. In other words, what has always been sidelined (I believe) is the Eleven. Unlike the way Peter stood among the brethren in the election narrative of 1.15-26, here the author makes clear that Peter and the Eleven stand together to deliver their defence against what has been misunderstood about them when they spoke in other languages.[46]

Aside from the issue of who is serving as representative for whom, the gesture of 'Peter standing with the Eleven' after the multitude had just been bewildered by what they have witnessed and heard, resulting in the accusation that the apostles were drunk (2.13), sets apart the Twelve apostles from the rest of the other characters. In other words, what I am suggesting is that the scene where Peter and the Eleven stood together with the purpose of explaining and defending themselves from the false accusation of the crowd, in some way legitimizes the status of the Twelve by presenting them as the ones responsible and accountable for what had just happened.[47] This responsibility and accountability rests only on the shoulders of appointed leaders. At this very juncture, the Twelve have finally assumed this role.[48]

45. Soards, *The Speeches in Acts*, p. 32.

46. Cf. Witherington, *The Acts of the Apostles*, p. 141.

47. It should be emphasized that Peter's speech was not necessitated primarily by the multitudes' amazement of hearing about God's mighty works through their own native languages. Rather, the speech was intended to explain (and defend) against the malicious accusation that the apostles were 'filled with wine'. *Contra* Stronstad, *Charismatic Theology*, p. 55.

48. This leads me to another aspect which is shared with other newly instated Spirit-inspired characters. I am specifically referring to the experience of rejection as one of the initial responses by the society to which leaders are being aggregated. For instance, the rejection of Jesus by the people in Nazareth synagogue echoes the rejection of Elisha after he had received the Spirit from Elijah (2 Kgs 2.23-25; Lk. 4.24-30). The same experience happened with the apostles. We find that after the Twelve had been baptized by the Spirit, the people who marvelled at them indirectly rejected God's message by accusing the apostles of simply being 'filled with wine'.

For Brawley, the Nazareth pericope is committed to introducing the role of Jesus as prophet (cf. Brawley, *Luke–Acts and the Jews*, p. 8). He adds that Luke does not really intend to present Jesus in the image of Elijah and Elisha, but rather, Luke cited the cases of Elijah and Elisha to prove that no prophet is accepted 'in his own country'. What Brawley is suggesting is that the rejection scene inadvertently promotes Jesus' role as prophet. This is also what we observe with the apostles in the accusation of

4. *The Society Recognizes the Twelve*

The apostles stand their ground. Peter delivers his speech. We now come to what is supposed to be the final phase of the apostles' aggregation—the response of the society in which the newly installed leaders are destined to serve. The figure below demonstrates how the narrative of Acts 2 has centred on Peter and the apostles, and also how the crowd has responded to them:

1. The apostles were filled by the Spirit and spoke in tongues (vv. 1-4).
   2. The crowd in Jerusalem accuse the apostles of being drunk (vv. 5-13).
      3. Peter and the apostles defend themselves:
         Three OT quotations,[49]
         (a) the first part of Joel 2.28-32 quotation (vv. 17-18).
         (b) the second part of Joel quotation (vv. 19-20).
         (c) the quotation from LXX Ps. 16.8-11 (vv. 25-28).
      3a. Peter and the apostles challenge the crowd to repent and be baptized (vv. 37-40).
   2a. The crowd receive the word and are baptized; devote themselves to the teaching of the apostles, having fellowship, breaking bread and prayers with the apostles (vv. 40-41).
1a. The apostles perform many wonders and signs (vv. 43-47).

My concern in this section is not about Peter's speech. Rather, my intention is to understand what the speech does for Peter and the rest of the apostles. From the structure suggested above, the speech brings the complete turnaround of the same people who have accused the apostles of being drunk. However, there is more to this than what the speech has done for the 'bewildered' people. Shifting the focus from the speech to the orator, it should be emphasized that the apostles were able to exonerate themselves from what could have been a malicious embarrassment. In other words, as Peter's sermon led to the mass conversion of the people, the same event should equally highlight the leadership abilities of the apostles. Their defence should not only be attributed to how the Spirit has endowed them with power to be witnesses, but due credit should also be

---

them 'being drunk'. And this is also where we see that the negative accusation against the apostles in Acts 2.14 inadvertently promotes their status.

49. These quotations are 'each marked off by a quotation formula and a renewed form of address' (vv. 16/22; vv. 25/29; vv. 34/36), Lüdemann, *Early Christianity*, p. 44.

given to the implicit leadership abilities which they have been trained for. Their ability to teach, as 2.42 states, is just one of them.

This kind of reading may also be applied to the people and their positive response to the apostles. Countless commentators have focused on the exegetical/historical issues which surround the sermon-response sequence of the story. From a social-scientific perspective, however, I suggest that the conversion of the '3,000 souls' is a figure intended, not only to bring out the magnitude of the event, but also the convincing vindication of the apostles from all the animadversions against them.[50] This would include (I believe) the leadership integrity of the apostles which was seriously damaged by Judas' betrayal of Jesus.

The summary statement in 2.42-47 does not only speak of how many people were added 'day by day' (cf. v. 46) to the Christian fold. Rather, this closing scene also impresses upon the readers of Luke–Acts how the apostles have successfully 'day by day' fulfilled their role as witnesses and leaders, the very role to which they have been appointed, trained, and transformed.

5. *Summary*

In this chapter I have attempted to understand the narrative of Acts 2 as the ritual process in the final stage of the apostles' rituals of status transformation. My study has led me to see some OT traditions which the author of Luke–Acts has employed in order to convey the apostles' process of installation as new leaders of the Christian community. One particular tradition is the status transformation of the seventy elders in Num. 11.

The installation of the seventy elders as leaders of the people of Israel in Num. 11 shares similar features with that of the apostles' experience in Acts 2. First, there was a leadership crisis which needed the help of new leaders. Second, there was a status transformation—from former followers to leaders. Third, there was the endowment of the Spirit during the process of the installation. And fourth, the leaders prophesied when the Spirit came upon them.

I also tried to explain the purpose of the catalogue of nations in Acts 2.5-13. I stated that despite the various suggestions concerning the function of this catalogue by NT scholarship, I proposed that only through

50. Cf. Lüdemann, *Early Christianity*, p. 47.

the rituals of status transformation can we put this pericope in its proper perspective. This perspective is that the catalogue of nations can actually function as representative of (1) how widely accepted was the leadership status of the apostles, and (2) the universal scope of the leadership responsibility of the newly installed leaders.

Likewise, I demonstrated that the author's depiction of the Peter standing with the Eleven in Acts 2.14 portrays the formal presentation of the initiands turned leaders of the Christian community. I emphasized that the picture of Peter standing with the Eleven supports my argument that the subject and focus of the narrative, from the time they were introduced in Acts 1.3 until they are formally presented here in Acts 2.14, are the Twelve apostles of Jesus.

Finally, I showed how the apostles were redeemed of their honour and leadership integrity by the form of response of the people once they have been installed as leaders. I mentioned how the apostles performed miracles and how the multitude were converted daily listening to the teachings of their new leaders.

CONCLUSION

I started this study with two important questions: Why were the apostles portrayed as having unanimity with the women disciples and Jesus' family in the upper room before the election of a new apostle (Acts 1.12-14)?; and Why was the election conducted before the arrival of the Spirit on the day of Pentecost (Acts 1.15-26)? My questions are supported and compounded by the fact that, apart from the directive to the apostles to wait in Jerusalem for the promise of the father, Jesus left no instructions to conduct a meeting with other groups and nor were there any orders to elect an apostle to replace Judas before Pentecost.[1] From this viewpoint, I suggested that the author was compelled to narrate these scenes of Acts 1.12-14 and 1.15-26 in the midst of the Ascension and Pentecost events because of an important reason. This reason has something to do with the apostles' change of status from being Jesus' followers to becoming the leaders of the Christian community.

The majority of studies have not explored the said pericopes from the perspective I proposed. One of the main reasons is the way most of these studies understand the structure of the narrative of Acts 1 and 2. This structure places over-emphasis on the individual stories of the Ascension and Pentecost resulting in a fragmented and disconnected narrative of the first two chapters of Acts.[2] In other words, because modern scholarship has primarily focused on the significance of the characters of Jesus and his ascension in Acts 1.9-11 and the Spirit and its arrival on the day of Pentecost in Acts 2.1-4, the role and function of the other characters in Acts 1–2 together with the stories they tell have been sidelined. This includes the stories about the meeting in the upper room (Acts 1.12-14) and the election of Matthias (1.15-26) which have been reduced to either simply providing continuity to the flow of the narrative—serving primarily to show continuity between the Ascension and Pentecost events—or, as

1. Section 1.3 following.
2. Section 5.1 and 7.2 following.

independent units of traditions inserted by the author because he could not find any other suitable places to put them.

The perspective I have suggested in this study has provided a plausible solution to the exegetical questions I mentioned. I proposed that, in order to understand the reasons why we find the pericopes of Acts 1.12-14 and 1.15-26 in the midst of the Ascension and Pentecost events, one needs to resolve the issue of the main focus of the narrative of Acts 1–2. The main focus, I believe, should be the apostles. The apostles are the primary characters, thus, making the other characters within the narrative of Acts 1–2 play secondary roles. These secondary characters inevitably include Jesus, the Spirit, and other groups or individuals mentioned in Acts 1–2. In doing so, the stories about Jesus' ascension and the Spirit's arrival on the day of Pentecost would all be on an equal level of importance with the other events in the same narrative. On the other hand, the character of the apostles would rise above any other characters or events as they are understood to be the reason why Acts 1–2 is structured as it is in the first place.[3]

So how did I go about proving that my perspective really works? First, I focused on the idea that the narrative of Acts 1–2 is primarily about the apostles and how they became leaders after Jesus' departure. This meant that all the events from the time the apostles were introduced in Acts 1.2 until they perform their first ministry by themselves are part of the whole process of the apostles' status transformation.

Second, I proposed that the apostles' status transformation was conducted, not essentially because of Jesus' departure, but because of the apostles' qualification to be leaders of the Christian community. It is this issue of qualification which necessitated the urgency to show the readers of Acts about the process of the apostles' transformation. My study suggested that the apostles' leadership qualification was in serious question because of their association with Judas—the apostle who betrayed Jesus. From this perspective, the whole Acts 1–2 narrative is viewed, not only from a historical but primarily from a sociological point of view. Acts 1–2, then, becomes a narrative highly apologetic in nature. It shows the effort of the author in promoting the leadership integrity of the apostles of Jesus. Judas' betrayal of Jesus has seriously marred, not only his reputation as an apostle, but also the reputation of the whole apostolate. The social embarrassment arising from Judas' betrayal of Jesus has prompted

---

3. Section 1.2.5.1; 8.2.

the author of Luke–Acts to launch his massive propagandic campaign to clear the name of the apostles.

What we have, therefore, is a crisis of leadership. It is a crisis which pertains to the moral integrity of the apostles who were expected to lead the community of Christians. It is also a crisis which needs to be immediately resolved before the apostles receive the fulfilment of the promise of the Father and attempt to begin doing the task which Jesus has commissioned them to undertake.

The perspective I have presented is just half of the task which is needed to answer the questions I have enumerated. The other half concerns finding the appropriate method and model to study the narrative. I found that the most appropriate is the social-scientific approach.[4] Specifically, I discovered that reading the narrative of Acts 1–2 from the model of a ritual answers all of the questions I have raised. In other words, the process of the apostles' change of status from followers to leaders can be understood from the structure of a modern-day ritual.

The idea to read the apostles' status transformation from the perspective of a ritual was inspired by three studies, two of which are from social anthropologists. The first of these two was Arnold van Gennep who, through his book *The Rites of Passage*,[5] has opened new insights into the study of rituals, particularly his identification of the three major stages through which an individual or group goes though the status transformation. Whether it be puberty rites, the passage from death to life, marriage rites, or any other status transformation ritual, Gennep identifies the three stages of the rite of passage as separation, transition, and incorporation.

The second is Victor Turner.[6] In his work *The Ritual Process*, Turner has expanded Gennep's work by introducing the idea of liminality and *communitas*. Liminality is the idea of statuslessness which the individual or group experience when they go through the rite of passage. At the same time, the initiands feel strong camaraderie as they continue to bond with each other. This, according to Turner, is *communitas*.

The third of these studies is most helpful in clearly defining my methodology. Mark McVann, in his application of Gennep's and Turner's work on the narrative of Lk. 3.1–4.30, showed me that it is possible to understand Jesus' encounter with John at the Jordan river, his baptism, and his confrontation with the devil in the wilderness as stages of a ritual.

---

4.   Cf. Section 1.1.1–1.1.3.
5.   Section 1.2.1.
6.   Section 1.2.2.

Jesus' change of status from private person to becoming the prophet of the nation can be read from the perspective of a status transformation ritual. McVann coined this as the Rituals of Status Transformation.[7] His contribution to Gennep's and Turner's work is his identification of the event of Jesus' encounter with the devil as a ritual confrontation (Lk. 4.1-13). He argued (a point which Gennep and Turner did not exploit) that the individual or group who goes through the ritual face mock confrontations as part of their initiation and training. These confrontations are designed to prepare the initiands to the real confrontations in the future.

From these three studies, I ventured to read the narrative of Acts 1–2 as the apostles' ritual of status transformation (RST). Through the model of the RST I was able to see how all of the events in the first two chapters of Acts fit together—clearly showing the ritual stages of the apostles' change of status from followers to leaders.

The description of the ritual stages I used basically follows McVann's. They are the *Separation, Transition* (which has two phases: Liminality-*Communitas*/Ritual Confrontation), and *Aggregation.* I also adapted McVann's descriptions of the major participants in the ritual—the ritual elder and the initiands.

The *Separation* stage[8] is the time when the initiands are taken away from any contact with society. In this stage, the initiands are ushered by the ritual elder into seclusion and training. The initiands are completely immersed into the teaching and instructions of the ritual elder. A significant phase in this time of training is what Turner has described as the cleansing of preconceived ideas of the initiands. All of the previous ideas which the initiand learned are totally wiped out in this stage of separation. These preconceived ideas need to be purged from the initiand in order for the ritual elder to instil his new teachings. This phase of cleansing is necessary if the initiand is to be successful in the status to which he or she is being transformed.

In Acts 1–2, I identified the time the apostles were said to have been with Jesus for forty days until Jesus completely leaves the Eleven by themselves when he ascended as the stage of separation (1.3-11).[9] In this stage, the apostles as initiands are said to have been completely with the ritual elder for forty days, receiving teachings about the kingdom of God

---

7. Section 1.2.3.
8. See Chapter 2 of this study.
9. Section 3.1.1.2.

(1.3b).[10] It is also during this stage that the initiands are cleansed from their preconceived ideas. This has been clearly demonstrated in 1.6-7 when the apostles asked Jesus if the restoration of the kingdom to Israel is now going to take place. As I have stated, Jesus' response is short of saying 'no' and instead gives them instructions to go back to Jerusalem and wait for the promise of the father (1.8).

The *Transition* stage is seen in Acts 1.12-26—the time between Jesus' departure and the Spirit's arrival on the day of Pentecost. This stage has two phases. The Liminality-*communitas* phase is seen especially in Acts 1.12-14 while the ritual confrontation phase is seen in Acts 1.15-26.

In the first phase (Acts 1.12-14), I indicated that the Eleven apostles returned to Jerusalem with no status at all. While it is true that they have already been commissioned by Jesus to be his witnesses, this role does not come to effect until they are baptized in the Spirit (Acts 2). The status of the apostles at this particular stage is unclear. They are, as I have stated, *betwixt* and *between*. The full picture of the apostles' liminal status is seen in the spatial and temporal setting of the 'upper room'. The initiands are completely secluded from society apart from the company of two distinct disciple groups—the women and Jesus' family.

It is at this point where I explained that there is something going on in the upper room other than just the expression of liminality-*communitas* of the apostles as initiands. I proposed that in order to fully appreciate the intent of the author behind the pericope of 1.12-14, other models from the social-scientific method should be employed. In other words, as the model of the Rituals of Status Transformation serves as my main theoretical framework, the models of patronage, networking, and the concept of honour and shame are working interactively within this main theoretical framework.

Recalling my study statement, I suggested that the author is promoting the apostles' leadership integrity by showing his readers that the apostles have gone through a serious transformation. The author needed to conduct this campaign in order to blot out the social shame created by one of the members of the Twelve—Judas and his betrayal of Jesus.

Integral to the author's campaign of promotion is the need to appeal to the other disciples of Jesus. I suggested that the reason why the women and Jesus' family were especially mentioned as those who were in unanimity with the Eleven in the upper room is due to their status as

10.   Section 3.1.2.

representatives of a wider clientele. This suggestion is best understood from the social concept of patronage and networking. I proposed that the leadership of the apostles would be that of a broker serving between God, the ultimate patron, and the people, as the clients. The author, therefore, needs to promote the apostles' leadership by appealing to the clientele of the other disciple groups. I have argued that the women disciples and the family of Jesus have their own network of clients. Showing the Eleven as having unanimity with these two disciple groups (1.14) is an invitation for the clients of these groups to render their support to the apostles whose reputation has been battered by Judas' betrayal of Jesus.

This perspective offers a plausible solution to the questions I have raised earlier. From the social-scientific method, I was able to show that contrary to the common view, Acts 1.12-14 is not simply the story of the group of Jesus' disciples praying in one room, waiting for the Spirit's arrival. Rather, it is one of the evidence which the author displays to prove that the apostles have the backing and support of two of the popular disciple groups after the Twelve.

The ritual confrontation happens in Acts 1.15-26—the narrative which NT scholarship simply understands as an election story. In this study, I have demonstrated that this is another episode where the author actively defends the apostles' leadership integrity. From the model of RST, I stated that the election narrative is the setting where the apostles face their ritual confrontation. The whole setting may be seen as a picture of a trial where the apostles are the defendants with Peter acting as their spokesman. Thus, contrary to the popular opinion that Peter speaks on behalf of all those in the assembly, I have proved that it is more logical to see that Peter delivers his speech on behalf of the Eleven apostles.[11]

On the other hand the 120 people who were part of the assembly, I suggested, represent the Christian community and therefore serve as those who stand to hear the defence of Eleven apostles. Their approval or disapproval thereof reflect how the community would also have responded to Peter and his defence speech.[12]

The case against the Eleven, as I have proposed, is a case which questions their leadership integrity in relation to the fact that it is from their group which Judas the betrayer came from. And, as I have suggested, the case can only be conceived in its full potential with a good under-

---

11.   Section 6.1.1 and 7.5.
12.   Section 7.5, no. 5.

standing of the concept of honour and shame.[13] In other words, when the setting in the election story is viewed from the perspective that the apostles were defending their honour rather than the more common suggestion of the need to replace Judas because the number of the apostles was down to eleven, one can understand why Peter had to give such a grotesque description of Judas' death, emphasizing that what Judas did was a fulfilment of scripture which nobody could have predicted and prevented (1.15-20).

From the method and model with which I have read the election narrative, I suggested that the pericope of Acts 1.15-26 ought to be understood as primarily the 'replacement of Judas' and not necessarily the 'election of Matthias'. Judas' replacement is actually a statement of excommunication and extirpation. It is a move which finally rids the apostles of a relationship with the traitor. It is a move which hopes to satisfy the readers of the apostles' sincerity and leadership integrity.

Finally, there is the stage of *Aggregation*.[14] I stated that I clearly see this stage in Acts 2. I indicated that the Spirit's baptism of the Twelve expresses God's approval and endorsement of the apostles' leadership status. I also argued that the setting of the aggregation is a setting which invites the readers of Acts to reflect on OT traditions.[15] In particular, I cited the OT account in Num. 11 where the aggregation in the status transformation of seventy elders of Israel strikes parallel scenarios with apostles in Acts 2.1-4. An instance is the distribution and endowment of the Spirit among the new leaders of Israel. And then there is the outburst of prophecy after the Spirit has rested upon the elders. Because of the parallels which Acts 2 share with Num. 11, the readers are helped to understand the apostles' aggregation as being ordained by God.[16]

The ultimate evidence which the author of Luke–Acts uses to prove to his readers that the apostles have been recognized in their new status is the positive response of the multitude who witnessed their preaching, teaching, and miracles after being baptized in the Spirit, and their formal presentation in 1.14. Acts 2.46-47 tells especially of how those who

---

13.   Section 6.2.1.

14.   Cf. Chapter 8.

15.   See my brief background study on the traditions surrounding Pentecost in 8.1.1 following.

16.   See section 9.1.1 following.

believed had gathered together, shared their possessions, and continued to grow in number.[17]

This study, I believe, is able to provide an alternative way of understanding the narrative of Acts 1–2. I showed specifically how the pericopes of 1.12-14 and 1.15-26 work within the two important events— the Ascension and Pentecost. I demonstrated that the story of the first two chapters of Acts is the story of the apostles' status transformation, and that through the social-scientific method, specifically the Rituals of Status Transformation, I showed how the change of status has taken place.

17. Section 9.3 following.

TWELVE APOSTLES FOR TWELVE THRONES?
THE REDACTION OF MATTHEW 19.28

In Chapter 7 of this study,[1] I argued that Acts 1.15-26 is not necessarily the fulfilment of Lk. 22.28-30. I stated that one of the important reasons is the silence of the text of Acts. In other words, the author gives no indication at all in the election narrative of Acts 1.15-26 that the choice of Matthias is an answer to the problem of the missing twelfth apostle which is alleged to be in line with Jesus' promise in Lk. 22.30.

The common view that Acts 1.15-26 is the fulfilment of Lk. 22.30 is based on the idea that the author of the gospel of Luke originally had the word δώδεκα before the word 'thrones'. Then the author altered his sources and dropped δώδεκα because he did not want to show that the betrayer Judas was rewarded with an eschatological rulership.[2] The suggestion that δώδεκα was omitted by Luke is understood only when compared with Matthew's version of the saying which has the word δώδεκα before 'thrones' in Mt. 19.28.[3]

---

1. See 7.3–7.4.

2. See my survey of scholars in 7.3.

3. This study assumes that there was indeed literary dependence between Matthew, Mark and Luke; specifically, that Matthew had the gospel of Mark as one of his major literary sources in shaping his gospel. This also meant the freedom of Matthew in altering the Markan source material in order to present his own theological agenda to the specific community he was ministering to. For further reading, see J. Fitzmyer, 'The Priority of Mark in Luke', in D.G. Miller *et al.* (eds.), *Jesus and Man's Hope*, I (Pittsburgh: Pickwick, 1970), pp. 131-70. Also J. Rohde, *Rediscovering the Teaching of the Evangelists* (London: SCM Press, 1968); N. Perrin, *What is Redaction Criticism?* (Philadelphia: Fortress Press, 1969); R.H. Stein, 'What is Redaktionsgeschichte?' *NovT* 13 (1971), pp. 181-98; *idem*, 'The Redaktionsgeschichtlich Investigation of a Markan Seam (Mc. 1.21f.)', *ZNW* 61 (1970), pp. 70-94; C.C. Black, *The Disciples according to Mark: Markan Redaction in Current Debate* (JSNTSup, 27; Sheffield: JSOT Press, 1989).

In the assumption that Lk. 22.30 is indeed a parallel to Mt. 19.28, this study will argue that it is possible to understand that the saying in Luke is closer to the original form of the saying. This means that, contrary to the common view, Matthew was the one who may have altered his sources by adding the word δώδεκα before the word 'thrones' in order to pursue his own agenda.[4] The section which follows is the study of this argument conducted from the redaction-critical perspective.

The Saying in Matthew 19.28

> Jesus said to them, 'Truly, I say to you, in the new world, when the Son of man shall sit on his glorious throne, you who have followed me will also sit on twelve thrones, judging the twelve tribes of Israel'.

Mt. 19 can be subdivided into at least five pericopes, namely the introductory statements (Mt. 19.1-2//Mk 10.1); the teaching on marriage and divorce (Mt. 19.3-12//Mk 10.2-12); attitudes toward children (Mt. 19.13-14//Mk 10.13-16//Lk. 18.15-17); the story of the young man (Mt. 19.16-22//Mk 10.17-22//Lk. 18.18-23); finally, Peter and his query on the fate of those who have decided to follow Jesus (Mt. 19.23-31//Mk 10.23-31//Lk. 18.24-30). The first and second pericopes speak of what Stephen Barton would call 'household ethics'.[5] They constitute Jesus' teaching on ethical values where each can be seen as independent from each other. Very different are the latter two pericopes.[6] These two pericopes are quite

---

4. Our goal is to find out if Matthew was consistently pursuing a specific agenda or developing and strengthening a strong theme for which the insertion of δώδεκα in Mt. 19.28 is just one in a cluster of other important redactions. But how does one particularly look for themes? What are the obvious signposts which can lead a reader to see an emphasis being delivered by the author? The answers are found in the process of isolating 'unique theological perspective' which entails the method of 'selection, modification, and expansion' of source materials; in other terms, a 'particular re-framing of tradition'. S. Moore, *Literary Criticism and the Gospels: The Theoretical Challenge* (London: Yale University Press, 1989), p. 183.

5. Barton, *Discipleship and Family Ties*, p. 204.

6. Following the lead of D.J. Harrington, 'The Rich Young Man in Matthew', in *Van Segbroeck* 2 (1992), pp. 199-208, and Schweizer, *The Good News according to Matthew* (ET; London: SPCK, 1976), pp. 384-85; W.D. Davies and D.C. Allison see three divisions in vv. 16-31 (i.e. vv. 16-22, 23-26, and 27-30) instead of my proposal of only two. Cf. *A Critical and Exegetical Commentary on the Gospel according to Saint Matthew*. III. *Commentary on Matthew XIX–XXVIII* (ICC; Edinburgh: T. & T. Clark, 1997), p. 38.

detached from the former two since they do not primarily promote family relationship issues. However, unlike the teaching on 'household ethics', the story of the 'Rich Young Man' in Mt. 19.16-22 and Peter's question to Jesus in Mt. 19.23-31 can actually be seen as one since they are what we might call 'didactically dependent' from each other. In other words, Peter's question to Jesus in the pericope of Mt. 19.23-31 is based on what had just transpired between Jesus and the young man in 19.16-22.[7] The plots of these two latter pericopes flow smoothly so that any attempt to establish the immediate context of the reward-saying in Mt. 19.28 should start reading from the story of the rich young man in 19.16-22.[8]

Nestle-Aland's 27th edition of *Novum Testamentum Graece* counts 279 words for Mk 10.17-31 while Mt. 19.16-31 only has 270. Matthew's count even includes the saying in 19.28 (a total of 33 words), a verse which Mark does not have. Luke's version, on the other hand, only has a total of 202. Matthew's version, therefore, is nine words shorter than that of Mark.[9] However, it would take more than just the counting of words to show us what Matthew (or even Luke for this matter) had in mind. It is not a question of how many words Matthew had dropped or omitted. Rather, what words or phrases has Matthew changed or replaced, and more importantly, why did he do this? The principal Matthean modifications of Mark are:

1. From 'Good Teacher, What Must I Do?' to 'Teacher, What Good Thing Must I Do?'

We find Mark's attributive διδάσκαλε ἀγαθε (Mk 10.17) repositioned by Matthew to διδάσκαλε, τί ἀγαθον in 19.16. Thus, instead of the vocative 'good teacher', Matthew has the simple address 'teacher' and places the adjective 'good' to qualify ποιήσω which asks 'what good thing must I do?' There are several suggestions as to why Matthew may have done this. Barton says that it may have been due to the author's 'ethicizing' intention, an attempt to be consistent with the 'household ethical' teachings in the previous pericopes.[10] Styler, on the other hand, suggests that Matthew seems to be avoiding the notion that Jesus is 'good'

---

7. Cf. D.A. Hagner, *Matthew 14-38* (WBC, 33b; Dallas: Word Books, 1995), p. 560.

8. For further discussions on the structural relationships of the said pericopes see B. Charette, *The Theme of Recompense in Matthew's Gospel* (JSNTSup, 79; Sheffield: JSOT Press, 1992), pp. 109-10.

9. A Matthean tendency to abbreviate?

10. Barton, *Discipleship and Family Ties*, p. 205.

or any claim to his divine nature because it is already a fact that Jesus is indeed divine.[11] On the contrary, Hagner believes that Matthew, with 'obvious christological interests, avoids the conclusion that Jesus is not to be considered "good" '.[12]

It is easy to fall short of putting emphasis on what Matthew may have wanted to emphasize rather than on what he did not. In other words, some exegetes have focused on the omission of ἀγαθός from διδάσκαλε, concluding that Matthew may have deliberately avoided describing Jesus as 'good', and as a result, given less attention to the association of ἀγαθός with ποιήσω. Would it not be possible to say that Matthew, though not wanting to minimize the attribute which ἀγαθός brings before the word διδάσκαλε, is more focused in attaining what he wanted to achieve by placing ἀγαθος before ποιήσω? Davies and Allison seem to agree. They have observed that,

> Matthew's version…gives us the impression that the adjective *good* was thrust in, in order to make occasion for the answer about *goodness*. That the answer is by no means relevant, seeing that the question asked was not concerning goodness in abstract, but concerning the conditions of obtaining eternal life; and, that the statement that God only is good, which is quite appropriate when used to exclude application of the title *good* to any other, does not by any means exclude the performance by another of at least one good deed.[13]

The moving of ἀγαθος from διδάσκαλε to ποιήσω focuses attention on the physical *doing*, in this case, the *things* which the young man can do 'in order to have eternal life'.[14] Could this be the reason why Matthew had

11. G.M. Styler, 'Stages in Christology in the Synoptic Gospels', *NTS* 10 (1963–64), pp. 404-406.

12. Hagner, *Matthew 14-38*, p. 555.

13. Davies and Allison, *Matthew*, p. 39, n. 4.

14. Consequently in 19.17, Matthew had to replace Mark's interrogative Τί με λέγεις ἀγαθον (Why do you call me good? 10.18) with Τί με ἐρωτας περὶ τοῦ ἀγαθοῦ (Why do you ask me about what is good?). He then also deletes θεός putting in place the simple substantive ὁ ἀγαθος. Charette believes that, 'The apparent contrast in 19.16 and 17 between the εἶς who seeks to *do* good and the εἶς who *is* good possibly intimates that the young man is one who thinks of goodness as resident in deeds. Ultimately he refuses to be perfect, which, according to 5.48 makes one like God.' *The Theme of Recompense*, p. 111. The replacements, I think, minimize the Markan focus on Jesus (hence the response of Jesus οὐδεὶς ἀγαθὸς εἰ μη εἰς ὁ θεος 'no one is good but God alone') favouring Matthew's emphasis on the *doing* over personalities.

to alter Mark's τὰς ἐντολὰς οἶδας (*know* the commandments, Mk 10.19) with τήρησον τὰς ἐντολὰς (*keep* the commandments)? Although one must beware of over interpreting the text, we cannot help but ask why the change from *knowing* to *keeping*, if not for the sense of *physical doing* over the *passive knowing*. The redaction also makes the Matthean insertion of λέγει αὐτ ποίας in 19.18 appropriate.

After stating to the young man that he should 'keep, observe, or fulfill' (τήρεω) the commandments, Matthew also gives a slightly different list of commandments. First, he omits the phrase μη ἀποστερήσῃς ('do not defraud'), probably due to its non-existence among the Ten Commandments.[15] And then, he adds the love commandment,[16] Ἀγαπήσεις τὸν πλησίον σου ὡς σεαυτόν which works well with what Jesus will be asking the young man to do in 19.21b: 'Go, sell what you possess and give it to the poor' (ὕπαγε πώλησόν σου τὰ ὑπάρχοντα καὶ δὸς τοῖς πτωχοῖς). This addition creates a context in which the act may be done with the decisive element of empathy and not simply an act of dry obedience to the command.

In 19.20, Matthew describes the man who queries Jesus as a νεανίσκος in contrast with Mark's ἐκ νεότητος. The reason for the change should be understood with Matthew's additions of τί ἔτι ὑστερῶ and Jesus' conditional statement of εἰ θέλεις τέλειος εἶναι.[17] In other words, the combination of the phrase 'young man' with the question 'what else do I lack?' or 'in what respect am I still inferior?'[18] prompts the utterance of the conditional challenge by Jesus 'if you would be perfect...' The invitation of Jesus to prove the young man's claim of having observed the law is further enhanced as Matthew omits Mark's portrayal of Jesus' sympathetic attitude towards the young man with the phrase ὁ δὲ Ἰησοῦς ἐμβλέψας αὐτ ἠγάπησεν αὐτον (Mk 19.21a). What we find in these additions, therefore, is the emphasis on the young man's 'deficiency in surpassing righteousness'.[19]

2. From 'What You Have' to 'What You Possess'.

Matthew's ὑπάρχοντα ('possessions'), a change from Mark's ὅσα ἔχεις ('what you have'), makes vivid the description of the material things the young man is told to give up (19.21a). The young man went away

---

15. This was also omitted in codices B, W, D, Ψ, etc.
16. Cf. Lev. 19.18.
17. Cf. Mt. 5.48.
18. BAGD, p. 848.
19. Gundry, *Matthew*, p. 387.

sorrowful. The reason for this 'sorrowful' response is his disinclination to sell his possessions and give to the poor, and not necessarily on the accompanying instruction of Jesus in 19.21c καὶ δεῦρο ἀκολούθει μοι ('and come follow me'). Such emphasis on selling possessions and loving the poor is consistent with the Gospel to the Hebrews in Origen's Latin commentary on Mt. 15.14. It speaks of a second rich man who approached Jesus and asked him the same question. This man went away, 'scratching his head' and displeased from what Jesus instructed him to do. Jesus then remarks,

> How can you say, I have fulfilled the law and the prophets, when it is written in the law: You shall love your neighbour as yourself; and lo, many of your brothers, sons of Abraham, are clothed in filth, dying of hunger, and your house is full of many good things, none of which goes out to them?[20]

3. From the 'Young Man's Sorrowful Exit' to the 'Difficult Entry to God's Kingdom'.

After Matthew has indicated that the young man had sorrowfully left the scene, he pictures Jesus responding with two traditional sayings. The saying in 19.23 is solely directed to the disciples as Matthew omits the Markan phrase of περιβλεψάμενος (looking around). In it, Jesus indicates that it is 'hard for a rich man to enter the kingdom of heaven'. And because this saying immediately follows the story of the young man (19.16-22), the assumption that the young man was 'materially' rich has commonly been accepted.[21] Coupled with 19.24, the analogy that 'it is easier for a camel to go through the eye of a needle than for a rich man to enter God's kingdom', compounds the degree of difficulty for a wealthy man to gain entry into the kingdom of God.[22]

There is a great deal of confusion about the point of this story. For instance, Francis Beare questions the 'astonishment' (ἐξεπλήσσοντο σφόδρα) of the disciples in 19.25, 'Has Jesus ever said anything to make them [the disciples] think that wealth is a prerequisite for entrance into the

---

20. Cited from A.F.J. Klijn, *Jewish-Christian Gospel Tradition* (Leiden: Brill, 1992), p. 56.

21. Matthew replaced Mark's rendering of Πῶς δυσκόλως οἱ τα χρήματα ἔχοντες ('how hard it is [for] those who have much') with πλούσιος δυσκόλως ('rich man, with difficulty').

22. The common proverbial saying has the 'elephant' instead of the καμηλον. *Berakoth: Hebrew–English Edition of the Babylonian Talmud* (trans. Maurice Simon; ed. I. Epstein; London: Soncino Press, 1965).

Kingdom?'[23] This is also where Stephen Barton draws over hastily the conclusion that discipleship means the 'detachment from possessions' and is a 'condition of entry into the kingdom'.[24] The fact is, the plot of the story does not suggest that wealth is the hindrance to enter God's kingdom. It is rather the inability to part from it in response to God's command which prevents an individual from gaining God's approval. Thus, if one is to equate that 'a man of wealth is blessed by God' (Deut. 28.1-14),[25] then, the disciples' 'astonishment' was a suitable response since if the rich young man cannot be saved, who could?

With reference to the story of the rich young man in 19.16-22, the sayings in 19.23 and 24 together with the responses of the disciples and Jesus in 19.25-26 attempt to explain that entering God's kingdom is not based on how much wealth a man has but how willing a man is in sacrificing and sharing his possessions. Moreover, the purpose of the whole plot does not primarily stress the 'how to enter God's kingdom' but also the fact of a 'corresponding reward' for those who are willing to give up their wealth. And this is what makes Peter's query in 19.27 very appropriate. Peter declares, 'Behold, we have left everything and followed you. What shall we have then?' Peter's question is not redundant. He is not asking for any assurance of whether they as disciples are qualified to enter God's kingdom. Rather, Peter wants to know what they get in return for having decided to leave everything they had and follow Jesus.[26] It is therefore from this query that Matthew employs the Q material of 19.28.[27]

One should bear in mind that Matthew's employment of the Q saying in 19.28 is in response to Peter's question in v. 27, and that the content of such response is the corresponding 'reward' to Peter and the disciples for their decision of having given up everything and followed Jesus. The need to stress this point is crucial since it has prevented some interpreters from properly understanding the meaning of the δώδεκα θρόνους and the scope of κρίνοντες in 19.28b. Thus, a summary of what had just preceded is helpful:

23. F.W. Beare, *The Gospel according to Matthew* (Oxford: Basil Blackwell, 1981), p. 397.

24. Barton, *Discipleship and Family Ties*, p. 206.

25. Cf. R.T. France, *Matthew* (Grand Rapids: Eerdmans, 1985), p. 287.

26. Davies surprisingly reads more into the text as he agrees with Cassian's statement that 'Actually what they left was, clearly nothing more than cheap and torn nets'. Davies and Allison, *Matthew*, p. 54.

27. Or, probably, that Matthew constructs the query as a link to the Q material.

First, the redactions displayed by Matthew, starting from the story of the young man (19.16-22) until the question of Peter (19.27), show that the issue is not only on the preparedness to give up wealth, but also on 'rewards' in return for earthly possessions given up for God's sake. While the issue includes the reward of entering God's kingdom, the idea of material remuneration is not necessarily sidelined.

Second, the focal lesson does not show or give any hint at any voluntary surrender of either social status, fame, political title, or any rulership position which is supposed to receive in return its eschatological equivalent.

Third, the reference to 'eternal life' in 19.16, 'treasures in heaven' in 19.21, 'enter the kingdom of heaven' in 19.23, 'enter the kingdom of God' in 19.24, shows that the reward is to be given not in the present age but in a setting that is clearly eschatological.

4. From 'One Throne' to 'Twelve Thrones'.

With the interpretative boundaries of 19.16-27 properly set, the reason as to why Matthew imports Q material is apparent. Verse 28 not only satisfies the query of Peter in 19.27 but is also faithful to the context of the whole narrative section of 19.16-27. Furthermore, 19.28 serves to link the rest of the reward sayings in 19.29 and 30.

If the Lukan saying (22.30) is closer to Q, we then can see two significant features original to Matthew. One is the strong eschatological content of the saying, and second, is the concreteness of the reward to the disciples. The eschatological tone of the saying is determined by Matthew's use of the phrase ἐν τῇ παλιγγενεσίᾳ (lit. 'in the regeneration'). This temporal dative phrase is familiar with the Stoics in the Greco-Roman period.[28] However, the phrase can be translated 'in the renewing of the world' which specifies a world in the time of the reign of the Messiah.[29] This translation is more reflective of the Jewish understanding of the word than of the previous Stoic concept.[30] For example,

28. Also used in different concepts such as 'reincarnation' (Nemesius, *De nat. hom.* 2), 'of the new world after the flood' (Philo, *Vit. Mos.* 2.65; 1 Clem. 9.4), 'of Christian rebirth' (Tit. 3.5; Corp. Herm. 13), 'of Israel's re-establishment after the exile' (Josephus, *Ant.* 11.66), 'of the afterlife' (Philo, *Cher.* 114); Davies and Allison, *Matthew*, p. 57.

29. BAGD, p. 606. The only other NT occurrence is in Titus 3.5.

30. A good discussion on the function of Παλιγγενεσία can be found in F.W. Burnett, '"Παλιγγενεσία" in Matt. 19.28: A Window on the Matthean Community?' *JSNT* 17 (1983), pp. 60-72.

Josephus *Ant.* 11.3.9 points to Israel's rebirth after life in exile.[31] The life after exile is enhanced by the reference to the title 'Son of man' (ὁ υἱος τοῦ ἀνθρώπου).

The second of the two significant features of this saying is most important. The addition of δώδεκα before θρόνους is not simply for the sake of strong parallelism.[32] The phrase δώδεκα θρόνους implies the concreteness and assurance of the reward by emphasizing the idea of equal appropriation to the Twelve. In other words, part of Matthew's purpose in utilizing this Q material together with his critical redactions, is not only to express 'rulership' but that each of them, and not only as collectively, will be rewarded. Modern scholarship has tended to see the meaning of κρίνοντες as primarily the sharing of rulership of Israel with Jesus in the eschatological kingdom. This share is the reward the disciples are to receive because of their loyalty to him. For example, Fred Burnett concludes that,

> The Matthean emphasis in this section is upon eternal life as the reward for discipleship. The theme of eternal life also is traditional (cf. Mark 10.27; Lk. 18.18), but it is enhanced both by the Matthean Jesus' conditional response to the young man (v. 17) and by the general statement that all who follow Jesus will inherit eternal life. [33]

However, such a view does not directly answer Peter's question in 19.27, nor is it consistent with the context of the story of the rich young ruler in 19.16-22. Burnett's conclusion only considers the part where 'following Jesus' is required. The emphasis on the willingness to give up wealth or possessions has been discarded. In addition, I have stated previously that the issue is also not the surrender of any rulership position which rightly deserves an equivalent rulership seat in the Messiah's kingdom. Peter asks what will be the corresponding reward for those who have given up their possessions and followed Jesus. Jesus, therefore, answers them with a direct reply[34] that the disciples will not only get to rule Israel with him, but that 'each of them will sit on individual thrones' and 'rule individually the twelve tribes of Israel'. The sense of 'individual

---

31. A comprehensive treatment of the phrase is effectively dealt by D.A. Hagner in his commentary of *Matthew 14–28*, p. 565.

32. *Contra* Davies and Allison, *Matthew*, p. 55.

33. Burnett, 'Παλιγγενεσία', p. 61.

34. Notice the corresponding response of Jesus οἱ ἀκολουθήσαντές μοι ('those who have followed me') 19.28 with Peter's earlier statement of ἠκολουθήσαμεν σοι ('we have followed you') in 19.27.

rulership and ownership' expresses equal appropriation and is strongly conveyed by Matthew's insertion of the word δώδεκα before the phrase θρόνους κρίνοντες τὰς δώδεκα φυλὰς τοῦ Ἰσραήλ, an item absent in its Lukan parallel.[35] In other words, having given up their possessions, the compensation of rulership for the apostles could be understood as both a material remuneration and an authoritative position.[36]

What I am suggesting is not necessarily the literal distribution of the twelve tribes amongst the Twelve apostles in the eschatological kingdom. What I am emphasizing is the element of assurance and the concreteness of the reward to the Twelve by Matthew's addition of the δώδεκα before θρόνους.

5.   From 'a House, a Family, and a Land' to 'a Hundredfold of Houses, Families and Lands'.

The emphasis on the assurance and concreteness of the reward is enhanced in 19.29. After addressing Peter's question, Jesus now turns to the πᾶς ὅστις who also followed him. Hagner sees this as, '...typical poetic language that employs hyperbole in the description of the bounteousness of eschatological blessing, the point being that the latter will exceed beyond calculation the losses incurred in the first place'.[37]

Everything that has been sacrificed for Jesus's sake will be bountifully compensated (ἑκατονταπλασίονα λήμψεται). The reward in 19.29 is not only of a relational content but also of material extent. The saying begins with οἰκίας and ends with ἀγρούς, both of which are material possessions.

Matthew ends the narrative scene with 19.30, probably an independent

---

35.   As I have argued earlier in the introduction to this study, it is Luke who has probably remained faithful to Q. The claim that it was Luke who deleted δώδεκα before θρόνους simply because Luke cannot allow the traitor Judas to be one of the recipients of Jesus' reward of rulership is unsubstantial.

36.   It seems likely that the idea of rulership with possession is strongly influenced by Dan. 7. The allusions of Matthew to Dan. 7 are evidenced by the following aspects. In Dan. 7.9, the first reference 'thrones' is plural which solicits the implication of one throne for God and the other for the Son of Man; again, Davies and Allison, *Matthew*, p. 54. The text of Daniel goes on further to stress that the 'Most High' take 'possession' of kingdoms forever. Possession of the kingdoms is shared with the 'people of the saints' of the Most High (Dan. 7.27). This concept of retribution is also reflected in Obadiah. In Obad. 11, 'strangers' took the wealth of God's people. However, when the 'day of the Lord' arrives, the 'house of Jacob' is empowered by the Lord to 'possess their own possessions' (17 following); cf. Wisdom 3.7-8.

37.   Hagner, *Matthew 14–28*, p. 566.

saying. This verse intends to show the prosperous fate for those who have denied themselves the fortunes of the present world for Jesus. The phrase πρῶτοι ἔσχατοι καὶ ἔσχατοι πρῶτοι shows not only the dramatic reversal of fortune but also the justice the new world has to offer.

So what have I accomplished so far? What is the significance of studying the saying of Mt. 19.28 in relation to the reward-promise of Lk. 22.30? Well, I have actually accomplished two significant issues. First, I was able to show that there are strong reasons to believe that Matthew had inserted the word δώδεκα before θρόνους. The primary reason is that the author of the first gospel desires to convey the message that those who are willing to give up 'earthly material possessions' for Jesus' sake will be rewarded bountifully with 'heavenly possessions'.

Second, the identification of reasons for the Matthean alterations narrows all other arguments as to why one cannot accept the possibility that Luke has remained faithful to Q. The truth is, the elimination of the argument that Matthew has the more primitive rendering of Q with regards to the 'twelve thrones' issue, leaves us no other probable reason why Luke cannot be more primitive than Matthew.

BIBLIOGRAPHY

Reference Works, Primary Texts, and Translations

Abercrombie, N., S. Hill and B.S. Turner (eds.), *The Penguin Dictionary of Sociology* (London: Penguin Books, 3rd edn, 1994).

Aristophanes (LCL; 2 vols.; trans. B.B. Rogers; Cambridge, MA: Harvard University Press, 1978).

Berakoth: Hebrew–English Edition of the Babylonian Talmud (trans. Maurice Simon; ed. I. Epstein; London: Soncino Press, 1965).

Blass, F., and A. De Brunner, *A Greek Grammar of the New Testament and Other Early Christian Literature* (trans. R.W. Funk; Chicago: Chicago University Press, 1961).

Bowker, J., *The Targums and Rabbinic Literature* (Cambridge: Cambridge University Press, 1969).

Brenton, L.C., *The Septuagint with Apocrypha: Greek and English* (Regency Reference Library; Grand Rapids: Zondervan, 1851).

Charles, R.H., *The Apocrypha and Pseudepigrapha of the Old Testament in English*, II (Oxford: Clarendon Press, 1913).

Charlesworth, J.H., *The Old Testament Pseudepigrapha* (London: Darton, Longman & Todd, I [1983]; II [1985]).

Danby, H., *The Mishnah: Translated from the Hebrew with Introduction and Brief Explanatory Notes* (Oxford: Oxford University Press, 1964).

Diodorus of Sicily (LCL; 12 vols.; trans. C.H. Oldfather; Cambridge, MA, Harvard University Press, 1963).

Dionysius of Halicarnassus (LCL; 7 vols.; trans. Ernest Cray; Cambridge: MA: Harvard University Press, 1953).

Dupont-Sommer, A., *The Essene Writings from Qumran* (trans. G. Vermes; Glouster, MA: Peter Smith, 1973).

Eliade, M. (ed.), *The Encyclopedia of Religion* (London: MacMillan, 1987).

Esler, P.F., *Modelling Early Christianity: Social-Scientific Studies of the New Testament in its Context* (London: Routledge, 1995), p. 4.

Etheridge, J.W., *The Targums of Onkelos and Jonathan Ben Uzziel on the Pentateuch* (New York: Ktav, 1968).

Glare, P.G.W. (ed.), *Oxford Latin Dictionary* (Oxford: Clarendon Press, 1982).

Grant, M., *Greek and Latin Authors: 800 BC—AD 1000* (New York: H.W. Wilson Co., 1980).

Hatch, E., and H.A. Redpath, *A Concordance to the Septuagint and Other Greek Versions of the O.T.: Including the Apocryphal Books* (Oxford: Clarendon Press, 1897).

Howatson, M.C. (ed.), *The Oxford Companion to Classical Literature* (Oxford: Oxford University Press, 2nd edn, 1989).

Josephus (LCL; 9 vols.; trans. H. St. J. Thackery; Cambridge, MA: Harvard University Press, 1965).
Lucian (LCL; 8 vols.; trans. A.M. Harmon *et al.*; Cambridge, MA: Harvard University Press, 1965).
Martínez, F.G., *The Dead Sea Scrolls Translated: The Qumran Texts in English* (trans. W.G.E. Watson; Grand Rapids: Eerdmans, 2nd edn).
Meecham, H.G., *The Letter of Aristeas: A Linguistic Study with Special Reference to the Greek Bible* (Manchester: Manchester University Press, 1935).
Milik, J.T. *et al.* (eds.), *Discoveries in the Judean Desert* (9 vols.; Oxford: Clarendon Press, 1955–1992).
Moulton, H.K. (ed.), *The Analytical Greek Lexicon Revised* (Grand Rapids: Zondervan, 1978).
Moulton, W.F., and A.S. Gedden, *A Concordance of the Greek Testament* (Edinburgh: T. & T. Clark, 1897).
Novum Testamentum Graece (ed. B. Aland *et al.*; Stuttgart: Deutsche Bibelgesellschaft, 27th edn, 1993).
Philo of Alexandria (LCL; 10 vols.; trans. F.H. Colson and G.H. Whitaker; London: Heinemann, 1935).
Plato: Plato the Laws (LCL; trans. Paul Shorey; Cambridge, MA: Harvard University Press, 1935).
Plutarch: Plutarch's Lives (LCL; 11 vols.; trans. Bernadote Perrin; Cambridge, MA: Harvard University Press, 1967).
Schechter, S., *Documents of Jewish Sectaries* (Cambridge: Cambridge University Press, 1910).
Strack, H.L., and P. Billerbeck, *Kommentar zum Neuen Testament aus Talmud und Midrasch*, II (Munich, 1956).
Talmud of the Land of Israel: A Preliminary Translation and Explanation (35 vols.; Chicago: University of Chicago Press, 1983).
The Apostolic Fathers (LCL; 2 vols.; trans. Kirsopp Lake; London: Heinemann, 1919).
The Aramaic Bible: The Targum, VI-XIII (eds. K. Cathcart *et al.*; Wilmington, DE: Michael Glazier, 1986).
The Babylonian Talmud (35 vols.; ed. and trans. I. Epstein; London: Soncino Press, 1935–1948).
The Midrash (10 vols.; trans. H. Freedman and M. Simon; London: Soncino Press, 1939).
The Mishnah (trans. H. Danby; London: Oxford University Press, 1989).
The Septuagint Version of the Old Testament and Apocrypha (With English Translation and Various Readings and Critical Notes) (London: S. Bagster, n.a.).
Xenophon (LCL; 7 vols.; trans. Carleton L. Brownson; London: Heinemann, 1922).

General Works

Abbott, F., and A. Johnson, 'Roman Egypt', in *idem*, *Municipal Administration in the Roman Empire* (Princeton: Princeton University Press, 1926).
Abercrombie, N., and S. Hill, 'Paternalism and Patronage', *BJS* 27 (1976), pp. 413-29.
Adams, B.N., 'Interaction Theory and Social Network', *Sociometry* 30 (1967), pp. 64-78.
Agnew, F.H., 'The Origin of the NT Apostle-Concept: A Review of Research', *JBL* 105 (1986), pp. 75-96.
Alexander, L.C.A., '*IPSE DIXIT: Citation of Authority in Paul and in the Jewish and Hellenistic Schools.*' A paper read at the proceedings of the 1997 Rolighed Conference

under the seminar title *Paul beyond the Judaism-Hellenism Divide*. Edited by T. Enberg-Pedersen.

—'Luke's Preface in the Context of Greek Preface-Writing', *NovT* 28 (1986), pp. 48-74.

—'Reading Luke–Acts from Back to Front', in J. Verheydey (ed.), *The Unity of Luke–Acts* (Leuven: Leuven University Press, 1999).

—'Sisters in Adversity: Retelling Martha's Story', in G.J. Brooke (ed.), *Women in Biblical Tradition* (Lampeter: Edwin Mellen Press, 1992).

—'The Preface of Acts and the Historians', in B. Witherington III (ed.), *History, Literature, and Society in the Book of Acts* (Cambridge: Cambridge University Press, 1996).

—*The Preface to Luke's Gospel: Literary Convention and Social Context in Luke 1.1-4 and Acts 1.1* (Cambridge: Cambridge University Press, 1993).

Alexander, P.S., and G. Vermes, 'Qumran Cave 4, XIX: Serekh Ha-Yahad and Two Related Texts', *Discoveries in the Judaean Desert*, XXVI (Oxford: Clarendon Press, 1998).

Alföldy, G., *The Social History of Rome* (trans. D. Braund and F. Pollock; London: Croom Helm, 1985).

Allen, O.W., Jr, *The Death of Herod: The Narrative and Theological Function of Retribution in Luke–Acts* (Atlanta, GA: Scholars Press, 1997).

Anderson, J.C., 'The Implied Reader in Matthew' (Unpublished seminar paper submitted to the Literary Aspects of the Gospels and Acts, SBL Annual Meeting, 1983).

Arbeitman, Y., 'The Suffix Iscariot', *JBL* 99.1 (1980), pp. 122-24.

Arlandson, J.M., *Women, Class, and Society in Early Christianity: Models from Luke–Acts* (Peabody, MA: Hendrickson, 1997).

Aronson, D.R. (ed.), 'Social Networks', *The Canadian Review of Sociology and Anthropology* (Special Issue 7 [1970]), pp. 221-86.

Ascough, R.S., *What Are They Saying about the Formation of Pauline Churches?* (New York: Paulist Press, 1998).

Ashley, T.R., *The Book of Numbers* (NICOT; Grand Rapids: Eerdmans, 1993).

Aune, D., *Prophecy in Early Christianity and the Ancient Mediterranean World* (Grand Rapids: Eerdmans, 1983).

—*The New Testament in its Literary Environment* (Philadelphia: Westminster Press, 1987).

—'The Significance of the Delay of the Parousia for Early Christianity', in G.F. Hawthorne (ed.), *Current Issues in Biblical and Patristic Interpretation* (Grand Rapids: Eerdmans, 1975).

Badian, E., *Foreign Clientele (264-70 B.C.)* (Oxford: Clarendon Press, 1958).

Bailey, K.E., *Through the Peasant Eyes: More Lucan Parables, their Culture and Style* (Grand Rapids: Eerdmans, 1980).

Bal, M., *Narratology: Introduction to the Theory of Narrative* (trans. C. Von Boheemen; Toronto: University of Toronto Press, 1985).

Baltzer, K., 'Considerations concerning the Office and Calling of the Prophet', *HTR* 61 (1968), pp. 567-91.

Banton, M. (ed.), *The Relevance of Models for Social Anthropology* (New York: Praeger, 1965).

Barbour, I., *Myths, Models, and Paradigms: A Comparative Study in Science and Religion* (New York: Harper & Row, 1974).

Barnes, J.A., 'Networks and Political Process', in J.C. Mitchell (ed.), *Social Networks in Urban Situations* (Manchester: Manchester University Press, 1969).

Barr, D.L., and J.L. Wentling, 'The Conventions of Classical Biography and the Genre of Luke–Acts', in C.H. Talbert (ed.), *New Perspectives from the Society of Biblical Literature* (New York: Crossroad, 1984).

Barrett, C.K., *The Acts of the Apostles*, I (Edinburgh: T. & T. Clark, 1994).

Barrett, S., *Anthropology: Student's Guide to Theory and Method* (Toronto: University of Toronto Press, 1996).

Barton, S.C., 'A Hellenistic Cult Group and the New Testament Churches', *JAC* 24 (1981), pp. 225-46.

—*Discipleship and Family Ties in Mark and Matthew* (Cambridge: Cambridge University Press, 1994).

—'Historical Criticism and Social-Scientific Perspectives in the New Testament', in J.B. Green (ed.), *Hearing the New Testament: Strategies for Interpretation* (Grand Rapids: Eerdmans, 1995).

—'Sociology and Theology', in I.H. Marshall and D. Petersen (eds.), *Witness to the Gospel: The Theology of Acts* (Grand Rapids: Eerdmans, 1998).

Bateson, G., *Naven* (Cambridge: Cambridge University Press, 1936).

Bauckham, R., *Jude and the Relatives of Jesus* (Edinburgh: T. & T. Clark, 1990).

Baumgarten, J., 'The Duodecimal Courts of Qumran, Revelation, and the Sanhedrin', *JBL* 95 (1976), pp. 59-78.

Beardslee, W., 'The Casting of Lots at Qumran and in the Book of Acts', *NovT* 4 (1960), pp. 245-52.

Beare, F.W., *The Gospel according to Matthew* (Oxford: Basil Blackwell, 1981).

Beasley-Murray, G.R., *Baptism in the New Testament* (London: Macmillan, 1962).

Benko, S., and J.J. O'Rourke (eds.), *Early Church History: The Roman Empire as the Setting of Primitive Christianity* (London: Oliphants, 1971).

Benoit, P., 'The Ascension', in *Jesus and the Gospel*, I (New York: Herder and Herder, 1973).

Berger, P.L., *The Sacred Canopy: Elements of a Social Theory of Religion* (New York: Anchor Books, 1990).

Berger, P.L., and T. Luckmann, *The Social Construction of Reality: A Treatise in the Sociology of Knowledge* (Harmondsworth: Penguin Books, 1966).

Black, C.C., *The Disciples according to Mark: Markan Redaction in Current Debate* (JSNTSup, 27; Sheffield: JSOT Press, 1989).

Black, M., *The Book of Enoch* (Leiden: E.J. Brill, 1985).

—*Models and Metaphors* (Ithaca, NY: Cornell University Press, 1962).

Blau, P.M., *Exchange and Power in Social Life* (New York: John Wiley & Sons, 1964).

Blok, A., 'Variations in Patronage', *Sociologische Gids* 16 (1969), pp. 365-78.

Blue, B., 'The Influence of Jewish Worship on Luke's Presentation of the Early Church', in I.H. Marshall and D. Peterson (eds.), *Witness to the Gospel: The Theology of Acts* (Grand Rapids: Eerdmans, 1998).

Bock, D., *Proclamation from Prophecy and Pattern: Lucan Old Testament Christology* (JSNTSup, 12; Sheffield: Sheffield Academic Press, 1987).

Boissevain, J., and J.C. Mitchell (eds.), *Friends of Friends: Networks, Manipulators and Coalitions* (New York: St. Martin's Press, 1974).

—*Network Analysis: Studies in Human Interaction* (The Hague: Mouton, 1973).

Bolt, B., 'Mission and Witness', in I.H. Marshall and D. Petersen (eds.), *Witness to the Gospel: The Theology of Acts* (Grand Rapids: Eerdmans, 1998).

Bornkamm, G., *Early Christian Experience* (New York: Harper & Row, 1969).

Boswell, D.M., 'Personal Crises and the Mobilization of the Social Network', in J.C. Mitchell (ed.), *Social Networks in Urban Situation* (Manchester: Manchester University Press, 1969).

Bott, E., *Family and Social Networks* (London: Tavistock, 2nd edn, 1971).

—'Urban Families: Conjugal Roles and Social Networks', *Human Relations* 8 (1955), pp. 345-83.

Bowker, J., *The Targums and Rabbinic Literature* (Cambridge: Cambridge University Press, 1969).

Bowman, J., 'Eschatology of the NT', in *IDB*, II, pp. 135-40.

Brawley, R., *Luke–Acts and the Jews: Conflict, Apology, and Conciliation* (Atlanta, GA: Scholars Press, 1987).

Brodie, T.L., 'Greco-Roman Imitation of Texts as a Partial guide to Luke's Use of Sources', in C.H. Talbert (ed.), *Luke–Acts: New Perspectives* (Edinburgh. T. & T. Clark, 1978).

—'Towards Unraveling the Rhetorical Imitation of Sources in Acts: 2 Kings 5 as One Component of Acts 8, 9-40', *Bib* 67 (1986), pp. 41-67.

Brooten, B.J., *Women Leaders in the Ancient Synagogue: Inscriptional Evidence and Background Issues* (BJS, 36; Chico, CA: Scholars Press, 1982).

Brown, P., 'The Rise and Function of the Holy Man in Late Antiquity', *JRS* 61 (1971), pp. 80-101.

—*Society and the Holy in Late Antiquity* (London: Faber & Faber, 1982).

Brown, R.E., *The Birth of the Messiah: A Commentary on the Infancy Narratives in Matthew and Luke* (London: Geoffrey Chapman, 1977).

—*The Death of the Messiah From Gethsemane to the Grave: A Commentary on the Passion Narratives in the Four Gospels* (New York: Doubleday, 1994).

Bruce, F.F., *The Acts of the Apostles* (Grand Rapids: Eerdmans, 1990).

Budd, P.J., *Numbers* (WBC; Waco, TX: Word Books, 1984).

Bultmann, R., *The History of Synoptic Tradition* (New York: Harper & Row, rev. edn, 1968).

Burke, P., *Sociology and History* (London: George Allen & Unwin, 1980).

Burnett, F.W., '"Παλιγγενεσία" in Matt. 19.28: A Window on the Matthean Community?', *JSNT* 17 (1983), pp. 60-72.

Burridge, R.A., *What Are the Gospels? A Comparison with Greco-Roman Biography* (Cambridge: Cambridge University Press, 1992).

Cadbury, H.J., 'Four Features of Lucan Style', in L.E. Keck and J.L. Martyn (eds.), *Studies in Luke–Acts: Essays Presented in Honor of Paul Schubert* (Philadelphia: Abingdon, 1966).

—*The Making of Luke–Acts* (London: SPCK, 1958).

—*The Style and Literary Method of Luke* (Cambridge, MA: Harvard University Press, 1920).

—'The Summaries in Acts', in K. Lake and F. Jackson (eds.), *The Beginnings of Christianity*, V (London: Macmillan, 1933).

Campbell, J.K., *Honour, Family and Patronage: A Study of Institutions and Moral Values in a Greek Mountain Community* (Oxford: Clarenden Press, 1964).

—*Honour and Shame: The Values of Mediterranean Society* (ed. J.G. Peristiany; London: Weidenfeld & Nicholson, 1965).

Campenhausen, H. von, *Tradition and Life in the Church* (London: Collins, 1968).

Capper, B., 'Reciprocity and the Ethic of Acts', in I.H. Marshall and D. Peterson (eds.), *Witness to the Gospel: The Theology of Acts* (Grand Rapids: Eerdmans, 1998).

Carney, T.F., *The Shape of the Past: Models and Antiquity* (Lawrence, KS: Coronado Press, 1975).

Carroll, J.T., *Response to the End of History: Eschatology and Situation in Luke–Acts* (Atlanta, GA: Scholars Press, 1988).

Cassidy, R.J., *Jesus, Politics, and Society: A Study of Luke's Gospel* (Maryknoll, NY: Orbis, 1978).

—*Society and Politics in the Acts of the Apostles* (Maryknoll, NY: Orbis Books, 1988).

Chance, J.B., *Jerusalem, the Temple, and the New Age in Luke–Acts* (Macon, GA: Mercer University Press, 1988).

Chapple, E.D., and C.S. Coon, *Principles of Anthropology* (New York: Henry Holt & Co., 1942).

Charette, B., *The Theme of Recompense in Matthew's Gospel* (JSNTSup, 79; Sheffield: JSOT Press, 1992).

Chatman, S., *Story and Discourse: Narrative Structure in Fiction and Film* (Ithaca, NY: Cornell University Press, 1978).

Chow, J.K., *Patronage and Power: A Study of Social Networks in Corinth* (JSNTSup, 75; Sheffield: JSOT Press, 1992).

Clark, A.C., 'The Role of the Apostles', in I.H. Marshall and D. Peterson (eds.), *Witness of the Gospel: The Theology of Acts* (Grand Rapids: Eerdmans, 1998).

Cohn, R.L., 'Liminality in the Wilderness', in *The Shape of Sacred Space: Four Biblical Studies* (Missoula, MT: Scholars Press, 1981).

Conzelmann, H., *Die Apostelgeschichte* (HNT, 7; Tübingen: J.C.B. Mohr, 1963).

—*The Theology of St. Luke* (trans. G. Buswell; New York: Harper & Row, 1961).

Crehan, J., 'Peter according to the D Texts of Acts', *TS* 18 (1957), pp. 596-603.

Crook, J.A., 'Women in Roman Succession', in B. Rawson (ed.), *The Family in Ancient Rome* (London: Croom Helm, 1986).

Cullmann, O., *The State in the NT* (New York: Scribner, 1956).

Culpepper, R.A., 'Redundancy and the Implied Reader in Matthew: A Response to Janice Capel Anderson and Fred W. Burnett' (Unpublished seminar paper read in the annual meeting of the SBL, 1983).

D'Angelo, M.R., 'Women in Luke–Acts: A Redactional View', *JBL* 109.3 (1990), pp. 441-61.

D'Arms, J.H., *Commerce and Social Standing in Ancient Rome* (Cambridge, MA: Harvard University Press, 1981).

Davies, E.W., *Numbers* (NCBC; Grand Rapids: Eerdmans, 1995).

Davies, J.G., 'The Prefigurement of the Ascension in the Third Gospel', *JTS* 6 (1955), pp. 229-33.

Davies, S., 'Women in the Third Gospel and the New Testament Apocrypha', in A. Levin (ed.), *'Women Like This': New Perspectives on Jewish Women in the Greco-Roman World* (Atlanta, GA: Scholars Press, 1991).

Davies, W.D., and Dale C. Allison, *A Critical and Exegetical Commentary on the Gospel according to Saint Matthew*. III. *Commentary on Matthew XIX-XXVIII* (Edinburgh: T. & T. Clark, 1997).

Dawsey, J., 'The Literary Unity of Luke–Acts: Questions of Style—A Task for Literary Critics', *NTS* 35 (1989), pp. 48-66.

De Jonge, M., 'The Book of Jubilees', in *idem* (ed.), *Outside the Old Testament World* (trans. J.C. Vanderkam; Cambridge: Cambridge University Press, 1985).

Denova, R., *The Things Accomplished among Us: Prophetic Tradition in the Structural Pattern of Luke–Acts* (JSNTSup, 141; Sheffield: Sheffield Academic Press, 1997).

DeSilva, D.A., *The Hope of Glory: Honor Discourse and New Testament Interpretation* (Collegeville, MN: The Liturgical Press, 1999).

De Ste. Croix, G.E.M., 'Suffragium: From Vote to Patronage', *British Journal of Sociology* 5 (1954), pp. 33-48.

Dibelius, M., *Studies in Acts of the Apostles* (ed. H. Greeven; trans. M. Ling; London: SCM Press, 1956).

Donne, B.K., *Christ Ascended: A Study in the Significance of the Ascension of Jesus Christ in the New Testament* (Exeter: Paternoster Press, 1983).

Downing, F.G., 'Theophilus' First Reading of Luke–Acts', in C.M. Tuckett (ed.), *Luke's Literary Achievements: Collected Essays* (JSNTSup, 116; Sheffield: Sheffield Academic Press, 1995).

Draper, J.A., 'The Twelve Apostles as Foundation Stones of the Heavenly Jerusalem and the Foundation of the Qumran Community', *Neotestamentica* 22 (1988), pp. 41-63.

DuBois, C.A., *The People of Alor* (Minneapolis, MN: University of Minnesota Press, 1944).

Dunn, J.D.G., *The Acts of the Apostles* (Valley Forge, PA: Trinity Press, 1996).

—*Baptism in the Holy Spirit* (London: SCM Press, 1970).

—*Jesus and the Spirit: A Study of the Religious and Charismatic Experience of Jesus and the First Christians as Reflected in the New Testament* (London: SCM Press, 1975).

—'Pentecost', in *Christ and the Spirit: Pneumatology*, II (Grand Rapids: Eerdmans, 1998).

—*Unity and Diversity in the New Testament* (London: SCM Press, 1977).

Dupont, J., 'La conclusion des Actes et son rapport à l'ensemble de l'ouvrage de Luc', in J. Kremer (ed.), *Les Actes des Apôtres: Traditions, redaction, theologie* (Leuven: Leuven University Press, 1978).

—'La destinee de Judas prophetisee par David (Act 1, 16-20)', *CBQ* 23 (1961), pp. 41-51.

—'La nouvelle Pentecote (Act 2, 1-11)', in *Nouvelles Études sur les Actes des Apôtres* (Paris: Cerf, 1984).

—'La question du plan des Actes des Apostres a la lumiere d'un texte de Lucien de Samosate', *NovT* 21 (1979), pp. 220-31.

—'The First Christian Pentecost', in *The Salvation of the Gentiles* (Ramsey, NJ: Paulist Press, 1979).

Earl, D., 'Prologue-Form in Ancient Historiography', *ANRW* 1.2 (1972), pp. 842-56.

Ehrhardt, A., 'Social Problems in the Early Church', in *The Framework of New Testament Stories* (Manchester: Manchester University Press, 1964).

Ehrman, A., 'Judas Iscariot and Abba Saqqara', *JBL* 97.4 (1978), pp. 572-73.

Eisenstadt, S.N., 'Patron-Client Relations as a Model of Structuring Social Exchange', *Comparative Studies in Society and History* 22 (1980), pp. 42-47.

—'The Study of Patron-Client Relations and Recent Developments in Sociological Theory', in S.N. Eisenstadt and R. Lemarchand (eds.), *Political Clientism* (London: Sage, 1981).

Eisenstadt, S.N., and R. Lemarchand (eds.), *Political Clientism, Patronage and Development* (Contemporary Political Sociology, 3; Beverly Hills: Sage, 1981).

Eisenstadt, S.N., and L. Roniger (eds.), *Patrons, Clients and Friends: Interpersonal Relations and the Structure of Trust in Society* (New York: Cambridge University Press, 1984).

Elliott, J.H., 'Patronage and Clientism in Early Christian Society', *Foundations and Facets Forum* 3 (1987), pp. 39-48.

—*Social-Scientific Criticism of the New Testament and its Social World* (Semeia, 35; Decatur: Scholars Press, 1986).

—'Social-Scientific Criticism of the New Testament: More on Methods and Models', *Semeia* 35 (1986), pp. 1-26.

—*What is Social-Scientific Criticism?* (Minneapolis, MN: Fortress Press, 1993).

Ellis, E.E., *Eschatology in Luke* (Philadelphia: Fortress Press, 1972).

—*The Gospel of Luke* (Grand Rapids: Eerdmans, 2nd edn, 1981).
Epstein, A.L., 'Gossip, Norms and Social Network', in J.C. Mitchell (ed.), *Social Networks in Urban Situations* (Manchester: Manchester University Press, 1969).
—'The Networks and Urban Social Organizations', in J.C. Mitchell (ed.), *Social Networks in Urban Situations* (Manchester: Manchester University Press, 1969).
Esler, P.F., *Community and Gospel in Luke–Acts: The Social and Political Motivations of Lucan Theology* (Cambridge: Cambridge University Press, 1987).
—'Glossolalia and the Admission of Gentiles into the Early Christian Community', *BTB* 22 (1992), pp. 136-42.
—'Introduction', in P.F. Esler (ed.), *Modelling Early Christianity: Social-Scientific Studies of the New Testament in its Context* (London: Routledge, 1995).
—'Review of D.G. Horrell, *The Social Ethos of the Corinthian Correspondence*', *JTS* 49 (1998), pp. 253-60.
—*The First Christians in their Social Worlds: Social-Scientific Approaches to New Testament Interpretation* (London: Routledge, 1994).
Estrada, N.P., 'A Redaction-Critical Study on the Relationship of the Spirit, Proclamation, and Miracle-Working Power in Luke–Acts' (Unpublished ThM thesis; Asia Graduate School of Theology, Philippines, 1994).
Evans, C., 'Luke's Use of the Elijah/Elisha Narratives and the Ethic of Election', *JBL* 106.1 (1987), pp. 75-83.
Farris, S., *The Hymns of Luke's Infancy Narratives* (JSNTSup, 9; Sheffield: JSOT Press, 1985).
Fearghus, F.O., *The Introduction to Luke–Acts: A Study of the Role of Lk. 1, 1-4, 44 in the Composition of Luke's Two-Volume Work* (Roma: Editrice Pontifico Istituto Biblico, 1991).
Ferrar, W., 'The Gospel according to Luke', in A. Carr (ed.), *Cambridge Greek Testament for Schools and Colleges* (Cambridge: Cambridge University Press, 1912).
Finley, M., *Ancient History: Evidence and Models* (London: Chatto and Windus, 1985).
Fischer, C.S., *Networks and Places* (New York: Free Press, 1977).
—*To Dwell Among Friends* (Chicago: Chicago University Press, 1982).
Fitzmyer, J., *Luke the Theologian: Aspects of his Teaching* (New York: Paulist Press, 1989).
—*The Acts of the Apostles: A New Translation with Introduction and Commentary* (New York: Doubleday, 1998).
—'The Ascension of Christ and Pentecost', in *idem*, *To Advance the Gospel: New Testament Studies* (Grand Rapids: Eerdmans, 2nd edn, 1998).
—*The Gospel according to Luke I–IX* (AB, 28; New York: Doubleday, 1985).
—'The Priority of Mark in Luke', in D.G. Miller *et al.* (eds.), *Jesus and Man's Hope*, I (Pittsburgh: Pickwick, 1970), pp. 131-70.
Fledderman, H.T., 'The End of Q', *SBL Seminar Papers* 29 (1990), pp. 1-10.
Flender, H., 'Heil und Geschichte in der Theologie des Lukas', *BEvT* 41 (1966), pp. 16-18.
—*St. Luke Theologian of Redemptive History* (trans. R.H. Fuller and I. Fuller; London: SPCK, 1967).
Flusser, D., 'Salvation Present and Future', in J.Z. Werblowsky and C.J. Bluker (eds.), *Types of Redemption: Contributions to the Theme of the Study-Conference Held at Jerusalem 14th to 19th July 1968* (Leiden: E.J. Brill, 1970).
Forkman, G., *The Limits of Religious of Religious Community: Expulsion from the Religious Community within the Qumran Sect, within Rabbinic Judaism, and within Primitive Christianity* (Lund: Gleerup, 1972).

France, R.T., *Matthew* (Grand Rapids: Eerdmans, 1985).

Francis, F., 'Eschatology and History in Luke–Acts', *JAAR* 37 (1969).

Franklin, E., *Christ the Lord: A Study in the Purpose and Theology of Luke–Acts* (London: SPCK, 1975), pp. 97-99.

Fuller, R.H., *The Mission and Achievement of Jesus: An Examination of the Presuppositions of New Testament Theology* (London: SCM Press, 1954).

Funk, R.W., 'The Apostolic Parousia: Form and Significance', in W.R. Farmer *et al.* (eds.), *Christian History and Interpretation* (Cambridge: Cambridge University Press, 1967).

Gager, J.G., *Kingdom and Community: The Social World of Early Christianity* (Englewood Cliffs, NJ: Prentice Hall, 1975).

—'Shall We Marry our Enemies?: Sociology and the New Testament', *Int* 37 (1982), pp. 256-65.

Gardner, J.F., *Women in Roman Law and Society* (London: Croom Helm, 1986).

Garnsey, P., *Social Status and Legal Privilege in the Roman Empire* (Oxford: Clarendon Press, 1970).

Garnsey, P., and R.P. Saller, *The Roman Empire: Economy, Society and Culture* (London: Duckworth, 1987).

Gellner, E., and J. Waterbury (eds.), *Patrons and Clients in Mediterranean Societies* (London: Duckworth, 1977).

Gelzer, M., *The Roman Nobility* (trans. R. Seager; New York: Barnes & Noble, 1969).

Genette, G., *Narrative Discourse Revisited* (trans. J.E. Levin; Ithaca, NY: Cornell University Press, 1988).

Giles, K., 'Is Luke an Exponent of "Early Protestantism?": Church Order in the Lukan Writings (Part 1)', *EvQ* 54 (1982), pp. 193-205; (Part 2) *EvQ* 55 (1983), pp. 3-20.

Gilmore, D.D., 'Anthropology of the Mediterranean Area', *Annual Review of Anthropology* 11 (1982), pp. 175-205.

—'Honor and Shame and the Unity of the Mediterranean', in *idem* (ed.), *American Anthropological Association Special Publication* 22 (Washington, DC: American Anthropological Association, 1987).

Gluckmann, M., *Essays on the Ritual of Social Relations* (Manchester: Manchester University Press, 1962).

Goulder, M., *A Tale of Two Missions* (London: SCM Press, 1994).

—*Type and History in Acts* (London: SPCK, 1964).

Gowler, D., *Host, Guest, Enemy and Friend: Portraits of the Pharisees in Luke and Acts* (New York: Peter Lang, 1991).

Grant, M., *Jesus* (London: Weidenfield & Nicolson, 1977).

Grasser, E., *Das Problem der Parusieverzogerung in den Synoptischen Evangelein und der Apostelgeschichte* (Berlin: Topelmann, 1957).

Gray, J., *I and II Kings: A Commentary* (London: SCM Press, 1977).

Green, J., *The Gospel of Luke* (Grand Rapids: Eerdmans, 1997).

Gundry, R.H., *A Commentary on His Literary and Theological Art* (Grand Rapids: Eerdmans, 1982).

Habel, N., 'The Form and Significance of the Call Narratives', *ZAW* 77 (1965), pp. 297-323.

Haenchen, E., *Die Apostelgeschichte* (Meyer, *Kritisch-exegetischer Kommentar* [Göttingen, 12th edn, 1959]).

—*The Acts of the Apostles* (Oxford: Basil Blackwell, 1971).

Hagner, D.A., *Matthew 14-38* (WBC, 33b; Dallas: Word Books, 1995).

Hallett, J.P., *Fathers and Daughters in Roman Society: Women and the Elite Family* (Princeton: Princeton University Press, 1984).

Hanson, K.C., and D.E. Oakman, *Palestine in the Time of Jesus: Social Structures and Social Conflicts* (Minneapolis: Fortress Press, 1998).

Harrington, D.J., 'Sociological Concepts and the Early Church: A Decade of Research', *TS* 41 (1980), pp. 181-90.

—'The Rich Young Man in Matthew', *Van Segbroeck* 2 (1992), pp. 199-208.

Hatch, E., *Essays in Biblical Greek* (Amsterdam: Philo Press, 1970).

Heil, C. (ed.), *Documenta Q: Reconstruction of Q through Two Centuries of Gospel Research Excerpted, Sorted, and Evaluated: Q 22.28, 30—You Will Judge the Twelve Tribes of Israel* (Leuven: Peters, 1998).

Hein, K., 'Judas Iscariot: Key to the Last Supper Narratives?', *NTS* 17 (1970–71), pp. 227-32.

Heine, S., *Women and Early Christianity: Are the Feminist Scholars Right?* (trans. J. Bowden; London: SCM Press, 1987).

Hellerman, J.H., 'Challenging the Authority of Jesus: Mark 11.27-32 and Mediterranean Notions of Honor and Shame', *JETS* 43 (2000), pp. 213-18.

Hemer, C., *The Book of Acts in the Setting of Hellenistic History* (Tübingen: J.C.B. Mohr, 1989).

Hengel, M., *Acts and the History of Earliest Christianity* (London: SCM Press, 1979).

—*Property and Riches in the Early Church: Aspects of a Social History of Early Christianity* (Philadelphia: Fortress Press, 1974).

Herman, G., *Ritualized Friendship and the Greek City* (Cambridge: Cambridge University Press, 1987).

Hiers, R., 'The Problem of the Delay of the Parousia', *NTS* 20 (1974), pp. 145-55.

Holmberg, B., *Sociology and the New Testament: An Appraisal* (Minneapolis, MN: Fortress Press, 1990).

Holwerda, D., 'Ascension', in *ISBE*, I, p. 311.

Horbury, W., 'Extirpation and Excommunication', *VT* 25.1 (1985), pp. 13-38.

—'The Twelve and the Phylarchs', *NTS* 32 (1986), pp. 503-27.

Horrell, D.G., 'Leadership Patterns and the Development of Ideology in Early Christianity', in *idem* (ed.), *Social-Scientific Approaches to New Testament Interpretation* (Edinburgh: T. & T. Clark, 1999).

—'Models and Methods in Social-Scientific Interpretation: A Response to P.F. Esler', *JSNT* 78 (2000), pp. 83-105.

Horrell, D.G. (ed.), *Social-Scientific Approaches to New Testament Interpretation* (Edinburgh: T. & T. Clark, 1999).

Horsley, R.A., *Sociology and the Jesus Movement* (New York: Crossroad, 1989).

Hubbard, B.J., 'Commissioning Stories in Luke–Acts: A Study of their Antecedents, Form and Content', *Semeia* 8 (1977), pp. 103-93.

—*The Matthean Redaction of a Primitive Apostolic Commissioning* (Missoula, MT: Scholars Press, 1974).

—'The Role of Commissioning Accounts in Acts', in C.H. Talbert (ed.), *Perspective on Luke–Acts* (Edinburgh: T. & T. Clark, 1978).

Humphreys, W.L., *Crisis and Story: Introduction to the Old Testament* (Palo Alto: Mayfield, 1979).

Hunter, A.M., *The Work and Words of Jesus* (London: SCM Press, 1950).

Ilan, T., *Jewish Women in Greco-Roman Palestine* (Tübingen: J.C.B. Mohr, 1995).

Jacobson, A.D., *The First Gospel: An Introduction to Q* (Sonoma, CA: Polebridge, 1992).

Jervell, J., *Luke and the People of God: A New Look at Luke–Acts* (Minneapolis, MN: Augsburg, 1972).

—*New Testament Theology: The Theology of the Acts of the Apostles* (Cambridge: Cambridge University Press, 1996).

—*The Unknown Paul: Essays on Luke–Acts and Early Christian History* (Minneapolis, MN: Augsburg, 1984).

Jewett, R., 'Paul, Phoebe, and the Spanish Mission', in J. Neusner *et al.* (eds.), *The Social World of Formative Christianity and Judaism: Essays in Tribute to Howard Clark Kee* (Philadelphia: Fortress Press, 1988).

Johnson, L.T., *Luke: The Literary Function of Possessions in Luke–Acts* (Montana: Scholars Press, 1977).

—*The Acts of the Apostles*, Sacra Pagina series. Vol. 5 (Collegeville, MN: The Liturgical Press, 1992).

Judge, E.A., 'The Social Identity of the First Christians: A Question of Method in Religious History', *The Journal of Religious History* 11 (1980), pp. 201-17.

Karris, R.J., 'Luke 23: 47 and the Lucan View of Jesus' Death', *JBL* 105 (1986), pp. 65-74.

—'Women and Discipleship in Luke', *CBQ* 56 (1994), pp. 1-20.

Kee, H.C., *To Every Nation under Heaven: The Acts of the Apostles* (Pennsylvania: Trinity Press, 1997).

Kenny, A.J.P., *A Stylometric Study of the New Testament* (Oxford: Clarendon Press, 1986).

Kirk, J.A., 'Apostleship since Rengstorf: Towards a Synthesis', *NTS* 21 (1975), pp. 249-64.

Kitz, A.M., 'Undivided Inheritance and Lot Casting in the Book of Joshua', *JBL* 119.4 (2000), pp. 601-618.

Klassen, W., *Judas: Betrayer or Friend of Jesus?* (London: SCM Press, 1996).

—'Judas Iscariot', *ABD* 3, pp. 1091-96.

Klauck, H.J., *Judas—Ein Junger des Herrn* (Freiburg, 1987).

Klijn, A.F.J., *Jewish-Christian Gospel Tradition* (Leiden: Brill, 1992).

Kloppenberg, J.S., *The Formation of Q: Trajectories in Ancient Wisdom Collections* (Philadelphia: Fortress Press, 1973).

—'The Sayings Gospel Q and the Quest of the Historical Jesus', *HTR* 89 (1996), pp. 307-44.

Knight, J., *Luke's Gospel* (London: Routledge, 1998).

Knox, A.D., 'The Death of Judas (Acts 1.18)', *JTS* 25 (1923–24), pp. 289-95.

Koester, H., *History and Literature of Early Christianity* (Philadelphia: Fortress Press, 1982).

Kopp, C., *The Holy Places of the Gospels* (New York: Herder and Herder, 1963).

Krodel, G.A., *Acts* (Minneapolis, MN: Ausburg, 1986).

Kümmel, W.G., *Introduction to the New Testament* (Nashville: Abingdon Press, 1975).

Kuntz, J.K., *The Self Revelation of God* (Philadelphia: Westminster Press, 1967).

Kurz, W., 'Luke 22.14-38 and Greco-Roman and Biblical Farewell Addresses', *JBL* 104 (1985), pp. 251-68.

—*Reading Luke–Acts: Dynamics of Biblical Narrative* (Westminster: John Knox Press, 1993).

—*The Acts of the Apostles* (Collegeville, MN: Liturgical Press, 1991).

Lake, Kirsopp, 'The Death of Judas', in F.J. Foakes Jackson and K. Lake (eds.), *The Beginnings of Christianity*. I. *The Acts of the Apostles* (London: Macmillan, 1933).

Lagrange, M.-J., *Evangile selon Saint Luc* (EBib; Paris: Gabalda, 8th edn, 1948).

Le Deaut, R., 'Pentecost and Jewish Tradition', *Doctrine and Life* 20 (1970), pp. 254-56.

Lüdemann, G., *Early Christianity according to the Traditions in Acts: A Commentary* (London: SCM Press, 1989).

Lull, D.J., 'The Servant-Benefactor as a Model of Greatness (Luke 22.24-30)', *NovT* 28 (1986), pp. 289-305.

Maccoby, H., *Judas Iscariot and the Myth of Jewish Evil* (New York: Free Press, 1991; Oxford: Maxwell-MacMillan, 1992).
—*The Sacred Executioner* (London: Thames & Hudson, 1982).
—'Who Was Judas Iscariot?', *JQR* (1991), pp. 8-13.
Maddox, R., *The Purpose of Luke–Acts* (Edinburgh: T. & T. Clark, 1982).
Malina, B.J., 'Early Christian Groups: Using Small Group Formation Theory to Explain Christian Organizations', in P.F. Esler (ed.), *Social Scientific Studies of the New Testament in its Context* (London: Routledge, 1995).
—'Patron and Client: The Analogy behind Synoptic Theology', *Foundations and Facets Forum* 4 (1988), pp. 3-33.
—'Reading Theory Perspective: Reading Luke–Acts', in J.H. Neyrey (ed.), *The Social World of Luke–Acts: Models for Interpretation* (Peabody, MA: Hendrickson, 1991).
—'The Individual and the Community: Personality in the Social World of Early Christianity', *BTB* 8 (1978), pp. 162-76.
—*The New Testament World: Insights from Cultural Anthropology* (Atlanta, GA: John Knox Press, 1981).
—'What is Prayer?' *The Bible Today* 18 (1980), pp. 214-20.
Malina, B.J., and J.H. Neyrey, 'Honour and Shame in Luke–Acts: Pivotal Values of the Mediterranean World', in J.H. Neyrey (ed.), *The Social World of Luke–Acts: Models for Interpretation* (Peabody, MA: Hendrickson, 1991).
Malina, B.J., and R.L. Rohrbaugh, *Social-Scientific Commentary on the Synoptic Gospels* (Minneapolis, MN: Fortress Press, 1992).
Marguerat, D., 'Soul's Conversion (Acts 9, 22, 26) and the Multiplication of Narrative in Acts', in C.M. Tuckett (ed.), *Luke's Literary Achievement: Collected Essays* (JSNTSup, 116; Sheffield: Sheffield Academic Press, 1995).
Marshall, A.J., 'Roman Women and the Provinces', *Ancient Society* 6 (1975), pp. 109-27.
Marshall, I.H., ' "Early Catholicism" in the New Testament', in R.N. Longnecker and M.C. Tenney (eds.), *New Dimensions in New Testament Study* (Grand Rapids: Zondervan, 1974).
—*The Gospel of Luke: A Commentary on the Greek Text* (Exeter: Paternoster Press, 1978).
—'The Significance of Pentecost', *SJT* 30 (1977), pp. 347-69.
Matill, A.J., *Luke and the Last Things* (Dillsboro: Western North Carolina Press, 1979).
May, D.M., 'Mark 3.20-35 from the Perspective of Shame/Honor', *BTB* 17 (1987), pp. 83-87.
McHugh, J., *The Mother of Jesus in the New Testament* (London: Darton, Longman & Todd, 1975).
McVann, M., 'Rituals of Status Transformation in Luke–Acts: The Case of Jesus the Prophet', in J.H. Neyrey (ed.), *The Social World of Luke–Acts* (Peabody, MA: Hendrickson, 1991).
Mead, M., *Growing Up in New Guinea* (New York: Blue Ribbon Books, 1930).
Meecham, H., *The Letter of Aristeas: A Linguistic Study with Special Reference to the Greek Bible* (Manchester: Manchester University Press, 1935).
Meeks, W.A., *The First Urban Christians: The Social World of the Apostle Paul* (New Haven: Yale University Press, 1983).
—*The Moral World of the First Christians* (Philadelphia: Westminster Press, 1986).
—'Understanding Early Christian Ethics', *JBL* 105 (1986), pp. 3-11.
Menninger, R.E., *Israel and the Church in the Gospel of Matthew* (New York: Peter Lang, 1994).
Menoud, P., 'Remarques sur les textes de l'ascension dans Luc-Actes', in W. Eltester (ed.), *Neutestamentliche Studien für Rudolf Bultmann* (BZNW, 21; Berlin: Töpelmann, 1957).

Menzies, R., *Empowered for Witness: The Spirit in Luke–Acts* (JPTSup, 9; Sheffield: JSOT Press, 1994).

Metzger, B.M., 'Ancient Astrological Geography and Acts 2.9-11', in W.W. Gasque and R.P. Martin (eds.), *Apostolic History and the Gospel* (Exeter: Paternoster Press, 1970).

—*The Text of the New Testament: Its Transmission, Corruption, and Restoration* (New York: Oxford University Press, 1964).

Meye, R., *Jesus and the Twelve* (Grand Rapids: Eerdmans, 1968).

Milik, J.T., *Ten Years of Discovery in the Wilderness of Judaea* (Naperville, IL: Allenson, 1959).

Mitchell, J.C., 'The Concept and Use of Social Networks', in J.C. Mitchell (ed.), *Social Networks in Urban Situations: Analyses of Personal Relationships in Central African Towns* (Manchester: University of Manchester Press, 1969).

Momigliamo, A., 'Patronus', *Oxford Classical Dictionary* (Oxford: Clarendon Press, 2nd edn, 1970).

Moore, S., *Literary Criticism and the Gospels: The Theoretical Challenge* (London: Yale University Press, 1989).

Mosala, I., 'Social Scientific Approaches to the Bible: One Step Forward, Two Steps Backward', *Journal of Theology for South Africa* 15 (1986), pp. 15-31.

Moule, C.F.D., 'Expository Problems: The Ascension—Acts 1.9', *ExpT* 68 (1957), pp. 205-209.

Moxnes, H., 'Patron-Client Relations and the New Community', in J. Neyrey (ed.), *The Social World of Luke–Acts: Models for Interpretation* (Peabody, MA: Hendrickson, 1991).

—*The Economy of the Kingdom: Social Conflict and Economic Interaction in Luke's Gospel* (Philadelphia: Fortress Press, 1988).

Mullins, T.Y., 'New Testament Commissioning, Forms, Especially in Luke–Acts', *JBL* 95.4 (1976), pp. 603-14.

Murphy-O'Connor, J., 'The Cenacle and Community: The Background of Acts 2.44-45', in M.D. Coogan *et al.* (eds.), *Scripture and Other Artifacts: Essays on the Bible and Archaeology in Honor of Philip J. King* (Louisville, KY: Westminster, 1994).

Nelson, P.K., *Leadership and Discipleship: A Study of Luke 22.24-30* (Atlanta, GA: Scholars Press, 1994).

Neusner, J., *The Talmud: A Close Encounter* (Minneapolis, MN: Fortress Press, 1991).

Newman, B., and E. Nida, *A Translator's Handbook on the Acts of the Apostles* (Help for Translators, 12; London: United Bible Societies, 1972).

Neyrey, J.H., 'Conflict in Luke–Acts: Labelling and Deviance Theory', in J.H. Neyrey (ed.), *The Social World of Luke–Acts: Models for Interpretation* (Peabody, MA: Hendrickson, 1991).

—*Honour and Shame in the Gospel of Matthew* (Westminster: John Knox Press, 1998).

—'Social Science Modelling and the New Testament', *BTB* 16 (1986), pp. 107-10.

Noack, 'The Day of Pentecost in Jubilees, Qumran and Acts', *ASTI* 1 (1962), pp. 73-95.

Nolland, J., *Luke* (2 vols.; WBC; Dallas: Word Books, 1993).

—'Salvation-History and Eschatology', in I.H. Marshall and D. Petersen (eds.), *Witness to the Gospel: The Theology of Acts* (Grand Rapids: Eerdmans, 1998).

Noth, M., *Numbers: A Commentary* (London: SCM Press, 1968).

Oakman, D.E., 'The Countryside in Luke–Acts', in J. Neyrey (ed.), *The Social World of Luke–Acts: Models for Interpretation* (Peabody, MA: Hendrickson, 1991).

Olson, D.T., *Numbers* (Louisville: John Knox Press, 1996).

Oppenheim, A.L., *The Interpretation of Dreams in the Ancient Near East* (Philadelphia: American Philosophical Society, 1956).

O'Reilly, L., *Word and Sign in the Acts of the Apostles* (Rome: Pontifical Biblical Institute, 1987).

Osiek, C., *What Are They Saying about the Social Setting of the New Testament?* (New York: Paulist Press, rev. edn, 1984).

O'Toole, R., *The Unity of Luke's Theology: An Analysis of Luke–Acts* (Good News Studies, 9; Wilmington: Glazier, 1984).

Painter, J., *Just James: The Brother of Jesus in History and Tradition* (South Carolina: University of South Carolina Press, 1997).

Parsons, M.C., *The Departure of Jesus in Luke–Acts: The Ascension Narratives in Context* (JSNTSup, 21; Sheffield: JSOT Press, 1987).

—'The Text of Acts 1.2 Reconsidered', *CBQ* 50 (1988), pp. 58-71.

—'The Unity of Luke–Acts: Rethinking the *Opinio Communis*', in '*With Steadfast Purpose*': *Essays on Acts in Honor of Henry J. Flanders* (ed. N. Keathley; Waco: Baylor University Press, 1990).

Parsons, M.C., and R.I. Pervo, *Rethinking the Unity of Luke–Acts* (Minneapolis, MN: Fortress Press, 1993).

Parvey, C.F., 'The Theology and Leadership of Women in the New Testament', in R.R. Reuther (ed.), *Religion and Sexism* (New York: Simon & Schuster, 1974).

Peristiany, J.G. (ed.), *Honour and Shame: The Values of Mediterranean Society* (London: Weidenfeld & Nicholson, 1965).

Perrin, N., *What is Redaction Criticism?* (Philadelphia: Fortress Press, 1969).

Pervo, R.I., *Profit of Delight: The Literary Genre of the Acts of the Apostles* (Philadelphia: Fortress Press, 1987).

Pilch, J., 'Praying with Luke', *The Bible Today* 18 (1980), pp. 221-25.

Plummer, A., *A Critical and Exegetical Commentary on the Gospel according to St. Luke* (eds. C.A. Briggs, S.R. Driver and A. Plummer; ICC Series; New York: Charles Scribner's Sons, 1906).

Powell, M.A., 'The Religious Leaders in Luke: A Literary-Critical Study', *JBL* 109.1 (1990), pp. 93-110.

—*What Are They Saying about Acts?* (New York: Paulist Press, 1991).

—*What is Narrative Criticism?* (Minneapolis, MN: Fortress Press, 1990).

Premerstein, A. von, *Von Werden und Wesen des augusteischen Prinzipats* (Munich: C.H. Beck'sche Verlagsbuchhandlung, 1937).

Quesnell, Q., 'The Women at Luke's Supper', in R.J. Cassidy and P.J. Scharper (eds.), *Political Issues in Luke–Acts* (Maryknoll, NY: Orbis Books, 1983).

Radcliffe-Brown, A.R., *The Andaman Islanders* (Cambridge: Cambridge University Press, 1922).

Rast, W., 'Joshua', in *Harper's Biblical Commentary* (New York: Harper & Row, 1988).

Reid, B.E., *Choosing the Better Part: Women in the Gospel of Luke* (Collegeville, MN: The Liturgical Press, 1996).

Reimer, I.R., *Women in the Acts of the Apostles: A Feminist Liberation Perspective* (trans. L.M. Maloney; Minneapolis, MN: Fortress Press, 1995).

Rengstorf, K.H., 'The Election of Matthias in Acts 1.15ff.', in W. Klassen and G.F. Snyder (eds.), *Current Issues in New Testament Interpretation: Essays in Honor of Otto Piper* (London: SCM Press, 1962), pp. 178-92.

Richardson, J. (ed.), *Models of Reality: Shaping Thought and Action* (Mount Airy, MD: Lomond Publications, 1984).

Reumann, J., *Mary in the New Testament: A Collaborative Assessment by Protestant and Catholic Scholars* (eds. R. Brown, K.P. Donfried, J.A. Fitzmeyer, and J. Reumann; Philadelphia: Fortress Press, 1978).

Rimmon-Kenan, S., *Narrative Fiction: Contemporary Poetics* (London: Methuen, 1983).

Robbins, V.K., 'The Social Location of the Implied Author of Luke–Acts', in J.H. Neyrey (ed.), *The Social World of Luke–Acts: Models for Interpretation* (Peabody, MA: Hendrickson, 1991).

Rodd, C.S., 'On Applying a Sociological Theory to Biblical Studies', *JSOT* 19 (1981), pp. 95-106.

—'Sociology and Social Anthropology', in R.J. Coggins and J.L. Houden (eds.), *The Dictionary of Biblical Interpretation* (London: SCM Press, 1990).

Rohde, J., *Rediscovering the Teaching of the Evangelists* (London: SCM Press, 1968).

Rohrbaugh, R.L., 'The Pre-Industrial City in Luke–Acts: Urban Social Relations', in J.H. Neyrey (ed.), *The Social World of Luke–Acts* (Peabody, MA: Hendrickson, 1991).

Royce, J.R., 'Scribal Tendencies in the Transmission of the Text of the New Testament', in B.D. Ehrman and M.W. Holmes (eds.), *The Text of the New Testament in Contemporary Research: Essays on the Status Quaestionis* (Grand Rapids: Eerdmans, 1995).

Sailhammer, J.H., *The Pentateuch as Narrative: Numbers* (Grand Rapids: Zondervan, 1992).

Sakenfield, K.D., *Journeying with God: A Commentary on the Book of Numbers* (Grand Rapids: Eerdmans, 1995).

Saller, R., *Personal Patronage under the Empire* (New York: Cambridge University Press, 1982).

Sanders, E.P., *Jesus and Judaism* (London: SCM Press, 1985).

Sandmel, S., 'Parallelomania', *JBL* 81 (1962), pp. 1-13.

Schille, G., *Die urchristliche Kollegialmission* (Zurich: Zwingli, 1967).

Schleiermacher, F., *The Life of Jesus* (Philadelphia: Fortress Press, 1975).

Schnackenburg, R., 'Apostles before and during Paul's Time', in W.W. Gasque and R.P. Martin (eds.), *Apostolic History and the Gospel: Biblical Historical Essays Presented to F.F. Bruce on his 60th Birthday* (Exeter: Paternoster, 1970).

Schneider, G., *Die Apostelgeschicte* (Freiburg: Herder, 1982).

Schottroff, L., *Let the Oppressed Go Free: Feminist Perspectives on the New Testament* (trans. A.S. Kidder; Westminster: John Knox Press, 1991).

Schüssler Fiorenza, E., *Discipleship of Equals: A Critical Feminist Ekklesia-logy of Liberation* (New York: Crossroad, 1993).

—*In Memory of Her: A Feminist Theological Reconstruction of Christian Origins* (New York: Crossroad, 1983).

Schweizer, E., *Church Order in the New Testament* (SBT, 32; London: SCM Press, 1961).

—'Pneuma', in G. Kittel (ed.), *TDNT*, VI (Grand Rapids: Eerdmans, 1968).

—*The Good News according to Luke* (ed. D. Green; London: John Knox Press, 1984).

—*The Good News according to Matthew* (ET; London: SPCK, 1976).

—'The Spirit and Power: The Uniformity and Diversity of the Concept of the Holy Spirit in the New Testament', *Int* 6 (1952), pp. 259-78.

Scroggs, R., 'The Sociological Interpretation of the New Testament: The Present State of Research', *NTS* 26 (1980), pp. 164-79.

Seccombe, D., 'Luke and Isaiah', *NTS* 27 (1981), pp. 252-59.

Shelton, J., ' "Filled With the Holy Spirit" and "Full of the Holy Spirit": Lukan Redactional Phrases', in P. Elbert (ed.), *Faces of Renewal: Studies in Honour of Stanley M. Horton* (Peabody, MA: Hendrickson, 1998).

—*Mighty in Word and Deed: The Role of the Holy Spirit in Luke–Acts* (Peabody, MA: Hendrickson, 1991).

Silverman, S., 'Patronage as Myth', in E. Gellner and J. Waterbury (eds.), *Patrons and Clients in Mediterranean Societies* (London: Duckworth, 1977).

Soards, M.L., *The Passion according to Luke: The Special Material of Luke 22* (JSNTSup, 14; Sheffield: JSOT Press, 1987).

—*The Speeches in Acts: Their Content, Context, and Concerns* (Louisville, KY: John Knox Press, 1994).

Sorensen, G.C., 'Beginning and Ending: The Virginians as a Sequel', *Studies in the Novel* 13 (1981), pp. 109-21.

Staden, van P., 'A Sociological Reading of Luke 12: 35-48', *Neotestamentica* 22 (1988), pp. 337-53.

Stambaugh, J.E., and D.A. Balch, *The New Testament in its Social Environment* (Philadelphia: Westminster Press, 1986).

Stanzel, F.K., *A Theory of Narrative* (trans. Charlotte Goedsche; Cambridge: Cambridge University Press, 1984).

Stein, R.H., 'The Redaktionsgeschichtlich Investigation of a Marcan Seam (Mc. 1.21f.)', *ZNW* 61 (1970), pp. 70-94.

—'What is Redaktionsgeschichte?', *JBL* 88 (1971), pp. 45-56.

—'What is Redaktionsgeschichte?', *NovT* 13 (1971), pp. 181-98.

Stempvoort, P.A. van, 'The Interpretation of the Acension in Luke–Acts', *NTS* 8 (1958), pp. 30-42.

Steyn, G.J., *Septuagint Quotations in the Context of the Petrine and Pauline Speeches of the Acta Apostolorum* (Netherlands: Pharos, 1995).

Stoops, R.F. Jr, 'Miracle Stories and Vision Reports in the *Acts of Peter*' (Unpublished PhD Dissertation; Harvard University, 1982).

—'Patronage in the *Acts of Peter*', *Semeia* 38 (1986), pp. 91-100.

Stowers, S.K., 'The Social Sciences and the Study of Early Christianity', in W.S. Green (ed.), *Approaches to Ancient Judaism* (Studies in Judaism and its Greco-Roman Context, 5; Atlanta, GA: Scholars Press, 1985).

Strange, W.A., *The Problem of the Text of Acts* (Cambridge: Cambridge University Press, 1992).

Strauss, M.L., *The Davidic Messiah in Luke–Acts: The Promise and its Fulfillment in Lukan Christology* (JSNTSup, 110; Sheffield: Sheffield Academic Press, 1995).

Streeter, B.F., *The Four Gospels* (London: Macmillan, 1924).

Stronstad, R., *The Charismatic Theology of St. Luke* (Peabody, MA: Hendrickson, 1984).

Styler, G.M., 'Stages in Christology in the Synoptic Gospels', *NTS* 10 (1963–64), pp. 404-406.

Sweetland, D.M., 'Luke the Christian', in E. Richard (ed.), *New Views on Luke and Acts* (Collegeville, MN: Liturgical Press, 1990).

Syme, R., *The Roman Revolution* (Oxford: Oxford University Press, 1939).

Talbert, C.H., *Literary Patterns, Theological Themes and the Genre of Luke–Acts* (SBLMS, 20; Missoula, MT: Scholars Press, 1974).

—*Reading Luke: A New Commentary for Preachers* (London: SPCK, 1982).

Talbert, C.H. (ed.), *What is a Gospel? The Genre of Canonical Gospels* (Philadelphia: Fortress Press, 1977).

Talmon, S., 'The Calendar Reckoning of the Sect from the Judaean Desert', in *Scripta Hierosolymitana*. IV. *Aspects in the Dead Sea Scrolls* (1967), pp. 177-79.

Tambling, J., *Narrative and Ideology* (Milton Keynes, UK: Open University Press, 1991).

Tannehill, R., *Luke* (Nashville, TN: Abingdon Press, 1996).

—'The Composition of Acts 3-5: Narrative Development and Echo Effect', *SBL Seminar Papers* (Chico, CA: Scholars Press, 1984).

—*The Narrative Unity of Luke–Acts* (2 vols.; Philadelphia and Minneapolis: Fortress Press, 1986, 1990).

Taylor, J.E., *The Immerser: John the Baptist within Second Temple Judaism* (Grand Rapids: Eerdmans, 1997).

Taylor, V., *Behind the Third Gospel: A Study of the Proto-Luke Hypothesis* (Oxford: Clarendon Press, 1926).

Theissen, G., *Social Reality and the Early Christians: Theology, Ethics, and the World of the New Testament* (Minneapolis, MN: Fortress Press, 1992).

Theissen, G., and Merz, A., *The First Followers of Jesus* (London: SCM Press, 1978).

—*The Historical Jesus: A Comprehensive Guide* (trans. J. Bowden; London: SCM Press, 1998).

Thornton, L.S., 'The Choice of Matthias', *JTS* 46 (1945), pp. 51-59.

Tidball, D.J., *An Introduction to the Sociology of the New Testament* (Exeter: Paternoster Press, 1983).

Torrance, T.F., *Space, Time and Resurrection* (Grand Rapids: Eerdmans, 1976).

—'Space, Time and Resurrection', *SJT Occasional Papers* 3 (1995).

Torrey, C.C., 'The Name "Iscariot" ', *HTR* 36 (1943), pp. 51-62.

Tozzer, A.M., *Social Origins and Social Continuities* (New York: Macmillan, 1925).

Turner, M., *Power from on High: The Spirit in Israel's Restoration and Witness in Luke–Acts* (JPTSup, 9; Sheffield: Sheffield Academic Press, 2000).

Turner, V., *Dramas, Fields, and Metaphors: Symbolic Action in Human Society* (Ithaca, NY: Cornell University Press, 1974).

—*The Forest of Symbols: Aspects of the Ndembu Ritual* (Ithaca, NY: Cornell University Press, 1967).

—*The Ritual Process: Structure and Anti-Structure* (New York: Aldine De Gruyter, 1995).

Tyson, J.B., 'The Emerging Church and the Problem of Authority in Acts', *Int* 42 (1988), pp. 132-45.

Uspensky, B., *A Poetics of Composition: The Structure of the Artistic Text and Typology of a Compositional Form* (trans. V. Zavarin and S. Wittig; Berkeley and Los Angeles: University of California Press, 1973).

Vanderkam, J.C., 'The Book of Jubilees', in *ABD*, pp. 1030-32.

Van Gennep, A., *The Rites of Passage* (trans. M.B. Vizedom and G.L. Caffee; Chicago: University of Chicago Press, 1960).

Van Seters, J., *The Life of Moses: The Yahwist as Historian in Exodus and Numbers* (Westminster: John Knox Press, 1994).

Van Unnik, W.C., *Luke–Acts: A Storm-Centre in Contemporary Scholarship: Studies in Luke–Acts* (eds. L.E. Keck and J.L. Martyn; London: SPCK, 1963).

Vaux, R. de, *Ancient Israel: Its Life and Institutions* (trans. J. McHugh; London: Darton, Longman & Todd, 1961).

Verheyden, J. (ed.), *The Unity of Luke–Acts* (Leuven: Leuven University Press, 1999).

Vermes, G., *The Dead Sea Scrolls: Qumran in Perspective* (Cleveland: Collins & World, 1978).

Via, E.J., 'Women, the Discipleship of Service and the Early Christian Ritual Meal in the Gospel of Luke', *St. Luke's Journal of Theology* 29 (1985), pp. 37-60.

—'Women in the Gospel of Luke', in U. King (ed.), *Women in the World's Religions: Past and Present* (New York: Paragon House, 1987).

Wallace-Hadrill, A., *Patronage in Ancient Society* (London and New York: Routledge, 1989).

Warner, M., *Alone of All her Sex: The Myth and Cult of the Virgin Mary* (London: Picador, 1976).

Waterbury, J., 'An Attempt to Put Patrons and Clients in their Place', in E. Gellner and J. Waterbury (eds.), *Patrons and Clients in Mediterranean Societies* (London: Duckworth, 1977).

Wedderburn, A.J.M., 'Traditions and Redactions in Acts 2.1-13', *JSNT* 55 (1994), pp. 27-54.

Weinstock, S., 'The Geographical Catalogue in Acts 2.9-11', *JRS* 38 (1948), pp. 43-46.

Wernberg-Moller, P., *The Manual of Discipline* (Leiden: E.J. Brill, 1957).

Whelan, C.F., 'Amica Pauli: The Role of Phoebe in the Early Church', *JSNT* 49 (1993), pp. 67-85.

White, L.M., (ed.). *Social Networks and Early Christianity* (Semeia, 48; Decatur, GA: Scholars Press, 1988).

—'Sociological Analysis of Early Christian Groups: A Social Historian's Response', *Sociological Analysis* 47 (1986), pp. 249-66.

Wilcox, M., 'The Judas-Tradition in Acts 1.15-26', *NTS* 19 (1972–73), pp. 438-52.

Wilder, A., 'Variant Traditions of the Resurrection in Acts', *JBL* 62 (1943), pp. 307-18.

Wilken, R., 'Collegia, Philosophical Schools and Theology', in S. Benko and J.J. O'Rourke (eds.), *Early Church History* (Valley Forge, PA: Judson Press, 1971).

Wilson, B.R., *Magic and the Millennium: A Sociological Study of Religious Movements of Protest among Tribal and Third-World Peoples* (London: Heinemann, 1973).

Wilson, S.G., 'The Ascension: A Critique and an Interpretation', *ZNW* 59 (1968), pp. 277-81.

—*The Gentiles and the Gentile Mission in Luke–Acts* (Cambridge: Cambridge University Press, 1973).

Winter, B., *Seek the Welfare of the City: Christians as Benefactors and Citizens* (Grand Rapids: Eerdmans, 1994).

Witherington III, B., *The Acts of the Apostles: A Socio-Rhetorical Commentary* (Grand Rapids: Eerdmans, 1998).

—*Women in the Ministry of Jesus: A Study of Jesus' Attitude to Women and their Roles as Reflected in his Earthly Life* (Cambridge: Cambridge University Press, 1984).

Witherup, R.D., 'Cornelius Over and Over and Over Again: 'Functional Redundancy in the Acts of the Apostles', *JSNT* 49 (1993), pp. 45-66.

—'Functional Redundancy in the Acts of the Apostles: A Case Study', *JSNT* 48 (1992), pp. 67-86.

Yadin, Y., *The Temple Scroll: The Hidden Law of the Dead Sea Sect* (London: Weidenfield & Nicholson, 1985).

Zahn, T., *Die Apostelgeschichte des Lucas* (2 vols.; Leipzig/Erlangen: Deichert, 1909).

INDEXES

INDEX OF REFERENCES

BIBLE

Genesis

7.4	50
7.12	50
7.17	50
11.28-30	39
12.1-4	39
13.6	137
15.1-6	39
17.1-14	39
17.15-27	39
22.3	80
22.6	137
24.1-9	39
26.1-6	39
26.23-25	39
28.10-22	39
30.14	191
35.9-15	39
41.37-45	39
44.18	169
46.1-5	39

Exodus

3.1–4.16	39
5.6	213
5.10	213
5.14-15	213
5.19	213
6.2-13	39
7.1-6	39
11.10-35	214
12	191
12.13	191
12.23	191

12.27	191
13.21	211
14.21	211
18	214, 215
18.13-26	214
18.24-26	214
19	195, 196
19.1	193
19.8	137, 197
19.16	197
19.18	197, 211
20	196
20.22	197
23.15	191
23.16	191
24.11	195
24.18	50
26.24	137
34.18	191
34.22	191
34.25	191
34.28	50
34.38	50

Leviticus

16.8	153
19.18	243
23.5-8	191
23.15-21	191
23.34	191
26	68

Numbers

11	211-19, 224, 226, 229, 237
11.4-25	226
11.4	212
11.6	212
11.10-30	212
11.10-13	212
11.11-15	212
11.11	219
11.14-17	218
11.14-15	212
11.14	219
11.16	213, 214, 216
11.17	217, 226
11.25	217, 219
11.26-30	217
16.14	176
18.21-26	176
22.22-35	39
24.24	137
26.55-56	154
26.55	176
27.21	137
28.16-25	191
28.26-31	191
33.53	176

Deuteronomy

4.11-12	197
4.33	30
8.2	50
8.4	50
9.9	50

9.25	50	*1 Kings*		*Psalms*		
16.1-8	191	17.17-24	128	2.1-2	140	
16.9-10	191	18.8	50	9.2	142	
16.11	195	18.21	191	12.5	142	
16.13	191	19.1-19	39	16.5	154	
16.16	191	19.16	223	16.8-11	228	
22.10	137			18.14	30	
28	68	*2 Kings*		19.5	142	
28.1-14	245	2	91	20.1	142	
31.14	39	2.9-14	96, 98	30.7	142	
31.31	39	2.11	96	39.16	142	
		2.12	96, 97	67.19	200	
Joshua		2.13	97	68.34	30	
1.1-11	39	2.15	215, 217			
1.10	213	2.23-25	227	*Isaiah*		
3.2	213			6	39	
7.10-21	153	*1 Chronicles*		34.17	154	
9.2	137	10.6	137	49.1-6	39	
18.6	154	22.1-16	39	58.6	222	
18.9-10	154	25.8	153	61.1-2	222	
		26.13	153	66.15-16	203	
Judges						
4.4-10	39	*2 Chronicles*		*Jeremiah*		
4.12	137	15.10-12	192	1.1-10	39	
6.11-24	39	15.10	192	5.5	137	
7.29	137	15.11	192	26.21	137	
13.17	137	15.12	193	29.26	217	
15.1	191			31.33	200	
15.2	137	*Ezra*				
15.5	137	1.1-5	39	*Lamentations*		
15.9	137	9.1-14	191	1.1	153	
		10.14	213	1.6	153	
1 Samuel				2.8	137	
3.1–4.1	39	*Job*				
4.3	213	2.11	137	*Ezekiel*		
6.13	191	3.18	137	1.1-n-3.15	39	
8.4	213	6.2	137	1.24	30	
10.6	217	9.32	137	36.26	200	
10.10-12	218	16.10	137	39.25-29	171	
12.17	191	17.16	137			
14.40-42	153	19.12	137	*Daniel*		
19.23	218	21.26	137	7	248	
19.24	217	24.4	137	7.9	248	
30.24	137	24.17	137	7.13	97	
		31.38	137	7.27	248	
2 Samuel		34.15	137			
4.4	191	38.33	137	*Joel*		
22.8-15	203	40.13	137	2.28-32	218, 228	

Obadiah
11   248

APOCRYPHA
1 Esdras
5.46   137
5.56   137
9.38   137

Tobit
2.1   192

Wisdom of Solomon
3.7-8   248
18.5   137
18.12   137

2 Maccabees
9.7-12   182
12.31-32   192

NEW TESTAMENT
Matthew
5.48   242, 243
8.5-13   127
9.5   191
10.1   175
10.2-4   123
10.2   157, 175
10.4   6
10.5   157
11.1   175
13.55   134
14.22-23   40
15.14   244
17.1-8   40
18.10-14   128
19   240
19.1-15   173
19.1-2   240
19.3-12   240
19.13-14   240
19.16-31   240, 241
19.16-27   246
19.16-22   173, 240,
            241, 244–
            47
19.16   241, 246

19.17   242, 247
19.18   243
19.20   243
19.21   243, 244,
            246
19.23-31   240, 241
19.23-30   173
19.23   244–46
19.24   245, 246
19.25-26   245
19.25   244
19.27   173, 245–
            47
19.28   157, 172,
            173, 187,
            239–41,
            245–47,
            249
19.29   246, 248
19.30   246
20.17   157, 175
24.40-41   128
26.14   6, 157,
            159, 160
26.20   157
26.25   6
26.27   159
26.47   6, 157
27.3-10   167, 181
27.55   112
28.1-8   40
28.9-10   40
28.10   42, 99
28.11-15   40
28.16-20   40
28.30   175

Mark
1.1-10   40
1.3   175
1.15   72
1.21-31   127
1.23-31   129
2.1-12   127
3.1-6   128
3.12-19   127
3.16-19   123
3.17   157

3.19-21   135
3.19   6
3.30-35   133
3.31-35   133, 135
4.10   157, 159
6.3   134
6.4   135
6.7   157
8.24   72
9.35   157
10.1-16   173
10.1   240
10.2-12   240
10.13-16   240
10.17-31   241
10.17-22   173, 240
10.17   241
10.18   242
10.19   243
10.23-31   173, 240
10.27   247
10.29   173
10.32   157
11.11   157
12.37-44   128
14.1-11   127
14.10   6, 157,
            160
14.17   157
14.20   157, 159
14.43   6, 157,
            159
15.21   128
15.40-41   128
15.40   112
15.41   112
16.1-8   128
16.9-20   40
16.19   98

Luke
1–3   29
1–2   132
1   82
1.1-17   29
1.1-4   46
1.1   47
1.3   80

1.5–2.52 46
1.5-25 40, 43
1.5-10 43
1.7-8 149
1.11 43
1.12-14 149
1.12 43
1.13-17 43
1.13 43, 149
1.14 142, 149
1.15-17 29
1.15 29, 220, 221
1.17 29, 220, 221
1.18 43, 88
1.19-20 43
1.26-38 40, 43
1.26-27 43
1.28 43
1.29 43
1.30 43
1.31-33 43
1.34 43, 89
1.35 43
1.36-37 43
1.38 43
1.39-56 221
1.41-45 221
1.41-44 29, 221
1.41 221
1.44 142
1.46-56 222
1.46-55 58
1.47 142
1.67 221
1.68-79 58
1.76 222
2.8-20 43
2.8-18 40
2.8 43
2.9 43
2.10 43
2.11-12 43
2.13-14 43
2.15-20 43
2.22-51 105
2.51 32
3 121
3.1–4.30 28, 35, 38, 233
3.1-22 29, 31
3.1-20 28, 29
3.1-2 132
3.1 46
3.3 29
3.7-8 29
3.8 29
3.10-14 29
3.15-17 35
3.18 74
3.19-20 29, 107
3.21-22 220
3.22 94
3.23-38 29
4.1-13 30, 31, 68, 69, 91, 115, 148, 222, 234
4.1-12 188
4.1-3 29, 104
4.1-2 49
4.1 30, 102, 148
4.2 35, 68
4.3-13 29
4.3 29
4.4 31
4.5 31
4.9 29
4.11 32
4.14-30 29
4.14-15 32
4.14 32, 222
4.16-30 222
4.16-19 59
4.16 32
4.18-19 29, 222
4.21-30 29
4.24-30 227
4.31-39 127
4.33-39 129
5.1-11 40, 43
5.1-2 43
5.3 43
5.4 43
5.8-10 43, 89
5.10 42, 43, 99
5.11 43
5.19-26 127
5.21 59
5.25-26 59
5.32 29
6.2 59
6.7 59
6.12-19 127
6.12-16 61, 121
6.13-16 159
6.13 47, 157
6.14-16 121, 123
6.15 157
6.16 6, 157
6.38 138
7.1-17 128
7.1-10 107, 127
7.11-17 127, 128
7.16 59
7.20-28 40, 43
7.20 43
7.21 43
7.22 43
7.23 43
7.24-28 43
7.25 107, 108
7.29 109
7.31-33 29
7.35-50 127
7.36-50 126
8.1-3 111, 112, 127
8.1 157
8.2 111, 112
8.4 138
8.9-17 128
8.19-21 132-34
9.1-6 61
9.1 138, 157
9.7-9 107
9.12 157
9.34 97
1.21-5 43
10.1-17 40, 43
10.1 43
10.2-15 43

10.9	75	18.18-23	240	22.30	2, 3, 166,
10.11	75	18.18	247		169–78,
10.16	43	18.24-30	240		187, 213,
10.17	43	18.28	173		239, 240,
10.21	142	18.31	157		246, 249
10.38-42	111	18.43	59	22.35	43
11.20	75	19.20	105	22.36	43
11.27-28	132	19.29	105	22.37	43
12	76	19.45-46	60	22.38	43
12.1	138	20.45–21.4	128	22.47-53	159, 161
12.16-21	108	21	73	22.47	6, 157,
12.19	108	21.8-9	74		159, 161
12.35-48	75	21.27	97	22.52	160
12.45	75, 76	21.30	3	22.54-62	7, 159,
13.3	29	21.34-36	75		161
13.5	29	21.37	105	22.55	138
13.10-17	126, 128	22	61, 161,	22.66	138
13.13	59		170	23.13	138
13.14	59	22.1-38	173	23.18	138
13.31-33	107	22.1-6	66, 159	23.26-32	128
13.34	138	22.2	160	23.27-31	74
14.1-6	128	22.3-6	5, 161	23.49	111–13,
14.8-10	128	22.3	6, 157,		128
15.1-7	128, 129		160, 161,	23.55-56	112
15.6	138		176, 181	23.55	51, 111,
15.8-10	129	22.4	160		113
15.9	138	22.5	160	24	49, 51, 52,
15.11-31	40, 43	22.6	160		82–89, 91,
15.11-20	43	22.7-13	40, 43		93, 94, 99,
15.20	43	22.7	43		101, 111,
15.21	43	22.8	43		116, 128,
15.22-24	43	22.9	43		149
15.25-30	43	22.10-11	43	24.1-43	83
15.31	43	22.12	43	24.1-11	100
16.13	58	22.13	43	24.1-9	43, 101
16.14	108	22.14-38	40, 43	24.1-3	43
16.16	72, 74	22.14	43	24.2-9	112
16.19-31	108	22.21-23	159, 161	24.2-3	51
16.19	108	22.24-30	171	24.4	43, 51, 88,
17.12-19	128	22.24-27	59, 61, 62		101
17.20-21	75	22.24	60	24.5	43, 51, 88
17.22-37	75	22.25-26	60	24.6-7	43
17.32-35	128	22.25	62	24.7	101
17.37	138	22.26	168	24.8-9	43
18.1-8	75, 129	22.27	59	24.10-11	125
18.9	90, 108	22.28-30	61, 170,	24.10	111–13
18.15-30	173		171, 175,	24.13-35	126
18.15-17	240		239	24.15	138

24.17	88	20.19	42, 99
24.20-21	126	20.21	42, 99
24.21	70	20.24	157, 159
24.22	88	20.25	159
24.24	126	20.26-31	159
24.33	138	21	7
24.34	7	21.24	80
24.36-53	40, 43, 87		
24.36-43	126	*Acts*	
24.36	43	1–2	5, 8, 9, 11,
24.37	43		20, 23, 24,
24.38	88		32, 39, 47,
24.41	43, 88		53, 77, 79,
24.44-53	86		81, 89,
24.44-49	83		109, 115,
24.44-48	43		120, 152,
24.46-49	83		179, 185,
24.47-49	11		205, 207-
24.47	84		209, 213,
24.48	84		220, 226,
24.49	43, 49, 84		231–34,
24.50-53	43, 85, 86,		238
	89, 91, 94,	1	14, 33, 39,
	99		51, 57, 64,
24.50-51	96		70, 82–87,
24.50	105		89, 91, 93,
24.51	84, 98		117, 148,
24.52-53	100		165, 180,
24.52	88		186, 213
24.53	99, 109	1.1-26	116
		1.1-14	44, 116–
John			18
1.14-16	80	1.1-12	40
1.42	157	1.1-11	87, 119
6.67	157	1.1-5	67
6.70-71	159	1.1-3	83
6.70	157	1.1-2	44
6.71	6, 157	1.1	82
7.2	191	1.2	47, 48, 67,
7.5	134, 135		93, 122
11.18	105	1.3–2.47	7, 8, 32–
12.4	6		34, 46, 53
13.2	6	1.3–2.14	14, 35, 37,
14.22	157		38
18.2	6	1.3–2.4	86
18.5	6	1.3-11	33–35, 46,
19.25	112, 134		65, 66,
20.19-21	40		101, 234

1.3-5	7, 33, 35,
	44, 46, 47,
	66, 69,
	116
1.3-4	49, 95
1.3	34, 35, 48,
	50, 67, 68,
	86, 152,
	177, 179,
	203, 230,
	235
1.4-5	11
1.4	49, 84,
	105, 121,
	177, 205,
	215, 216
1.5	49, 117
1.6-11	116
1.6-8	33, 35, 46,
	66, 70, 76
1.6-7	102, 235
1.6	44, 70, 87,
	138, 171
1.7-8	44, 47, 97,
	104, 121,
	185, 205,
	207
1.7	71, 87, 97
1.8	1, 11, 24,
	52, 71, 84,
	90, 97,
	116, 117,
	147, 148,
	192, 199,
	216, 235
1.9-12	86
1.9-11	1, 7, 33,
	35, 46, 47,
	66, 81, 86,
	90–92,
	94–100,
	104, 118,
	120, 121,
	231
1.9-10	100
1.9	44, 84, 98
1.10-11	51, 96,
	99–101,

119, 120

1.10   44, 52, 88

1.11-13   208

1.11   44, 83, 97, 99–101, 205

1.12-26   33, 34, 46, 66, 91, 102, 104, 115, 119, 120, 213, 215, 235

1.12-14   1, 3-6, 8–10, 20, 23, 33, 35, 36, 38, 44, 52, 80, 104, 105, 114–21, 124, 125, 148, 179, 207, 231, 232, 235, 236, 238

1.12   33, 104–106, 117, 147, 216

1.13-14   104, 109, 117, 120, 124, 147

1.13   33, 36, 47, 109, 117, 119, 121–24, 157

1.14-15   205

1.14   33, 34, 48, 105, 110–12, 115, 125, 132–36, 138, 139, 142, 146, 147, 179, 205, 236, 237

1.15-26   1, 2, 5, 6, 8, 9, 12, 20, 23, 33, 36, 38, 104, 105, 110, 115–20, 124, 136, 148, 151, 152, 165–67, 170–72, 175–79, 186, 187, 205, 207, 227, 231, 232, 23–39

1.15-22   79, 80, 119, 120, 216

1.15-20   237

1.15   4, 10, 34, 36, 105, 109, 116, 132, 140, 146, 147, 152, 179, 180, 204, 206, 210

1.16-22   147

1.16-20   5, 36, 80, 105, 115, 124, 159, 181

1.16   7, 178, 179, 181

1.17-20   122

1.17-19   167

1.17   6, 169, 176, 177, 178, 183, 185

1.18-19   147, 176

1.20   115, 167

1.21-26   122, 177, 184, 185

1.21-22   48

1.21   47, 132, 214

1.22   48, 120, 122, 156

1.23-26

1.23   147

1.24   205

1.26   176, 185, 205

2   2, 4, 14, 33, 36, 57, 119, 148, 170, 177, 187, 190, 192, 196, 197, 199, 202–204, 206–209, 211, 212, 215, 218, 224, 226, 228, 229, 235, 237

2.1–8.1   116

2.1-47   33, 46

2.1-27   192

2.1-14   34

2.1-13   202

2.1-4   1, 8, 10, 11, 24, 33, 37, 38, 48, 104, 120, 121, 124, 171, 207, 211, 215, 216, 218, 224–26, 228, 231, 237

2.1   10, 139, 140, 197, 202, 204–209, 215

2.2-4   205

2.2   139, 197, 206, 215

2.3   197, 216

2.4   198, 211, 219–21

2.5-47   8, 33

2.5-14   37

2.5-13   199, 205, 224, 225, 228, 230

Ref	Pages	Ref	Pages	Ref	Pages
2.5-11	208	2.42	142, 207, 208, 229	6.2-3	223
2.5	198			6.2	157
2.6-7	77, 88	2.43-47	228	6.5-6	184, 223
2.6	138, 139, 197, 198, 208	2.43	142, 170, 207, 208	6.5	223
		2.44	138–40, 142, 170	6.7-8	119
2.7-11	140			6.10	223
2.7	197, 198, 205	2.45	140	7.30-36	40, 43, 44
		2.46-47	77, 237	7.30	44
2.8	198	2.46	88, 90, 101, 138, 140, 143, 146, 185, 229	7.32	44
2.9-11	225			7.33-34	44
2.9	198			7.34	44
2.10	198			7.35-36	44
2.11	38, 198, 199, 207, 218	2.47	33, 35, 102, 140	7.47	206
				7.55	223
				7.57	138, 144, 146
2.12	198, 218	3.11	138, 141	8.1–15.35	116
2.13	198, 227	4.1	143	8.1-3	143
2.14-47	207	4.5-32	140	8.4-13	44
2.14-42	216	4.5-11	143	8.6	138, 143, 146
2.14-40	142	4.5	138		
2.14	35, 102, 152, 179, 205, 207, 208, 226–28, 230	4.8	221	8.26-30	43, 44
		4.13-25	143	8.26	44
		4.23	140	8.27-28	44
		4.24	138, 140, 143, 146	8.27	44
				8.29	44
2.15-16	205	4.25-27	140	8.30	44
2.15	208	4.26	138, 140	8.39	44
2.17-36	218	4.27	138	9.1-9	44
2.17-18	228	4.31	138, 141, 221	9.1-8	40
2.17	10, 72, 206, 207	4.32-37	170	9.1-3	44
				9.3	44
2.19-20	228	4.36	157	9.4-5	44
2.19	199	5.1-11	141, 170	9.4	44
2.22	199	5.9	138	9.6	44
2.23	128	5.12-16	142	9.7	44
2.25-28	228	5.12	138, 141, 142, 146	9.8-9	44
2.26-27	37			9.9-18	40
2.32-33	205	5.13	141	9.10-19	44
2.33	200, 215	5.17-21	43, 44	9.10	44
2.37-40	228	5.17-18	44	9.11-12	44
2.37	205, 207, 208	5.19-20	44	9.13-14	44, 89
		5.19	44	9.15-16	44
2.39	10, 206, 207	5.20	44, 227	9.17-19	44
		5.21	44, 138	9.17	221
2.40-41	228	5.25	143	9.32	119
2.41	139, 142	5.38-39	128	9.37	109
2.42-47	229	6	223, 224	9.39	109

10.1-8	40, 44	12.17	134	19	224
10.1-2	44	12.20	138, 146	19.6	208
10.3	44	12.23	182	19.20-21	119
10.4	44	12.24-25	119	19.25	138
10.5-6	44	13	223	19.29	138, 144,
10.7-8	44	13.1-3	40, 44		146
10.9-29	40	13.1-2	44	19.32	138
10.9-23	44	13.2	44, 223	20.1–28.31	116
10.9-10	44	13.3	44	20.5-15	80
10.10-12	44	13.7	223	20.7	138
10.13	44	13.8	223	20.8	109
10.14	44	13.9	221, 224	20.17-35	224
10.15-16	44	13.36	128	20.20	50
10.17	44	13.44	138	20.27	50, 128
10.19-20	44	15	135, 145–	20.28	224
10.20	44		47, 186	20.31	50
10.21-23	44	15.2	147	21.1-18	80
10.24	138	15.5-6	147	21.28	134
10.30-33	40, 44	15.6	138, 147	21.30	138
10.30	44	15.7-11	147	22.6-11	40, 44
10.31	44	15.7	147, 200	22.6	44
10.32	44	15.13	134, 186	22.7-9	44
10.33	44	15.16-18	147	22.7	44
10.41	122	15.22-29	145	22.10	44
10.45-46	208	15.22	146, 147,	22.11	44
11.4-17	40		157	22.12-16	40, 44
11.4-12	44	15.25	138, 146	22.12	44
11.4-5	44	15.26	186	22.13	44
11.5-6	44	15.28	186	22.14-15	44
11.7	44	15.30	138	22.15	44
11.8	44, 89	15.36–19.40	116	22.16	44
11.9	44	16.5-6	119	22.17-21	40, 44
11.10-12	44	16.8-10	44	22.17	44
11.13	227	16.8	44	22.18	44
11.27-30	223	16.9	44	22.19-20	44
12.2	3, 122,	16.10-17	80	22.21	44
	173, 185	16.10	44	23.11	40, 44
12.6-12	44	16.13	138	25.17	138
12.6-11	141	16.24-34	40	25.18	227
12.6-10	40	17–18	110	26.12-20	40, 44
12.6	44	17.22	227	26.12	44
12.7-8	44	18.7-11	43, 44	26.13	44
12.7	44	18.7-8	44	26.14-15	44
12.9	44, 89	18.9	44	26.14	44
12.11	44	18.10	44	26.15-18	44
12.12	44, 109,	18.11	44	26.17	44
	138, 141	18.12	138, 144,	26.19-20	44
12.13-17	141		146	27.1–28.16	80

27.21-26	40, 44	*1 Corinthians*		*Hebrews*	
27.21-23	44	15.5	7, 157	4.14	98
27.21	227	15.7	134	6.19-20	98
27.24	44			9.24	98
27.25-26	44	*Galatians*			
28.17	138	3.28	127	*James*	
28.31	119			1.1	159
		2 Thessalonians			
Romans		3.6-13	74	*1 Peter*	
15.6	137, 143			3.22	98
16.1-3	130	*Titus*			
16.1	131	3.5	246	*Revelation*	
				1.10-20	40
				3.21	175

OTHER ANCIENT LITERATURE

PSEUDEPIGRAPHA		QUMRAN		5.3	155
1 Enoch		*1QH*		6.3	180
14	203	3.11-23	154	6.16	155
39.1-14	98	4.13	154	6.21-22	155
				9.7	155
3 Maccabees		*1QM*			
4.4	137	13.12	154	*1QSa*	
4.6	137	18.1	154	1.9	155
5.50	137	2.13.5	154	1.16	155
6.39	137	2.13.9	154	222	180
4 Ezra		*1QS*		*4Q266*	
13.1-10	203	1.1	140	17-18	195
		1.8–2.18	201		
Letter of Aristeas		1.8–2.16	194	*Damascus Document*	
172	143	1.9-11	154	13.3-4	155
178	143	1.13-20	194	13.12	154
		1.19	194		
Jubilees		2.2	154	*11QTemple*	
1.1-2	194	2.4	154	18.10-13	195
1.1	201	2.17	154	19.11-14	195
6	193	2.23	155	21.12-16	195
6.1-20	201	3.7	140		
6.15-18	193	3.24	154	TARGUMS	
6.18-19	194	4.18	155	*Neof. Exod.*	
6.19	201	4.24	154	19.16	199
15.1-24	201	4.25-26	155		

Targ. Ps.-J. Exod.
20.2   199

MISHNAH
Sanh.
1.6   180, 181

BABYLONIAN TALMUD
B. Bat.
106b   153

Pes.
68b   196

Šab. 88b   199

PHILO
De cherubim
114   246

De decalogo
4.1.151   154
32–36   197
33   197
35   198
36   198
44   198
46   198

De specialibus legibus
2.189   199

De vita Mosis
2.65   246
2.291   101

JOSEPHUS
Antiquities of the Jews
4.323-336   96
7.7.366-367   153
11.3.9   246
11.66   246
15.277   145

17.6.5   182
20.169   105

The Jewish War
1.1-2   78

EARLY CHRISTIAN
LITERATURE
1 Clement
9.4   246

Acta Pilati
16.6   98

The Apocryphon of James
14-16   98

Barnabas
15.9   98

Corpus Hermeticum
13   246

Epistula Apostolorum
51   98

The Martyrdom &
        Ascension
        of Isaiah
11.22-33   98

RABBINIC WRITINGS
Seder 'Olam Rabba
5   195

CLASSICAL
Aristotle
Ath. Resp.
8   154

Cicero
On Divination
1.25   63

Epiphanius
Panarion
78   134

Lucian
Alexander the False
        Prophet
24   63
Hermotimus
7   63
How to Write History
55   83

Martyrdom of Polycarp
7.1   109

Nemesius
De Nat. Hom.
2   246

Ovid
Fasti
2.481-509   98, 101
Metamorphoses
14.805-851   98

Plautus
Menaechmi
571   108

Plutarch
Romulus
27.7-8   100
Timoleon
31.3-4.251   154

Tertullian
Against Marcion
4.19   134

Index of Authors

Abbott, F. 154
Abercrombie, N. 13, 20
Abraham, R.D. 23
Alexander, L.C.A. 4, 18, 83, 84
Alexander, P.S. 155, 156
Alföldy, G. 54
Allen, O.W. Jr. 182
Allison, D.C. Jr. 240, 242
Anderson, J.C. 93
Arbeitman, Y. 157
Ascough, R.S. 18
Ashley, T.R. 212, 213, 215–17
Aune, D. 78

Badian, E. 54
Bal, M. 79
Balch, J.L. 56
Baltzer, K. 39
Barbour, I. 15
Barr, D.L. 78
Barrett, C.K. 1, 3, 47, 110, 116–19, 121,
    123, 136, 139, 167, 174, 179, 180,
    206, 208, 225
Barrett, S. 17
Barton, S.C. 9, 12, 175, 240, 241, 245
Bateson, G. 22
Bauckham, R. 114, 135, 136
Bauer, W. 226
Baumgarten, J. 174
Beardslee, W. 155, 156
Beare, F.W. 244, 245
Benoit, P. 86
Berger, P.L. 19, 67
Billerbeck, P. 195
Black, C.C. 239
Black, M. 15
Blue, B. 181
Boissevain, J. 55

Bowman, J.W. 75
Brawley, R. 222, 228
Brenton, L.C.L. 137
Brooten, B.J. 4
Brown, P. 58
Brown, R.E. 28, 133, 134
Bruce, F.F. 92, 134
Bultmann, R. 32, 126
Burnett, F.W. 246, 247
Burridge, R.A. 78

Cadbury, H.J. 92, 112, 119, 120, 126,
    174, 180, 208
Campbell, J.K. 55, 163
Capper, B. 212, 225
Carney, T.F. 15–18, 54
Carroll, J.T. 76
Cassidy, R.J. 127
Chance, J.B. 106, 170–72
Chapple, E.D. 22
Charette, B. 241, 242
Chatman, S. 85
Chow, J.K. 56
Clark, A.C. 1, 53, 90
Cohn, R.L. 23, 27, 68, 69, 104
Conzelmann, H. 71–75, 110, 225
Coon, C.S. 22
Crehan, J. 167
Cullmann, O. 157
Culpepper, R.A. 87

D'Angelo, M.R. 127, 128
Davies, E.W. 212, 214, 217, 219
Davies, J.G. 85, 92
Davies, S. 125, 126, 128–30
Davies, W. 245, 246, 248
Davies, W.D. 240, 242
De Jonge, M. 193, 194

Denova, R. 2, 170–72
DeSilva, D.A. 67, 162
Dibelius, M. 120
Dodd, C.H. 75
Donfried, K.P. 134, 152
Donne, B.K. 68, 87
Douglas, D.E. 150, 163, 164
Downing, F.G. 57
DuBois, C.A. 22
Dunn, J.D.G. 3, 117, 120, 131, 137, 152,
176, 193
Dupont, J. 116, 167, 196, 200

Earl, D. 83
Ehrman, A. 156, 157
Eisenstadt, S.N. 55
Elliott, J.H. 9, 15–18, 54–56
Ellis, E.E. 174
Esler, P. 8, 9, 13–19
Estrada, N.P. 221
Etheridge, J.W. 199
Evans, C. 222

Farris, S. 28
Fearghus, F.Ó. 118
Ferrar, F.W. 126
Finley, M. 16
Fiorenza, E.S. 129
Fitzmyer, J. 3, 6, 48, 70, 71, 82, 86, 92,
97, 109, 112, 116, 123, 134, 139,
140, 147, 153, 173, 176, 180, 182,
192, 195–97, 200, 206, 208, 218,
221, 225, 239
Fledderman, H.T. 175
Flender, H. 92, 127
Foucault, M. 86
Fowler, D.B. 108, 109
France, R.T. 245
Francis, F.A. 73
Freedman, H. 199
Fuller, R.H. 30

Gellner, E. 55
Gelzer, M. 54
Genette, G. 79
Gennep, A. van 20–24, 26, 52, 215, 233,
234
Giles, K. 168

Gilmore, D.D. 55, 163
Goulder, M. 121
Gowler, D. 58
Grant, M. 30
Grasser, E. 72
Gray, J. 97
Green, J.B. 61, 133, 160, 161, 205
Grodel, G.A. 93
Gundry, R.H. 175, 243

Habel, N. 39
Haenchen, E. 3, 48, 73, 78, 92, 112, 119–
21, 168, 225
Hagner, D.A. 241, 242, 247, 248
Hanson, K.C. 150, 163, 164
Harnack, A. 208
Harrington, D.J. 240
Hatch, E. 136, 137, 146
Heidland, H.W. 143
Hein, K. 160
Hellerman, J.H. 162, 163
Hemer, C. 78
Hiers, R. 74
Hill, S. 13, 20
Horbury, W. 158, 183
Horrell, D.G. 8, 17, 66
Hubbard, B.J. 39–43, 88, 89, 118
Humphreys, W.L. 69
Hunter, A.M. 30, 174

Ilan, T. 126

Jacobson, A.D. 175
Jervell, J. 2, 157, 169–73
Jewett, R. 130, 131
Johnson, A. 154
Johnson, L.T. 2, 3, 6, 83, 87, 98, 105,
110, 113, 117, 134, 139, 142, 146,
170, 172, 176, 179, 184, 208, 222
Judge, E.A. 13, 14

Karris, R.J. 126
Käsemann, E. 73
Kenny, A.J.P. 137
Kimball, S.T. 21, 22
Kirk, J.A. 158
Kitz, A.M. 154
Klassen, W. 5, 123, 157, 158, 160, 178,

181–83
Klauck, H.J. 157
Klijn, A.F.J. 244
Kloppenborg, J.S. 174, 175
Knight, J. 79, 81, 87
Knox, A.D. 167
Kopp, C. 206
Kuntz, J.K. 39
Kurz, W. 83, 84, 119

Lake, K. 5, 91, 112, 120, 123, 180, 208
Le Deaut, R. 195
Lemarchand, R. 55
Luckmann, T. 19, 67
Lüdemann, G. 110, 111, 196, 225, 228,
    229
Lull, D.J. 62

Maccoby, H. 5, 158, 161
Maddox, R. 196
Malina, B.J. 15, 56, 135, 162–65
Marguerat, D. 88
Marshall, A.J. 4
Marshall, I.H. 32, 57, 160, 174, 191,
    193–95, 211, 221, 222
Martinez, F.G. 194
Matill, A.J. 73, 74
May, D.M. 213
McHugh, J. 134
McVann, M. 20, 24–32, 37, 46, 49, 50,
    70, 94, 151, 190, 233, 234
Mead, M. 22
Meecham, H.G. 143
Meeks, W.A. 18, 19, 56, 164
Menninger, R.E. 175
Menoud, P. 91
Menzies, R. 10, 196, 201–204, 206, 207,
    220, 221
Merz, A. 107
Metzger, B.M. 47, 113, 225
Meye, R. 158
Milik, J.T. 154, 195
Mitchell, J.C. 55, 150
Momigliamo, A. 107
Moore, S, 240
Moule, C.F.D. 92
Moxnes, H. 53, 56, 57, 59–62, 107, 109,
    162

Mullins, T.Y. 39–43, 88, 89, 99, 100, 118
Murphy-O'Connor, J. 206

Nelson, P.K. 53, 171, 173, 174, 178
Neusner, J. 196
Newman, B. 111, 136, 142, 205
Neyrey, J.H. 24, 135, 162–65
Nida, E.A. 111, 136, 142, 205
Noack, B. 194
Nolland, J. 76
Noth, M. 212–14, 218, 219

Oakman, D.E. 106
Oppenheim, A.L. 39
O'Reilly, L. 196
O'Toole, R. 128

Parsons, M.C. 11, 50, 81–85, 88–94, 97,
    98, 100
Parvey, C.F. 127, 130
Peristiany, J.G. 163
Perrin, N. 239
Pilch, J. 56
Plummer, A. 126
Powell, M.A. 78, 80, 90
Premerstein, A. von 54

Quesnell, Q. 48, 109, 127

Radcliffe-Brown, A.R. 22
Rast, W. 154
Reid, B.E. 130
Reimer, I.R. 126
Rengstorf, K.H. 167, 168
Reumann, J. 113, 132–35
Richardson, J. 18
Rimmon-Kenan, S. 79–81
Rodd, C.S. 13
Rohde, J. 239
Rohrbaugh, R.L. 106
Roniger, L. 55
Royce, J.R. 204

Saller, R. 54
Sanders, E.P. 5
Sandmel, S. 202
Schechter, S. 155
Schille, G. 158, 161

Schnackenburg, R. 158
Schottroff, L. 126
Schweizer, E. 1, 28, 220, 240
Seccombe, D. 223
Shelton, J. 220, 221
Silva, D.A. de 105
Silverman, S. 57
Soards, M.L. 167, 181, 227
Sorensen, G.C. 83
Staden, P. van 10
Stambaugh, J.E. 56
Stanzel, F.K. 78
Ste. Croix, G.E.M. de 54
Stein, R.H. 239
Steyn, G.J. 167
Stoops, R.F. Jr. 62–64
Strack, H.L. 195
Streeter, B.F. 174
Stronstad, R. 1, 211, 218, 224, 227
Styler, G.M. 241, 242
Sweetland, D.M. 127
Syme, R. 54

Talbert, C.H. 78, 85, 92
Talmon, S. 195
Tambling, J. 77, 78
Tannehill, R. 67, 84, 91, 119, 170, 172
Taylor, J.E. 30
Taylor, V. 126
Theissen, G. 107
Thornton, L.S. 167
Torrance, T.F. 68
Torrey, C.C. 156
Tozzer, A.M. 22
Turner, B.S. 13, 20
Turner, M. 11, 195–97, 199, 203, 220

Turner, V. 22–27, 34, 67, 70, 71, 77, 104,
    233, 234
Tyson, J.B. 2, 122

Uspensky, B. 84, 86

Van Seters, J. 214
Van Stempvoort, P.A. 92
Van Unnik, W.C. 73
VanderKam, J.C. 193
Vaux, R. de 191, 200, 201, 214
Verheyden, J. 82
Vermes, G. 155, 156, 195
Via, E.J. 127

Wallace-Hadrill, A. 108
Waterbury, J. 55
Wedderburn, A.J.M. 193
Weinstock, S. 225
Wentling, J.L. 78
Wernberg-Moller, P. 155
Whelan, C.F. 4, 131
Wilcox, M. 120, 167–69
Wilder, A. 92
Wilken, R. 19
Wilson, B.R. 14
Wilson, S.G. 92
Winter, B. 62
Witherington III, B. 6, 7, 47, 48, 83, 110–
    12, 116, 117, 126, 140, 142, 143,
    146, 182, 205, 207, 226, 227
Witherup, R.D. 88, 94

Yadin, Y. 195

Zahn, T. 206